Killer Tomatoes

Killer Tomatoes

Fifteen Tough Film Dames

Ray Hagen *and* Laura Wagner

FOREWORD BY JANE RUSSELL

McFarland & Company, Inc., Publishers

Jefferson, North Carolina, and London

Library of Congress Cataloguing-in-Publication Data

Hagen, Ray, 1936–
Killer tomatoes : fifteen tough film dames / Ray Hagen and Laura Wagner ;
Foreword by Jane Russell
p.   cm.
Includes bibliographical references and index.

ISBN 0-7864-1883-4 (softcover : 50# alkaline paper) ∞

1. Actresses—United States—Biography.
I. Wagner, Laura, 1970–   II. Title.
PN1998.2.H345   2004   791.4302'8'092273—dc22   2004013463

British Library cataloguing data are available

Cover photograph: Publicity shot of Ann Sheridan in 1939

Manufactured in the United States of America

*McFarland & Company, Inc., Publishers
Box 611, Jefferson, North Carolina 28640
www.mcfarlandpub.com*

For all my Barbaras
—Ray Hagen

To my mentor, the late *Doug McClelland*, for his brilliance,
friendship and encouragement
and to
My *Mother*. Unlike Marie Windsor in *The Killing*, I'd never
sell you for a piece of fudge
—Laura Wagner

Acknowledgments

RAY HAGEN: My *sincerest* gratitude to Jane Russell for patiently spending so many hours answering so many questions, and for being the first person in *many* years to call me "kiddo." Also to her close friends and co-workers—Beryl Davis, Connie Haines, Hal Schaefer, Jack Singlaub and the late Portia Nelson—for helping me add so much to Jane's story.

To the family and friends of Jean Hagen (no relation) who went out of their way to help me tell Jean's story: her children, Aric Seidel and Christine Seidel Burton; her sister, LaVerne Verhagen Steck; and "the Northwestern girls" who became her friends for life—Patricia Neal, Nathalie Brown Thompson, Mimi Morrison Tellis, Helen Horton Thomson and Nancy Hoadley Salisbury.

To Peter Bren for taking the time to give me new and important information about his loving and beloved stepmother, Claire Trevor.

To the ladies with whom I lunched all those years ago: Mercedes McCambridge in 1963, Ann Sheridan in 1966 and Jean Hagen in 1975. I tried to pass myself off as a distinguished film scholar but they knew I was just a star-struck nervous wreck in the presence of a Goddess. And speaking of the 1960s ...

To my old friend Jean Barbour for allowing me to raid the back issues of her late husband Alan G. Barbour's wonderful *Screen Facts* magazine, where my interview with Ann Sheridan was first published in the November 1966 issue (vol. 3, #2), and where the earliest version of my Gloria Grahame article was published in May 1964 (vol. 1, #6).

To editors Leonard Maltin (*Film Fan Monthly*) and the late Henry Hart (*Films in Review*) for giving us fellow movie freaks a place to write about and an excuse to meet our movie icons whilst cleverly disguised as grown-ups. (Did we *ever* fool *anyone*?) My first attempts at profiling Jane Russell, Claire Trevor and Mercedes McCambridge appeared in, respectively, the April 1963, Nov. 1963 and May 1965 issues of *Films in Review*. An early profile of Jean Hagen was in *Film Fan Monthly*, Dec. 1968. Those pieces were the genesis of my chapters on these ladies in this book.

To Colin Briggs, Bob Robison and Jeff Gordon for their help with my Lynn Bari chapter.

And of course to comely Laura Wagner, first for getting me into this, and then for helping to get me out of it.

LAURA WAGNER: Thanks are due to the friends who put up with my insane demands for information and movies: Mida Baltezore, John Cocchi (The Credit

King), Christine Corsaro, Earl Hagen, G.D. Hamann, Richard Hegedorn, Frances Ingram, David Marowitz, Marvin of the Movies, Jim Meyer, James Robert Parish, Bob Robison (ACCOLADES), Morty Savada, George Shahinian, Eleanore Starkey, Charles Stumpf, Dan Van Neste and Tom Weaver.

To those who consented to interviews: George Dean, Marsha Hunt, Sybil Jason, Virginia Mayo, Lina Romay, Jack Smith, Martha Tilton and George Ward.

To all my photo dealers through the years: Gene Massimo (of Fan*Fare), Hal Snelling, Milton T. Moore, Jr., Jerry Ohlinger's Movie Material Store and Larry Edmunds Bookshop (Mike Hawks).

To Steve Tompkins. This poor man uncomplainingly sent me tons of videos, even trading with others to get me my needed films. His friendship is much appreciated.

To Christina Rice, creator of the fabulous AnnDvorak.com website, who was of immeasurable help with the Dvorak chapter. Christina, you are my hero.

To the late Barbara Whiting-Smith, bless her, who was not only a terrific actress, but also a terrific person.

To Ben Ohmart, always ready to be supportive.

To Bob King, my editor at *Classic Images* (where an abridged version of my Marilyn Maxwell essay appeared in the February 2000 issue) and *Films of the Golden Age*, who was the first to give me a chance. He deserves special mention; no one could ask for a nicer editor or a funnier guy to chat with. His colleague at *CI*, my buddy Carol Peterson, is funny, indispensable—and one tough dame.

To Ray Hagen, who made this project maddening but fun. His shrewdness, editing, humor and Barbara Stanwyck impersonations are unmatched.

To my family: my wonderful mother, Frances Wagner, who is consistently my best audience, but never much of a critic. Which is a good thing. I'd be lost without my brother, Tom Wagner, a whiz at finding photos and information. He always comes through, and I treasure him. My nephews, Jake and Luke Vichnis, are the lights of my life, even if they're too young to read this book. And to my outrageous aunt, Charlotte Rainey, who bears a striking resemblance to Ida Lupino. How cool is that?

Last, and certainly never least, my great pal, the late Doug McClelland, the finest film writer ever. From the moment I met him, he was my guiding star. In the last months of his life he was there helping, as usual, and lending support to a project he believed in. He said this would be the one movie book he "was looking forward to." I hope we didn't disappoint him.

Contents

Foreword

by Jane Russell

When I was a kid I adored Katharine Hepburn, especially when she played Jo, the ballsy sister in *Little Women*. All the kids in school started calling me "Jo." I also loved Barbara Stanwyck, Ann Sheridan, Bette Davis, Claire Trevor—I didn't know them but after seeing them in so many movies, I felt like I knew them. They weren't feminists, they were just strong women, and I always admired anyone who had some guts. All those sweet, quiet, polite, ladylike little things just bored me to death.

Back then there were so many wonderful women's stories being filmed, and so many strong actresses. But by the time I started doing movies they were mostly making men's stories. It has always saddened me that I never got to work with directors like George Cukor and William Wyler, directors who could really pull such marvelous performances from actresses. For example, I'd love to have played Lillian Roth in *I'll Cry Tomorrow*. She wanted me to play her, but they decided to go with Susan Hayward instead. So many of us were typecast then and that was hard to fight. I was usually "the girl in the piece" and it was the guys' stories, but I was always the gal with a smart answer.

That was fine with me because I was used to holding my own in the company of guys; it was second nature to me. My cousin Pat and I grew up as the only two girls among twelve boys, including my four younger brothers, and we raised them. I understood boys, and I understood men. I was married to a football star, Bob Waterfield, and there were always guys around the house. So I guess I had an advantage over many women who weren't raised around men and didn't understand them, because the movie business was run by men—studio heads, directors, most of the writers. If you couldn't handle these guys on an equal footing, you weren't going to last very long in pictures.

Why were these strong actresses, and the characters they played, so popular? Why are women like that popular when you know them? Well, maybe not the really tough ones, the killers, but even they're interesting to watch. Sometimes even Barbara Stanwyck was *too* nasty, but I liked her so much.

I love the idea of a book about strong women and I'm so glad it's here.

Introduction

The only way to conquer Barbara Stanwyck was to kill her, if she didn't kill you first. Lynn Bari wanted any husband that wasn't hers. Jane Russell's body promised paradise but her eyes said, "Oh, please!" Claire Trevor was semi-sweet in Westerns and super-sour in moderns. Ida Lupino treated men like used-up cigarette butts. Gloria Grahame was oversexed evil with an added fey touch—a different mouth for every role. Ann Sheridan and Joan Blondell slung stale hash to fresh customers. Ann Dvorak rattled everyone's rafters, including her own. Adele Jergens was the ultimate gun moll, handy when the shooting started. Marie Windsor just wanted them dead. Lucille Ball, pre–Lucy, was smart of mouth and warm as nails. Mercedes McCambridge, the voice of Satan, used consonants like Cagney used bullets. Marilyn Maxwell seemed approachable enough, depending on her mood swings. And Jean Hagen stole the greatest movie musical ever made by being the ultimate bitch. These wonderwomen proved that a woman's only place was not in the kitchen. We ain't talkin' Loretta Young here.

When movies began to talk in the late 1920s, the women talked back (and snarled back and slapped back and shot back), and audiences adored them. Tough guys and tougher gals quickly replaced the suave sweeties of the silent era as a new, slangy form of screen acting catapulted truckloads of brand new and mostly stage-trained actors to screen stardom. The wisecrack had entered its golden age. Sound suddenly made the saucy flirtations of Clara Bow, the lugubrious vamping of Theda Bara and the imbecilic innocence of Mary Pickford seem instantly dated and even laughable, and they were replaced in the public's affections by actresses who behaved and *sounded* like actual people (even as they continued to look heavenly beyond all reason).

Some of the ladies in this book were among the very first wave of muscular maidens who set patterns that are being copied to this day. These hot tamales weren't dependent on men to get where they wanted to go, though they weren't above pretending to be if necessary. They'd been through a mill or two and they'd learned the ropes.

(Oddly, one of the most popular on-screen professions for these babes was not the first one that comes to mind, but that of *singer*. Cinematographers lingered lovingly over these Circes in gorgeous gowns, impeccably coiffed and made up, crooning seductive torch songs—dubbed if necessary, but who cared? Singing was apparently a code occupation for women of dubious ambition and, though one might question the connection, it made for some fabulous visuals.)

By 1933 Mae West had come on the scene and things had gotten so out of hand that bluenoses in general, and the Catholic Church in particular, were threatening boycotts if the movie studios didn't clean up their act. There had been a Production Code all along but now it was put solidly into effect. There were still plenty of unwed mothers and gun-totin' seductresses but now they had to *pay* for their sins. Impurities now had to be artfully suggested rather than shown, so the world would be safe for Shirley Temple.

Then, in the '40s, *film noir* created a sensation and the ladies of *noir* were certainly no ladies. It wasn't called *film noir* then, it wasn't called anything, they were just detective movies or whodunits or mysteries, and the women were as strong as the men. Often, deliciously, stronger.

We offer here 15 *femmes fatale* from the late 1920s to the early 1950s, roughly the first quarter-century of American sound films. All played their share of heroines and housewives, but they really caught fire when the gutsy parts came along. Conspicuous by their absence here are Bette Davis and Joan Crawford, who have been written about so extensively that there isn't a single word left to say about them. (Surprisingly, you won't even find Ruby Keeler here. After all, who knows *what* was going on behind that blank stare?) We've included a number of big stars here but we also wanted to celebrate the careers of some lesser known actresses who, along with the superstars, helped to define the genre.

There were many other hard-boiled Hollywood hotties, of course, but with only so much time and space we had to whittle the list down to a precious few. And it must be grudgingly admitted that a wee tad of personal preference dictated not a few choices.

So here they are, a gaggle of highly skilled and utterly unique actresses whose pre-feminist strength and independence were awesome to behold. Whether with gags, glares or gats, they railed, they ranted, they raved, they rode roughshod. They *ruled*.

—R. H. and L. W.

Lucille Ball: Red Ball Express

by LAURA WAGNER

> Pretty Lucille Ball, who was born for the parts Ginger Rogers sweats over, tackles her "emotional" role as if it were sirloin and she didn't care who was looking.
> —Critic James Agee on *The Big Street* (1942)

"I regret the passing of the studio system," Lucille Ball once said. "I was very appreciative of it because I had no talent. Believe me. What could I do? I couldn't dance. I couldn't sing. I could *talk*. I could barely walk. I had no flair. I wasn't a beauty, that's for sure." Most people agree with Lucy's assessment of her film career. The millions of fans who still watch her, via reruns, on *I Love Lucy*, believe the character she played on the popular comedy—crazy about breaking into show business, yet possessing none of the talent required.

She's such a TV icon it's hard for some to separate the two Lucys—the gorgeous, snappy actress of film and the wacky, slapstick queen of television. On TV she was a middle-aged housewife, on film she was a dazzling beauty. The difficulty with her movie career wasn't that she was bad or not up to the roles. Quite the contrary: They were rarely up to *her*.

She was born Lucille Desiree Ball on August 6, 1911, in Jamestown, New York. Her father, Henry Ball, was a telephone lineman, and her early childhood was spent in Butte, Montana, and Wyandotte, Michigan. Henry died in a typhoid epidemic when Lucy was three, so her mother, Desiree (nicknamed DeDe), expecting her second child (Fred), worked in a factory to support her family. It was there she met Ed Peterson, who would become her second husband in 1918. The whole family eventually settled in with DeDe's father in Celoron, New York.

Lucy went from organizing shows in high school to attending the Robert Minton–John Murray Anderson School of Drama in Manhattan in 1926. The star pupil was an 18-year-old Bette Davis. Lucy, homesick and out of her league, quickly returned home. Financial troubles there led her to venture back to New York City. She auditioned in vain as a showgirl for Earl Carroll and Florenz Ziegfeld. Instead she found luck in modeling, dropping out of school.

The Player's Club, Jamestown's theater group, gave Lucy a supporting role in *Within the Law* in 1930. By all accounts she was a hit, and moved with the show when it played the Chautauqua Institution, a summer resort.

Even with this small-town success, Lucy concentrated instead on her modeling

5

(for Hattie Carnegie, among others). It took prompting from agent Sylvia Hahlo to lead a reluctant Lucy into film. There was a call for models to go to Hollywood to appear in producer Samuel Goldwyn's *Roman Scandals* (1933), starring Eddie Cantor. Feeling sure there was no hope for her at the auditions, convinced she was "the ugly duckling of the lot," she was, to her surprise, hired for the six-week shoot. Lucy would meet actress Barbara Pepper, an enduring friend, during filming.

She secured a contract with Goldwyn lasting six months. She attributed this to her "stick-to-itness." She told Kathleen Brady in 1986: "Suddenly I was in show business. It interested me because I was learning, and because I was learning I never complained. Whatever they asked, I did. I did one line, two lines, with animals, in mud packs, seltzer in the face. Eddie Cantor noticed it first at Goldwyn. He'd say 'Give it to that girl, she doesn't mind.' I took it all as a learning time."

The platinum blonde Ball was thought during this early period to resemble Constance Bennett, a fact which contributed to Goldwyn signing her, and she doubled for the star in *Moulin Rouge* (1934). Lucy was being paid around $300 a week as "atmospheric background" for Goldwyn and loan-outs to Fox.

Her Goldwyn contract was coming to a close and she asked for and got a release. "I didn't want to be a showgirl any more," she said later. "I wanted to get on with it and I had a chance to be a contract player at Columbia, although I was making a lot less money than I did as a showgirl." Columbia was only a slight improvement. Lucy appeared in comedy shorts and more bits. Her stay at the studio was abruptly cut short, says Lucy, when "one day at six o'clock they fired about 15 of us. We were out lock, stock and barrel. We were on the street. We just stood there. What happened? Nobody knew."

In need of work, she reluctantly heeded RKO's call for girls with modeling experience for *Roberta* (1934). It was only a dress bit, but the studio was sufficiently impressed by

Portrait of Lucille Ball, 1944.

her looks—blonde, very lean and lanky—to sign her in late '34. "I was a stock girl at RKO," she wryly told a reporter later. "Down in the small print it said I had to sweep out the office if they wanted me to."

At first there wasn't much change. The bits were no different than the ones Lucy had handled earlier. Momentum was gained when Lela Rogers, Ginger Rogers' mother, took an interest. According to Ginger, her mother, who conducted acting classes at RKO, intervened on Lucy's behalf. "The studio told my mother they were thinking of letting Lucy go. My mother said firmly, 'You fire Lucy ... then I'll quit. Lucille Ball is one of the most promising youngsters on this lot. If you're stupid enough to do that, the minute you let her go, I'll snap her up and take her to another studio and see that she gets the roles she deserves."

The studio listened, probably not in fear of losing Lela Rogers but, more likely, Ginger, one of the top stars at RKO at that time. Lucy's roles built in prominence. Her early parts presented her as a rough-around-the-edges, sometimes bitchy blonde. At least the size of her roles was improving.

RKO gave her permission to star in the stage musical comedy *Hey Diddle Diddle*, opening in Princeton, New Jersey, on January 21, 1937 with Conway Tearle. *Variety* praised "her sense of timing," but the show never made it to Broadway due to Tearle's health, and closed a month later in Philadelphia. This disappointment was tempered by producer Pandro S. Berman's interest in Lucy's comedic abilities. He wanted her right away for *Stage Door* (1937), a revamped version of Edna Ferber and George S. Kaufman's play.

Stage Door was an important turning point for Lucy, her snappy flippancy adding immensely to the diversity of showbiz hopefuls at the boarding house.

Co-star Ann Miller became a good friend, always crediting Lucy with getting RKO to sign her. In her autobiography she remembered the set being "very friendly," despite "quite a lot of tension between Ginger Rogers and Katharine Hepburn. Lucy helped relieve a lot of the strain because she would always laugh and joke and kid. Eve Arden was the same way, and thank God for them." Miller added to writer Eve Golden that Lucy "was a wonderful lady, loads of fun. She was like a showgal, you know, that great, rare sense of humor."

After the good response she drew from *Stage Door*, Lucy languished in uninteresting supporting parts and her first lead, opposite Joe Penner, in *Go Chase Yourself* (1938).

What gave her a boost was *The Affairs of Annabel* (1938), just another product from RKO's B-unit. Everyone was surprised when this congenial spoof of the movie world became a breakout hit.

Ball plays movie star Annabel Allison for Wonder Pictures ("If It's a Good Picture—It's a Wonder"), long-suffering victim of her press agent's (Jack Oakie) wild schemes to get her publicity. Still smarting from his previous gag to promote her last picture, *Behind Prison Bars*, by getting her arrested, the put-upon actress is hired out by Oakie as a maid in preparation for *A Maid and a Man*. *The Affairs of Annabel* was Lucy's first chance to really show how well she could handle light comedy. Two months later, *Annabel Takes a Tour* (1938) was released, with the same popular response. RKO envisioned a series, but the idea was nixed when Oakie demanded more money than the B-budget could handle.

The studio suddenly got serious on her in 1939, casting her in four straight dramas. The soapy saga *Beauty for the Asking* was about a jilted girl rising to cosmetic queen. *Twelve Crowded Hours* was a newspaper yarn with Richard Dix; considering their age difference (Dix, 44, Ball, 28), the two were surprisingly agreeable together. RKO reteamed them the next year in *The Marines Fly High*.

At first glance Lucy's role in *Panama Lady*, originated by Helen Twelvetrees in *Panama Flo* (1932), doesn't seem to fit the normally spirited Ball, but she gave an effectively subdued performance. Lucy once referred to this South American–set drama as "a dog," but the *New York Daily News* regarded it as a "minor triumph" for her, even if box office proved otherwise.

The part of the hardboiled floozy in *Five Came Back* was pure Lucy, at this point in her career anyway. Considered a sleeper, the tense film maintains its rep today. With this success, Lucy earned the right to climb out of the second feature trenches, but no go. RKO gave her what amounted to a cameo in Kay Kyser's *That's Right— You're Wrong* (1939).

In December 1939, Orson Welles began work on his first movie, one which never reached fruition. Before his classic *Citizen Kane*, he was keen on *The Smiler with a Knife*, a thriller Welles thought, after rewrites, had the makings of *The Thin Man*. He first wanted Carole Lombard, but she declined. He was intrigued by the possibility of casting Ball, but faced opposition from RKO, who didn't feel she could carry the picture. Which just proved she was at the wrong studio. This was confirmed most eloquently by her casting in the turkey *You Can't Fool Your Wife* (1940).

Not since her supporting days at RKO had she handled a role as bitchy as *Dance, Girl, Dance* (1940), mopping the floor with Maureen O'Hara in the process. Lucy is a burley queen (singing "Mother, What Do I Do Now?"), with an attitude as plain as her name: Tiger Lily White. The movie itself, however, is notable today solely for introducing her, in an indirect way, to Desi Arnaz.

She had just finished filming a scene with O'Hara. Desi, in Hollywood to reprise his stage role in *Too Many Girls*, later remembered, "The first time I saw Lucy was in a Hollywood studio lunchroom. Lovely, dazzling Lucille Ball was to be one of the stars of *Too Many Girls*. I was eager to meet her. Then she walked in. She had a black eye, frowzy hair and was wearing a too-tight black dress with a rip in it. She had been playing a dance-hall floozy in a free-for-all fight scene. I groaned, 'Oh, no!' That afternoon, when she showed up on the set where I was working, I said, 'Oh, yes!' She had fixed her hair and make-up and put on a sweater and skirt. She was a dream. I took one look and fell in love."

Lucy broke off her longtime relationship with director Alexander Hall, saying it wasn't love at first sight when she met Desi, "it took a full five minutes." The whirl-wind courtship cumulated just after *Too Many Girls* premiered when the couple was wed on November 30, 1940, in Greenwich, Connecticut.

Before this, however, RKO had paid $100,000 for the screen rights to *Too Many Girls*. When Mary Martin refused the role, played on stage by Marcy Westcott, Lucy was penciled in, with Trudy Erwin ghosting on vocals. Employing members of the theater cast, and retaining the show's director (George Abbott), the movie added Frances Langford and Ann Miller.

The movie revealed a likable Lucy at her most relaxed. She plays the headstrong daughter of Harry Shannon, making him suspicious when she insists on going to his alma mater Pottawatomie, all the way out in Stop Gap, New Mexico. He hires four All-American football players to monitor her, and, of course, she falls in love with one of them (Richard Carlson). The plot was threadbare and a bit silly, but fast-paced, filled with "youthful effervescence and spontaneity" (*Variety*), and a score by Rodgers and Hart ("I Didn't Know What Time It Was").

She tested for Howard Hawks' *Ball of Fire* (1941) with Gary Cooper, but lost out to Barbara Stanwyck. After this major disappointment, Lucy starred in the zany *A Girl, a Guy and a Gob* (1941). "The important thing," wrote *The New York Times*, "is not who gets the girl, but how much fun they have along the way," which summed up the amiable story nicely. This underrated comedy wasn't a high point in her career, but an improvement over some of the stuff RKO was giving her.

And it was much better than Charlie McCarthy-Edgar Bergen's *Look Who's Laughing* (1941); it was material like this Lucy wanted to break free of. *Valley of the Sun* (1942), a comedy Western directed by old hand George Marshall, was better. It was RKO's most expensive ($650,000) Western since *Cimarron* (1931). Top-billed Ball ("The prettiest girl in Arizona") is engaged to unscrupulous Indian agent Dean Jagger, until attractive Indian scout James Craig shows up.

Valley of the Sun (RKO, 1942) was one of Lucy's better RKO films. "The prettiest girl in Arizona," she gets involved with attractive Indian agent James Craig.

Andy Warhol called *The Big Street* (1942), based on Damon Runyon's story *Little Pinks*, "the sickest film ever made," and he isn't far off-target. At first, Lucy, who won the part over suggested star Merle Oberon, was concerned about the unsympathetic nature of her character, a nightclub singer with a mean streak as wide as the Grand Canyon. She consulted Charles Laughton because she considered her role "so bitchy. It's so unrealistically rude, crude and crass." But Laughton allayed her fears: "My advice to you is to play the bitchiest bitch that ever was! Whatever the script calls for. And don't try to soften it. Just play it!" She definitely did.

Lucy plays a gorgeous, self-absorbed singer (her song "Who Knows?" is dubbed by Martha Mears), worshiped by clearly sadomasochistic busboy Little Pinks (Henry Fonda), whom she treats like a doormat. "Her Highness," as Fonda calls her, doesn't lack for admirers but she's after cash, adoration and position, in the whole package of William T. Orr.

She snaps, growls and snarls at Little Pinks—"that's not a name, that's a toothbrush"—but he moons and swoons over her. More so when jilted Barton MacLane knocks her down stairs, leaving her crippled. Here, it gets even sicker.

Fonda pays her hospital bills, goes into hock, cares for her, caters to her every whim—while Lucy insults and taunts him. Then she decides on a change of climate; with no money to travel, Lucy suggests—this is the kicker—that Fonda *push* her wheelchair the more than one thousand miles to Florida. And he does it.

But Lucy's performance isn't just that. She shows that some of her nastiness stems from her uncertainty of ever walking again, allowing the facade to break down for … just … a … few … seconds … then—*wham*, she's back in the groove, treating everyone like dirt. Her death scene is very affecting. Credit Lucille Ball for making a heartless shrew a figure of pity at the conclusion.

Lucy called her character "a girl with a foolish, unhealthy obsession which made her more ruthless than Scarlett O'Hara. It was anything but a sympathetic part, but it was exciting because it was so meaty—so rich in humor, pathos and tragedy." It was anything but a hit.

Nor was shooting helped by the coolness between her and Fonda. "I didn't know Henry Fonda all that well before we began *The Big Street*, and I sure didn't want to know him all that well when we were finished. He hardly talked to me the whole time, and when he did, well…"

One problem was the scene where Lucy learns for the first time that her legs are paralyzed. "The director [Irving Reis] and I rehearsed the scene. I started swaying my shoulders, and tried dancing with only my arms. I try to make my legs move, but they won't. I'm dancing, sitting up in bed, looking at my paralyzed legs. Irving was terrific. He said that I had done it perfectly and he wanted to shoot it right away while we still had the mood. I looked over to the door, and Fonda was standing there. He had watched the rehearsal, and as soon as Irving started setting up the shot, he came over to me and said, 'You're *not* going to do it like that, are you?' I said, 'Well, Irving said it was good.' Fonda just shook his head back and forth and walked away. Try to do a scene after that."

Louella Parsons talked her up as Oscar-worthy, but it never happened. At RKO it meant nothing. They thought her salary ($1500) unwarranted. Her films were doing poorly and she was refusing movies, like a loan-out to Fox for the Betty Grable musical *Footlight Serenade* (1942). With the bust of *The Big Street*, it was clear: Lucy was out.

As her last picture under contract, she replaced Rita Hayworth in the musical comedy *Seven Days Leave* (1942). All was not happy on the set. Victor Mature, dating Hayworth at the time, made his displeasure over the casting known. It was a shaky time, not only because of the contract termination, but because of Desi's absences traveling with his band.

If RKO failed to recognize her abilities, MGM was more than willing to sign her. It was MGM, by way of hair stylist Sydney Guilaroff, who would change her career. She was elevated to full-fledged star in bigger-budgeted productions, with Technicolor only enhancing her beauty. As for her blonde (sometimes brown) hair: "I felt she needed to stand out,"

Lucy's first for MGM, the Technicolor musical *DuBarry Was a Lady* (1943) with Red Skelton, was also the first with her soon-to-be-famous red hair, courtesy of hair stylist Sydney Guilaroff.

related Guilaroff in his autobiography, "so I mixed a variety of hair-dyes into a henna rinse that transformed her into a shimmering golden redhead."

First at MGM was *DuBarry Was a Lady* (1943), an Arthur Freed production adapted from the smash 1939 Cole Porter show starring Ethel Merman. Of course, Lucy was no Merman; she was dubbed on the title song (Martha Mears again), but sang with her own voice on "Friendship."

Red Skelton is smitten with money-conscious Ball, asking her to marry him after he wins the lottery, with only Gene Kelly standing in their way. Red plans on slipping Kelly "a Rooney"—"a high-powered Mickey"—but mistakenly drinks it himself. He's dreamily transported to France where he's King Louis XV and Ball is his mistress Madame DuBarry.

As singer May Daly, Lucy is serious and practical, trying to suppress her love for penniless Kelly, while he croons Cole Porter's lovely "Do I Love You, Do I?" But in Red's dream, her manner changes: she's wacky, sassy, visibly in love with "The

Black Arrow" (Kelly). She's also hell bent on keeping Red at arm's length, especially during their romp "Madame, I Love Your Crepes Suzettes." The dance suddenly becomes a mad chase, with Red and Lucy flopping down exhausted at the end. "This ain't a love affair," he sighs. "This is a track meet."

DuBarry Was a Lady proved to be a major hit for MGM.

Working with producer Arthur Freed again, Lucy copped the lead in *Best Foot Forward* (1943), another Broadway hit, from originally slated Lana Turner; Lana had to bow out due to pregnancy. Lucy plays herself, a Hollywood star asked by Winsocki Military Academy student Tommy Dix to be his prom date. She accepts, through the prodding of her press agent William Gaxton, and things get a little crazy.

Ball is at her wry best, flipping the insults and quips left and right, at what she correctly perceives to be a bad situation. In need of a new contract, she reluctantly plays along. Envisioning huge crowds mobbing her as she steps off the train, Ball looks over the deserted station with disgust. "Well, I don't mind the band playing," she notes sarcastically, "but if this crowd doesn't stop shoving, I'll *scream*." One lone barking dog greets her. "My public," Lucy regally gestures.

Best Foot Forward's script was teeming with wisecracks, certainly better than

Movie star Lucy wants out of her press agent William Gaxton's ploy to get her publicity by being a prom date in *Best Foot Forward* (MGM, 1943).

anything RKO gave her, and she made the most of them. She also gets to "sing" again, this time with Gloria Grafton's voice, on "You're Lucky," written for the film by the Broadway composers Hugh Martin and Ralph Blane.

Her luck ran out with *Meet the People* (1944). It was a strange concept for a musical: factory worker Dick Powell co-writes a musical play about "the common man," wanting glamorous Broadway actress Lucy to star. But even after she becomes a shipyard worker, only the "common man" can put on *his* play; wealthy Lucy must humble herself to matter in Powell's life. "The hero is the people," songwriter-producer E.Y. Harburg explained. "The story takes the point of view that the people, after all, are running the country." It was all a lot of hooey, far too preachy to appeal to musical fans. Lucy looks gorgeous, but she and staid, pretentious Powell (who sings "In Times Like These" superbly) were not a good match.

She next did three cameos in a row. In the all-star *Thousands Cheer* (1943), she joined Ann Sothern and Marsha Hunt in an unfunny skit about a barber (Frank Morgan) posing as a doctor giving physicals to potential WAVEs. Lou Costello, eluding studio police, invades the movie set where Lucy, Preston Foster and director Robert Z. Leonard are shooting a fictional movie in *Abbott and Costello in Hollywood* (1945).

Most famous, for sheer camp value, is *Ziegfeld Follies* (1946, filmed in 1944). In the opening number "Here's to the Girls," sung by Fred Astaire, newcomer Cyd Charisse's ballet bit gives way to an exquisite Lucy on top of a live merry-go-round horse, stunning in pink. After gracefully moving around the stage, she pulls out a whip and "lashes" a group of female dancers dressed as cats. Costumer Helen Rose later remarked, "I created lavish outfits of pink sequins, using twelve hundred ostrich feathers. With Lucille Ball's flaming red hair, I thought it was the best number in the picture."

MGM bought Philip Barry's 1942 play *Without Love*, which had starred Katharine Hepburn and Elliott Nugent on Broadway, as a vehicle for her and Spencer Tracy. To Barry's displeasure it was rewritten for the screen by Donald Ogden Stewart, and to Tracy's displeasure the movie was stolen by the supporting players: Lucille Ball and Keenan Wynn. After her lavish Technicolor movies, she was there mainly to supply comedy asides in a black-and-white movie, and she did her job. This was a sure sign that her days at MGM were numbered.

She was loaned out to Fox for the well-liked *The Dark Corner* (1946). Ball gives her role, secretary to private investigator Mark Stevens, a quiet, warm strength that holds the tough movie together, as her jaded boss is framed for murder. "I sharpen pencils, I do the typing, answer the phones—and mind my own business," she calmly tells a cop, until circumstances, and a blossoming love between her and Stevens, gets her involved.

While it doesn't dull memories of its source *Libeled Lady* (1936), *Easy to Wed* (1946) gave Lucy her best comedy showcase, reprising, and greatly enriching, Jean Harlow's part in the original. The story: Esther Williams sues a newspaper for libel for claiming she stole somebody's husband. Editor Keenan Wynn gets lady-killer Van Johnson to set her up in the same situation she's denying. Lucy, Wynn's long-suffering fiancée, stood-up at the altar too many times, reluctantly marries Van at Keenan's urging. At the appropriate time, she'll barge in and ... Esther can't sue. Except, Van falls for Esther and Lucy falls for Van, causing expected complications.

When we first meet jilted bride Ball, she's storming through the newsroom in full wedding regalia, like a tornado, to Wynn's office, papers flying and swirling in her path. Fiery, gorgeous, starved with neglect, Lucy falls for smooth-talking Romeo Van. Their drunk scene is high comedy at its best, as is the wacky one where Van is taught duck calls; after Van lamely does the "Lazy Hen Call," Lucy cracks, "She's not lazy. She's *dead.*" She madly giggles, noodles on the piano, acts like a female duck responding to mating calls—in short, she's sensational. Lucy's speaking voice is used here to fun effect. Harlow had said the word "subtle" correctly; Lucy, her character none-too-bright, mispronounces it haughtily as "*sub*-tul." It's a small change, but effective—and very funny. In fact, aided by writer Dorothy Kingsley's enhancement of her part, Lucy is the only player to bring freshness to her role, the only player to improve on the classic original.

We can look back now, in view of her success on TV, and say MGM was unfair. Sure, she was terrific, but the moviegoing public just didn't warm up to her. *Easy to Wed* showed what she was comically capable of, but, MGM was just being practical when they released her after the minor *Two Smart People* (1946).

Without the big push of MGM, Ball freelanced (at $75,000 per). After *Lover Come Back* (1946) at Universal, she found herself in the first-rate *Lured* (1947), co-starring George Sanders. It was a neat atmospheric thriller about a killer lurking around London nabbing young, innocent girls via the personals. He is dubbed "The Poet Killer" for the poems he posts to the police foretelling his murders. Lucy is a flippant taxi dancer engaged by Scotland Yard to help smoke out the culprit by playing female detective.

She went over to Columbia for the slight comedy *Her Husband's Affairs* (1947). It was directed by Ball's friend S. Sylvan Simon, and would eventually earn Lucy a non-exclusive three-picture deal with the studio, on Simon's request.

In late 1947, she returned to the stage, touring regional theaters in Elmer Rice's *Dream Girl.* The show had been a hit on Broadway with Betty Field and a flop on film starring Betty Hutton, but Lucy took the role as her own, gaining excellent notices. *The Los Angeles Times* praised her "efficiency as a comedienne," adding that "she can tinge a scene delicately with pathos. She has special facility in dealing with sharp-edged repartee." Author Rice was duly impressed, later crediting Lucy's "expert timing" for keeping "the play bright and alive," and her performance "delighted" him. The successful run was cut short, due to Ball's health, when a virus spread through the overworked cast.

Radio opened up new opportunities. She'd been a regular on radio going back to the '30s, and had done some excellent dramatic work in the medium (*Lux Radio Theater*'s "They Drive by Night," in Ida Lupino's part, and "A Little Piece of Rope" from *Suspense* are sides of Lucy never seen on film). In 1948 she secured her own CBS show with Richard Denning, *My Favorite Husband.* This successful comedy, a precursor to *I Love Lucy*, had behind it four people who would become very important to Ball and her future TV successes: writers Madelyn Pugh, Bob Carroll, Jr., producer-director Jess Oppenheimer and actor Gale Gordon. It would run until 1951.

There were rumors that she turned down the lead in *Born Yesterday* (1950) for the chance to do *Sorrowful Jones* (1949), her first of four movies with Bob Hope. Other sources say she desperately wanted the part of Billie Dawn, which won Judy

Holliday an Oscar, but that Columbia chief Harry Cohn was against it. Instead, the first of her deal with Columbia was *Miss Grant Takes Richmond* (1949), a not-bad comedy of a wacky secretary who unwittingly uncovers a gang of bookies.

She did a cameo as herself in Rosalind Russell's *A Woman of Distinction* (1950), followed by her best role at Columbia, the title role in *The Fuller Brush Girl* (1950). It was a frantic, slapstick-heavy showcase for her comedic abilities, particularly her hilarious masquerade of a burlesque dancer with heavy fake eyelashes.

Over at Paramount, she romped through *Fancy Pants* (1950) with Bob Hope. In this reworking of *Ruggles of Red Gap*, Hope is an inept actor posing as a butler. One marvelous sight gag has Hope styling Lucy's hair. When he finishes, she's sporting an enormous bird cage, complete with live bird, embedded within her coiffure. One critic observed, "She is a fine foil for the star, building up bits of business to a point where they are comically consequential even though they have next to nothing to do with the original plot."

Cecil B. DeMille, noting her work, sought her for *The Greatest Show on Earth* (Paramount, 1952). Lucy asked Harry Cohn for a postponement on her commitment, which had one film to go. With her Columbia booster S. Sylvan Simon passing away in 1951, and Cohn resenting Ball's high-priced deal ($85,000 a picture), the mogul had other plans.

Pre–*I Love Lucy*, **Ball had one of her best comedy roles in the slapstick-heavy** *The Fuller Brush Girl* **(Columbia, 1950) with Eddie Albert.**

He gave her *The Magic Carpet* (1951), a screenplay she said made her "hysterical with laughter." Her friend director Edward Sedgwick termed it "a lease breaker." "He expects you to turn it down," he advised Ball, "then he's automatically free of paying you eighty-five thousand dollars. Tell him you'll do the picture. It'll break [producer Sam] Katzman. His whole budget is less than your salary."

Lucy surprised them all by accepting. When revisions were suggested by a bewildered Katzman, Lucy shrugged them off—no changes, she "liked" it just as it was; she wanted it over with as quickly as possible. A real potboiler, it took just a week to shoot, and the same amount of time to forget.

Lucy wasn't able to accept DeMille's offer after all. She found, after a decade of marriage, she was pregnant. She was overjoyed, DeMille less so. After being informed of the event, the director sighed to Desi, "Congratulations, Mr. Arnaz. You are the only man who has ever screwed his wife, Cecil B. DeMille, Paramount Pictures, and Harry Cohn, all at the same time." Gloria Grahame was assigned Ball's role in the Oscar-winning movie.

Since 1950, CBS had been interested in transferring *My Favorite Husband* to television. During most of her marriage, Lucy and Desi had been separated due to Desi's band tours, and Lucy was anxious for him to join her on TV. Executives at CBS couldn't see it. *My Favorite Husband* was about a "typical all–American couple," and Cuban-born Desi certainly didn't fit that description. "From all sides," Lucy remarked, "we were told that the idea was ridiculous and were advised to give it up." The couple, undeterred, personally paid for the pilot, now called *I Love Lucy*, formed their own company, Desilu, and went out on a vaudeville tour to show the network that people would accept them as a duo. After some heavy negotiations with CBS, eventually giving the Arnazes ownership of the series and half of the profits, it was a go. In an unprecedented move, even surprising Lucy, the couple would later buy RKO Studios for $6,000,000 to house their production company.

Meanwhile, Ball gave birth to daughter Lucie Desiree on July 17, 1951. A few months later, *I Love Lucy* premiered. Lucille Ball, 40, show business vet of almost 20 years without any major success, became a mega-star overnight. The show validated what her few loyal film fans knew all along: She was a top comedienne. She would win two Emmy Awards (1952, 1955) for her zany portrayal of Lucy Ricardo, a showbiz-crazy housewife always ready to crash her bandleader hubby's act.

The show was a phenom. The same audiences unable to relate to Lucy the glamorous movie star took her to heart on television. She was one of them, a typical, funny, middle-class woman with dreams and schemes. When Lucy became pregnant for a second time, it was incorporated into the show's storyline, despite protest from the network. She gave birth in real life to her son Desi, Jr. on January 19, 1953. That same night, in a show filmed in October, Lucy Ricardo also gave birth to a boy. The show made television history and 44 million tuned in to see the event.

Because of their TV schedule, there wasn't much time for feature films. Then in 1954 Lucy and Desi were approached by MGM to do *The Long, Long Trailer,* directed by Vincente Minnelli and produced by Lucy's old RKO colleague Pandro S. Berman. Newlyweds buy a trailer, almost damaging their marriage. It turned out to be MGM's highest-grossing comedy up to that time.

Successful, yes. Good, no. Lucy gets one wild scene trying to mix salad in the back of the speeding trailer, but it's basically Desi's movie. Ball gave a strange, almost irrational performance, with a touch of underlining bitterness that hardly fit her "new bride" role.

Perhaps the sharp edge that Lucy displayed was an early sign that the Arnaz marriage was hitting rock bottom. TV's "perfect couple" had troubles going back to 1944 when Lucy had filed for divorce, only to reconsider. The oft-cited difficulties were Desi's womanizing, but now his drinking was an added factor. Lucy's friend, author Bart Andrews, informed *People Weekly,* "She told me that by 1956 it wasn't even a marriage any more. They were just going through a routine for the children. She told me that for the last five years of their marriage, it was 'just booze and broads.' That was in her divorce papers, as a matter of fact."

The overload of work placed on Desi didn't help. As president of Desilu, he was supervising at least 229 series *(Our Miss Brooks, Make Room for Daddy, The Ann Sothern Show,* etc.). He had little time to attempt damage control on his ailing marriage.

According to author Charles Higham, "Desi was busier than ever, fighting off headaches and tics caused by pressure... It is scarcely any wonder that his hair went white or that his headaches, violent outbursts of temper, and quarrels with Lucy increased..."

Lucy was no innocent. "She was vulnerable," said her friend Ann Sothern. "But if she didn't respect you, she could be tough." Many describe her as a controlling, demanding and difficult perfectionist. When Joan Crawford later guested on TV with Lucy, she was incredulous: "And they call *me* a bitch!" Ball had a love-hate relationship with co-star Vivian Vance, one that reportedly put Vance in therapy. During one assertive moment, Vance supposedly cracked, "I'd tell you to go fuck yourself, if Desi hadn't already taken care of that."

Her friend Phyllis McGuire remarked, "She was very much in love with Desi, but she went through absolute hell with him." It was heartbreaking for her to see the unraveling of a relationship that many thought, even to the end, was the love of her life. It was said that money, enterprise, and power had wrecked their personal happiness.

MGM agreed to another picture, this time with Desi producing: *Forever, Darling* (1956). It was directed by the same Alexander Hall cast off by Lucy so many years ago for Desi, and it again featured them as a couple in conflict. *Forever, Darling* was not a hit, a puzzlement since it was much better than *The Long, Long Trailer.*

The still very popular *I Love Lucy* went off the air in 1957 to public disapproval, and was replaced by one-hour specials *(The Lucy-Desi Comedy Hour)* featuring them as the Ricardos. It lasted until 1960, by which time they were deep in divorce proceedings.

It was, according to Lucy, "the worst period of my life. I really hit the bottom of despair—anything from there on had to be up. Neither Desi nor I have been the same since, physically or mentally, though we're very friendly, ridiculously so ... " To keep herself busy, she accepted two offers, a Broadway musical *Wildcat* and her third movie with Bob Hope, *The Facts of Life* (1960).

The Facts of Life told the story of Hope and Ball, married to others (Ruth Hussey and Don DeFore), whose attempts at an affair are foiled. Much praised at the time, today it just doesn't play. However, Lucy looks terrific, very un–Lucy Ricardo–ish, and her maturity and warmth were sparkling.

Hedda Hopper said of *Wildcat*: "She knew she couldn't sing, admits she was too old to dance, but for her Broadway debut she would sing, dance and have to hold the whole thing together." The musical comedy, written by Richard Nash, with music and lyrics by Cy Coleman and Carolyn Leigh, directed by Michael Kidd, rested squarely on Ball's very slight musical shoulders. "It's a challenge," she admitted. "I'd gone as far as I wanted in TV. I know I'm sticking my neck out—but I stuck it out in TV, too. It won't kill me if the play flops, but I'm not anticipating failure."

The show opened in New York on December 16, 1960. It wasn't what everybody hoped for, but Ball got great reviews. This was attributed to writer Nash's reluctant revision of Lucy's character. "We found out the audience had come to see 'Lucy,' not Lucille Ball playing in *Wildcat* ... I was writing against my own views as a writer, but I had to," Nash remarked.

By the sheer force of Lucy's personality and hard work, *Wildcat* did outstanding business. A long run was likely, but she got sick; viruses, exhaustion and strained vocal chords that developed nodes (the reason for her eventual raspy voice) became too much. The show closed after 171 performances. Though Lucy was certainly no singer, she effectively put over the show's big hit, "Hey, Look Me Over."

The Arnaz marriage was officially over on May 4, 1960, but months later she met stand-up comedian Gary Morton. Everyone was surprised when they married on November 19, 1961; they seemed oddly matched. Gary took over managing her career and, it was whispered, stayed out of her way; the conflicts between her and Desi were now history. They would remain married until her death. Desi also married again in 1961 to (many say Lucy lookalike) Edie Hirsch.

She was unable to accept Frank Sinatra's offer to play Laurence Harvey's mother in *The Manchurian Candidate* (1962) because of TV work, a loss considering what a stretch it would have provided her. Angela Lansbury nabbed the part, but it would have been fascinating to see Lucy pull off the unsympathetic role.

Lucy stayed on friendly terms with Desi, and it was Desilu who produced her next series *The Lucy Show* (1962). But, a month after its premiere, Lucy bought out Desi's share of Desilu, becoming its sole controlling force, the first woman to hold such a position. Lucy continued on with her popular show, while astutely and firmly guiding Desilu. *The Lucy Show* was revamped as *Here's Lucy* in 1968, again with Gale Gordon (a perfect foil) and her two children Lucie and Desi, Jr.; Lucy won two more Emmys (1967 and 1968) before the show went off in 1974. Lucy would sell Desilu to Gulf + Western in 1967 for $17 million.

Her last movie with Bob Hope, *Critic's Choice* (1963), had flopped, and future films worried her. Finally in 1968 a project materialized. The idea of filming the life of Frank and Helen Beardsley was tossed around Desilu for years after their story was chronicled in *Life*—a widow with eight children and a Navy lieutenant–widower with ten kids, who also have children together. Lucy owned the rights, and when she was finally pleased with a script, the project went full speed ahead. Henry Fonda was signed on, the pair obviously over their cold feelings during *The Big Street*. The funny, warm comedy *Yours, Mine and Ours* was a smash, grossing over $17 million.

Still nervous, Lucy turned down *Cactus Flower* (1969), which went to Ingrid Bergman. She didn't return to the big screen until the dismal, problem-plagued

Mame (1974). Based on Patrick Dennis' novel *Auntie Mame*, this musicalization (score by Jerry Herman) was first presented on Broadway in 1966 with Angela Lansbury. *Auntie Mame, sans* music, would have been a fine Ball vehicle. Composer Herman later said, "She was a nice lady and she tried, so you can't punish her for not being able to sing or dance." But everyone did. Ball heatedly asked author Charles Higham at the time, "Why am I doing this? I must be out of my mind." The movie was critically savaged. It would be her last theatrically released film.

The '70s and '80s brought her semi-retirement. She appeared on television, mostly with Bob Hope and her own specials for CBS and NBC. Now considered "The First Lady of Television," awards came her way (Entertainer of the Year, Television Academy's Hall of Fame, Kennedy Center Honors). Lucille Ball had become an American institution.

Lucy unwisely turned down two film projects going to Jessica Tandy: *Driving Miss Daisy* and *The Story Lady*, but she made a gutsy choice by accepting the telefilm *Stone Pillow* (1985), portraying a homeless woman. Lucy was unfairly criticized for going against type. *I Love Lucy* was still playing in syndication (and will continue to play forever), and everyone wanted to remember her as the zany redhead, not someone picking through garbage. The same response met her 1986 return to series TV, *Life with Lucy*. At 77 she was still trying to play the Lucy everyone remembered, not a woman her own age. It was painful to watch, and the ABC show was off the air quickly.

Desi Arnaz passed away in 1986 of cancer. Even though they had been divorced for over 20 years, the feelings were still there. Lucy's friend Betty White told *People Weekly*, "The day that Desi died she and I were doing *Password* together. She was being real funny on the show, but during a break she said, 'You know ... it's the damnedest thing. Goddamn it, I didn't think I'd get this upset. There he goes.' It was a funny feeling, kind of a lovely, private moment."

She was in and out of the hospital in her last years, especially with heart problems, passing away after a ruptured aorta on April 26, 1989. The whole world felt the loss.

Lucy's friend and most frequent co-star (four movies, 20-plus TV shows) Bob Hope dedicated a NBC special to her; *Bob Hope's Love Affair with Lucy* aired on September 23, 1989. He said at the time to Kay Gardella, "[S]he was cute and could throw a line. She was always there with an amusing quip, and we always did a lot of laughing."

Which is what Lucy will always be remembered for, making people laugh. But her movie work shows vividly that she was much more than that. The many people unfamiliar with her largely neglected film work are in for a marvelous surprise.

1933: Broadway Thru a Keyhole (Fox), Roman Scandals (UA), Blood Money (UA). **1934:** Moulin Rouge (UA), Nana (UA), Bottoms Up (Fox), Hold That Girl (Fox), Bulldog Drummond Strikes Back (UA), Affairs of Cellini (UA), Kid Millions (UA), Broadway Bill (Columbia), Jealousy (Columbia), Men of the Night (Columbia), Fugitive Lady (Columbia), The Whole Town's Talking (Columbia), Perfectly Mismated (Columbia short), Three Little Pigskins (Columbia short). **1935:** I'll Love You Always (Columbia), His Old Flame (Columbia short), Carnival (Columbia), Roberta (RKO), Old Man Rhythm (RKO), Top Hat

(RKO), The Three Musketeers (RKO), I Dream Too Much (RKO), A Night at the Bilt-more Bowl (RKO short). **1936**: Dummy Ache (RKO short), One Live Ghost (RKO short), Swing It (RKO short), Chatterbox (RKO), Follow the Fleet (RKO), The Farmer in the Dell (RKO), Bunker Bean (RKO), That Girl from Paris (RKO), Winterset (RKO), So and Sew (RKO short). **1937**: Don't Tell the Wife (RKO), Stage Door (RKO). **1938**: Joy of Living (RKO), Go Chase Yourself (RKO), Having Wonderful Time (RKO), The Affairs of Annabel (RKO), Annabel Takes a Tour (RKO), Room Service (RKO), The Next Time I Marry (RKO). **1939**: Beauty for the Asking (RKO), Twelve Crowded Hours (RKO), Panama Lady (RKO), Five Came Back (RKO), That's Right, You're Wrong (RKO). **1940**: The Marines Fly High (RKO), You Can't Fool Your Wife (RKO), Dance, Girl, Dance (RKO), Too Many Girls (RKO). **1941**: A Girl, A Guy and a Gob (RKO), Look Who's Laughing (RKO). **1942**: Valley of the Sun (RKO), The Big Street (RKO), Seven Days Leave (RKO). **1943**: DuBarry Was a Lady (MGM), Best Foot Forward (MGM), Thousands Cheer (MGM). **1944**: Meet the People (MGM). **1945**: Without Love (MGM), Abbott and Costello in Hollywood (MGM). **1946**: Ziegfeld Follies (MGM), The Dark Corner (TCF), Easy to Wed (MGM), Two Smart People (MGM), Lover Come Back (Universal). **1947**: Lured (UA), Her Husband's Affairs (Columbia). **1949**: Sorrowful Jones (Paramount), Easy Living (RKO), Miss Grant Takes Richmond (Columbia). **1950**: A Woman of Distinction (Columbia), Fancy Pants (Paramount), The Fuller Brush Girl (Columbia). **1951**: The Magic Carpet (Columbia). **1954**: The Long, Long Trailer (MGM). **1956**: Forever, Darling (MGM). **1960**: The Facts of Life (UA). **1963**: Critic's Choice (WB). **1967**: A Guide for the Married Man (TCF). **1968**: Yours, Mine and Ours (UA). **1973**: Mame (WB). **1985**: Stone Pillow (TVM).

Lynn Bari: *The* Other Woman

by RAY HAGEN

Lynn Bari appeared in 128 movies. How many can you name? One or two? Good for you. More than three? Come sit by me.

A strikingly beautiful woman, she was repeatedly referred to as a Claudette Colbert lookalike. (A British writer once called her "Claudette Colbert with biceps.") But unlike Colbert, Lynn never had the smash hit or breakout role that shot her to the top ranks of movie superstardom. Nonetheless, after making a modest film debut as a chorus girl, she did rise to a certain degree of fame, built up a stalwart and loyal fan base, and managed to remain a working professional for 40 years.

She was born Marjorie Schuyler Fisher in Roanoke, Virginia, on Dec. 18, 1917 (1913 and 1919 are also often given). Her parents were Marjorie Halpen and John Maynard Fisher, and she had an older brother, John Owen. When Mr. Fisher died in 1925, his widow moved with her children to her family's home in Boston where she soon met and married a Religious Science minister, Robert H. Bitzer. Marjorie attended the Prince School in Boston and grammar school in Melrose.

Bitzer left his Boston pulpit to head the Institute of Religious Sciences in Los Angeles, where Mrs. Bitzer enrolled her tomboy daughter in a drama school. Marjorie already had dreams of becoming an actress and made her acting debut doing Portia's big speech from *The Merchant of Venice*. She graduated from Beverly Hills Grammar School.

In 1933 she saw a newspaper ad for chorus dancers 5'6" or taller for MGM's new Joan Crawford-Clark Gable musical, *Dancing Lady*. (When studios were overwhelmed by thousands of hopefuls answering such ads, the practice was permanently discontinued.) Marjorie eagerly reported to MGM, along with hundreds of other girls, not knowing a thing about dancing. Dance director Sammy Lee thought she'd be an effectively statuesque showgirl and hired her at $8.43 a day. It was the Depression and, at $50 a week plus overtime, she felt like the richest kid on the block.

She now decided that neither Marjorie Fisher nor Marjorie Bitzer were to her liking, so she changed her name. She took "Lynn" from Lynn Fontanne and "Barrie" from British playwright Sir James M. Barrie, being a great fan of his *Peter Pan*. She later modified the spelling when she read about the Italian city of Bari.

Lynn was a chorine in the lavish production number "Heigh Ho, the Gang's All Here," prancing, rather than dancing, in the chorus behind Crawford and Fred

Astaire (in his own film debut). She's clearly recognizable when the camera pans across the showgirls as each one talks a line of the song's lyric. Lynn's immortal line: "The grand old cheer." She'd lightened her dark hair and there's still some baby fat, but the striking smile and throaty voice are definitely in place.

She told Richard Lamparski in 1968, "Mr. Gable used to buy me ice cream cones and pat me on the head and call me 'J.B.' I never found out what that meant 'til it was too late to do anything about it. Jail bait."

She did another chorus bit in Metro's *Meet the Baron*. Sammy Lee, who was on loan to MGM, had taken a liking to Lynn and when he returned to his home lot, Fox, he took her with him and persuaded them to give her a stock contract.

Lynn became a utility girl. In 69 Fox movies released between 1933 and 1938 she played chorus girls, showgirls, sales clerks, telephone operators, waitresses, students, nightclub patrons, party and wedding guests, tourists, even incidental extra bits and appearances with other hopefuls in their screen tests. Sometimes she'd even get a word or two to speak, but not often. Rarely, if ever, did she get billing. "So I started studying," she said in the August, 1942 *Hollywood Magazine*. "I was serious about acting and treated it like a business. I went to school on the lot after Fox signed me." It was an apprenticeship that yielded little glory, but she paid attention and learned her business. It didn't hurt that she was a friendly, good-natured girl who became, and remained, popular and well-liked on the lot.

In 1937 she moved up a step into playing actual roles. She was cast in *The Baroness and the Butler* as Klari, a flirtatious maid who tries her wiles on William Powell. In *Walking Down Broadway*, a cheapie about six chorus girls and their respective fates, she was the one of the sextette who got bumped off early in the plot. She was given her first female lead, as a reporter, in *Mr. Moto's Gamble*, and left the B unit to give a solid performance as the gold-digging schemer trying to

Portrait of Lynn Bari, circa 1942.

steal Ian Hunter from star Barbara Stanwyck in *Always Goodbye*. All were released in 1938 and both moviegoers and fan magazines began to take notice of this "new girl," Lynn Bari. From this point on, she was always given billing.

It became clear to Fox chief Darryl F. Zanuck that Lynn's years of studying and observing had paid off. She turned out to be adept at both drama and comedy, her voice was deep down and distinctive, and of course she did look awfully good. She had become, in the studio's eyes, useful, and use her they did.

By this time, Claire Trevor had refused to re-sign with Fox and had left the lot. She had been the frustrated queen of Sol Wurtzel's busy B unit (she played the lead in *Walking Down Broadway*) and decided to try her luck elsewhere. So now Lynn Bari took over where Trevor had left off—grinding out dozens of quickie dramas and comedies year after year, mostly starring as heroines in the B's and playing under-the-title meanies in occasional A's. Her image as Hollywood's prototypical Other Woman had begun to take hold. She later told Lamparski, "I was always leering over my fan at John Payne or Don Ameche, and poor Alice Faye would be crying over the telephone or something. Many times if we were doing benefits, and I'd be with the leading lady, the ingenue, she'd get all the applause and the kids would hiss at me. I loved it."

But she came to resent being tagged "Queen of the B's." Though the studio thought it was a great publicity gambit, she considered it a stigma and would much rather have played decent roles in good movies. "I made as many as three at a time," she told Lamparski. "I'd go from one set to another, shooting people and stealing husbands. I never knew what the hell the plots were. We'd have as much as 20 or 30 pages a day of dialogue to do. Never had any time off. They got their money's worth." She played spies, actresses, waitresses, murderesses (suspected and actual), madcap working girls and that hallowed staple of B movies, spunky girl reporters. Fox's top actors (Tyrone Power, Don Ameche, Henry Fonda, John Payne) eschewed the B unit, so Lynn had to settle for such lower-case leading men as Lloyd Nolan, Donald Woods, John Sutton and Alan Curtis. She was averaging seven films a year.

On March 15, 1939, probably on lunch break, Lynn married actors' agent Walter Kane. They had met the previous year while she was agent-shopping.

It was during 1939–40 that Lynn finally grew into her own distinctive "look" on screen, having now lost all traces of her youthful baby fat. Her roundish face was now strong and angular, with wide cheekbones, flashing eyes and strongly defined features. The boxy, shoulder-padded '40s styles certainly suited her better than the fussy '30s frocks, and her tightly curled, marcelled hairdos now gave way to a softly waved, shoulder-length brunette bob. At 5'7" in bare feet, and with one of the most perfect figures in Hollywood, she went from pretty ingenue to stone knockout. Her height may have been somewhat responsible for her typecasting, since the common wisdom around Hollywood was that the prime requisites for Other Woman roles were to be tall and wear clothes well. She was and she did.

The titles tell the story of Lynn Bari's screen life during these years: *Speed to Burn, Meet the Girls, Pardon Our Nerve, Chasing Danger, City of Chance, Charter Pilot, We Go Fast, Secret Agent of Japan, The Perfect Snob, Earthbound*—well, you get the idea.

Amid the fluff was *Blood and Sand* (1941), a big-budget hit. Bullfighter Tyrone Power juggled new Fox star Linda Darnell and former Fox bit player Rita Hayworth while Lynn played the small role of his sour sister, Encarnacion, a role she disliked.

George Montgomery lights Lynn's fire in *Orchestra Wives* **(Fox, 1942).**

She confessed to having a violent crush on Power—who didn't?—but had to settle for a few brotherly pecks on the cheek. It was Hayworth's part she'd really wanted.

She caught a break in '42 when she was given the lead in an A picture: *The Magnificent Dope* with Henry Fonda, a *Meet John Doe* knockoff. She acquitted herself well enough for Fox to guarantee that from then on she would have over-the-title star billing. The previous year she'd played the tart-tongued singer with Glenn Miller's band in *Sun Valley Serenade* and now they were reunited in possibly Lynn's most popular film, the entertaining *Orchestra Wives*. Both were Other Woman roles in which she made mincemeat of sweet Sonja Henie in the former and sweet Ann Rutherford in the latter. She was a dazzling sight as she belted out her songs, though in both her singing was dubbed by Pat Friday, to Lynn's disappointment. She later told Colin Briggs, "Glenn Miller was very kind, and do you know he preferred my own voice to the trained one I mimed to, as he thought I sounded more like a band singer."

Her final 1942 release was another A production, *China Girl*. She was a sympathetic spy, Capt. Fifi, and delivered the goods with a strong, well-received performance. Her unrequited love for George Montgomery was played without frills, and her strength and humor made his choice of the wan Gene Tierney difficult to fathom. But they *were* the stars and Lynn *was* the Other Woman, so the deck remained stacked. She was billed third, but above the title as promised. Director Henry Hathaway, never noted for over-praising his actors, told Polly Platt in 1973 that he thought Lynn was "a marvelous actress."

It couldn't have been easy for Lynn to watch so many new girls come to Fox and quickly rise to A-list stardom (Gene Tierney, Linda Darnell, Betty Grable, Jeanne Crain, June Haver) while Lynn gamely soldiered on in lower-tier projects, but if it did bother her she never let on publicly.

In 1942 Lynn filed for divorce from Walter Kane. They had separated on August 10 and the divorce was granted November 25. Lynn testified "Mr. Kane acted like he didn't want to be married to me. Frequently he didn't get home 'til 3 A.M. And it wasn't business that kept him." As Lynn's agent, Kane was to have continued receiving ten

Lynn pins John Payne in *Hello, Frisco, Hello* (Fox, 1943).

percent of Lynn's $500,000 contract, but he agreed on a settlement of $7,500. She later explained, "I always wanted to be with somebody that I loved, but it was a tempestuous marriage and lasted only a few years. I was working very hard in pictures; at that time we worked six days a week. I'd get up at 4:30 in the morning, and sometimes I worked 'til seven at night and sometimes 'til midnight. With the full work load I had and the exhaustion I felt, the marriage was just too much for me to absorb."

That year, radio announcer–actor Bill Goodwin introduced her to Sid Luft, a test pilot at Douglas Aircraft, formerly of the Royal Canadian Air Force and, after Pearl Harbor, the Ferry Command. They were married at producer William Perlberg's Bel-Air home on November 28, 1943, three days after her divorce from Kane was final.

She was seen in only one film in '43, the lavish Alice Faye musical *Hello, Frisco, Hello*. She looked smashing in Technicolor, but was still playing the menace, vainly trying to steal John Payne from sweet Alice. But this time her name was above the title, albeit fourth of four.

Alice and Lynn remained close friends over the years. As Faye told Colin Briggs, "Lynn and Jane Wyman were chorus girls in *King of Burlesque* and she had a couple of lines in *On the Avenue*. With *Lillian Russell* and *Hollywood Cavalcade* she'd moved up to good supporting roles, though they cut her part in *Hollywood Cavalcade*. When we co-starred in *Hello, Frisco, Hello* we were old friends and I was so happy she got to be a star in that, probably my favorite movie."

Lynn returned the compliment: "Alice Faye and Vivian Blaine were the nice gals, always pleasant. Linda Darnell was not one of my favorite people and I didn't care for Carole Landis."

During the war years, Lynn endeared herself to GIs everywhere by visiting many training camps for the Hollywood Victory Committee and the USO. In September 1942 she did a much-publicized three-week Stars Over America War Bond tour across the U.S. with Ronald Colman, Greer Garson, Hedy Lamarr, Joan Leslie, Irene Dunne and Ann Rutherford. In January 1943 she and young Roddy McDowall were guests at President Roosevelt's Birthday Ball.

Her velvety alto voice made her ideal for radio and throughout the '40s she was a frequent guest on variety and dramatic shows, including a half-dozen *Lux Radio Theatre* appearances.

The July 1944 issue of *Silver Screen* featured cover girl Lynn Bari in military mufti, holding an oversized War Bond. It was her one and only U.S. fan magazine

Lynn overlooking Francis Lederer in *The Bridge of San Luis Rey* (UA, 1944).

cover (she did better overseas). That was the year producer Benedict Bogeaus bought the rights to Thornton Wilder's *The Bridge of San Luis Rey*, planned as a prestige item for United Artists, and he wanted Lynn Bari to be his star. Fox was then in need of a special electric camera crane for one of their musicals, and Bogeaus had the only one in town. He said he'd give it to them if they'd loan him Lynn. It was forever after known at Fox as the Bari Boom.

Lynn received tons of publicity hailing her overdue ascent to the big time. "A star at long last," gushed reporters. But it turned out to be a rushed production and the reviews—for the film and for Lynn—were tepid. In her interview with Colin Briggs, Lynn said, "The director [Rowland V. Lee] was old-fashioned and wanted acting with lots of hammy gestures, just like the silents. My singing, except for the song at the harpsichord, was dubbed. I did try out with the orchestra for the Donkey song but my nerves got the better of me, so they dubbed a soprano who sounded nothing like me."

She went back to Fox and picked up right where she'd left off. *Tampico* was a naval adventure in which Lynn was unjustly suspected of being an enemy agent but was actually the good girl who got the guy. The guy, however, was Edward G. Robinson. Her final 1944 release was *Sweet and Low-Down*, another big band gumdrop, this time singing with Benny Goodman's orchestra (and Lorraine Elliot's voice) and losing the nondescript leading man to Linda Darnell.

In an interview with columnist Lee Mortimer, Lynn explained what can be charitably referred to as her career arc: "I made a career of leering at Linda Darnell, Betty Grable and Alice Faye. Usually I'd corner my woman backstage and say to her in a very nasty tone, 'He's mine, all mine, you see? I've got him and you'll never take him away from me!' Then I'd stalk away, leaving Linda or Betty or Alice to slowly begin to cry in a gorgeous, Technicolor close-up. I went to the front office and asked for a chance at a lead. They told me, 'Our leading women play clinging vine roles. You look like you could eat a tree.'"

Due to pregnancy, her only 1945 release was the Eddie Rickenbacker biography *Captain Eddie*, starring Fred MacMurray. He had sole star billing and Lynn, as nice Mrs. Eddie, was back under the title again. When MacMurray signed with Fox to do the film, he specifically asked for Lynn as his leading lady. MacMurray was six feet three so Lynn didn't need to "scrunch down until I look like a question mark" as she did to play scenes with shorter actors. "I can wear my highest heels and my broadest shoulders and he'll still make me look tiny."

The Lufts' daughter was born on Aug. 15, 1945, three weeks before the due date, but died several hours later.

By 1945 Lynn had been at Fox for 12 years. "I've been at this studio longer than any actress on the lot," she told Inez Wallace in February of '46. "I've lived through two regimes for the reason that my job was so insignificant, when they were firing big names they didn't even notice me, just kept me on like the furniture and other props." She mentioned a pair of upcoming Fox projects. "I'm the only actress on the lot who doesn't want to play Amber." (Linda Darnell played *Forever Amber*, and it was a notorious flop.) But she did want to play opposite Tyrone Power. "If he does *Captain from Castile*, as is rumored, I'd love to play Catana. Come to think of it, I'd love to play Catana with or without Ty." Power did *Castile* but newcomer Jean Peters played Catana. *Laura* was another plum she wanted but lost.

Fred MacMurray flirts with Lynn in *Captain Eddie* (Fox, 1945).

Lynn was loaned to RKO for *Nocturne* (1946), co-starring with George Raft. It was a standard-issue *noir* thriller and Lynn was the good girl, but ads showed her in a sexy black negligee looking luscious and lethal. Back on her home turf she appeared in her final three Fox films, all released in '46. She was a baddie in *Shock*, a B thriller with Vincent Price, and played a librarian in *Margie*. The latter was a favor to the director, Henry King, who asked her to do it. *Margie* was a big hit but was strictly a Jeanne Crain vehicle with Lynn in a pleasant but unrewarding supporting role.

Her last role at Fox was as a harried mother of three who wrote crime novels in the comedy-mystery *Home Sweet Homicide*. She played the mother of Dean Stockwell, Connie Marshall and teenaged Peggy Ann Garner. Barbara Whiting was another of the teens in the cast and recently recalled that Lynn "was a good actress. Oh, she was beautiful. And nice. People liked her at the studio, everyone thought she was a good woman. She was good with the kids. In talking to me, she would kid about Sid [Luft]. She knew that my family knew him."

The following year, Lynn asked to be let out of her contract and was given her release after a record 14 years as a Fox contract player.

Lynn filed suit for divorce from Sid Luft in May 1947, informing Superior Court, "During our marriage I was the only breadwinner in the family." But after six months' separation, they reconciled. Their son, John Michael, was born September 18, 1948.

Now a freelance actress, Lynn wasn't finding much to do of any importance. Between 1948 and 1950 she made only three small movies for two small studios.

In January 1950 Lynn made her stage debut, joining a road company of Moss Hart's *Light Up the Sky* for a lengthy tour, and followed that with a Chicago run of *Goodbye, My Fancy*.

By June she was in New York, diving head-first into television as the star of a CBS live summer replacement series, *The Detective's Wife* (7/7/50–10/6/50). Lynn played the wife of a private eye (Donald Curtis) who helped her hubby solve crimes. As she told Colin Briggs in 1987, "This was the hardest work of my entire life. No one knew much about TV then and the whole thing was done with everyone's hands clasped in prayer."

As soon as the series ended, Lynn filed for divorce from Sid Luft, who had already begun his tempestuous relationship with Judy Garland. Louella Parsons reported that, on noon of Christmas Eve, Luft abducted their two-year-old son from Lynn's home. "I had told Sid that he could see Johnny at 10 o'clock Sunday morning," she told Louella. "At 12 o'clock he came to the door. I said the baby was asleep and could not be disturbed then. He went outside, kicked the window in, knocked my mother down, struck me, grabbed Johnny and ran with him. A spokesman for Sid telephoned to say that if I would promise not to prefer charges against Sid for striking my mother, breaking into the house and taking the baby he would return Johnny to me." She refused to agree to any such thing, and Johnny was returned to Lynn at 8:00 that evening.

The divorce was granted on December 26. Lynn was given custody of John and Luft was ordered to pay support payments of $500 a month for the first year and $300 per month thereafter, plus a $1,500 cash settlement. By mid–1951 Lynn had asked for a contempt citation, stating that Luft had fallen behind in his support payments. In September he paid the amount due. The divorce became final on the last day of 1951. For 18 more *years* Lynn and Luft would be in and out of court over delinquent support payments, and the Garland connection assured heavy press coverage.

There were three films in 1951. *I'd Climb the Highest Mountain* brought her back to Fox and damned if it wasn't another Other Woman role, trying to steal Susan Hayward's husband (William Lundigan). *On the Loose* at RKO had her playing teenager Joan Evans' selfish mother (she would play plenty of those), and Columbia's bottom-drawer *Sunny Side of the Street* wasted her in a trivial wisecracking receptionist role that any bit player could have (and should have) done.

Universal gave her a mother role in *Has Anybody Seen My Gal*, entertaining piffle about a family's war over an inheritance. For a mother role it was unusually strong, even central. Universal's contract pin-ups Rock Hudson and Piper Laurie were top-billed but Lynn and Charles Coburn had no trouble commanding every scene they were in.

It was becoming clear that as good as her film career had gotten at 20th Century-Fox was as good as it was ever going to get. She made ten more movies between 1952 and 1968 and not one is worth discussing. She was far better served by TV and live theater.

Her second TV series, *Boss Lady* (7/1/52-9/23/52), was a summer replacement for NBC's *Fireside Theatre*, filmed in Hollywood. Lynn starred as the head of a construction company with fellow ex–Fox player Glenn Langan as her boyfriend and Lee Patrick as her secretary.

On August 8, 1955, Lynn married Dr. Nathan Rickles, a Beverly Hills celebrity psychiatrist .

Lynn found herself back in court (and back in the papers) in September 1958 when Sid Luft, now married to Judy Garland, sued for and won custody of their son John. He somehow managed to convince a judge that the famously chaotic Garland-Luft home would be a healthier environment for John, but another judge took a more careful look and overturned the decision two months later, on November 26.

Lynn appeared in a 1959 TV commercial for an Ovaltine weight-loss program, smiling happily and holding up a flouncy period costume. "Remember this dress?" she asks. "I wore it in *The Bridge of San Luis Rey* 15 years ago." And guess what, it still fit, thanks to Ovaltine's miracle diet plan. Truth to tell, there weren't many people in 1959 who even remembered *The Bridge of San Luis Rey*, much less the dress.

That year Lynn sang in a Pasadena Playhouse production of the Broadway musical *Plain and Fancy*. For the next 14 years she concentrated her energies on what became her favorite performing venue, the stage. She would pause long enough to do her two final movies, *Trauma* (1964) and *The Young Runaways* ('68), both minor efforts, and occasional guest shots on episodic TV series (*Ben Casey, Bronco, The World of Disney, Perry Mason, Death Valley Days, Lux Video Theatre, The Girl from U.N.C.L.E., The FBI*, etc.). But it was live theater that excited and reinvigorated her as an actress. She toured in *Bye Bye Birdie, Enter Laughing, A Clearing in the Woods, Anniversary Waltz, Horace, The Bad Seed, All the Way Home, Simon and Laura, Adam & Id, French Postcards* and *Ballad of a City*.

She received great acclaim for a 111–city tour throughout the U.S. and Canada of *Barefoot in the Park* (1965-66). When the show played in Los Angeles, critic Margaret Harford wrote in *The L.A. Times* (1/27/66): "Miss Bari takes charge as the young bride's terribly practical mother. The minute she comes puffing up the five-and-a-half flights to her newly married daughter's nest, prospects for an evening's fun brighten visibly. She is an artful comedienne, a real pro with a cool, ironic style and the wit to time a laugh just long enough without letting it get cold."

Lynn divorced Dr. Rickles on July 26, 1972. As she later explained, "There must have been something wonderful about this man or I wouldn't have married him. But I hadn't realized how difficult the life of a psychiatrist can be. I acted as his secretary and his nurse; I was also taking care of the six-bedroom house in which we lived, and of Johnny, and of Nathan's young daughter by a previous marriage, trying to give her love and a feeling of emotional security. I stood it as long as I could; then, to preserve what was left of my sanity, I decided I'd better get a divorce.

"I'll never marry again," she correctly predicted. "I think that after you've been married three times, you're out. Each time I felt that I was marrying for a good reason but I was wrong."

She quickly returned to the stage and received the best notices of her career as a sharp-tongued alcoholic in a six-month tour of Neil Simon's *The Gingerbread Lady* (1972). The *Dallas Herald* commented: "She is a terrific actress. No one could question that after having seen Miss Bari so dominate the stage, giving so much power, poignancy and biting comic emphasis to the role."

A long-time political liberal, in 1972 she went public and made it known that she was supporting the candidacy of Dr. Benjamin Spock for president.

The following year Lynn, hit the road for the last time, joining Vivian Blaine, Robert Alda, Selma Diamond, Hildegarde and Jane Kean in Stephen Sondheim's *Follies*, playing Carlotta and singing "I'm Still Here" with skill and, God knows, conviction. Forty years earlier she had signed on as a starry-eyed MGM showgirl, and yes, by golly, Lynn Bari was still here.

But poor health, arthritis and a chronic back problem soon forced her retirement. She moved from Beverly Hills to Santa Barbara in 1982, where she shared an apartment with her son John, by then a successful artist.

Lynn died on November 20, 1989, of a heart attack. She was cremated, as per her instructions, and two days later her ashes were scattered at sea off the Santa Barbara coast. Her brother John Owen survived.

Back around the late 1960s, this writer was mindlessly watching some long-forgotten game show where celebrity panelists were asked to identify personalities whose photos were shown. I jumped as the TV screen was suddenly filled with one of Lynn's foxy Fox glamour portraits. Just as suddenly, panelist Joan Rivers screamed out, "*Lynn Bari!* She had the blackest lips in Hollywood!" I recall wondering if Lynn might be watching. She'd have loved it.

1933: Dancing Lady (MGM), Meet the Baron (MGM). **1934:** I Am Suzanne (Fox), Search for Beauty (Paramount), David Harum (Fox), Coming Out Party (Fox), Bottoms Up (Fox), Stand Up and Cheer (Fox), Handy Andy (Fox), Caravan (Fox), 365 Nights in Hollywood (Fox), Music in the Air (Fox). **1935:** Charlie Chan in Paris (Fox), Under Pressure (Fox), The Great Hotel Murder (Fox), George White's 1935 Scandals (Fox), Ten Dollar Raise (Fox), Spring Tonic (Fox), Doubting Thomas (Fox), Ladies Love Danger (Fox), Orchids to You (Fox), Curly Top (Fox), Charlie Chan in Shanghai (TCF), Dante's Inferno (TCF), Metropolitan (TCF), Welcome Home (TCF), Redheads on Parade (TCF), The Gay Deception (TCF), Music Is Magic (TCF), The Man Who Broke the Bank at Monte Carlo (TCF), Way Down East (TCF), Thanks a Million (TCF), Show Them No Mercy (TCF), King of Burlesque (TCF). **1936:** My Marriage (TCF), It Had to Happen (TCF), The Song and Dance Man (TCF), Everybody's Old Man (TCF), Private Number (TCF), Poor Little Rich Girl (TCF), 36 Hours to Kill (TCF), Girls Dormitory (TCF), Star for a Night (TCF), Sing, Baby, Sing (TCF), 15 Maiden Lane (TCF), Ladies in Love (TCF), Pigskin Parade (TCF). **1937:** Crack Up (TCF), Woman Wise (TCF), On the Avenue (TCF), Fair Warning (TCF), Timeout for Romance (TCF), Love Is News (TCF), Wake Up and Live (TCF), Cafe Metropole (TCF), This Is My Affair (TCF), Wee Willie Winkie (TCF), Sing and Be Happy (TCF), She Had to Eat (TCF), The Lady Escapes (TCF), You Can't Have Everything (TCF), Life Begins in College (TCF), Wife Doctor and Nurse (TCF), Ali Baba Goes to Town (TCF), Lancer Spy (TCF), Forty Five Fathers (TCF), Love and Hisses (TCF). **1938:** Rebecca of Sunnybrook Farm (TCF), City Girl (TCF), The Baroness and the Butler (TCF), Walking Down Broadway (TCF), Battle of Broadway (TCF), Mr. Moto's Gamble (TCF), Always Goodbye (TCF), Josette (TCF), Speed to Burn (TCF), I'll Give a Million (TCF), Meet the Girls (TCF), Sharpshooters (TCF). **1939:** Pardon Our Nerve (TCF), The Return of the Cisco Kid (TCF), Chasing Danger (TCF), News Is Made at Night (TCF), Elsa Maxwell's Hotel for Women (TCF), Hollywood Cavalcade (TCF), Pack Up Your Troubles (TCF), City in Darkness (TCF). **1940:** City of Chance (TCF), Free, Blonde and 21 (TCF), Lillian Russell (TCF), Earthbound (TCF), Pier 13 (TCF), Kit Carson (United Artists), Charter Pilot (TCF). **1941:** Sleepers West (TCF), Blood and Sand (TCF), Sun Valley Serenade (TCF) We Go Fast (TCF), Moon Over Her Shoulder (TCF), The Perfect Snob (TCF). **1942:** The Night Before the Divorce (TCF), Secret Agent of Japan (TCF), The Falcon Takes Over (RKO), The Magnificent Dope (TCF), Orchestra Wives (TCF), China Girl (TCF). **1943:** Hello, Frisco, Hello (TCF). **1944:** The Bridge of San Luis Rey (United Artists),

Tampico (TCF), Sweet and Low-Down (TCF). **1945:** Captain Eddie (TCF). **1946:** Shock (TCF), Margie (TCF), Nocturne (RKO), Home Sweet Homicide (TCF). **1948:** The Man from Texas (Eagle Lion), The Amazing Mr. X aka the Spiritualist (Eagle Lion). **1949:** The Kid from Cleveland (Republic). **1951:** I'd Climb the Highest Mountain (TCF), On the Loose (RKO), Sunny Side of the Street (Columbia). **1952:** Has Anybody Seen My Gal? (Universal), I Dream of Jeannie (Republic). **1954:** Francis Joins the WACS (Universal). **1955:** Abbott and Costello Meet the Keystone Kops (Universal). **1956:** The Women of Pitcairn Island (TCF). **1958:** Damn Citizen (Universal). **1964:** Trauma (Parade). **1968:** The Young Runaways (MGM).

Joan Blondell: Trouper

by LAURA WAGNER

If any actress best represents the snappy 1930s dame, it's Joan Blondell. During that era she played a lively assortment of chorus girls, waitresses, golddiggers, reporters and secretaries in a total of 53 movies, 44 of them for Warner Bros. "Yet, for all that overwork," Mick LaSalle writes in *Complicated Women*, "Blondell hardly ever had a false moment. Self-possessed, unimpressed, completely natural, always sane, without attitude or pretense ... the greatest of the screen's great broads. No one was better at playing someone both fun-loving yet grounded, ready for a great time, yet substantial, too."

She was fun-loving, but sometimes there were limits. As a flip waitress in *Other Men's Women* (1931), Joan puts the breaks on a fresh customer:

BLONDELL: Anything else you guys want?

CUSTOMER (*checking her out as she bends over*): Yeah, give me a big slice of *you*—and some french fried potatoes on the side.

BLONDELL: Listen, baby, I'm A.P.O.

CUSTOMER (*turning to friend*): What does she mean, A.P.O.?

BLONDELL: Ain't Putting Out.

"I was the fizz on the soda," she once said. "I just showed my big boobs and tiny waist and acted glib and flirty." While that's a fair assessment of most of her early roles, it wasn't the whole story.

By the time she was born on August 30, 1906, as Joan Rosebud Blondell, in New York City, show business had a solid hold on her family. Her father was the "original Katzenjammer Kid," vaudevillian Eddie Blondell, and, at the time of Joan's birth, he had a popular routine ("The Lost Boy") with his wife Kathryn Cane. It was said that Joan was born during a matinee at the theater.

Naturally, she would soon join the act. "At three I went on the stage for the first time in Sydney, Australia," Joan said in 1970. "Then I continued with the act on through Europe ... with zillions of trips back to the States on the Orpheum Circuit and the Pantages Circuit. Then my brother [Eddie, Jr.] was born and when he grew up he got into the act, and when vaudeville got bad my sister [Gloria] came in and we all struggled in the act. We sang, we danced, we did comedy sketches, we did everything. Always on the stage, always going, a week in each town and then finally a night in each town, then split weeks when it got bad. But we were always together, always together."

Her education consisted of a week here, a week there, at various schools along the traveling road. Main concern, however, centered on just surviving between shows. "I had to go make the rounds," Joan told John Kobal. "I got a few punk jobs here and there on a small salary which kept us going [librarian, sales clerk, waitress]." She also won $2000 in a beauty contest during a stopover in Dallas, Texas, earning the title "Miss Dallas."

She kept auditioning and seeking work on the stage. When she was 21, Joan landed a small role on Broadway in *Tarnish* (1927). After she appeared at the Provincetown Theatre in Greenwich Village in a rotating group of shows, she declined a scholarship to the Robert Minton–John Murray Anderson School of Drama because her "family needed whatever I could earn and the scholarship was for tuition only." This disappointment was softened by a seven-month gig in the road company of *The Trial of Mary Dugan*.

Joan returned to Broadway for George Kelly's *Maggie the Magnificent* in a supporting part, along with an up-and-coming James Cagney. Opening the same week

Portrait of Joan Blondell, c. 1939.

as the stock market crash during October of '29, the play flopped miserably, ending its run after just 32 performances. *The New York Times* made mention of "the gum-chewing, posing, brazen jade played by Joan Blondell—inclining toward caricature, but highly amusing in a drama that needs tangible vitality."

This standout appearance led to two other short-lived but important Broadway parts: *Sporting Blood* and *Penny Arcade*.

William Keighley, soon to be directing both Cagney and Blondell over at Warners, had seen the two in *Maggie* and felt they were "manna from heaven." He told Cagney later, "I was looking for an attractive yet tough young cookie and a strong, beautiful broad, and here were you and Joanie on that stage, the living, breathing counterparts of the two I needed for *Penny Arcade*."

The play opened on March 11, 1930. For their supporting roles in *Penny Arcade*, Cagney and Blondell got most of the notices. It lasted only 24 performances, but it would propel both actors to Hollywood.

"Al Jolson saw the show," Joan explained later, "and he bought it, then sold it to Warner Brothers with the stipulation that they take and use two people from the Broadway company, Cagney and Blondell. So they had to take us, and that's how we got into pictures. We arrived in Hollywood the same day and we were signed the same day, for just that one picture, of course, which ended up being [retitled] *Sinner's Holiday*."

Contrary to popular belief (and Joan herself), Cagney and Blondell didn't switch their original roles with Grant Withers and Evalyn Knapp for the film version; they played the same roles they had on Broadway. Cagney plays a weak-willed son shielded from a murder rap by an over-protective mother, while Joan is his snappy girlfriend ("Don't do anything while I'm gone you couldn't do on a bicycle").

The two might have come to Warners for just one picture, but it didn't take long for the studio to act. "[The] whole bunch of them saw the first day's rushes," Joan recalled. "We were shooting on the back lot—I'll never forget that day… Cagney and I had done our scene the day before and we were there to do a little more. All the bosses came down: Warner, Zanuck and all of them, with a contract, a long-term, five-year contract, and they signed us on that back lot in the broad daylight. So that's how that started, and from then on, it was one picture after another." Her starting salary would be $200 to Cagney's $400 a week.

No time was wasted. Blondell started making movies at a fast and furious clip, although at first her parts were minimal. Before *Sinner's Holiday* was released, she was rushed into *The Office Wife* (1930). She played either wisecracking pals to the heroines, sexy dames, or both, in *Illicit*, *Millie*, *My Past* and *God's Gift to Women* (all 1931). Today Joan is just barely in existing prints of the then-controversial, now-classic *The Public Enemy* (1931), as Eddie Woods' gal pal. After mandatory cuts from censors, several of her scenes were removed, including one where she and Woods share a bed.

Blondell was the only bright spot in the otherwise dreary *Big Business Girl* (1931), appearing in the last ten minutes as a professional divorce correspondent ("My life is just one hotel room after another"). Her bawdy, earthy presence ("Well, I'll be a dirty drink of water!") was a relief, and numerous critics took note of that fact. In *Night Nurse* (1931), an unsavory story of an attempt to starve a wealthy child, Joan was a flippant nurse (she chews gum during her nurse's oath) who joins star Barbara Stanwyck in uncovering the conspiracy. Many reviewers at the time, and still today, fondly recall *Night Nurse* for the scenes where the girls strip down to their scanties.

Columnist Jimmy Starr was one of those taking notice of this lively film newcomer. "Joan Blondell, in her favorite role of the wisecracking sister, again saves the day, or cinema, in this case," Starr wrote about *The Reckless Hour*. "Miss Blondell has a way about her that is fascinating because she can spout off the most obvious lines without making them the least bit obvious. It's her knack—and a good one."

She was rewarded with her first lead (replacing Marian Marsh), opposite James Cagney, in *Blonde Crazy* (1931). Bellboy Cagney teams up on the road with Blondell to "take from a lot of wise guys. Cheat a lot of cheaters." It was an ebullient pre–Coder with sex, brash banter, frame-ups and two stars totally in control and having fun with their material—and each other. Their chemistry was so good that Warners eventually placed them together three more times (*The Crowd Roars, Footlight Parade* and *He Was Her Man*), as well as announcing them for all sorts of projects (*Saturday's Children, Blessed Event*).

The year 1932 would be her busiest. Gathered together with *Blonde Crazy*, these ten films solidified Blondell's screen persona to her growing audience. "I'm no Pollyanna, or sweet 16 either," she tells Doug Fairbanks, Jr., in *Union Depot*. "I've been around, I know what it's all about. But, gee, I always try to keep decent. There's a few things I draw the line at." Or put more simply in *Central Park*, "Of course I've got nerve, but I've got a little principle too." It was a principle that took her through most of her films. If she was a tart, as in *Three on a Match, The Crowd Roars* and *Big City Blues*, and, later, *Gold Diggers of 1933*, the love of a good man (Warren William, Eric Linden) would eventually redeem her. In *Three on a Match*, her mother is adamant: "She's not a bad girl, she's just not serious enough. She's too full of fun." Joan eventually learns, and tries to knock some sense into her married friend Ann Dvorak, who is sowing some wild oats. "You're a fool, Vivian. Take it from someone who's been one. How can you do this to a man who's been on the square?"

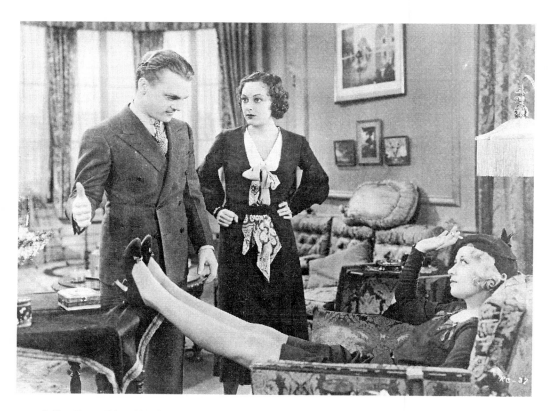

A flip Joan Blondell (right) defies an angry James Cagney, as a concerned Ann Dvorak watches, in *The Crowd Roars* (WB, 1932).

Joan's image-defining roles in '32 included a loan-out to Samuel Goldwyn, *The Greeks Had a Word For Them*, a delectably crude comedy about three fun-lovin', hard-drinkin' gals (top-billed Ina Claire, J.B. and Madge Evans) who are "always together, thicker than thieves, out for no good." Joan plays the somewhat dim Schatze, peacemaker between the always bickering Claire and Evans, who says flippantly of one man, "He's my fiancé. Not that we're engaged or anything like that." It was later reissued, retitled *Three Broadway Girls*, with Blondell gaining top billing. More than anything, the film was notable for introducing Joan to its cameraman, George S. Barnes. The couple would marry on January 4, 1933.

The Depression was at its peak in 1933, and so was Blondell. She exemplified the average woman of that dismal period. Audiences could relate to her honesty, her drive, and her humor and strength in the face of adversity. She came across as one of them—a down-to-earth gift she never lost. "I related to the shopgirls and chorus girls, just ordinary gals who were hoping. I would get endless fan mail from girls saying, 'That is exactly what I would have done, if I'd been in your shoes, you did exactly the right thing.' So I figured that was my popularity, relating to the girls."

A futile trip to welfare and her mother's needless death at the start of *Blondie Johnson* prompts a fed-up Joan to no longer stick by the rules, telling racketeer Chester Morris, "I know all the answers and I know what it's all about. I found out that the only thing worthwhile is dough, and I'm gonna get it, see? This city is gonna pay me a living, a good living, and it's gonna get back from me just as little as I have to give." She eventually elevates herself to head of the rackets. Blondell gave a smart, honest, sympathetic portrayal of a woman whose hard life urges her on.

Blondie Johnson was the second of three movies pitting Claire Dodd, Warners' resourceful temptress, as nemesis to Blondell for the affections of the leading man. Introduced to Dodd in *Johnson*, an unimpressed Joan dryly remarks, "Yeah, I think we've been introduced four or five hundred times. How do you do." More catty is their intro in *Footlight Parade* (1933): "I know Miss Bi…Fitch," Joan quickly states. When Cagney finally wakes up to Dodd's insincerity, it's Blondell who triumphantly gives her the heave-ho (and a kick on the rear):

DODD: But where do I go?

BLONDELL: Outside, Countess. As long as they have sidewalks, *you* have a job.

Many of Blondell's characters always felt the need to give short histories of themselves, often to the men they loved and felt unworthy of. In *Gold Diggers of 1933* she lays it on the line to Warren William: "Carol, that's my name. Cheap and vulgar Carol. Daughter of a Brooklyn saloon keeper and a woman who took in washing. Carol, the torch singer at Coney Island. Cheap and vulgar."

Gold Diggers is best known today for Busby Berkeley's seven-minute, dramatically staged anthem for war veterans hit by the Depression. The poignancy Blondell brought to the song didn't surprise Berkeley one bit: "I knew Joan couldn't sing when I decided to use her in the 'Remember My Forgotten Man' number. But I knew she could act the song, talk it, and put over its drama for me." Author Charles Higham wrote: "She symbolizes, in that sequence, the thirties, just as Crawford in broad-shouldered mink on a fog-cloaked wharf in *Mildred Pierce* moodily symbolizes the forties."

As 1933 was coming to a close, Warners hit comic pay dirt with *Havana Widows*, the first teaming of Blondell with Glenda Farrell. It was an inspired idea—two golddiggers, one devious (Glenda), the other more favorable to love (Joan)—tearin' up the screen and demonstrating some lively chemistry. It was so good it's a shame Warners didn't do even more.

Joan and Glenda, formerly with "Iwanna Shakitoff—Direct from Russia with her 40 Beautiful Hip Hip Hooray Girls" in burlesque, seek wealthy husbands in Havana: "A couple of smart dames like us can take over the joint," boasts Glenda. When they arrive, Joan falls for Lyle Talbot (not bad), but Glenda, always the schemer, wants her to go after Guy Kibbee instead. Farrell devises a slick blackmail ploy in an abandoned building:

FARRELL: If he's cold at first, don't get discouraged. Remember, Nero played a fiddle while Rome burned.

BLONDELL: Well, you better act fast because I'm not going to burn long enough for him to do much fiddlin'.

Farrell was always getting Blondell into trouble. Her advice to Joan in the frisky *Kansas City Princess* (1934) says it all: "A girl's gotta have three things nowadays: money, jack and dough. About time you learned it." *Princess* had a brief, but priceless, scene where the girls, manicurists hiding from Robert Armstrong, disguise themselves as Girl Scouts.

Joan gave a pithy summation of their characters in *We're in the Money* (1935), where they were lady process-servers: "I've got the nobleness, she's got the ambition." They were ex-chorus girls working in a carnival in *Miss Pacific Fleet* (1935), which was filled with the usual deadpan deliveries and merriment, as well as gorgeous Warren Hull ("I know my weakness," Joan sighs).

Warners seemed to lose interest in the duo, which is puzzling. Joan and Glenda would have only minimal contact in *I've Got Your Number* (1934), *Traveling Saleslady* (1935) and *Gold Diggers of 1937* (1936). The ads for *Saleslady* were deceptive: "The gimme girls are at it again! They get their biggest orders after office hours! They make business a pleasure ... and how they love their work!" They were not a team in the picture, a fact that greatly diminished its entertainment value. When Warners did put them together, they were the snappiest gals on screen.

They were also, not surprisingly, the best of friends off-screen. Glenda's son Tommy Farrell told Dan Van Neste in 1998, "Joan and my mother were 'bosom buddies.' When they were at Warners together, during their lunch hours, they would go out shopping, and the director would say, 'Where are the girls?' They'd have to go chasing them."

Joan became pregnant in the beginning of 1934, giving birth to a son, Norman, on November 2. But Warners was unrelenting; she made five films that year.

It was an exhausting schedule, but she showed the usual spunk in *Dames*, as a former member of the Jolly Widows burlesque troupe ("I've got 17-cents and the clothes I stand in, but there's life in the old girl yet"). She blackmails Guy Kibbee (again) to help Dick Powell and Ruby Keeler put on a show. The top-billed Blondell gets to talk-sing one of her best known numbers, "The Girl at the Ironing Board," as well as "Try to See It My Way, Baby."

Warner Brothers' snappy golddiggers Glenda Farrell and Joan Blondell, seven-time co-stars and best friends off-camera, share a laugh on the set of *Traveling Saleslady* (WB, 1935).

She was untypically out-of-control, as well as "spoiled, selfish, and headstrong" in *Smarty*. "Wounds are nicely healed," her husband Warren William tells her, "and you gotta take out the stitches and see if everything is bleeding nicely inside." Antagonizing him unceasingly, her ambiguous reference to "dice carrots," possibly a sexual reference, finally freaks him out and he slugs her. Before this odd, but very funny, comedy is through, it's quite naively clear: women should be slapped regularly to keep them in line. The seductive ending probably caused censors at the time some headaches. Making up with William, Blondell lies on the coach with open arms. As he moves down on her, Joan coos, "Tony dear, *hit* me again."

The fun on-camera didn't transfer to real-life. She sued George Barnes for divorce on August 12, 1935, claiming "he went hours without speaking to her, drove his car while intoxicated, and ignored guests at their home." It was also revealed later that he made Joan submit to abortions because he didn't want children.

Almost immediately Joan was seen around town with singer Dick Powell, her co-star in five previous films. During their much publicized romance in '36 they would be seen together in three more. They married on September 19, 1936; Powell would eventually adopt her son.

It was around this time that Blondell started to get a little antsy about what she felt was the heavy reliance on comedy and the sameness of her roles. She wanted dramatic parts. She was given a nice, non-comic role in *Bullets or Ballots* (1936), but it was strictly an Edward G. Robinson picture. She admitted to the *L.A. Evening Herald Express* that she didn't "want to do heavy things, to die or be stabbed or starve to death," but, added bitterly, "I'll probably be a comic until the day I walk out of Warner Brothers."

Which was essentially true. Yet who could resist Blondell, more madcap than usual, in *Stage Struck* (1936)? It was a part, played to the hilt by a zany and willing Blondell, of a hammy, temperamental socialite-actress who runs around with three dogs on a leash—and a loaded gun:

BLONDELL: I'm Peggy Revere.

POWELL: The girl who shot her husband?

BLONDELL: Nothing. A mere flesh wound.

The problem with Blondell's character, besides her attitude, is, according to all, "she can't sing, she can't dance and she can't act—and she'll murder this show!" To get her out, Dick Powell and the show's producer Warren William try to make her believe she's seriously ill. In a hilarious scene, a right-on-target, over-dramatic Blondell relishes the seriousness of her "illness": "Gentlemen, no x-rays. I don't look well enough for pictures." When it seems Jeanne Madden will go on in Joan's place, Blondell shows up backstage shouting valiantly, "Once a trouper, always a trouper!" All ends "happily" when she is detained backstage shooting her equally hammy boyfriend (Craig Reynolds) and being led away in handcuffs.

She was Sam Levene's Brooklynese girlfriend, whose mama "was a strip goil in burlesque," in *Three Men on a Horse* (1936), based on the stage hit. Even though her part was not the best, Joan projected a sweet quality in *Gold Diggers of 1937* (1936), especially in her scenes with Dick Powell, who sang to her "With Plenty of Money and You." Not good was *Back in Circulation* (1937), her second of four with Pat O'Brien. As with the upcoming, even more dismal *Off the Record* (1939), also with O'Brien, Joan plays a reporter out for the big scoop. The funniest bit in the whole picture had Blondell laying two right hooks on a guy trying to rough up O'Brien.

Two of her best during her waning days at Warners were, not surprisingly, loan-outs: *Stand-In* (UA, 1937) with Leslie Howard, and her first Columbia comedy with Melvyn Douglas, *There's Always a Woman* (1938). The latter in particular showed off Joan, the spry, delightful comedienne, in a tailor-made vehicle. If Warners was sticking her into the same routine, as good as that routine was in her capable hands, Columbia wrote above the norm for her. And she excels. With a smooth, very compatible Douglas, they do a bickering take-off on Powell and Loy from the *Thin Man* series; Blondell, playing detective, and hubby Douglas, working for the D.A., aid and abet each other on a murder case. One scene stands out because of its sheer absurdity: the interrogating of Blondell, who won't give up a clue, by the police. After hours of the "third degree," it is the cops, not Joan, who crack; she remains bright and cheery throughout it all. A weary detective finally admits defeat. "Unless I can use a hose on her—I give up." The film was so popular, a follow-up, *There's*

That Woman Again, was set in motion, but Warners refused to loan her; Virginia Bruce subbed.

When Joan became pregnant again, giving birth to daughter Ellen on July 1, 1938, Warners simply "squashed" her into a girdle, she told John Kobal later, and "I thought I was gonna die. I passed out a couple of times from it." They kept her working non-stop and she was hospitalized at one point with extreme exhaustion. She claimed she didn't feel mistreated, but all this had to get some ideas moving around.

Especially since her roles were getting more generic. She was seeing important roles easily played by herself go to others, both contract and non-contract players. Warners was also building up Ann Sheridan, who was the same type. The pickings, if they were slim before, would get even slimmer.

Dick Powell was likewise sick of his musical parts, wanting roles with more substance to them. It was he who made the decision for the both of them to leave Warners in the beginning of 1939. Joan never fought for better roles or more money. She would have stayed contentedly at Warners if Powell didn't move, simply because of the atmosphere. "We were all brothers and sisters, Pat O'Brien and I told each other everything, one experience and one joke after another. We'd work together and help each other. There was a camaraderie and professional way of working that's lost now, it seems to me... We were family, so in front of that camera it was really teamwork."

Joan's last under contract, *The Kid from Kokomo*, was made in December of '38. It was, luckily, a very funny movie, with Joan as a wisecracking ex–bubble dancer engaged to fight manager Pat O'Brien, but the ace part was handled by an untamed May Robson. It did nothing for Blondell's rep, but it was a nice exit from the studio.

Director David Butler requested her for Bing Crosby's *East Side of Heaven* (1939), her first freelancer, but one wonders why. You get Blondell, you anticipate spunk, wisecracks and the like, but the part wasn't written in that direction; it was simply flat, a typical Crosby leading lady, not the kind of role she had hoped for. But this was followed by two lively Columbia Melvyn Douglas comedies, *Good Girls Go to Paris* and *The Amazing Mr. Williams* (both 1939).

Dramatically, Joan got what she wanted in an unusual place: *Two Girls on Broadway* (MGM, 1940), a reworking of *Broadway Melody of 1929*. As Lana Turner's self-sacrificing sister, Blondell, effortlessly, with her sincerity, sensitivity, warmth and likability, takes the acting honors away from her co-stars Turner and George Murphy.

For a minor success like this (after all, *Two Girls* was a Turner vehicle), there were two features, co-starring her husband, that were bottom of the barrel: *I Want a Divorce* (1940) and *Model Wife* (1941); unsurprisingly these would be her last with Powell. The chemistry they exuded at Warners was now shot to hell. Married life, soon to be over anyway, had put a serious crimp into their once playful pairings on-screen.

Another collaboration in between their ghastly films together was the play *Goodbye to Love* (1940), a "comedy-farce," which Powell financially backed. It played briefly and closed in California, without sticking to its original plan of a tour before New York.

Of her four films released in 1941, only *Three Girls About Town* gave Joan a good opportunity. It was frantic, pointless and tasteless, but a laugh riot, about a dead body shuttled around different hotel rooms. It was her fourth for Columbia, a studio who clearly always made Blondell feel at home with good material and show-case roles. She would have been wise to pursue more with that studio, but, unfortunately, she would make only two more (*The Corpse Came C.O.D.*, another irrepressible chance for Joan to be smart and take-charge funny; and, decades later, *Ride Beyond Vengeance*).

Lady for a Night (1941) was memorable in at least one respect. It hearkened back to her days at Warners, where her heroines rose from nothing. "Just because I was born in the Mississippi Hollow," she bitterly tells John Wayne, "because Mother wore her eyes out doing plain sewing, because my father died of swamp fever trying to make a few potatoes grow—is that why I'm being punished?" In typical Blondell fashion she dreams of "being respectable, to live up there with those fine people, to be a civilized human being. I don't want to be a gambling house gal all my life. I want to be quality folk." But, again, she ultimately realizes she's better than the snobs. "I'm Jenny Blake," she defiantly announces at the conclusion, with pride in her voice, "and no lady." Few but Blondell (and Barbara Stanwyck) could make dialogue like that work.

The year 1942 was spent entertaining the troops and doing radio work. Blondell, like many in Hollywood, did all they could during WWII to build morale, and she traveled extensively with the USO. Her bond-selling efforts earned her the name "Miss Hollywood Victory Committee."

Back in Hollywood, she did a fine job in *Cry Havoc* (1943), a harrowing, moving story of nine volunteer nurses in Bataan. Joan is, of course, a down-to-earth ex–burlesque stripper: "Do'ya know what you do to a banana before you eat it? Well, I do it to music." It was a part rich in humor and underlining pathos, a rare, well-rounded character for her to play. Trying to stay brave in the face of bombing attacks on their outpost, and stuck in the small shelter, Joan, fighting back tears, tries to take the severity out of the situation by showing the girls how she used to strip. It was a affecting scene handled with restraint by Blondell.

MGM was so impressed they offered her a five-picture deal. She turned them down. Dick Powell was in an awkward transitional period in his career; he was finding it difficult getting the serious fare he craved to change his image. Joan realized it wouldn't do to wave an important contract like that in front of him, making him feel inferior. Fat lot of good it did her in the long run.

A turning point in her career was slowly occurring. And that turning point involved two people: June Allyson and Mike Todd.

Producer Mike Todd has been described as "the gaudiest, brashest, most controversial showman" in New York. He was a wheeler-dealer, "broke one day, a millionaire the next, broke again, but never poor." He had successes on Broadway, including *Something for the Boys* with Ethel Merman, and he was now, in 1943, starting up *The Naked Genius*, co-written by Gypsy Rose Lee. Joan took the dubious sounding part of Honey Bee Carroll, a burlesque queen posing as a novelist, at her husband's urging.

The show was a mess on the road and still a mess when it reached Broadway on October 21, 1943. It didn't seem to matter how awful it was, business was excellent; some say on Blondell's name alone. Todd, conscious of the play's shortcomings, played it up in the ads: "Guaranteed Not to Win the Pulitzer Prize. It Ain't Shakespeare But It's Laffs." When Todd did close the show, after 36 performances, it wasn't because of failure; he had sold the film rights to Fox, where it eventually became *Doll Face* (1945).

Meanwhile, back in Los Angeles, Dick Powell had started a relationship with newcomer June Allyson, who had a small role in his *Meet the People* (1944).

When Joan returned to California, she filed for divorce from Powell on July 14, 1944, reminding one of a quote from *Broadway Gondolier*: "People don't marry crooners," Blondell told one character, "they only divorce them." Todd, back in New York, was unable to obtain a divorce from his wife, with whom he had a son, Mike Todd, Jr. Joan went back to film work. Powell and Allyson would marry on August 19, 1945.

Joan found the role of a lifetime with *A Tree Grows in Brooklyn* (1945). She was given this plum assignment after Alice Faye supposedly turned it down.

Beautifully helmed by first-time director Elia Kazan, it was based on Betty Smith's nostalgic novel set in 1912, of a family's struggles to survive amid poverty. Author Smith could have modeled Aunt Sissy, the most colorful character in her book, after Joan: "When Sissy was around, everything was gay and glamorous ... She spoke in a low, soft, warmly melodious voice that soothed those who listened ... She was bad. But she was good. She was bad where the men were concerned. But she was good because wherever she was, there was life, good, tender, overwhelming, fun-loving and strong-scented life ... There was something true and direct about Sissy."

To those who knew the private Blondell, who

Blondell comforts Peggy Ann Garner in *A Tree Grows in Brooklyn* (Fox, 1945), the role of her lifetime as "Aunt Sissy."

"rushed home" to be with her two children after working on movie sets all day, the character of Sissy was also apropos. "She had so much tenderness in her," Smith wrote, "so much of wanting to give of herself to whoever needed what she had, whether it was her money, her time, the clothes off her back, her pity, her understanding, her friendship or her companionship and love. She was mother to everything that came her way."

Blondell's Aunt Sissy radiates a sweetness, a calm common sense that is so appealing, she steals every scene she's in. Flirtatious in spots, serious in others, Blondell fully captures her character's "reckless good sense and her clear way of straightening out troubles." She was justly proud of her work: "Kazan let me have a moment or two of tenderness, of maturity, that nobody had ever given me before." She said in 1972: "I remember that one with fondness."

It is shocking today to realize that Joan's subtle, beautiful performance wasn't even nominated for a supporting Oscar. James Dunn, as the alcoholic father, won a deserved Best Supporting Actor trophy, and Peggy Ann Garner was awarded a special juvenile award, but Joan was inconceivably passed over.

It also didn't lead to better roles. She was wasted in the bigamy comedy *Don Juan Quilligan* (1945), as one of William Bendix's two wives, and the notoriously horrendous *Adventure* (1945), Clark Gable's first picture back from the service.

Her relationship with Mike Todd also wasn't steady. He was a violate personality and fiercely possessive of Joan. She admitted that she knew what she was getting into when they were finally able to wed on July 4, 1947. Their short-lived union was marked by physical abuse and Todd's dependency on Blondell financially. "He not only insisted I give up my career, but when his shows were in trouble, he made me give up my money and my jewelry. Or so I thought. Fifteen years later he was married to Liz Taylor and I saw my big ring on her finger!"

Joan made only three movies during this disastrous marriage. *The Corpse Came C.O.D.* was a fun '30s throw back of two bickering, romantically drawn reporters solving a murder. Joan and George Brent, old pros at this sort of thing, worked well together; they were previously paired back in '32 for *Miss Pinkerton*. She wasn't so lucky with Brent in the not-so-jolly *Christmas Eve*.

That step backwards was more than made up for with *Nightmare Alley*. The film was considered risky material in 1947, but star Tyrone Power fought for the unusual role of an ambitious man whose rise to success ultimately hurls him down a destitute path, where he becomes a circus geek—a man who bites the heads off chickens. Not an ordinary movie, by any means, especially for matinee idol Power. Ty romances Joan to get her unique mind-reading act, which leads briefly to prestige, but also to other forms of illegal fakeries before his downfall and his redemption with Coleen Gray.

Blondell was cast at Power's insistence; he considered her one of Hollywood's sexiest women. And she comes through, showing that with good material like this, *Cry Havoc* and *A Tree Grows in Brooklyn*, she was a dramatic actress with real and vital talents. The film was not a hit, but it was an artistic success, and is now regarded as a classic. It's certainly one of Blondell's best.

She was in no position to appreciate that in the late '40s. Todd wasn't keen about her working. He wanted her close by—to watch over her, really. Some say he "persuaded" producers not to hire her. But money was getting tight from inactivity and Todd's lavish spending and gambling, so Joan decided to go back to work.

In Connecticut she did a summer stock run in *Happy Anniversary* during 1949. She and Todd were now split, and although he tried to reconcile, "I had to get away from what had become a life of unreason and brutality," Joan would write later. "There was too much fury to this man. The turbulence, the rages were more than I could bear, even though I loved him. So I left, heartsick and drained. It was the toughest thing I ever did. It meant trying to reactivate a career."

The divorce was granted on June 8, 1950. Financial worries would plague her for some time because of him. She also began to suffer health problems brought on by rheumatoid arthritis, an affliction she kept a secret from producers, out of fear of being uninsurable.

Returning briefly to the screen, Joan was a playwright in *For Heaven's Sake* (1950). Looking trim and glamorous, she portrayed an ambitious actress neglecting her daughter (Natalie Wood) in *The Blue Veil* (1951), starring Jane Wyman. Of this movie, Joan indifferently remarked, "That was the worst piece of trash I ever made. I did it in a day-and-a-half in New York." A piece of trash, unquestionably, but just try to keep a dry eye. It also garnered Joan her only Oscar nomination. Reviewers who claimed to have missed her during her Todd-induced absence from the screen were full of praise and "welcome back" salutes. Her part was short and a little unremarkable, so the nomination was probably a testament to her popularity with Hollywood professionals.

The years leading up to 1956 saw Blondell turn exclusively to television and the stage. She toured in the shows *Come Back, Little Sheba, I Give You My Husband, Call Me Madam* and, in her old role as Aunt Sissy, in the touring company of the musical version of *A Tree Grows in Brooklyn*.

Film work resumed in the late '50s, when she saw the star roles she had once enjoyed give way exclusively to character parts. "It takes all the talent you've got in your guts to play unimportant roles," Blondell said in 1971. "It's not degrading, just tough to do. It's fine to start out as a curvy biz-wiz, but unfortunately, when you can't do those roles any more, people think you're finished.

"But I accept change. I say, all right, it's a new generation growing up. So you support the young kids, and you have great respect for them because that's the way you were at one time ..."

The once-curvaceous Blondell was now "plump" by Hollywood's standards and getting roles that fit that image: wisecracking friends (*Desk Set, Will Success Spoil Rock Hunter?*) and madams/saloon keepers (*Advance to the Rear, Support Your Local Gunfighter, Waterhole No. 3*). Most of her roles during the remaining period of her career were trivial, allowing Joan to show up periodically to brighten the proceedings, then leave. She was always a welcome sight, and her stock in trade became a more bawdy, more earthy, a more *everything*, version of herself. Knocking back shots of whisky became high art in her hands, adding a comic twitch after the alcohol had taken its effect on her. Blondell was always enjoyable to watch.

Her best performances during this period were in *Lizzie* (1957) and *The Cincinnati Kid* (1965).

Lizzie came out six months before the similar *The Three Faces of Eve*, the film for which Joanne Woodward won an Oscar. Then, as now, unjustly overlooked because of *Eve*'s publicity and big budget, *Lizzie* merits more respect today, not least for Eleanor Parker's mesmerizing, frightening performance of the girl harboring three very distinct personalities within herself. Plus, the three-week shoot on a limited budget created a taut, disturbing and much more realistic atmosphere than *Eve*. Blondell gamely plays Parker's bourbon-guzzling, quip-ready, seriously bitter aunt who's at first unsympathetic and disbelieving to her niece's plight. It's hard to forget Joan's unnerved first reaction to seeing Parker dressed up as the evil Lizzie or her non-stop, self-centered chattering about herself as Eleanor suffers.

"Lady Fingers?," an incredulous Edward G. Robinson asks Karl Malden in *The Cincinnati Kid*. "I haven't seen that old bitch ... oh, it must be at least ten years. Long enough to think of her almost fondly."

Blondell is, of course, Lady Fingers, hired by Malden as relief dealer in Robinson's much-anticipated stud poker game with young card-wiz Steve McQueen. If *Lizzie* didn't do well, *The Cincinnati Kid* was a smash, grossing over $10 million; it's the role, together with the later *Grease*, that modern movie audiences know Blondell for.

Blondell's card dealer Lady Fingers in *The Cincinnati Kid* (MGM, 1965) was one of her best known later roles. Left to right: Karl Malden, Blondell, Edward G. Robinson.

She and Robinson in the story have a history, implied as formerly romantic. Blondell, spicy and sardonic, ribs him every so often about his age and his shaky status as "The Man." Vets Joan and Eddie G. show the youngsters how it's done in their tangy scenes together. Perhaps too well. "The sad part about that was that they cut our stuff. The pictures now run so long, and they had to cut something, so they cut our *meaning* to each other, which had made the thing interesting." Some of the edge of their past relationship is there, and nothing can change Blondell's salty attitude: "You wanna deal?," she challenges McQueen, after hours of game-playing. "Then deal 'em yourselves. I'm going to the john, I'm going to get something to eat and I'm gonna take a nap. If you don't like it—you can both go to hell!"

Stage work was always there. She played Nancy Walker's mother in the musical *Copper and Brass*, but Blondell left the troubled production in Philadelphia. Soon afterwards the well-regarded *The Rope Dancers* opened on Broadway (November 20, 1957). *The New York Journal-American* raved, "The most rewarding part in the play is that allotted Joan Blondell, the heart-of-gold neighbor, and she scores consistently. She has almost all the laugh lines, and she is one character that I understood all the way." The play ran 189 performances. Other shows featuring Blondell: *Crazy October* (an out-of-town dud with Tallulah Bankhead), *Gypsy, Bye, Bye Birdie, The Dark at the Top of the Stairs, Time of the Cuckoo, New Girl in Town* and, much later, an off–Broadway show she regretted, *The Effect of Gamma Rays on Man-in-the-Moon Marigolds* (she disliked her unsympathetic character).

Joan Blondell as an axe-murderess? The heart leaps with joy at the very prospect. That fascinating concept almost became a reality when producer-director William Castle cast her in *Strait-Jacket* (1964). She was replaced when Joan Crawford, considered a bigger "name," suddenly showed interest. This role could have saved her largely undistinguished movie work in the '60s; at least it was a lead. She was typically feisty, but the films were hardly worth her effort.

ABC-TV's *Here Come the Brides* (1968-70) put Joan back in the limelight; she would be Emmy-nominated for her saucy role of saloon keeper Lottie in 1969. "I find making features dull," she said at the time. "Hopefully this series will run 12 years and I won't have to worry about films to keep busy." Joan Barthel, writing in *Life*, said that Blondell's part on the show "was an afterthought, a last-minute write-in when they needed someone to counterpoint all those dewy brides, but Blondell played Lottie with no apologies and a gorgeously rowdy charm ..."

Television turned out to be a good, busy source of work, and continued to be right until her death: *Medical Center, That Girl, Police Story, McCloud, Love, American Style, The Rookies, The Love Boat, Starsky and Hutch* and more.

The year 1972 saw the publication of her novel *Center Door Fancy*. It was a thinly veiled autobiography, colorfully chronicling her early days in vaudeville and her career in Hollywood. Names were changed, but it was clear who everyone was; no one was spared, including herself. It was a bestseller, but Joan was unhappy with some aspects of it, especially the publisher's addition of profanities.

That same year, Blondell had high hopes for NBC's detective show *Banyon*, starring Robert Forster, but it lasted only four months. What made it memorable was that it was being filmed at Warner Bros., where Joan hadn't stepped foot for over 30 years. "I looked for the old dressing rooms at Warners," she reminisced with

Charles Higham at the time, "where Kay Francis and Eddie Robinson, Bette Davis and Ann Dvorak lived and breathed, and there was nothing left. I try, really try not to gaze too far into the past. But then it all floods in, the grips and the gaffers from the old days step by and take me in a big bear hug and they say, 'Oh, Joanie, it's good to have you back.' And I feel so tender I could cry."

There is an inside joke regarding the name of her character on *Banyon*, Peggy Revere, head of the secretarial school; it was the name of her over-theatrical actress in *Stage Struck* back in '36.

Blondell's health declined progressively in the '70s, first from a stroke, then when she was diagnosed with leukemia. Through it all she looked ahead and continued to work, on television and in motion pictures.

"Without work, what is life?" was trouper Blondell's motto. "Retirement doesn't really come into my way of thinking," she remarked. "I don't think I could do it. I've never stopped working in my life. Even in all the years since Warner Brothers, I have worked somewhere. There was only a period of three years when I didn't; I was married to someone who wanted me to quit and that was perfectly all right with me. But aside from that, even if I wasn't in pictures, I started on the road taking shows out, then coming back and starting in again here."

And she stayed active until December of 1979, when she passed away on Christmas Day. Surrounding her was her family: son Norman, daughter Ellen and sister Gloria, herself a successful radio and TV actress. Joan had always kept it real, always kept her priorities straight. "I wasn't that ambitious. I enjoyed a home life more than a theatrical career. I just took what they gave me, because I wanted to get home quickly."

Joan, said one writer, personified everyone's "good friend," on- and off-camera. "Of all the stars I have interviewed," wrote Charles Higham, "I have liked Joan Blondell the best. She is unique in my experience in being an actress who is devoid of ego, self-congratulation and self-pity, and would not dream of quoting a favorable review of herself. She is down-to-earth and human and real. This is almost unheard of in Saran-wrapped Hollywood." Her accessibility, straightforwardness and her quick-with-a-comeback attitude was her appeal, and it never diminished as she got older.

In a candid 1971 interview, Joan, typically realistic, remarked: "I live a quiet life now; I've earned the right to live the way I want to. I can relax and enjoy my $34 set of silverware, and every time I see a gorgeous hunk of silver, or a painting, I can think, I've had all that. I don't have it now, but I *did* have it, and the hell with it."

1930: Broadway's Like That (WB short), Devil's Parade (WB short), The Heart Breaker (WB short), The Office Wife (WB), Sinner's Holiday (WB). **1931:** Illicit (WB), Millie (RKO), My Past (WB), God's Gift to Women (WB), Other Men's Women (WB), The Public Enemy (WB), Big Business Girl (WB), Night Nurse (WB), The Reckless Hour (WB), How I Play Golf #10 (WB short), Blonde Crazy (WB). **1932:** Union Depot (WB), The Greeks Had a Word for Them (Goldwyn/UA), The Crowd Roars (WB), The Famous Ferguson Case (WB), Make Me a Star (Paramount), Miss Pinkerton (WB), Big City Blues (WB), Three on a Match (WB), Central Park (WB), Lawyer Man (WB). **1933:** Broadway Bad (Fox), Blondie Johnson (WB), Gold Diggers of 1933 (WB), Goodbye Again (WB), Footlight

Parade (WB), Havana Widows (WB), Convention City (WB). **1934:** I've Got Your Number (WB), He Was Her Man (WB), Smarty (WB), Dames (WB), Kansas City Princess (WB). **1935:** Traveling Saleslady (WB), Broadway Gondolier (WB), We're in the Money (WB), Miss Pacific Fleet (WB). **1936:** Colleen (WB), Talent Scout (WB), Sons O'Guns (WB), Bullets or Ballots (WB), Stage Struck (WB), Three Men on a Horse (WB), Gold Diggers of 1937 (WB). **1937:** The King and the Chorus Girl (WB), A Day at Santa Anita (WB short), Back in Circulation (WB), The Perfect Specimen (WB), Stand-In (Wanger/UA). **1938:** There's Always a Woman (Columbia). **1939:** Off the Record (WB), East Side of Heaven (Universal), The Kid from Kokomo (WB), Good Girls Go to Paris (Columbia), The Amazing Mr. Williams (Columbia). **1940:** Two Girls on Broadway (MGM), I Want a Divorce (Paramount). **1941:** Topper Returns (UA), Model Wife (Universal), Three Girls About Town (Columbia), Lady for a Night (Republic). **1943:** Cry Havoc (MGM). **1945:** A Tree Grows in Brooklyn (TCF), Don Juan Quilligan (TCF), Adventure (MGM). **1947:** The Corpse Came C.O.D. (Columbia), Nightmare Alley (TCF), Christmas Eve (UA). **1950:** For Heaven's Sake (TCF). **1951:** The Blue Veil (RKO). **1956:** The Opposite Sex (MGM). **1957:** Lizzie (MGM), This Could Be the Night (MGM), Desk Set (MGM), Will Success Spoil Rock Hunter? (TCF). **1961:** Angel Baby (AA). **1964:** Advance to the Rear (MGM). **1965:** The Cincinnati Kid (MGM). **1966:** Paradise Road/Big Daddy (Syzygy/United), Ride Beyond Vengeance (Columbia). **1967:** Waterhole No. 3 (Paramount), Winchester '73 (TV). **1968:** Kona Coast (WB), Stay Away, Joe (MGM). **1970:** The Battle at Gannon's Bridge (TV), The Phynx (WB). **1971:** Support Your Local Gunfighter (UA). **1975:** The Dead Don't Scream (TV), Winner Take All (TV). **1976:** Won Ton Ton, the Dog Who Saved Hollywood (Paramount), Death at Love House (TV). **1977:** Opening Night (Faces Distribution, Inc.), The Baron/Black Cue (Paragon). **1978:** Grease (Paramount), Battered (TV). **1979:** The Champ (MGM), Family Secrets (TV), The Glove (Pro-International; released 1981). **1980:** The Woman Inside (TCF).

Ann Dvorak: A Life of Her Own

by LAURA WAGNER

> She was thrilling, every inch of her a great actress on the order of ... Ann Dvorak.
>
> —Gore Vidal, in his novel *Myra Breckinridge.*

In 1932, Ann Dvorak was poised for great stardom. Just a chorus girl at MGM when she was discovered by Howard Hughes in 1931, she was cast as Paul Muni's sister in Howard Hawks' now-classic *Scarface.* Her striking, highly intense performance made her the talk of the town.

An impressed Warner Brothers bought her contract and important things were promised. Jack Warner was struck by her "dainty, unworldly quality," believing that she had a "dazzling future" ahead of her.

Then, it all went haywire.

She was born Annabelle McKim on August 2, 1911, in New York City. Her father was Edwin Samuel McKim, a silent-era director. Her mother, Anna Lehr, had a respectable acting career, working in over 40 films from 1912 to 1928. At least one is known to still exist, *Jesus of Nazareth* (1928), in which she played the Virgin Mary. The surname "Dvorak" originated from her mother's family.

The McKims were separated in 1916, divorcing by 1920. Her father disappeared shortly thereafter.

Due to her mother, five-year-old Ann made her film debut in *Ramona* (1916) as Baby Anna Lehr, the name she would use in *The Man Hater* (1917) and *The Five Dollar Plate* (1920).

Ann's educational history is unclear. Studio bios tell us that she was put in a succession of boarding schools, convents, Los Angeles Page School for Girls (editing the school newspaper *The Pagette*) and Hollywood High (Dvorak's biographer Christina Rice found no record of her having gone there). Ann claimed in later interviews that she "majored in journalism and edited a school newspaper" at Occidental College. Publicity states that she was also briefly a cub reporter with *The Los Angeles Times.* Since this period is clouded by studio elaborations, it's hard to tell what's what. However, buried in a *Movie Mirror* article, Ann lets slip that "I supported myself and my family ever since I left school at 15."

Ann's lack of education might explain her later, almost fanatical thirst for reading, her studying of languages and various subjects.

She had long been serious about dancing and singing, taking extensive lessons, but she was also interested in following her mother's footsteps. In 1928, Ann unsuccessfully tested for the film *The Iron Mask* (1929).

Undaunted, she sought work as a chorus girl at the Pom Pom Club in Los Angeles. With what would become typical Dvorak moxie, she managed to up her salary from $25 to $65 a week, minutes after landing the job.

MGM's call for chorines for *The Hollywood Revue of 1929* motivated Ann to audition. When she was turned down, Dvorak approached dance director Sammy Lee. "Are you running this show?" she asked. "Well, I'm as good as the ones you chose. Why didn't you pick me? I'm going to get somewhere. I'm sincere. I work. I have ambition." This fire-in-the-belly drive worked, she was hired. Six months

Portrait of Ann Dvorak, 1938.

later, she was Lee's assistant. In addition to her 20-plus film appearances at MGM during 1929–31, she coached Conchita Montenegro in *La Sevillana* and Joan Crawford in *Dance, Fools, Dance.*

Crawford is often credited with tipping off Howard Hughes, who was producing *Scarface*, to Ann, but that distinction goes to actress Karen Morley. The two girls had become friends at MGM, and Morley, who was already cast in *Scarface* as Paul Muni's moll, advised Ann that the part of Muni's sister was still open. Ann tested for Hughes.

But according to *Scarface* director Howard Hawks, it was George Raft who finally secured Ann's hiring. The scene was a party at Hawks' house. "Ann asked [Raft] to dance with her but he said he'd rather not," Hawks later recalled. "She was a little high and right in front of him starts to do this sexy undulating dance, sort of trying to lure him on to dance with her. She was a knockout. She wore a black silk gown almost cut down to her hips. I'm sure that's all she had on. After a while George couldn't resist her suggestive dance and in no time they were doing a sensational number which stopped the party."

An impressed Hawks cast her as Tony "Scarface" Camonte's sister Cesca, for whom he has obsessive, incestuous feelings. Hughes, too, signed her to a five-year contract at $250 a week, starting in September of 1931. She was on her way.

Considering that she didn't seem to have any acting lessons or experience, Dvorak's arrival as a fierce, excitingly emotional actress in *Scarface* was a revelation. Where did all that smoldering fire come from? Her scenes with Muni were fervent and uncomfortably real for that time, making all too clear his motives and her fearful, restless nature.

Trying to break free of her brother's terrifying emotional bonds, she boldly acts out, pursuing an interested but cautious George Raft. Her provocative dance for him out in front of a nightclub, mirroring their real-life party dance, is a terrific pre–Code moment.

Howard Hawks was wowed by Dvorak's "sprightly, direct, unbashful manner" off-camera, and the two began an affair that would last into their next picture together, *The Crowd Roars*.

Before *Scarface* was completed, Howard Hughes assigned Ann to the lighter *Sky Devils* (1932). She was as far away from Chicago gangsters as she could get: an American chorus girl in France who joins in the adventures of two WWI fliers (Spencer Tracy, William Boyd). She got to dance, do pratfalls and act highly amused—and was a natural.

By the time it was released in January of 1932, ahead of *Scarface*, which was encountering censorship problems, Dvorak was being treated to some high-gear publicity. Jerry Hoffman, in his *Los Angeles Examiner* review of *Devils*, stated that he could "understand now the why and wherefore" regarding all the buzz about her.

This quickie was followed by one of Ann's best early roles, a loan-out to Warner Bros. for *The Crowd Roars* (1932).

"I can't play a neurotic," protested Joan Blondell.

Concurred Dvorak, "I can't play an ingénue."

With these words, the two actresses, with Howard Hawks' consent, switched roles. Ann plays the long-suffering, high-strung mistress of race car driver James Cagney, while Blondell is the attitude-heavy tramp in love with his brother. Ann's best scene is also her most intense. Believing her a bad influence on his younger brother, Cagney dumps her. Ann's already frayed emotions escalate until they explode into a torrent of desperation, slapping him and then pitifully sobbing for his forgiveness. Wow. No one had an emotional meltdown quite like Dvorak.

Warners was delighted with her performance, and in late January of 1932, they paid $40,000 to Hughes for her contract. Her weekly salary stayed at $250.

She was put to work immediately in *The Strange Love of Molly Louvain* (1932), a strong showcase for her talents as a dramatic actress—and singer. Ann, who first sang on-screen in *Scarface* ("The Wreck of the Old 97"), here gets to do a scat version of "Penthouse Serenade," and a song she herself wrote, "Gold Digger Lady."

The scene in which the two songs are sung together is a transitional one: "Penthouse," reflecting her lost dreams of a happy family life with the man who left her pregnant, and "Lady," her acceptance of following a wanton path, getting involved with a crook and leaving her child behind.

It's Ann's movie all the way—a heartbreaking, highly effective role, allowing

"Three on a match means one will die soon." Ann Dvorak, Joan Blondell and Bette Davis in *Three on a Match* (WB, 1932). The role was Ann's finest at Warners.

her to run a wide gamut, from youthful exuberance to bitterness, regret, pain and passion, to mother love, sacrifice and redemption.

It was during filming that Ann met actor Leslie Fenton, fifth-billed as the man who sets her off onto the wrong road. In view of future events in Dvorak's personal life, that was quite fitting.

The British-born actor was ten years older and had been in film since the early '20s. The intellectual, moody Fenton was a world-traveler, a bit eccentric, and to Dvorak he might have represented the ultimate man of the world. And a father figure. He also had an attitude when it came to Hollywood, preferring to follow his own path rather than conform to studio demands. It was an attitude that, coupled with Ann's own fiery determination, would prove disastrous.

She was rushed right into *Love Is a Racket* (1932), a film reeking of sophistication and pre–Code hijinks. Ann is simply there to supply her striking presence, pine for Douglas Fairbanks, Jr., and toss off some witty asides.

About two weeks into filming, on March 17, 1932, she and Fenton flew to Yuma, Arizona, and were married. It was a whirlwind month-long courtship, catching everyone by surprise. Especially Gladys Freeman. Several days after the announcement of the nuptials, Gladys, who acted under the names Julie Carter and Gladys Belmont, sued Fenton for $250,000 in a breach of promise and betrayal suit. She alleged that he "promised to marry her, and induced her to live with him for several months." Fenton had also been guiding Freeman's career.

Warners kept Ann working on a hectic schedule, just as they did with all their contract players. Before July she had finished three more films. Both *Stranger in Town* and *Crooner* were standard-issue female leads, meant simply to put her in front of the public. *Three on a Match* was quite a different story. It was the role which would become her crowning achievement at the studio.

Bette Davis, playing one of the three, called it "a dull B picture." The reason was simple: Davis had a minuscule role. Quite the contrary, *Match* was an unforgettably powerful drama realistically depicting Ann's swift debasement from booze, drugs and the sexual magnetism of Lyle Talbot.

When she starts the film, she is the beautiful, pampered wife of rich Warren William and has a child. Yet she is restless, life is "tiresome and pointless" and she is "fed up with everything." Then gorgeous Talbot appears. That's it, she's *gone*. Ann leaves her family, shacks up with Lyle and gets her party on.

The remarkable aspect of Dvorak's performance is her physical and mental deterioration, which she does with expert subtlety; drunk, lying wasted on her bed, she eventually advances to full-blown cocaine addict. Ann has all of the addict's tics, groggy visage and pauses down brilliantly.

Her role could have easily been overacted—if Davis had done it, God *knows* the hysterics which would have resulted. Even in her final gut-wrenching scenes, when Ann realizes the hoods are going to kill her kidnapped son, she brings a simmering, beautifully controlled intensity to her desperation. Murmuring to herself in prayer, crying and trembling uncontrollably, she shakily scribbles a message in lipstick on her nightgown. When the crooks suddenly approach, a screaming Ann bolts for the window, crashing through the glass and falling to her death—to save her child.

Her vivid performance deserved at least an Oscar nomination. It didn't come, but an "unlimited future" was predicted, and Warners was ready to give her the projects that would propel her to real stardom.

No one reckoned on ill-timed temperament.

Obviously, resentment had been building, possibly spurred on by her maverick husband. Warners had no inkling when, on July 4, 1932, they received a wire:

> Going to Europe via New York. Ann tired and unhappy over studio conditions. She must have rest. Take care of things for us. See you later. Leslie and Ann.

In New York, Ann confronted reporters. Of her many gripes, the biggest was that Buster Phelps, the child who played her son in *Three on a Match*, made double her salary. Ann wanted a raise and a rest. (Truth be told, Phelps was paid the same amount as Dvorak.)

By leaving when she did, Ann lost out on several important roles, including a few that went to Bette Davis (*20,000 Years in Sing Sing*); Samuel Goldwyn had wanted her for *Cynara* with Ronald Colman.

Fan magazines seized on a different angle for her departure—love. The romantic "young runaways" were having their belated honeymoon, seeing the world together and learning about each other. When Dvorak returned, a full nine months later, she was glad, she said, that she had put Fenton ahead of her career. "Love is more important than fame," she gushed.

But, *still* ...

If only Ann had waited until she had a firmer foothold at the studio; she had only been at Warners six months when she went on strike. When Bette Davis later rebelled for better parts and salary, she was several years into her contract; Bette lost her case, but earned the respect of the studio *and* worthier roles. Dvorak acted too soon.

They returned to America in March of 1933. Meetings with Warners were arranged to iron out her contract. Her weekly salary would eventually be advanced to $1,500.

There had to be some lingering animosity. Her future roles at Warners, with a few exceptions, would be of inferior quality, and one wonders if they were punishment for her hasty rebellion. That Dvorak was able to rise to these occasions is a testament to her versatility and professionalism.

A number of projects were promptly proposed: *Upper World, British Agent, Merry Wives of Reno, Twenty Million Sweethearts* and the never-filmed *Broadway and Back*.

Any one of them would have been better than the one she was finally assigned: *College Coach* (1933), as Pat O'Brien's neglected wife. Her only other role that year was with Maurice Chevalier in *The Way to Love*, a loan-out to Paramount; she was replacing Sylvia Sidney, who had fled to New York in the midst of production. Ann, as a mistreated knife thrower's assistant, looked quite striking and elicited much sympathy.

In December 1933, Ann made a public plea seeking her father, whom she hadn't seen since she was a small child. He was finally located in 1934 living in Philadelphia, supposedly unaware she was a star. After some publicity regarding their reunion, nothing more was heard of him.

The year 1934 would be her busiest and most uneven, with nine Warner features hitting theaters. They couldn't decide whether they wanted to bury her (*Side Streets, Midnight Alibi, I Sell Anything, Gentlemen Are Born*), give her standard parts (*Massacre, Heat Lightning, Friends of Mr. Sweeney, Murder in the Clouds*) or reward her (*Housewife*).

"A point often ignored in cinema history studies of [Bette] Davis," wrote Jim Parish and Don Stanke years later of *Housewife*, "is that Ann Dvorak, who plays the film's title role, was established as a strong dramatic actress *long* before Bette, and it was she who set the standard for battling with the studio for better roles. In her quiet performance as Nan Wilson Reynolds, it is Miss Dvorak and *not* the already mannered Bette, who woos the audience's attention and affection. It is Dvorak who provides the proper artistic control for the feature..."

The big difference between the two actresses was maturity. Bette, in these early movies, was very rough around the gills; she became polished, but always tended to slip into campy tirades. Dvorak was a natural; she was intense, but always in control, even in highly emotional situations.

Case in point is their confrontational scene in *Housewife*. While Bette, clearly struggling to steal the moment, bounces around the room with flailing arms and mannerisms galore, much like a top ricocheting from one object to the other, Ann steadily stands her ground. She is quiet, thoughtful and direct, effectively under-playing—and in the process, the scene is hers. Bette, frustrated at the lack of atten-tion she received, later referred to the picture as "a horror." She was, after all, upstaged.

It is puzzling that Warners never took advantage of Ann's musical abilities until 1935, what with her melodic, husky singing voice and her dancing skills. Her only full-blown musical at Warners was *Sweet Music* (1935), co-starring an obnoxious Rudy Vallee, who sings most of the score. Ann shares a duet with Vallee on "Fare Thee Well, Annabelle," which is notable for her dynamic moment of waving a baton and exuberantly leading a girl chorus into a swinging dance.

The film also shows her rarely displayed quippy side; her constant verbal jabs directed toward Vallee are done with expert comic timing. Ann has a marvelously antagonistic attitude that, considering Rudy's wooden acting, is totally justified: "There ought to be a law against guys like that breathing in the first place." *Sweet Music* was one of her better studio assignments, and when she asks in the film, "What am I supposed to be—a singer, a dancer or an actress?," the satisfying answer is that Warners allowed her to be all three in the same movie.

The same went for the punchy *G-Men* with James Cagney. Ann's memorable part was small, but she gets to sing and dance to the playful "You Bother Me an Awful Lot," act cute, and finally do some fantastic emoting that leads to her being shot to death in a phone booth.

Bright Lights (1935) earmarked just a few moments for her singing and danc-ing ("Toddlin' Along with You"), but she was fine as the wife of vaudevillian-turned-Broadway star Joe E. Brown. Even better was a loanout to Fox for *Thanks a Million* (1935). It was typical leading lady stuff, but she and Patsy Kelly stole the show singing and energetically tapping to "Sugarplum."

It looked like she was at last gaining lost ground. Better parts seemed inevitable. Then it came crashing down.

Assigned to Howard Hawks' *Ceiling Zero* in September of '35, she rejected the minor role because of illness. Ann acknowledged that she was also sick of the roles being offered her. In a letter dated September 30, she wrote to Jack Warner: "I must insist that you place me in productions of dramatic merit, in which my artistry, per-sonality, intelligence and experience may be displayed. Failure to do so will be con-sidered as a breach of contract on your part."

Hospitalized in October with extreme exhaustion, she was told by her doctors to rest a couple of months, but she reported back to work on November 1. The stu-dio put her on suspension.

In early February 1936, Dvorak took Warners to court to "construe the terms of her contract." She said that the studio refused to give her work when she was well in November, suspended her salary, but "still claimed the right to her exclusive services." Ann alleged that the studio had breached her contract when they had suspended pay-ment on her salary. She asked for damages and the cancellation of her contract. Ann said in court, "I told Mr. Warner if I was not worth my salary, for him to release me."

Warners countered, charging her with temperament, with refusing roles, and that she was "growing thinner and thinner from ill health" and was "unfit to work in pictures." Ann denied these allegations, stating that Warners put her on suspension in "an asserted effort" to cut her salary.

Ann's motion that her contract be terminated was rejected by the court, who claimed Warners was justified in their actions. But that wasn't the end of it.

In August she was still fighting, this time privately. Part of the suspension period, she said, was incorrect: February 27 to July 2, 1936. Early in March, Ann offered to work, but was dismissed. "From that time until July," she wrote, "Warner Bros. did not accept my tender of service and did not request me to report for service and did not utilize my services. That was the choice of Warner Bros. and was not my choice. I am not responsible for actions and decisions of your managers; and I do not believe that I could fairly be penalized because your representative did not choose to permit me to work." She also declined to accept that the 126-day period was to be added to her present contract, which was originally set to run until September of '38.

Through all this squabbling, Warners' solution was to loan Ann to RKO for back-to-back B pictures, *We Who Are About to Die* (1936) and *Racing Lady* (1937).

If her strike in 1932 caused hard feelings, this new (and very public) rift was the final straw. In 1937 other Warner contract actresses were getting Dvorak-perfect material like *Confession, Marked Woman, It's Love I'm After, They Won't Forget* and *Tovarich*, but Ann was being hauled over to Bryan Foy's B unit. She was cast as Della Street (to Donald Woods' Perry Mason) in *The Case of the Stuttering Bishop* and played John Litel's ex-wife in *Midnight Court*. She looked and acted elegant in both, her final films for Warners. Her contract was terminated by mutual consent on February 26, 1937.

How much say did Fenton, her co-plaintiff in the '36 suit, have in her Warners trouble? Fenton was seen as a controlling force, transferring his disdain for studio politics to his wife. Dvorak's mother told a reporter, "She's always liked people, been a friendly approachable girl. Now, in the short time they've been married, I can notice the change in her personality. She talks with Leslie's tongue and sees things through Leslie's eyes. There was a time when her work and career were the most important things in her life. Now there isn't anything important but Leslie, who has never cared anything about the things that matter to most people."

She had a terrific chance when Goldwyn sought her for *Dead End* (1937), but she was suddenly, without explanation, replaced by Sylvia Sidney. Had Ann's fights with Warner Bros. frightened producers? Or, as has been hinted, did Warners indulge in a little sabotage?

Her output slowed drastically, not helped by frequent trips overseas with her husband. Ann got leads in some B pictures (*Manhattan Merry-Go-Round, She's No Lady, Gangs of New York*), and had a minor but attractive part in *Merrily We Live* (1938)—but these productions had short shooting schedules.

Thanks to her husband, who was directing, she secured a role in *Stronger Than Desire* (1939), a remake of *Evelyn Prentice* (1934). Ann painted a powerful portrait of a mentally abused wife, giving the film its most vivid moments, especially in her concluding courtroom scene confessing to her husband's murder. All the desperation, suffering and anguish bursts forth in a deeply affecting, two-and-a-half-minute *tour de force*. Holding back her sobs until the end, Ann's contained intensity is easily the movie's best acting.

Ann obtained a three-picture deal from Columbia, starting with the psychological thriller *Blind Alley* (1939). Dvorak played Chester Morris' moll forcefully, but with a soft edge, humanizing her character to show her deep devotion. Her low-key intensity overshadowed a snarling Nina Foch in the 1948 remake *The Dark Past*.

The closest Ann ever came to a Joan Blondell role was in *Cafe Hostess* (1939), as a hard luck gal trying to make a living in a dive. "I'm fed-up playing glamour girl to a lot of poor saps sneaking out on their wives for a cheap thrill," she tells shady Club 46 owner Douglas Fowley. It is Fowley who taught her "to play up to 20 different men every night ... 30 on Sunday." She doesn't think she's good enough to reform, warning the man she loves (Preston Foster) how "I was born in a room while a jazz band was playing, raised in an alley where kids graduated to the hot seat. That I never knew who my mother was. I've been around. I know how men are." It was a cheapie, but well worth it to see a jaded Dvorak wisecrack, have a brawl with another girl, act sincere and be the center of attention.

The same goes for the surprisingly thoughtful *Girls of the Road* (1940). What promised to be a tawdry exploitation feature was elevated, thanks to Robert D. Andrews' empathetic script and the straightforward playing of Dvorak and Helen Mack, into a sincere social indictment. Ann is a governor's daughter who takes to the road to learn first-hand the conditions of runaway "road girls" in an effort to help them. Ann's subdued, sensitive performance was one of her best.

Fenton, who was born in Liverpool, had gone back to enlist in the British Navy, and Ann felt it only natural that she join her spouse during wartime. On December 14, 1940, she left the U.S. for England.

Again she was dropping her career. Her absence from Hollywood this time would be almost four years.

Those years were hardly idle or unimportant. She enlisted in the British Women's Land Army and drove an ambulance under heavy bombing during the Nazi blitz. Ann wrote articles for the *London Daily Illustrated* and the *London Herald*, did commentary on the BBC, while also participating in U.S.O. shows in England and Ireland. She added to this busy schedule four patriotic British films: *This Was Paris*, *Squadron Leader X*, *Escape to Danger* and *There's a Future in It*. She made her stage debut in London in a GI production of *The Eve of St. Mark*.

Fenton served as a PT boat commander, and was seriously wounded in the commando raid on the port of St. Nazaire; he was awarded the Distinguished Service Cross.

They returned to America in late May of 1944.

By July, Ann was filming *Flame of Barbary Coast*. All seemed fine until September 5, 1944, when Ann announced her separation from Fenton. "Put it down to a war casualty," she told Louella Parsons. "We just couldn't get along and our unhappiness started in England while we were working on the war effort there." It is entirely probable, with Fenton off fighting, that Ann, independently alone for the first time in her life, took a step back and reassessed their relationship. They attempted to reconcile, but their divorce was granted on August 2, 1946.

Meanwhile, *Flame of Barbary Coast* (1945), set in San Francisco during the earthquake of 1906, reintroduced film audiences to Dvorak in a big way. It was one of Republic's most lavish films of the year, costing $600,000. John Wayne co-starred, but Ann's the focus here, playing Flaxen Terry, the fiery star singer at the El Dorado. In addition to Ann's "totally unexpected quips in many scenes" (*Hollywood Citizen News*), it would be her finest musical role: "Love, Here Is My Heart" (in French and English), "Carrie," "On Moonlight Bay" and "That Man (Is Always on My Mind)." Ann, looking gorgeous in her period costumes, seems to be enjoying herself immensely. She's at turns sly, self-possessed, spirited and poignant—in short, dominating the whole production.

She was irresistibly bitchy in *Masquerade in Mexico* (1945), director Mitchell Leisen's remake of his classic *Midnight* (1939), as Patric Knowles' amused, glamorous and very amoral wife. Ann is foolin' around with bullfighter Arturo de Cordova, so Knowles hires Dorothy Lamour to pose as a contessa to distract Arturo. Then Ann's claws come out: "Join us downstairs when you've fixed your face, will you?" she purrs to the newly-arrived Lamour. "But don't do a complete job, because here in the country we usually go to bed by one o'clock." Before the film is through she gets to dance, slap people, bounce digs about with her partner-in-crime Natalie Schafer, and show how deliciously nasty she could be.

Post–Civil War Kansas is the setting for another of Dvorak's best, *Abilene Town* (1946). In it, Marshall Randolph Scott must choose between two women: scrappy barroom singer Dvorak and church-going Rhonda Fleming. Ann is tangy, vigorous and feisty, knocking soft-spoken Scott for a loop when she isn't kicking his shins. Dvorak the firecracker also gets to sing three songs: "Snap Your Fingers," "I Love It Out Here in the West" and "Everytime I Give My Heart."

As another singer in *The Bachelor's Daughters* (1946), Ann was, for the first and only time, voice-doubled. It was an enjoyable, if little-seen, movie, and Ann handled her slight part pleasantly.

The outrageous *Out of the Blue* (1947) more than made up for it. Ann is the brandy-swilling, weak-hearted eccentric picked up by lonely George Brent in a bar. Once at his apartment, the fun begins.

DVORAK: You know, brandy is very good for my heart. My doctor says that it's a vascular dilator. And my heart is liable to stop like *that* if I don't have brandy periodically.

BRENT: You don't think you had too much?

DVORAK: Not *too* much—or I couldn't say "periodically."

His wife due home, Brent, trying to get rid of her, attempts to sober her up with coffee. "Caffeine," Ann deadpans, "is very bad for my heart." After a struggle, Ann passes out cold, with Brent dumping her presumably dead body on neighbor Turhan Bey's patio. It starts a merry-go-round of body-swapping, with the constantly fainting Dvorak getting jostled from room to room. When another neighbor, Elizabeth Patterson, takes pity and wants to call the police, Ann stresses weepily, "Oh no, think of my family... my reputation ..."

Dvorak gave a hysterical film-stealing portrayal as a brandy-swilling oddball in the black comedy *Out of the Blue* (Eagle-Lion, 1947). Left to right: Dvorak, Virginia Mayo, Turhan Bey.

PATTERSON: Are you a debutante, dear?

DVORAK: Yes. I came out in '38 and I haven't been home since.

A socko comedy performance that drew raves all around, it was unlike anything she had ever done. However, it was made by Eagle-Lion, not a major studio, and the rest of the cast just wasn't on par with Dvorak's off-center, inebriated antics; she was the whole damn show.

This was followed, and contrasted, by her lovely performance in *The Private Affairs of Bel Ami* (1947). As John Carradine's (then George Sanders') "keen, clever and intriguing" wife, Ann gives a classy, elegantly stylish portrayal, but it's debatable if the movie even deserved her. *The Long Night* (1947) was more interesting, telling, via flashbacks, the circumstances leading to Henry Fonda murdering Vincent Price. Ann was formidable as magician Price's tough, seen-it-all assistant, tempering her characterization with vulnerability.

It really looked like Ann was at last serious about her career, with seven movies completed in three years. With perhaps a touch of bitterness and regret in her voice, she insisted, "I'm going to give my career a chance this time. No pulling out across the world again. I'm going to pull all the stops and give it everything!"

Easier said than done. A few days after Ann's divorce from Fenton became final, on August 7, 1947, she wed Igor Dega, a young, attractive Russian dancer, who was seen briefly dancing with her in *The Bachelor's Daughters*.

It became the same old story. Dega took priority. Ann's "complete absorption" with his dancing was understandable, but it didn't help her own career.

A couple of months after the wedding, she did *The Walls of Jericho* (1948). Her role, that of country lawyer Cornel Wilde's insecure wife, was small and underwritten, so Ann effectively conveyed her emotions silently. Unlike her amiable drunk in *Out of the Blue*, here her alcoholism is pathetically heartbreaking, as her inability to fit into Wilde's "social circle" leads to deadly

The Long Night (RKO, 1947) featured Ann as magician Vincent Price's jaded assistant and ex-lover.

resentment. Late for a party, Wilde goes upstairs, where she is locked in the bathroom. Suddenly, an intoxicated, mean-eyed and quietly determined Dvorak comes out and ferociously rips her party gown to pieces. It was a brilliantly played scene, fully capturing her intense frustration.

In September of '48 she made her Broadway debut, taking over for Meg Mundy in the controversial play *The Respectful Prostitute*. Ann got raves for the high-profile part, and stayed with the show until it closed on December 18. One of the few other jobs she took during her marriage was another controversial play headed for Broadway, *People Like Us*. It opened on October 4, 1949, in Toronto, Canada, and collapsed on the road on October 15 in Detroit.

Also collapsing was her marriage. She had enthused to Louella Parsons, "He's very sweet, and sunny tempered," but when they separated in December 1949, Ann told reporters that, far from sunny, Dega was "sullen and morose." To columnist Harrison Carroll she said, "We just couldn't live each others' lives ... I have come back to Hollywood to resume my screen career. I tried but I just can't go on night after night sitting in these cafes." She was finally awarded a divorce on August 7, 1951.

Back in Hollywood, her short but sweet role as Ann Blyth's biological mother in *Our Very Own* (1950) was a heart-wrenching vignette in a dull little movie.

This was followed by *The Return of Jesse James* (1950), a Lippert potboiler, and a clear indication of her waning status. Ann is the "lowdown ornery" daughter of Henry Hull. Dealing cards to no one in particular in a saloon, she meets up with Jesse James lookalike John Ireland and they fall in love. Or do they? She tries to turn Ireland on to some big dough, sneering after a petty hold-up, "Chicken feed. Small change for beer. I'm playing for champagne." Well, it *almost* works. Trying to betray the mortally wounded Ireland for his reward, she is instead shot down. Ann's uniquely choreographed death is the movie's only bright spot.

Mention *A Life of Her Own* (1950), a Lana Turner vehicle, and many film fans will only cite Ann's performance. Such is the impact that she made, and continues to make, with her astonishing 13½-minute Oscar-worthy contribution.

On her first day in New York aspiring model Turner sees the dark side of the modeling world through the eyes of has-been Dvorak. Ann is urgently seeking to get "back in harness," but she knows better; years of drink and debauchery have taken their toll. Lana can only sit by speechless as Dvorak unravels before our very eyes, every raw nerve exposed as she desperately clings to what she once had. "My last

Lana Turner can only stand by and watch as a riveting Dvorak steals *A Life of Her Own* (MGM, 1950) away from her.

chance ... nothing left ... nothing to show ... nothing to show for *any* of it ..." It's a stunning turn, made even more disturbing because of her haggard, no-holds-barred appearance—no glamour here. Lana is haunted by her suicide during the remaining 96 minutes, and so is the viewer.

She played real-life WWII spy Claire "Highpockets" Phillips in *I Was An American Spy* (1951). Posing as a nightclub singer in Manila (introducing the now-standard "Because of You"), she is caught and tortured by the Japanese. The colorful leading role gave Ann one of her best chances to show her emotional depth, as she commits herself to helping the Allies when her husband is killed by the Japanese.

In *The Secret of Convict Lake* (1951), playing a woman older than her years, spiteful, repressed, love-starved Ann is one of eight women up in the California mountains, waiting for their menfolk to return from a silver strike. Fugitives invade the camp, and Ann gets recklessly involved with Zachary Scott, even betraying the other women for him. She was excellent expressing her pent-up bitterness, her fear of old age and her attraction to bad-to-the-bone Scott. In an awesomely intense scene, she violently smashes a mirror with Scott's cologne bottle.

It was a great, neurotic way to end a movie career.

In what was now typical, Ann promptly married again; she couldn't even wait for her final decree to come back from the Dega union. Explaining that she had supplemented her California divorce with a Nevada one, she married architect Nicholas A. Wade on November 1, 1951, in Las Vegas.

The career suddenly stopped short in 1952, after a bit of television work. Her husband's business sent him around the world and Ann followed. They underwent divorce proceedings in 1956 but reconciled, moving to Honolulu in 1959, while maintaining a house in Malibu.

She stayed in retirement. They traveled extensively, became "avid bibliophiles," collecting rare first editions, and lived well. Nothing is really known about these later years because the couple kept a low profile, choosing to lead a very private life. They would remain married for 26 years, until Wade passed away in 1977. Ann followed on December 10, 1979, of cancer. Her ashes were scattered off the beaches of Waikiki.

Contrary to reports, instigated by a 1980 *National Enquirer* article, Ann did not live in poverty during her final years. Writer Christina Rice went to Hawaii to talk to a close friend of Dvorak's, who told Rice that the actress did not become the hopeless alcoholic the *Enquirer* article made her out to be. Ann was never a resident of "The Jungle," a slum where she was supposed to be living at the time of her death; her real home was several blocks away. This poverty rumor has become the thing people most often bring up in discussions of Dvorak. It simply wasn't true.

Dvorak could have had it all. She was a hot young actress, considered by Warners more valuable in the early '30s than Bette Davis. The buzz was so strong about Ann that reportedly an excited Ruth Chatterton peeked onto the set of *Molly Louvain* just to get a gander at her.

Ann did manage to carve a nice niche for herself—a talent like that can never be truly defeated. And she was a fighter. Before Davis, Sheridan, Lupino and de Havilland, she set the stage for the many future female rebellions at Warner Bros.

We'll never know if Ann ever regretted her stalled career. She had the guts and ability but the sustained drive just didn't seem to be there; she was always too willing to drop everything. What she apparently wanted in the long run was, not stardom, but a stable home and husband. She finally got it and a life of her own.

As Baby Anna Lehr: **1916**: Ramona (Clune). **1917**: The Man Hater (Triangle). **1920**: The Five Dollar Plate (three reels, Harbaugh/Oliver). **As Ann Dvorak**: **1929**: The Hollywood Revue of 1929 (MGM), Song of the Rose (MGM short), Gus Edwards International Colortone Revue (MGM short), Mexicana (MGM short), The Doll Shop (MGM short), The Song Shop (MGM short), Shooting Gallery (MGM short), The General (MGM short), So This Is College (MGM), It's a Great Life (MGM), **1930**: Manhattan Serenade (MGM short), They Learned About Women (MGM), Pirates (MGM short), Flower Garden (MGM short), Clock Shop (MGM short), The Woman Racket (MGM), Chasing Rainbows (MGM), Lord Byron of Broadway (MGM), Free and Easy (MGM), Children of Pleasure (MGM), Our Blushing Brides (MGM), Way Out West (MGM), Good News (MGM), Love in the Rough (MGM). **1931**: The Snappy Caballero (MGM short), Crazy House (MGM short), Free and Easy (MGM, Spanish version), Devil's Cabaret (MGM short), Dance, Fools, Dance (MGM), Just a Gigolo (MGM), Politics (MGM), This Modern Age (MGM), Susan Lenox, Her Fall and Rise (MGM), The Guardsman (MGM), A Tailor Made Man (MGM), Son of India (MGM), La Sevillana (MGM). **1932**: Sky Devils (UA), Scarface (UA), The Crowd Roars (WB), The Strange Love of Molly Louvain (WB), Love is a Racket (WB), Stranger in Town (WB), Crooner (WB), Three on a Match (WB). **1933**: College Coach (WB), The Way to Love (Paramount). **1934**: Massacre (WB), Heat Lightning (WB), Housewife (WB), Friends of Mr. Sweeney (WB), Side Streets (WB), A Trip Thru a Hollywood Studio (WB short), Midnight Alibi (WB), I Sell Anything (WB), Gentlemen Are Born (WB), Murder in the Clouds (WB). **1935**: Sweet Music (WB), G-Men (WB), Dr. Socrates (WB), Thanks a Million (TCF), Bright Lights (WB). **1936**: We Who Are About to Die (RKO). **1937**: Racing Lady (RKO), The Case of the Stuttering Bishop (WB), Manhattan Merry-Go-Round (Republic), She's No Lady (Paramount), Midnight Court (WB). **1938**: Gangs of New York (Republic), Merrily We Live (MGM). **1939**: Stronger Than Desire (MGM), Blind Alley (Columbia), Cafe Hostess (Columbia). **1940**: Girls of the Road (Columbia). **1942**: This Was Paris (WB/British). **1943**: Squadron Leader X (RKO/British). **1944**: Escape to Danger (RKO/British), There's a Future in It (Strand). **1945**: Flame of Barbary Coast (Republic), Masquerade in Mexico (Paramount). **1946**: Abilene Town (UA), The Bachelor's Daughters (UA). **1947**: Out of the Blue (E-L), The Private Affairs of Bel Ami (UA), The Long Night (RKO). **1948**: The Walls of Jericho (TCF). **1950**: Our Very Own (RKO), The Return of Jesse James (Lippert), Mrs. O'Malley and Mr. Malone (MGM), A Life of Her Own (MGM). **1951**: I Was an American Spy (AA), The Secret of Convict Lake (TCF).

Gloria Grahame:
Those Lips, Those Eyes

by RAY HAGEN

The photographic files on Gloria Grahame reveal an astonishing assortment of faces. Although she was considered one of the sexiest creatures ever to amble across a screen, Gloria was oddly dissatisfied with her small features, and her enthusiasm for variously oversized mouths resulted in her becoming artistic to the point of virtuosity with a lipstick brush. During those pre-collagen days, she also tried altering her appearance by stuffing wads of Kleenex under her upper lip, and a series of wholly unnecessary cosmetic surgeries left her scarred and mutilated at a time when she should have been looking her best.

Her feral, feline sort of sex appeal ideally suited her to "bad girl" roles (she had more than her share) and proved an interesting contrast in more sincere parts. Producers tried at first to cover up her odd semi-lisp, a funny catch noticeable on certain consonants, but later encouraged it when they found that, coupled with her intriguingly girlish voice, it sounded sexy. But there was nothing girlish behind her eyes when she looked at a man. No coy flirtation here, this babe clearly meant business.

Gloria had more to offer than a set of unique physical qualities. She was a genuinely accomplished actress, and a versatile one. But she allowed herself to become typed as a bored, petulant, willful siren, and—though she did an awfully good job of it—the pattern wore thin.

Her Hollywood career was building slowly but steadily until she had one smashingly successful period, topped off by an Academy Award. From there on it was downhill all the way as her career took a spectacular nosedive. Her personal problems and those unaccountable cosmetic surgeries also hampered her progress.

She always wanted to be an actress, and seems to have come by that ambition naturally. Her mother was Jean Grahame, a Glasgow-born actress who had attained some success on the London stage. Jean gave up her career when she married Michael Hallward, a writer and commercial and industrial designer, and traveled with him to Canada where their first daughter, Joy, was born sometime around 1917. While Joy was still an infant, the Hallwards relocated to the U.S. It was there, in Los Angeles, that Gloria was born on November 28, 1923 (not 1925 as she claimed for many years). She was named Gloria Grahame Hallward.

Gloria's first schooling was at a San Diego nursery school. The Hallwards then moved to Pasadena where Gloria's mother became a director at the Pasadena Playhouse. In 1979, while in London, Gloria (interviewed by Ian Woodward for *Woman's Weekly*) spoke of those days: "I was more or less reared on Shakespeare. I'd come home from school and there they were, rehearsing Shakespeare and Chekhov in the front parlor ... My mother was then a director and she was teaching me how to act practically from the moment I could walk and talk ... So, when I discovered the local drama school, I just wanted to be a part of that world ... Gradually I joined in on some of my mother's productions. I played the page in *The Merry Wives of Windsor* and the child in *The Toymaker of Nuremberg*. I played Ophelia on the back lawn when I was about six, and the little lame girl in *The Bluebird* when I was seven. I never had any doubt, none at all, about what I wanted to do."

But all was not well at home. The Depression had hit Michael Hallward hard, and he and his wife divorced.

It was while attending Hollywood High School that Gloria began to make professional progress. She won a summer scholarship to the Guy Bates Post School of the Drama, and won two National Forensic League theatrical competitions. In 1940 she appeared in a cornball rural comedy, *Maid in the Ozarks*, at the Grand Playhouse in Los Angeles. Also in the cast was future Hollywood co-star Robert Mitchum. (Her niece Vicky, Joy's daughter, later married Mitchum's brother Jack.)

Hollywood High's 1942 senior class play was *Ever Since Eve*, and Gloria had a featured role. Among those attending the performance was producer Howard Lang. After the play, Lang spoke to Gloria and offered her an understudy spot in his production of *Good Night, Ladies*, then playing in San Francisco. She had one more month to go before graduating and the offer was for her to begin immediately, so arrangements were hurriedly made with the school authorities for Gloria to complete her studies by mail. With the consent of the school board and her parents, she left for San Francisco within 24 hours.

She understudied one of the leading actresses for six weeks when, in true Ruby Keeler tradition, the actress took ill and Gloria got to go on. She stayed on for the last few weeks of the California engagement, and continued in a leading role when the show moved to Chicago for a year's run. *Good Night, Ladies* was a rehash of *Ladies Night in a Turkish Bath*, and Gloria (her name was still Gloria Hallward) frequently appeared in an all-enveloping sheet.

The show closed in '43, and Gloria decided to head for Broadway. Once in New York, she quickly got another understudy job, this time to Miriam Hopkins, who had just taken over Tallulah Bankhead's role of Sabina in Thornton Wilder's *The Skin of Our Teeth*. Miss Hopkins, however, was quite less destructible, so Gloria's performance never got beyond the wings.

But she impressed the play's producer, Michael Meyerberg, who took her out of the show and gave her a role in his new play, *Star Dust*. (Her understudy was another future movie siren, Marie Windsor.) It closed during the out-of-town tryouts.

Gloria got her first film work in three "Soundies" produced in New York during 1943–44. They were precursors to today's music videos, short musical films featuring popular recordings of the day made to be shown on jukeboxes specially configured with small screens. She served primarily as background set decoration.

She finally got a chance to be seen on Broadway when she got a role in Jed Harris' production of Nunnally Johnson's *The World's Full of Girls*. It opened at the Royale Theatre on December 6, 1943. The critics gave it an especially apathetic reception, but three of them singled out Gloria's performance. *The Daily News* said: "Gloria Hallward is a flamboyant and amusing floozy," and the *World-Telegram* noted that "the cast was fair—Frances Heflin, Gloria Hallward and Virginia Gilmore outstanding." *The Herald-Tribune* commented: "Gloria Hallward conceives a particularly dreadful portrait of a slut," which may or may not have been a compliment. In any event, the show folded six days later.

She was next hired by George Abbott for a role in his production of *A Highland Fling*, which opened April 28, 1944, at

Portrait of Gloria Grahame, 1948.

the Plymouth Theatre. John Ireland, another future movie cohort, was also in the cast of this rather tepid comedy-fantasy, and Gloria spoke her lines in a Scottish burr. The closest she came to a personal rave notice came from the *Herald-Tribune*'s Howard Barnes, who said simply: "Gloria Hallward does an excellent job as a barmaid." It closed a month later, on May 20.

But she was seen in this show by a Metro scout. He liked her work, signed her to a contract and *then* brought her to the Coast for a screen test. As of July 1944, Gloria became an MGM contract player. Her salary was $250 per week, and her new name was Gloria Grahame. (L.B. Mayer thought Gloria Hallward sounded "too theatrical.")

She was immediately cast as the saucy title blonde in *Blonde Fever* (1944), playing a fickle, flighty waitress whose affections were vied for by Marshall Thompson and Philip Dorn. It was merely a Metro B programmer, but a Metro B was often the equivalent of most other studio's A's, so it seemed a fairly promising beginning. They then gave her a microscopic one-scene bit in *Without Love*, a 1945 Tracy-Hepburn vehicle—and that was it. The studio did keep her busy in the portrait gallery where they shot many leggy pin-ups, as they did with all their starlets. One of them wound up on the cover of the October 22, 1946, *Life*, with an accompanying feature on the newcomer. But Gloria's looks, while certainly striking, didn't quite fit the lush MGM glamour stereotype (think Lana), and not even a prestigious *Life* cover prompted them to give her more work.

She busied herself these years by doing USO tours. It was while doing one of these camp shows that she met 20th Century-Fox contract actor Stanley Clements, known mainly for playing supporting roles as jockeys and thugs. They were married in Wichita Falls, Texas, on August 29, 1945. It was by all accounts a turbulent union and Clements seemed to take his thuggish movie persona quite seriously. He was a heavy drinker, a compulsive gambler and wildly jealous. Two violent years later, after they had separated for the fourth time, Gloria sued for divorce.

In 1946 Frank Capra was trying to cast a young actress as Violet Bick, the town trollop in *It's a Wonderful Life*, which he was about to begin at RKO. He wasn't having much luck so he called Billy Grady, MGM's casting director, and asked if he knew of a "young blonde sexpot." According to Capra, in his autobiography *The Name Above the Title*, Grady replied: "Do I know any? For chrissake I'm up to here in blonde pussies that've never been to the post. Let me show you some tests." Capra continued, "The second test was that of a sultry, surly young blonde that seemed undecided whether to kiss you or knock you down. 'Hey Bill, who's *that* dame?' 'Who is she, for chrissake? She's a star. But do you think I can get any of our jerk directors to listen? Two years she's been around here snapping her garters. You can have her for a cuppa coffee. Her name's Gloria Grahame.' Another loanout from MGM [the other was Donna Reed]. And another star was born." Gloria later told interviewer Myrtle Gebhart that if it hadn't been for *It's a Wonderful Life* and Frank Capra, "I'd still be yawning my way to old age. For a year and a half I hadn't done a thing but wait around."

Crossfire with George Cooper (RKO, 1947).

Back at Metro after her new beginning, Gloria was now put to work. She was a shawp-tawkin'

Brooklyn girl who won current teen rage Frank Sinatra in *It Happened in Brooklyn*, a funny silent screen vamp in Red Skelton's *Merton of the Movies* and a nightclub singer, dubbed by Carol Arden, who was murdered (the first of her many violent screen deaths) in *Song of the Thin Man*. All were released in 1947.

RKO borrowed her again to play another tart, Ginny, the worldly B-girl in *Crossfire*. Again, a small part, but a key one. She worked for all of two days, but this time attracted a good deal of attention, both critical and public. Her strikingly sharp, unusual features and lisping baby voice were used to great advantage, and she acted the weary, angry dance hall girl with far more than the usual clichéd characteristics. In addition, *Crossfire* was one of the year's most important, most discussed films. Gloria was nominated for a 1947 Best Supporting Actress Academy Award. She lost to Celeste Holm for *Gentleman's Agreement*, but just being nominated put her solidly on the Hollywood map.

RKO's Dore Schary offered to buy her MGM contract and upped her salary (then $500) to a weekly $750. In June 1947, she became an RKO-Radio player. Schary was decidedly impressed with her work in *Crossfire*, but six months later he left RKO.

Her first films under her new RKO contract were *Roughshod* and *A Woman's Secret*, both released in 1949. *Roughshod* was a trivial Western with Gloria as a been-through-the-mill frontier babe and she was prominently featured glowering sexily in all the ads. In *A Woman's Secret* she played an ambitious nightclub singer (dubbed by Kaye Lorraine) taken under the wing of a famous former singer (Maureen O'Hara, not dubbed) who wound up murdering her protégé. It was at this time that her incredible repertoire of mouths began to appear. She enlarged her upper lip to mammoth proportions in *A Woman's Secret*, and also began an endless assortment of hair styles. Her director was Nicholas Ray.

Her divorce from Stanley Clements became final on June 2, 1948, and just a few hours later she and Nicholas Ray were married. Ray, like Gloria's first husband, was also quick-tempered and a heavy drinker. Their son, Timothy Nicholas, was born on November 11. Tongues wagged.

Ray arranged to get Gloria a loanout to Columbia and again directed her as Humphrey Bogart's leading lady in *In a Lonely Place*, seen in 1950. (Their marriage had already reached the rocky stage and her contract specified that while on the set Ray would be her undisputed boss in every detail.) It was a moody, unconventional Hollywood melodrama *without* a happy ending, and was one of the year's most interesting (if not profitable) pictures. She paired wonderfully with Bogart and her strikingly sincere performance was given wide critical approval, but the public stayed away. *Screen Album* called her performance one of the year's finest, "because when she looked, she really looked, and when she listened, she really listened, and her appearance in a scene guaranteed that scene a certain mood value, and vitality. As an actress, she's well trained, as a woman she has an original quality which sets her apart from a good many of the other young blonde starlets that infest Hollywood. In a melodramatic situation, she quite admirably refuses to be melodramatic, and when she's in love, you trust her, and when she's in trouble, you're worried. A bit player until *Lonely Place*, Gloria's shown she's got more than enough for better things."

But critics had been calling her exceptionally promising for six years.

In 1950, RKO wasn't the best studio for her to be tied to. Howard Hughes was then running the place and he wouldn't release Gloria to even test at other studios for roles that she desperately wanted—Billie Dawn in Columbia's *Born Yesterday* (which won Judy Holliday an Oscar), the Shelley Winters role in Paramount's *A Place in the Sun*, Eve Harrington in *All About Eve* at Fox. The latter is especially vexing. Gloria had played a similar role in *A Woman's Secret*, an ambitious young performer wanting to replace an older mentor, and she'd have made a far more believable threat to Bette Davis' Margo Channing than the rather bland Anne Baxter, who was the weakest link in an otherwise perfect cast.

Instead Hughes assigned her to a secondary role as a dice-roller in *Macao*, a potboiler filmed in 1950 but not released until 1952. It reunited Gloria with Robert Mitchum, her fellow player from *Maid in the Ozarks*, but she didn't want to do a subservient role in a Mitchum–Jane Russell vehicle, arguing in vain that after being nominated for an Oscar and co-starring with Humphrey Bogart she deserved something better. Autocratic director Josef von Sternberg was fired in mid-production and the script was heavily rewritten by Mitchum and Gloria's husband Nicholas Ray, and it was Ray who, uncredited, finished directing the picture.

She was not seen on screen in '51, but the following year was the most successful of her entire screen career. She appeared in *Macao*, was Joan Crawford's scheming but ill-fated nemesis in *Sudden Fear* (these were her last RKO films), was Angel the Elephant Girl in Cecil B. DeMille's mammoth *The Greatest Show on Earth* (replacing a pregnant Lucille Ball), and was Dick Powell's unfaithful Southern wife in Vincente Minnelli's *The Bad and the Beautiful*. *Macao* got deservedly short shrift but she won wide acclaim for each of the other films, all of which were grade-A, big-budget, widely attended hits.

She got a barrage of publicity for refusing a double in *Greatest Show* and allowing an elephant to poise an enormous foot inches above her face in a circus sequence. She more than held her own in an all-star cast and her on-screen rivalry with Betty Hutton for Charlton Heston's affections (go figure) produced a quintessential Grahame moment. "I'll take Brad the way he is," says Gloria. "That is, if you're his type," sniffs Hutton, to which Gloria barks, "*Who you callin' a type?*"

Many critics thought she stole *Sudden Fear* from under the top-starred Miss Crawford's flaring nostrils. She takes a savage delight in helping her adulterous lover (Jack Palance) plan the murder of his wife (Crawford). Instead, he kills Gloria by mistake. The two ladies did not exactly become the closest of friends during shooting since Joan wanted an off-camera fling with Palance but Gloria got there first.

And her chilling study of the flighty, self-willed Southern belle who came to a nasty end in *The Bad and the Beautiful* topped off her perfect year by winning her the Academy Award as 1952's Best Supporting Actress. (By the end of '52 there was absolutely no doubt that Gloria was going to get an Oscar nomination, the only question being for which performance.) She also won *Film Daily*'s supporting performance award for *Sudden Fear* in their poll of the nation's movie critics. *Greatest Show*'s surprise Oscar win as the year's Best Picture did her booming stock no harm, either.

This Oscar ceremony was the first one to be televised and Gloria's win came early in the evening, making her the first actor to win an Oscar on TV. (Anthony Quinn's Supporting Actor win was announced first but he was on location and couldn't be there to accept.) Gloria's nerves got the better of her and her acceptance speech was limited to four breathless words: "Thank you very much."

Her personal life was less perfect. In August 1952 she and Nick Ray had divorced. They'd been separated for a year after he caught her being more than step-motherly to his 14-year-old son Tony, though this was hushed up at the time. She appeared in court wearing a startlingly low-cut dress and news photographers had a field day.

Gloria Grahame was now a hot property. She was paid a small fortune to do a five-minute bit (with her Academy trophy) as her TV debut on *The Eddie Cantor Colgate Comedy Hour*, seen on April 11, 1953.

Grahame was not making herself any too popular with her fellow workers. Her attitude toward such inconsequentials as winning friends and influencing people, including publicity people, was always somewhat cavalier at best, but now she appeared to be developing a disease common to the chosen few, cunningly dubbed "Oscaritis" by the tradefolk.

Columbia had first penciled in Gloria's name for the role of Alma in their upcoming *From Here to Eternity* (1953), but the part went to Donna Reed. Instead, that year she appeared in four pictures that were not as successful.

The Glass Wall was a minor though well-intentioned chase thriller with a sympathetic Grahame on the lam with Vittorio Gassman. The ads capitalized on her Oscar.

Elia Kazan's *Man on a Tightrope*, filmed in Munich, had Gloria as Fredric March's discontented, quite unglamourous wife. Her distinctive personal qualities and natural abilities were put to ideal use, but the public wasn't interested in the trials of a beleaguered circus troupe being stalked through Communist-controlled Czechoslovakia. It didn't make a dime, although the film and Grahame's performance were critical successes.

She was superb in *The Big Heat*, the best of her '53 releases. An exceedingly violent film, directed impeccably by Fritz Lang, it's a classy and classic thriller in which she played an irresponsible gun moll in an intriguingly casual manner. When cop Glenn Ford is trying to pump her for information on a ganglord's underworld activities, she flips him off with "When Vince talks business I go out and get my legs waxed." Midway through the proceedings, her enraged hoodlum boyfriend (Lee Marvin) brutally disfigures her by throwing a potful of scalding coffee in her face, and she spends the remainder of her footage with half her face bandaged. Now on Ford's side, she tracks down the blackmailing widow of a corrupt cop who'd committed suicide, leaving her with enough incriminating evidence to blow the gang apart, and shoots her dead so that the evidence will now become public. At the finale she gives Marvin the same treatment he gave her, scalding his face and ripping off her gauze to show him what he can expect (and what a zealous makeup man can really do). Then he shoots her. C'est la vie. Classic Gloria Grahame.

Next came as trivial a mess of claptrap pottage as was ever filmed, *Prisoners of the Casbah* ("Searing Sensations in Technicolor"). She played an Arabian princess in a long brown wig, saying at the time that the chance to play a glamour girl who

The Big Heat (Columbia, 1953) with Adam Williams, Alexander Scourby and Lee Marvin.

didn't come to a bad end was a refreshing relief. But it's difficult to see why she indulged herself in such nonsense at this point in her career.

Late in '53 she went to London to make *The Good Die Young* (released in 1955) at Shepperton Studios. Again she's a faithless wife, but this time she avoided paying her usual ultimate price as her hubby (John Ireland) merely tosses her, fully clothed, into a full bathtub.

She had started to grow increasingly more careless about her appearance, and her brusque attitude did not endear her to the British press.

She was married for the third time on August 15, 1954. The groom was Cy Howard, the prolific writer-producer-director who created such radio comedy diehards as *My Friend Irma* and *Life with Luigi*. They had conducted a long and stormy courtship for over two years. As with her two previous flings at wedded bliss, the marriage was even stormier.

She was in two films in 1954—*Human Desire*, in which she was Broderick Crawford's two-timing wife (he strangled her at the finish) and *Naked Alibi*, where she was a third-rate singer in a booze joint before getting shot by Gene Barry. Jo Ann Greer dubbed Gloria's vocal of "Ace in the Hole," but Gloria's moves were what sold the number. She delivered good performances in both films, but critics and audiences had begun to notice a certain stereotype she had created.

At this time it began to be noised about that she had taken to stuffing bits of

Kleenex or cotton wool under her upper lip for that luxuriant look. Between that and the flaring lipstick, she was producing a puffy effect that altered her speech and rendered her lower jaw area practically immobile. She had always been a pouty type, but now began to look half-drugged as well.

By 1955, her appearance on screen as well as off began to dissipate badly. Now with straggly dark brown hair, she was seen in the same sort of role (bored, petulant, bleary-eyed, puffy-lipped and oversexed) in *The Good Die Young*, *The Cobweb* and *Not As a Stranger*. In *Stranger* she was the other woman who had her way with Robert Mitchum in one of the most hilariously erotic seduction scenes ever filmed, with wild whinnying horses cueing the action. She received uniformly poor notices for the first time in her career. And she looked dreadful.

Always profoundly dissatisfied with her appearance, Gloria had started on a series of plastic surgeries back in the mid–1940s, trying to conform to a standard of perfection known only to her secret self. It had begun with a nip here on her lips, a tuck there on her chin, but had now escalated into major surgeries, one of which all but paralyzed her upper lip. Gloria's niece, Vicky Mitchum, was quoted by Grahame biographer Vincent Curcio in 1989: "Over the years, she carved herself up, trying to make herself into an image of beauty she felt should exist but didn't. Others saw her as a beautiful person, but she never did, and crazy things spread from that."

When she reported for work on MGM's *The Cobweb*, this gratuitous carving had reached critical mass. Curcio quoted *Cobweb* producer John Houseman: "Gloria gave us problems on *Cobweb*. She became obsessed with a passionate desire to be sexy, and to achieve it through cosmetic surgery, which made her self-conscious and defensive. Everyone, including the cameraman, worried about her looks. She had started with cotton under her lip, and I imagine she thought it so irresistible, she had the effect done surgically. In fact, she showed up for the first day's shooting with stitches in the lip, which threw people into a minor panic. The airbrushing of scars on the sides of her lip is visible in the publicity shots taken at that time. She thought she could achieve this sexy look by being bee-stung, and so she had her lip surgically disfigured into a bee-stung lip. She looked awful, and it was hard to understand her."

She regained some lost ground in her last '55 release, *Oklahoma!* She was certainly an unlikely choice to play the droll soubrette Ado Annie, but Richard Rodgers insisted on having her. Unexpectedly, she handled her first and only musical-comedy role with fine high spirit. Said William K. Zinsser in his *New York Herald-Tribune* review: "Gloria Grahame steals the acting honors as Ado Annie, getting great humor by underplaying the role. When she confesses that she has suddenly become alarmingly fond of men, when she sings 'I Cain't Say No' to illustrate this point, there is a look of pure pleasure in her eyes and a small secret smile around her mouth. Her subtle performance is one of the movie's biggest treats." Jack Karr of Canada's *Toronto Daily Star* thought, to his surprise, that she "has turned out to be remarkably funny, but there is the strangest impression that Miss Grahame has played every scene with a shot of novocain in her upper lip, so immobile is her face." Her off-key, meter-beating renditions of "I Cain't Say No" and "All 'Er Nothin'" were delightful, but non-singer Gloria was the first to admit it was a painstakingly slow

Oklahoma! with Gene Nelson (Magna, 1955).

process to record the songs practically one phrase at a time, leaving it up to the sound crew to paste all the pieces together.

In '55 she went to London to film *The Man Who Never Was*, released the following year. The picture was based on Ewen Montague's story about a corpse launched at sea by the British in an effort to mislead German intelligence during World War II. Grahame played an American librarian in love with an RAF pilot. She gave a sensitive, emotional performance in an uncustomarily sincere role, but her facial appearance was ghastly. "Gloria Grahame as the American girl is very good," said the *New York Mirror*, "but her makeup is nothing short of horrible. She is seen as an oily-skinned, dark-haired attraction."

This marked the end of her "movie star" phase. Her personal eccentricities and continued facial alterations finally alienated Hollywood and exhausted the patience of her fan base.

After Gloria completed *The Man Who Never Was*, the Howards decided to remain in Europe. They moved to Paris, and lurid reports of her escapades, with and without Howard, began to leak back to the U.S. press. Their violent marriage seemed headed for a violent divorce more than once, but in September '56 she bore a daughter, Mariana Paulette, in France.

Several papers reported that she'd had yet more plastic surgery on her lips and chin. Photographs taken of her upon her return to the States in December '56, holding her new daughter, showed her smiling happily but looking shockingly mutilated. Her hair, still unkempt, was again blonde.

In March '57, she announced to the papers that her marriage to Cy Howard was over and done, adding: "I'm going to concentrate on my baby, Mariana, and I'm going to resume my acting career."

Ride Out for Revenge, a minor 1958 Western, showed her looking quite pretty but decidedly different, and she was not happily cast as an Indian-hating widow. A year later she was back in her old mold in *Odds Against Tomorrow*, a brief spot as a friendly neighbor with the hots for Robert Ryan. Gone forever, thankfully, were the overpainted lips.

Beginning in 1961 she began doing guest appearances on various TV series (*G.E. Theatre*, *The New Breed*, *Sam Benedict*, *Burke's Law*, *Name of the Game*, *The Fugitive*, *The Outer Limits*, etc.). She was no longer the glamourous siren of the 1950s, nor was she trying to be, and she was now digging full-tilt into character roles. Hectic TV shooting schedules no longer allowed for the carefully lit close-ups of her movie prime and there were occasional glimpses of her surgery scars.

In January 1962 she revealed that on May 13 of the previous year she'd secretly married her former stepson, Tony Ray, in Tijuana, Mexico. Ray was a sometime actor who played one of the leads in John Cassavetes' *Shadows* (filmed in 1957), and was Nicholas Ray's son by a marriage previous to Gloria's. This meant that her ex-husband was now her father-in-law, and that their son Timothy had become both his mother's brother-in-law and his half-brother's stepson. And she was now her own sister-in-law. To add to the tangle, Gloria bore her husband two sons, Anthony, Jr. (4/30/63), and James (9/21/65). Her former husband was their grandfather. Where, one wondered, could she go from here? Many were scandalized by this almost-but-not-quite incestuous union and it made for some titillating publicity (to Gloria's distress), but this marriage lasted for 14 years.

In 1966, after a seven-year absence from films, she had a small role as another cheating wife in another lower-case Western, *Ride Beyond Vengeance*. It didn't make a ripple.

Beginning in the early '60s Gloria had returned to the stage, doing live theater all over America and England. She had always wanted to do great parts in great plays, and for the rest of her life cheerfully abandoned her movie image to do plays by Shakespeare (Mistress Page in *Merry Wives of Windsor*, Lady M in *Macbeth*), Chekhov (*The Three Sisters*), Noël Coward (Amanda in *Private Lives*), Edward Albee (Martha in *Who's Afraid of Virginia Woolf*), Alan Ayckbourne (*How the Other Half Lives*), Tennessee Williams (*The Glass Menagerie*), Arthur Miller (*The Price*), Somerset Maugham (*Rain*), Clifford Odets *(The Country Girl)*, George S. Kaufman *(The Man Who Came to Dinner)*, Moss Hart *(Light Up the Sky)* and William Saroyan *(The Time of Your Life)*. The latter starred Henry Fonda, who later said, "The highlight of my recent tour was the ten-minute scene I played with Gloria Grahame. She's a most riveting actress." She also appeared in productions of *A Shot in the Dark*, *Laura*, *The Marriage-Go-Round*, *Bell, Book and Candle* and a new play called *A Tribute to Lili Lamont*.

A touch of lipstick—1947 to 1966.

In 1971 she returned to regular filmmaking, though mostly in low-budget thrillers, and she continued to pop up regularly on television in episodic series, TV movies and miniseries. She was now playing psychotics, eccentrics, killers, daffy mothers, over-the-hill actresses, aging mistresses—basically, anything that was handed to her. In 1973, James Robert Parish quoted an ambivalent Gloria as saying, "I don't know how I feel about it. It's hard to get a good script. Maybe I should just keep doing housework and not try to come back at all, you know what I mean?"

One of these projects is worth noting, a 1974 TV movie, *The Girl on the Late, Late Show*. The cast was headed by Don Murray and featured other stars from Gloria's era in assorted cameos—Van Johnson, Yvonne DeCarlo, Walter Pidgeon, John Ireland, Cameron Mitchell and Ralph Meeker. The movie involved a search for Carolyn Parker (Gloria), a former movie star who mysteriously dropped out of sight 20 years ago at the height of her fame. Throughout the movie, people are discussing her and watching scenes from the star's glory days—"Carolyn" co-starring with Humphrey Bogart, Broderick Crawford and Glenn Ford in clips from *In a Lonely Place, Human Desire* and *The Big Heat*. (Gloria also shot a quick scene with Van Johnson, shown as a black and white outtake from Carolyn's final uncompleted movie, and a brief shot as the younger Carolyn running down a flight of stairs and screaming as she witnesses a murder.) She's described as "a girl you'd see in a polo coat at a football game, talk to her for five minutes and lose her in the crowd, but remember the rest of your life." At the end of the film, all the mysteries are solved and Carolyn is found. Don Murray enters a dilapidated old mansion and sees her from the back, sitting and watching *In a Lonely Place* on TV. She turns slowly to face her visitor (and the camera), her face skeletal and tear-stained. She looks up at Murray and wearily asks, "Who were you expecting to find here? Carolyn Parker?" Slow curtain, The End. For any Hollywood historian, or Gloria Grahame fan, this is all most disquieting, not to say downright spooky. For her part, Gloria was thrilled. She had practically nothing to do, her character was the center of the film, and she was paid quite handsomely.

In 1975, at age 51, Gloria was diagnosed with breast cancer. She spent the next few years in and out of court battling with Tony Ray over their divorce, and steadfastly refusing to divulge her condition as she continued working on TV and doing plays both here and in England.

"I find England quite extraordinary," she told Ian Woodward. "I grew up in such an English atmosphere, with both my parents being English themselves. I feel at home here. I have a British passport; I've had it quite awhile. And I belong to British Equity, the actors' union." She added, "I've had a very beautiful life. A very interesting life. A very lucky life. I realize it especially when I consider others' lives— so boring and grey and motionless. I care *passionately* for the job I do."

Through painful setbacks, she muscled her way through a grueling work schedule until collapsing in England during rehearsals for a second production of *The Glass Menagerie*. She was flown to St. Vincent's Hospital in New York, where she refused all aggressive attempts to prolong her life.

She died on October 5, 1981, just short of what would have been her fifty-eighth birthday. The death certificate listed her "approximate age" as 41. Her sister Joy said, "Gloria would have been smiling at that one."

Thanks to the ever-growing public interest in what we now call *film noir*, Gloria Grahame's reputation as the genre's ultimate femme fatale has continued to grow. In 1979, a full biography of Gloria was published, Vincent Curcio's (hideously titled) *Suicide Blonde*. Then, in 1986, yet another Gloria Grahame book was published. A short volume titled *Film Stars Don't Die in Liverpool*, it was Peter Turner's affectionate memoir of his relationship with Gloria during her final days in England as her illness was progressing.

Yes, she was probably the most blatantly carnal vixen ever filmed. And yes, she led a private life of considerable vitality and color. But let it not be forgotten that she was a stage-trained actress of greater power and range than moviegoers saw. Under all the Hollywood frou-frou, and her own misguided insecurities, Gloria Grahame was one killer tomato.

1943: Pin-Ups on Parade (Soundies). **1944:** Oh! Please Tell Me Darling (Soundies), Loads of Pretty Women (Soundies), Blonde Fever (MGM). **1945:** Without Love (MGM). **1946:** It's a Wonderful Life (RKO). **1947:** It Happened in Brooklyn (MGM), Merton of the Movies (MGM), Crossfire (RKO), Song of the Thin Man (MGM). **1949:** A Woman's Secret (RKO), Roughshod (RKO). **1950:** In a Lonely Place (Columbia). **1952:** Macao (RKO), The Greatest Show on Earth (Paramount), Sudden Fear (RKO), The Bad and the Beautiful (MGM). **1953:** The Glass Wall (Columbia), Man on a Tightrope (TCF), The Big Heat (Columbia), Prisoners of the Casbah (Columbia). **1954:** Human Desire (Columbia), Naked Alibi (Universal), The Good Die Young (UA). **1955:** Not as a Stranger (UA), The Cobweb (MGM), Oklahoma! (TCF). **1956:** The Man Who Never Was (TCF). **1958:** Ride Out for Revenge (UA). **1959:** Odds Against Tomorrow (UA). **1966:** Ride Beyond Vengeance (Columbia). **1971:** The Todd Killings (National General), Chandler (MGM), Blood and Lace (AIP), Escape (ABC-TV), Black Noon (CBS-TV). **1972:** The Loners (Fanfare). **1973:** Tarot (Vagar). **1974:** Mama's Dirty Girls (Premiere), The Girl on the Late, Late Show (NBC-TV). **1976:** Mansion of the Doomed (Group 1), Rich Man, Poor Man (ABC-TV). **1977:** Seventh Avenue (NBC-TV). **1979:** Chilly Scenes of Winter AKA Head Over Heels (UA), A Nightingale Sang in Berkeley Square (AIP). **1980:** Melvin and Howard (Universal). **1981:** The Nesting (Feature Films).

Jean Hagen: After the Rain

by RAY HAGEN

I think it was the voice that did it for me when I saw this new girl, Jean Hagen, in her first two movies. In both she played floozies, one wearily battered and one sharply comic, and there was a complete shift in sound as well as attitude from one to the other. She was clearly a skilled and experienced actress with an offbeat beauty and an intriguing off-center smile, not the typical run of starlet the studios usually presented. But it was that warm and pliable voice, womanly rather than girlish, that riveted my attention. I find it both reasonable and ironic that Jean Hagen's greatest fame rests on her performance as a bubbleheaded shrew with the most insanely hideous voice ever to hit a soundtrack.

Jean made only 19 feature films, and only two of lasting importance. But those two—*The Asphalt Jungle* and, especially, *Singin' in the Rain*—assure her some small niche in cinema history. They also display her unique versatility, ranging from brutally honest pathos to knockabout farce. It's regrettable that, during her four years as an MGM contract player, she was used mostly in slick B programmers, usually playing drabs, trollops or colorless second leads. Her looks, and her skill, seemed to suit her to strong character roles while still in her twenties, but most of the parts she did play in films were anything but strong.

Jean Shirley Verhagen was born in Chicago, Illinois, on August 3, 1923. Her father, Christian M. Verhagen, was born in Holland and came to the U.S. when he was 25 "as an adventure," says Jean's sister, LaVerne Verhagen Steck. He settled in Illinois and became a mechanical engineer. "He first saw Mom walking across the street, holding a tennis racquet," says LaVerne, "and said to a friend, 'I'm gonna marry that girl.'" Christian and Marie Verhagen raised five children—in order of arrival, LaVerne, Donald (who was killed in World War II), Jean, Roger and Paul. There were also three infants who died in childbirth. Roger and Paul are both retired optometrists in, respectively, Indiana and Florida, and LaVerne lives with her husband on their farm in Pelham, New Hampshire.

LaVerne recalls, "Our childhood was wonderful, nothing but happiness. Our parents were very family-oriented people, very close. And I can't remember when Jean wasn't interested in acting. We used to put on plays in our basement in Chicago. We wrote them and acted in them and charged five cents." The family moved to Elkhart, Indiana, when Jean was 12.

Jean attended Chicago's Northwestern University, majoring in drama. Not coming from a wealthy family, she was there on a limited budget, and helped defray costs by working the freshman dorm's switchboard. While still at school she obtained her first professional job on radio as an eccentric teenager, appearing irregularly on a daily afternoon series called *The Brewster Boy*. Her part-time radio work also helped finance her education.

During her years at Northwestern, Jean met five other aspiring actresses who, though their lives would take very different directions, would become her close friends for the rest of her life—Patricia Neal, Helen Horton, Nancy Hoadley, Nathalie Brown and Mimi Morrison. Helen Horton (now Helen Thomson) remembers, "Except for Pat, who was two years younger, we all met in a play we did together during our first year, *Cry Havoc*. Jean played the cigarette-smoking, wisecracking, smarty-pants girl. Then she did Sabina in *Skin of Our Teeth* and she was terrific, she was extremely talented. She was at her best when she was being funny or tough. Jean was the one who brought us back down to earth if we got a bit flighty." Jean also appeared in *Twelfth Night*, and in one of Northwestern's annual satirical revues with Mimi and Paul Lynde.

Patricia Neal joined this group when she came to Northwestern, rooming briefly with Jean and two other students. She later said that "people used to tell us we looked like sisters."

During their last year at college, Jean and Mimi Morrison teamed up as a comedy duo in nightclubs around Chicago. "The act was very silly," says Mimi (now

Cry Havoc at Northwestern University, 1943. Seated at left, front: Nancy Hoadley and Jean Hagen. Standing at far right: Helen Horton and Nathalie Brown. All became lifetime friends (courtesy Nathalie Brown Thompson).

Mimi Tellis). "The agent who booked us said to Jean, 'Now, you're very pretty,' and said to me, 'and you're not.' [*laughs*]. We did a patter song together, then we were two gum-chewing girls who walked through the audience selling cigars and cigarettes with short skirts and black stockings and all that, and we'd toss repartee back and forth, 'Hey, Maisie' kind of stuff. We were all very impressed that Jean was already a professional radio actress while at college." They continued doing their club act during their first year out of school.

In December 1945, Jean set out to conquer New York, arriving with Helen Horton. The whole Northwestern group, except Mimi, was in New York by then, sharing inexpensive apartments in various combinations. Jean did not have instant success crash-

Portrait of Jean Hagen, 1949.

ing Broadway, but managed to continue working in radio in such series as *Grand Central Station, Hollywood Story* and *Light of the World*.

In 1946, after a real-life stint selling cigarettes in a nightclub, she became an usher at the Booth Theater, where the Ben Hecht-Charles MacArthur play *Swan Song* was running. She had made some outspoken (and decidedly negative) comments about the show, and at a theater gathering was overheard by the authors. They engaged her in conversation and, far from being offended, offered her a chance to try out for a small role as a replacement for an ailing cast member. Jean promptly came down with appendicitis and wound up in the hospital. But the job was kept open for her and, upon her recovery, she took over the part.

The show closed on September 28, 1946, and she quickly won the role of Laurette Sincee in Lillian Hellman's *Another Part of the Forest* (a prequel to *The Little Foxes*), which opened on November 20 of that year. Also in the cast was Patricia Neal. They were now roommates in New York (eventually sharing three different apartments together) and were ecstatic when they learned that both had won roles in the same play. To celebrate, they shopped 'til they dropped. Said Ward Morehouse in his

New York Sun review: "There is a superb performance from Patricia Neal as the young Regina, another from Jean Hagen as the brazen trollop sought by the weakling Oscar." Hagen and Neal had cemented their friendship and, along with the other four Northwestern girls, would remain lifelong best friends.

Early the following year Jean began dating actor Tom Seidel. They were married on July 3, 1947, while she was playing in *Dear Ruth* in a Connecticut summer stock company. Seidel had played small parts and uncredited bits in films since 1938, mainly in B pictures (*Gone with the Wind* being a prime exception).

Back in New York, Jean obtained a job as Judy Holliday's understudy in *Born Yesterday*, and late in 1947 played Billie Dawn for a month while Holliday was on vacation. Her next Broadway assignment was as Regina in Eva Le Gallienne's translation of Ibsen's *Ghosts*, in which Le Gallienne and Alfred Ryder starred. It opened on February 16, 1948. Critical reaction was divided, about Jean's performance as well as about the production. Brooks Atkinson wrote in *The New York Times*, "Jean Hagen's scheming servant-girl is well played, the commonness harshly breaking out of the demure reserve in the last scene." But Richard Watts, in *The New York Post*, said, "I cannot say that Jean Hagen as Regina and Robert Emhardt as Engstrand offer exactly subtle performances, but at least they give some show of alertness to the proceedings." It closed five days later.

Jean had better luck in her next show, Jed Harris' production of Herman Wouk's *The Traitor*, which opened March 31, 1949. She was seen in the play by Sam Zimbalist and Anthony Mann, who were in New York doing location work on an about-to-be-produced MGM crime drama, *Side Street*. They were immediately impressed with Jean and tested her the following morning. The test was flown to the coast for a quick okay, which it got.

She was signed at once to a Metro contract, and the next morning she was at work in the picture, playing a dipso nightclub singer who got throttled for her misplaced loyalty to gangster James Craig. In her first scene in her first film, set in the seedy club in which she sang, she delivered a prophetic line with mushy, boozy dignity: "An entertainer has to put up with a lot for the sake of her profession."

"Both my parents were very driven, strong people," says their son, Aric Seidel. "When they came to California from New York, they knew exactly what they wanted. In retrospect it reminds one of the old saying, watch out what you wish for."

On the completion of *Side Street*, MGM sent her to Hollywood and cast her as a lanky homewrecker ("that tall job") in *Adam's Rib*. Spencer Tracy and Katharine Hepburn starred, and considerable attention was paid to the four featured Broadway recruits who were all appearing in their first important Hollywood roles—Judy Holliday, Tom Ewell, David Wayne and Jean Hagen. *Adam's Rib*, released in 1949 just before *Side Street*, was a substantial hit and served as an effective springboard for all their careers.

She was next seen as a brutalized pioneer wife in *Ambush* (1950), a competent if unremarkable Western, and was then given the poignant role of Doll Conovan in John Huston's *The Asphalt Jungle* (1950). Huston chose Jean for the part of the pathetic drab in love with a crook "because she has a wistful, down-to-earth quality rare on the screen. A born actress."

Jean was sitting with Huston while he was screening test footage of various

Jean sparring with lawyer Spencer Tracy in *Adam's Rib* (MGM, 1949).

unknown actresses for the role of Louis Calhern's young blonde mistress. A few minutes into Marilyn Monroe's test, they turned and looked at each other at the same moment. "Her?" asked Huston. "Yep," said Jean. Both the picture and Jean's touching performance were widely admired, but Monroe got quite the lion's share of the publicity. Jean told people who didn't remember who she played in *The Asphalt Jungle* that "there were only two girl roles, and I obviously wasn't Marilyn Monroe."

Metro then let her languish in three minor efforts. *A Life of Her Own* (1950) was a Lana Turner dud in which Jean was seen briefly—very briefly—as a friend of Lana's. Jean's husband was played by real-life hubby Tom Seidel. She had a few scenes as a loose lady on the make for Ray Milland in *Night Into Morning* (1951), and in *No Questions Asked* ('51) she mooned over Barry Sullivan, who only had eyes for Arlene Dahl. These programmers kept her working but hardly advanced her career, though critics were paying her favorable notice. The *New York Herald-Tribune*, in its *No Questions Asked* review, commented: "It is Jean Hagen who is responsible for the one real performance in the picture. With little or nothing to work with, she manages to make the sincere girl both believable and sympathetic. She is excellent and admirably restrained in the drunk scene, a temptation to any actor."

In 1952, following these trifles, *Singin' in the Rain* was released. Jean's hilarious performance as Lina Lamont, the egomaniacal silent screen vamp ("I am a shimmering, glowing star in the cinema firma-*mint"*) whose screechy voice was not okay for sound, is still considered one of the big reasons for that film's lasting success. Her lines have been quoted endlessly: "I make more money than Calvin Coolidge! *Put tigither!*," 'I cahn't git him outta my mind," "If we can bring a little happiness into your humdrum lives, it means our hard work ain't been in vain fer nothin'."

The satire on Hollywood's early talkie days was an altogether happy blending of talents meshing perfectly to produce what many filmgoers still feel is the finest musical comedy Hollywood has made. Hagen drew raves for her deliriously spot-on performance, and was nominated for a Best Supporting Actress Academy Award (Gloria Grahame won for *The Bad and the Beautiful*). Her lampoon was perhaps too effective; most movie fans who saw her as the idiotic blonde with the piercing voice never even connected her with the Jean Hagen they saw in subsequent films.

The vocal credits for *Singin' in the Rain* are interesting, and rather confusing. In the film, Debbie Reynolds has been hired to re-dub Jean's dialogue and songs in the latter's first talking picture. We see the process being done in a shot of Reynolds,

back to camera, matching her dialogue to Jean's and synchronizing it while watching the sequence on film. But the voice that is used to replace Jean's dialogue is not Reynolds', but Jean's own quite lovely natural voice. Director Stanley Donen explained, in Hugh Fordin's *The World of Entertainment*: "We used Jean Hagen dubbing Debbie dubbing Jean. Jean's voice is quite remarkable and it was supposed to be cultured speech, and Debbie had that terrible western noise." To further confuse matters, the voice we hear as Jean sings "Would You?," also supposedly supplied by Reynolds, is that of yet a third girl, unbilled studio singer Betty Noyes.

When I met Jean in 1975 (about which more later), I asked her how, after she'd played so many

Gene Kelly trying to silence Jean in *Singin' in the Rain* (MGM, 1952).

drudges, MGM thought to even consider her for this splashy part. She told me, "L. B. Mayer's wife, of all people, had the idea from seeing me in *No Questions Asked*, one of my lesser efforts. How she ever got the idea of me for Lina from *that*, I'll never know. I discovered later that they'd tested loads of actresses before they decided on me. But I was very pleased that during the filming they were working so hard on the dance numbers, and with Debbie, that they left me pretty much on my own." (Among the other MGM actresses considered were Nina Foch, Arlene Dahl and Jane Greer.)

In a recent interview on the Turner Classic Movies channel, co-star Donald O'Connor paid Jean a sincere tribute: "She was a consummate actress. She was the sweetest gal in the world but she was on the quiet side, not like Lina Lamont at all with that high-pitched voice. No, she was a straight, legit actress. They didn't get a ditzy blonde to play the part, they got a great actress to play the ditzy blonde. That's why that part is so dynamic and so wonderful."

And shortly before her death in 2002, in an interview for *Singin' in the Rain's* 50th anniversary DVD release, actress Kathleen Freeman (Lina's frustrated vocal coach) said, "Jean Hagen was never appreciated for her capabilities. If you see her in this and you see her in *The Asphalt Jungle*, most people didn't know it was the same person. That's pretty good work. She was extraordinary, and a good friend. And *beautiful*—good Lord almighty, she was a pretty thing."

Despite the extremely favorable reaction to Jean Hagen in *Singin' in the Rain*, MGM neither publicized her nor gave her roles half as worthwhile. In *Carbine Williams* (1952), an A picture but a dull one, she was the gently understanding wife of James Stewart, who played the beleaguered inventor of the carbine rifle. According to Mimi Tellis, "Jean never wanted to be typed as hard-boiled, she got very tired of those roles in movies. She loved those insipid roles like Jimmy Stewart's sweet wife. She liked straight roles better than character parts."

She played the outdoorsy hometown girlfriend of shell-shocked war veteran Ralph Meeker in *Shadow in the Sky* ('52), but had to withdraw from the role of the vixenish farm wife in *Letter from the President* when she became pregnant. (Claire Trevor replaced her, and the film was released as *My Man and I*.) Her son, Aric Philip, was born on August 19, 1952. (They named him Aric because, he says, "my parents wanted something that would look good on a marquee.") He was the Seidels' second child; their first, Christine Patricia, named for Patricia Neal, was born August 26, 1950.

Jean was seen in three more minor Metro pictures in 1953: *Latin Lovers*, stooging again for Lana Turner; *Arena*, a mopey role in a dreary 3-D rodeo Western; and opposite Red Skelton in the witless *Half a Hero*. It was Skelton's swan song at MGM, and Jean's as well.

When I showed Jean a list of her films she said, "I'd almost forgotten some of these. I guess on purpose." Noticing *Latin Lovers* on the list, she said, "Every time Mr. Mayer would get mad at me, he'd punish me by putting me in a Lana Turner movie." But she greatly enjoyed watching Lana's utterly futile off-camera efforts at wooing her notoriously scandal-free, mated-for-life leading man, Ricardo Montalban.

In June 1953, Jean's MGM contract expired, but the previous month she began a three-year stint as Danny Thomas' wife in his weekly ABC-TV comedy series, then called *Make Room for Daddy*. The show was a hit, and brought her more popular recognition than she had gotten from her four years at MGM. (She was nominated for an Emmy as Best Supporting Actress in a Series in 1955, and the next year was nominated for two Emmys, as Best Actress *and* as Best Supporting Actress, both for the Thomas show. Three losses in two years.) She played a strong, hip brand of comedy on the show, but felt that a housewife by any other name was still second fiddle, so she took the opportunity to appear in the film version of Clifford Odets' *The Big Knife* (1955) as Connie Bliss, a feral nympho tramp on the make for Jack Palance. The film was uneven but Jean was decidedly on-heat. ("That hurts, boyfriend. I'm a naughty girl, I wish I could say I didn't like it.") Being cast back in the same mold she had once been stuck in was now a change of pace.

According to Danny Thomas, in his 1991 autobiography *Make Room for Danny*, he and Jean were less than soulmates. He objected to her preference for sloppy clothes and jeans on rehearsal days, at one point admonishing her to "for God's sake, put on high heels, put on a little lipstick," when network exec Robert Kintner was about to visit the set. Kintner had insisted on Jean for the role and "considered her the pivotal character in the series," which rankled Thomas. He found Jean aloof, though granting that she worked as hard as anyone else. He was a bit daunted by her Broadway and Hollywood resume, and Jean did indeed feel straitjacketed in her sitcom wife-and-mom role. Her husband (who had quit acting and was now an actors' agent) was wreaking havoc by staging some bitter arguments with the producers, which didn't help matters. According to Mimi Tellis, "Tom was hard on Jean, he drove her to do work she didn't want to do. She hated doing that Danny Thomas show for so many years. There was terrible tension, and the pressure finally got to her."

Ill feelings and the professional confines of the series, plus a genuine desire to spend more time with her children, prompted her decision to leave the Thomas show in 1956 after completing its third season. (Thomas returned the following season as a widower and eventually "married" Marjorie Lord, in whose hands the part became more that of a bland straight woman than when Jean played it.)

Jean now mostly stayed home, raising her family. Her son Aric says, "Her family was her passion. If she was upset about not getting work, I never knew it."

Some feel that Jean was fired from the Thomas show because of Seidel's interference, and that she had already started drinking heavily, but her daughter Christine Burton says, "She quit *Make Room for Daddy* because she wanted to spend time with my brother and me. But by then we were in school, so she didn't have anything to do all day. She didn't play bridge, she didn't do the PTA or the Brownies or the Girl Scouts. She'd worked all her life, and now all of a sudden she's got nothing to do. That's when she started drinking. She didn't drink in front of us, ever. She was a closet drinker. I didn't even know about it until I found a bottle of Scotch in a drawer in my bedroom, and I confronted her about it."

During these years she got a variety of TV jobs, but not many movies. She had a "best friend" role in *Spring Reunion* (1957), a dreary attempt to introduce a dramatic Betty Hutton to an audience that no longer cared about any Betty Hutton, and was back doing housework in Disney's *The Shaggy Dog* (1959). That year she returned to the stage, co-starring with Keefe Brasselle in *Who Was That Lady I Saw You With?* at the Dayton, Ohio, Theatre Festival. She had a thankless part as Missy LeHand,

Roosevelt's loyal secretary, in *Sunrise at Campobello* (1960); was Ray Milland's troubled wife in a nuclear holocaust low-budgeter called *Panic in Year Zero!* (1962); and had a small part as a shallow, matronly social butterfly in Bette Davis' *Dead Ringer* (1964).

By this time Jean had been drinking quite heavily and her marriage to Tom Seidel was unraveling. As Patricia Neal recently explained it, "Tom was a big drinker, and Jean kept up. It's terrible how much they drank. She became an alcoholic but I don't think Tommy did. You know the story of *Days of Wine and Roses?* That was Jean. He drank and she drank, but she suffered and he really didn't. It was just so sad."

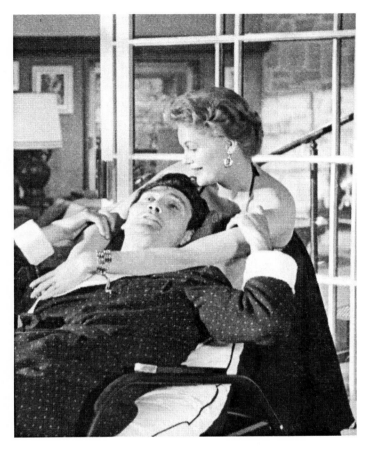

Jean pawing Jack Palance in *The Big Knife* (UA, 1955).

Seidel sued her for divorce in 1965, winning custody of the children. "I remember my father's explanation of why he divorced my mother," says Aric Seidel. "He said he hoped to shock her out of drinking by way of the divorce. I know he felt very badly about it and he spent a couple of years 'on the couch' trying to come to grips with the guilt."

Jean's Northwestern chum Nathalie Brown (now Nathalie Thompson) said, "Tom was a very difficult guy. I remember when they split up. He dumped her and set her up in a small apartment. She lost custody of the children and ended up in the hospital after a friend found her passed out unconscious in her apartment."

Jean's daughter Christine says of this period, "Our parents never argued in front of us. We were so protected that we didn't have a clue until they separated. He never drank during the day, only at night. He wasn't an alcoholic, not addicted to alcohol like she was. She stopped drinking after she went into a coma, this was around 1968. She was in the UCLA Hospital and they told me she'd be dead in a couple of weeks. It wasn't a shock to me because she'd been in and out of rehab hospitals before. She'd dry out, stay with my aunt LaVerne at her New Hampshire farm for a couple of weeks, come back and start all over again. One day I went to visit her in UCLA and all of a sudden she came out of the coma and sat up—'What day is it? Where's a newspaper?'—and she never touched another drop of liquor ever again."

Says Mimi Tellis, "Jean took a lot of comfort in LaVerne and she loved going back to that farm. It was very healing for her."

"It's something I don't like to talk about," says LaVerne about those visits. "It was emotionally hard to see her like that. Her husband put her on a plane and sent her here. She could barely stand but every day we walked, a little bit farther every day, and eventually to the center of town four miles away. She loved walking through the woods, we'd have such a good time. She built up her strength and seemed in good health and good spirits, but apparently it didn't last because she came back two or three more times. Once she came in a wheelchair. Each time I sent her home she was strong again. She was very resilient. She tried so hard."

In her 1988 autobiography, *As I Am*, Patricia Neal wrote: "Jean had started out with a bang at MGM, but Hollywood had left her nursing hopes of fulfillment, and when the teat dried up, she started on the bottle. Eventually Tom left her. My dear friend did finally quit drinking, but there were many heartbreaks to come before she made it."

They lost touch with each other for awhile but reunited in 1974. "Jean wasn't drinking now," wrote Neal, "and looked the best I had seen her in years. Unfortunately, she had another problem. My beloved Jean had throat cancer and was going to Germany for laetrile, a supposed cure unavailable in the States. But she was bubbly and bright and so much the way I remembered her from the old days."

She had by now dropped completely off the map professionally. Then, late in 1974, the fifth volume of Richard Lamparski's *Whatever Became Of…?* series included an interview with Jean, then a resident of the Motion Picture Country Hospital in Woodland Hills, California. It noted that she'd been ill for some time, and I was moved to write her a letter telling of my admiration for her work. To my delight she answered, and we began a lengthy correspondence by mail and spoke often on the phone. It was during this period that she was operated on for a malignant tumor on her upper soft palate. Two weeks after the surgery, she wrote: "Please excuse the writing as I'm lying flat on my back at the Motion Picture Hospital. Well, into every life some rain must fall, but I swear, too much is falling on me! One always feels that cancer somehow happens to other people, not yourself. But despite having to be fed through a tube I really feel quite good."

Three months later, in August '75, she felt strong enough to visit New York, staying at the Fifth Avenue apartment of her old Northwestern friend Nancy Hoadley (now Salisbury), and we arranged to meet there one morning. To my surprise and relief, Jean looked and sounded surprisingly healthy, heavier than in her movie days, and we settled down to having a fine old chin wag, but since it was such a beautiful day she wanted to get outside and walk about. I was a bit concerned about her stamina but we continued chatting merrily as we walked, and walked, and walked—all though Central Park, down Fifth Avenue, a long stroll through the Museum of Modern Art, then over to the West 40s theatre district. Her old MGM pal Rita Moreno was currently on Broadway in *The Ritz* and Jean decided she'd like to see if we could get last-minute tickets for a matinee. They were sold out, so instead she made a call to another actress friend, Kay Medford, and we walked over to Medford's apartment for a delightful visit until early evening, the two old pros exchanging ribald war stories and I happily drinking them in. Finally I *walked* her back home, Jean still feeling cheerful and energetic and seemingly indestructible. She'd talked frequently of her desire to get back into harness, of how much she loved and missed acting, and now seemed to me quite capable of doing just that.

She returned to California. Helen Thomson flew in from her home in London and visited Jean in the Motion Picture Hospital: "I invited Jean to come see me in London. So she came over, stayed three weeks and she was an absolute delight, so funny, and my children adored her. Never went near a drink. She mostly forgot to take all the pills they'd been stuffing into her, and she was fine. She'd been in that Motion Picture Hospital for I think about five years. She wanted to see how she'd do on her own, so she found an inexpensive hotel, stayed there for a few nights, went to see a few shows—and she was *recognized!* Oh, she was so thrilled. The whole trip turned her around because she realized she didn't have to be in that hospital. She went back to California, got a flat, and was taking tap-dancing lessons! Karl Malden offered her a part in *Streets of San Francisco*, and she got more offers."

After being out of commission for a dozen years, she now rallied enough to appear on the Malden series, plus episodes of *Good Heavens* and *Starsky and Hutch*. All were seen in 1976, and Jean seemed to me as sharp and sturdy as she had when I last saw her.

But by 1977 the cancer had clearly taken its toll. When her sister LaVerne visited Jean in the Motion Picture Hospital, "she was very ill. I'd been in contact with her doctor during that time. My brother, my daughter and I went to see her and I knew she didn't have long to live. The large cancerous growth on her neck was very obvious, and she couldn't swallow. We wheeled her around the hospital and she was in good spirits despite the pain, greeting all the patients she knew. Very brave, so brave. She was always that way, even as a child. When I was leaving, she said, 'Please don't come back, I want you to remember me the best you can.' I knew there was no hope. She was dying."

Nathalie Thompson, along with her 17-year-old daughter Kristin, also visited her. Kristin had become as close to Jean as her mother had always been, but neither were prepared for this visit. "She'd had the operation on her throat and had a scarf covering her scar," Nathalie says. "She'd lost weight, she was a wraith. She looked like she was dying. Kristin took one look at her and was just terrified. She couldn't handle it. Jean was a completely different looking person. It was upsetting to me, to Jean and to Kristin."

After her throat operation, Jean did a small role as a vicious landlady in a TV movie, *Alexander: The Other Side of Dawn*. In it she appeared ravaged, and that beautiful, mellow voice was now a hoarse rasp, but she was stubbornly determined to go down fighting. It was her final performance.

"I visited her a couple of times in the Motion Picture Home," says Mimi Tellis. "The last time, I went down there to kind of rescue her. She was playing poker with one of the Three Stooges, who was her pal. I walked past her several times before I recognized her. In her drinking days she had a weight problem but now she was quite wasted away, very thin. I took her out to dinner and to visit some friends and she had the most wonderful time. I don't think anybody was paying a whole lot of attention to her, she was just sort of buried at the Home. When I left her she said, 'It's amazing to see you and know that there's still some life out there. We're not finished, Mimi.' Of course I didn't have any idea of being finished. She'd forgotten there was a world out there, which was so sad to me. Later I was talking to her one night on the phone when she had this tumor in her throat, and she was all excited about a doctor who'd invented a laser tool that could go in and zap it. She was on a long waiting list, but she'd just gained one or two pounds and I thought, 'Oh, she's on the mend, she's going to make a comeback.' Nathalie called me the next morning and said, 'Did you hear about Jean?,' and I said 'Yes, isn't it great, she's gained weight.' And she said, 'No, she died last night.' It was such a shock."

Jean Hagen died of throat cancer on August 29, 1977. She'd just turned 54. The month before, Gene Kelly and some friends gave her a birthday party in the San Fernando Valley. They knew how seriously ill Jean had become and weren't sure she'd make it to her actual birthday (August 3), so they held it for her in July.

Jean's daughter Christine remembers that "after she was diagnosed with cancer, my mom never had another cigarette again, just as after she awoke from the coma she never had another drink. She'd been an alcoholic and a smoker, and that's what it took for her to quit. A year or so before she died, she went to Germany by herself to get laetrile, got it, came back, and the Motion Picture Hospital took it away from her because it wasn't an approved treatment in the U.S. So she went to all that trouble and didn't get to keep it. She had a pretty miserable middle-age and it was such a sad end, but she always had a really incredible attitude. She was such a great lady."

Tom Seidel died of a stroke at 75 on December 7, 1992. "He married and divorced again twice before his death," says Aric Seidel. "During the last year or two of his life he had found an old picture of my mother. He framed it and kept it on his desk. Although he never said so, it was obvious he realized Mom was the only one he was ever truly in love with."

(Neither of Jean's children went into the family profession. Christine, formerly a tennis instructor, now shows and breeds dogs and trains them for work with the ill and elderly. Aric was a representative with American Tobacco and Hyatt Hotels and is now a wine distributor. "What I am mostly is a father and a husband," he says, "the two jobs that are most important to me. My 15-year-old daughter Ariel, a sometimes aspiring actress, heaven forbid, is like my mother; beautiful, has a great voice, and is way too much fun to be around.")

Her lifelong Northwestern friends all paid tribute to Jean:

HELEN THOMSON: "Jean was extremely courageous. Twenty-five years later we all still think about her and talk about her and miss her. And I'm delighted that you're writing about her."

MIMI TELLIS: "Jean had higher aspirations for her acting career and she could have expanded more but she was always typecast. The other thing she wanted was one real love in her life before she died. But she always kept an absolutely marvelous humor and was always great fun to be with. Always."

NATHALIE THOMPSON: "We got to really know one another over the years and had many reunions together. I used to wonder what the Hollywood big shots did with their garbage, so I once called Jean from Connecticut and asked her. She said, 'Oh, we wrap it up in a mink coat and throw it over a cliff.' She was so pretty and so much fun, even during the bad times. A very funny, wonderful girl."

NANCY SALISBURY: "She was a trusted and loving friend. My daughter was very fond of Jean, there was always a lovely bond between Jean and all our children. They had such good times being with her, as the rest of us did. Such a great sense of humor, so much fun to be around. I remember her with great warmth and joy. She lives vividly in my memory and always will. She had a great spirit."

PATRICIA NEAL: "Jean was clear at the end of her life. She was a good woman. I understand your loving her, I loved her too. I adored her."

1949: Side Street (MGM), Adam's Rib (MGM). **1950:** Ambush (MGM), The Asphalt Jungle (MGM). **1951:** A Life of Her Own (MGM), Night Into Morning (MGM), No Questions Asked (MGM). **1952:** Singin' in the Rain (MGM), Shadow in the Sky (MGM), Carbine Williams (MGM). **1953:** Latin Lovers (MGM), Arena (MGM), Half a Hero (MGM). **1955:** The Big Knife (UA). **1957:** Spring Reunion (UA). **1959:** The Shaggy Dog (Buena Vista). **1960:** Sunrise at Campobello (WB). **1962:** Panic in Year Zero! (AIP). **1964:** Dead Ringer (WB). **1977:** Alexander: The Other Side of Dawn.

Adele Jergens: A Lot of Woman

by LAURA WAGNER

Adele Jergens' brief part in *Somebody Loves Me* typifies her hard-edged screen persona. Playing Nola Beech, a singing star with plenty of attitude, she heads the vaudeville bill that newcomer Betty Hutton, as Blossom Seeley, starts out with. She steals Betty's best song, and despite pathetic pleas to give it back, Adele is more than a little annoyed as she turns to a stagehand for assistance with this nuisance.

ADELE: Hey, tell this stage struck brat she's in vaudeville, not Sunday school.

STAGEHAND (*to Hutton*): You're wasting your breath, kid. She'd murder her own mother for an extra bow.

ADELE: *I did.* But I gave the old lady a real stylish funeral.

The tramp, the haughty star, the two-timer, the dance hall queen, the crook—Adele Jergens played them all. She was an absolutely gorgeous blonde but her height (varying sources say between 5'7" and 5'10"), strong aura and Brooklyn accent invariably placed her in the company of thugs and gamblers. It's a typecasting people have responded to; today Jergens is considered hot stuff among *film noir* and crime movie fans. She played her sexy roles with an edginess that could make many a *femme fatale* blush. She seemed to be the real thing on screen, especially in the '50s when her voice lowered, and she made it quite clear: Don't mess with this gal.

She was born Adele Louisa Jurgens on November 26, 1917, in the Ridgewood section of Brooklyn, New York, the youngest (and only girl) of four children. She was a self-professed tomboy, playing baseball and dreaming of being a newspaper reporter. Dancing lessons at seven years old changed all that. The stage was her new ambition. At 14 she won a scholarship to Manhattan's Albertina Rasch Dance School and became, she would say later, "all wrapped up in my dancing." Despite later reports from studio bios and other articles devoted to her, Adele never studied singing in her youth; she always utilized a voice double when she was called on to sing in movies.

Adele would also claim in interviews that she first appeared in a Broadway show when she was 15 during summer vacation. If so, there is no record of its name. Three years later, at almost 18, she racked up her first known Broadway credit as a chorus girl: *Jubilee*, which opened on October 12, 1935.

Her beauty didn't go unnoticed. She signed with the John Robert Powers Agency in New York, becoming a top model. She also became known as "New York's

92

No. 1 Showgirl," appearing in successful shows like *Leave It to Me!* (1938) and *DuBarry was a Lady* (1939), as well as dancing in local clubs. She traveled abroad in cabaret and, when she returned to the U.S., garnered some publicity by being named "Miss World's Fairest" at New York's 1939 World's Fair. It was during this period that she also briefly became a Rockette at Radio City Music Hall. Adele continued on as a showgirl in *Louisiana Purchase* (1940) and *Banjo Eyes* (1941), and, a big break, understudying Gypsy Rose Lee in *Star and Garter* (1942), going on just once.

That's all it took and Hollywood was plenty interested.

Adele's time spent under contract to Twentieth Century-Fox is always

Portrait of Adele Jergens, 1946.

misjudged, sources citing it somewhere before *Star and Garter*, yet failing to turn up any credits. The problem is that she and Virginia Mayo, friends since *Banjo Eyes*, are often mistaken for each other, a striking resemblance both actresses admit to. However, checking the Fox movies attributed to Mayo (1943-44), the actress in question is clearly Adele in either large groups or choral dance numbers: *Hello, Frisco, Hello, The Gang's All Here, Sweet Rosie O'Grady* and *Pin-Up Girl*. The only Fox movie ever officially credited to Adele is *Jane Eyre* (1944), but if she is indeed in that film, she's not easily discernible. It's possible that she made other Fox films during this period.

After Fox failed to pick up her option, Columbia promptly signed her to a seven-year contract, starting with *Together Again* (1944), as a stripper. From this small part she snared the sweet, well-mannered female lead—where's the fun in that?—in the serial *Black Arrow* (1944). After being seen as chorines in *Dancing in Manhattan* and *Tonight and Every Night* (both 1945), Adele was given her first starring part in a feature, *A Thousand and One Nights* (1945), an underrated spoof of Arabian Night pictures, as the Princess of Baghdad.

She got reams of publicity (labeled "The Eyeful"), everyone marveling at this new, gorgeous find. But despite this success in a popular movie, Columbia was slow to act. No further films were released with Adele in 1945, and in 1946 just one made it to the screen. Luckily, it was in an amusing comedy starring Rosalind Russell.

In *She Wouldn't Say Yes* (1946), Adele displayed a comedic gift never fully exploited on screen. She's the temperamental Allura, aptly named author of *Biography of a Blonde*, a racy 300-page autobiography with "a different romance on every page." She consults psychologist Russell after a series of beaux die: "I kiss dem, dat's all, and dey die," Adele intones in an exaggerated Bolivian accent. Jergens briefly complicates Roz's relationship with Lee Bowman, but in the end she is cured to romance another day. Aggressive Allura is described as "quite a terrifying young woman" by butler Harry Davenport, who marvels to Bowman, "She's so *blonde*, isn't she?"

In the fantasy *Down to Earth* (1947), Adele is the actress portraying Terpsichore, the Goddess of Dance, in Larry Parks' Broadway musical *Swinging the Muses*, until competition arrives in the form of Terpsichore herself (Rita Hayworth). Adele's in her glory as the tough-talking star who isn't about to lose her part to some nervy upstart. Parks has to separate the two. "Sister," Adele growls forcibly, fists clenched, "you're about to lose some teeth." Well, this being Columbia and not the real world, Adele is fired and Hayworth takes over, thus ending Jergens' seventh-billed role. But, while she's on screen, Adele does a little tap dancing and sings (with the bluesy voice of dubber Kay Starr) "The Nine Muses."

In *The Dark Past* (Columbia, 1948), Adele is an unfaithful wife dallying with Stephen Dunne. Left to right: Lee J. Cobb, Jergens, Dunne, Lois Maxwell.

With four more movies on her schedule, 1947 turned out to be a very productive, if less than inspiring, year. She played a chiseling secretary in *Blondie's Anniversary*, but was better served as the musical lead in the obscure *When a Girl's Beautiful*, her singing courtesy of Suzanne Ellers. She exuded toughness in *I Love Trouble*, but was limited to one scene with star Franchot Tone, pulling out a revolver and coolly remarking, "This was for when I got bored with you." Her best movie that year was *The Corpse Came C.O.D.*, an airy murder mystery, portraying a glamourous Hollywood star implicated in homicide and diamond smuggling. This self-assured performance alone should have alerted Columbia to her possibilities.

But, again, she was stuck in only one scene in *The Fuller Brush Man* (1948) with Red Skelton, and had a limited part in the intriguing *The Dark Past* (1948), a well-played remake of *Blind Alley* (1939). She's an unfaithful wife who, in her best scene, confronts gun moll Nina Foch. Looking Adele over, Foch cracks, "You don't look like any angel to me." Truer words were never spat out.

Crazy casting 101: Jergens plays Marilyn Monroe's mother in *Ladies of the Chorus* (Columbia, 1948).

Many thought her role as Marilyn Monroe's burlesque dancer mother in *Ladies of the Chorus* (1948) a mistake at this point in her career (Adele was 31 to Monroe's 22). Wearing a blonde wig over gray hair, she's referred to more than once as "an old hag," which doesn't ring true. Yet despite the slight age gap, Adele ably projects the right amount of life experience and motherly instinct to make her role believable. She's also allowed a great youthful flashback from her days as a headliner. Looking sensational, a brunette Adele socks over "Crazy for You," dubbed by Virginia Rees. Showing infinitely more charisma than newcomer Monroe, Adele really sizzles. Yet, for all the fuss about Marilyn later, and Adele's crazy casting as her mother, Nana Bryant stole *Ladies of the Chorus* out from under them both.

The "Crazy for You" number in *Ladies* took excellent advantage of Adele's dancing skills, something Columbia played down probably due to Rita Hayworth. In fact, some say Harry Cohn had originally put Adele under contract to keep his top star Hayworth in line. Her roles at the studio reflected this backhanded interest. She had supporting parts in *Prince of Thieves* (1948), *Law of the Barbary Coast* (1949), *Slightly French* (1949, a funny bit as a temperamental French star) and *Make Believe Ballroom* (1949), but headed the casts of *The Woman from Tangier* (1949), *The Crime Doctor's Diary* (1949) and *The Mutineers* (1949), certainly not a distinguished group. The latter film featured Adele as the seductive secretary-nurse (uh-huh) of counterfeiter George Reeves. When Reeves takes over a freighter, Jergens plays up to first mate Jon Hall to keep him preoccupied. "I hate rules," she coos to the befuddled Hall. "Isn't it strange that the best things in life are either a sin or make you fat?" *Variety*, who disliked the film, complained, "The actors perform with a singular lack of enthusiasm. All, that is, save Miss Jergens, who comes out quite well as a loose wench who frankly likes men."

The Treasure of Monte Cristo (1949), a loan-out to Lippert, was notable solely for introducing her to handsome ex–Fox contract player Glenn Langan; the couple, who exhibited a few sparks on camera, would have an on-again, off-again personal relationship for a couple of years. Adele would first get seriously involved with then-actor Ronald Reagan in December of 1949, which, according to Adele's friend Virginia Mayo, almost led to the altar. "He was crazy about her," Mayo says. "He gave her a lot of jewelry." Adele as First Lady of our country?

If her personal life was smooth, her career surely wasn't. The contract at Columbia failed to turn her into an important name in A features. Despite this, Adele was seemingly content. "I liked working there very much," she told Dan Van Neste shortly before her death in 2002. "It was my home studio and I knew everyone and they knew me. Everybody was very nice, but they worked us hard. I only recall one film in which we were able to rehearse. They would put me in three pictures at one time but I didn't mind. I enjoyed it; and besides it was a steady income. Columbia was really a learning experience for me. I had been on the stage but never acted in films before. I was learning with each movie I made even though many were B pictures."

Half of 1950 saw Jergens freelancing, with mixed results. Because of Columbia's misuse, Adele was relegated to the second feature pile, except that odd occurrence *(Edge of Doom, Show Boat, The Cobweb)* when she cinched tiny roles at the major studios. "I still keep practicing," she said of her neglected dancing, "but if someone doesn't give me a good dancing part pretty soon I'll stop and concentrate on being a champion screen home-wrecker." Which is what would happen after her next film.

The actress was busy little crook in 1950, a year which saw her in ten films. In *Armored Car Robbery* she had the showy role of Yvonne LeDoux, a "strictly high-rent" burlesque queen. Her second-billed part was minimal, but very effective, seen mostly seductively dancing on stage, and playing around, of course, on her hubby. "That's a lot of woman," howls one interested male.

She dabbled in some blackmail in *Side Street*, but was dumped into the East River as thanks for her services rendered. *Radar Secret Service*, her best role that year, had Adele involved with radium thieves and two-timing Tom Neal with boss Tristram Coffin. When Neal finds out, he pulls a gun on the both of them. Ever resourceful, she aids Coffin by sneaking him a pistol. Walking in on the scene moments later, Myrna Dell looks down dumbfounded at Neal's dead body. "When you're through

A handy gal to have around, Adele passes a pistol to Tris Coffin in *Radar Secret Service* (Lippert, 1950). Won't Tom Neal be surprised?

with a boyfriend, you're *really* through," she says to Jergens. She played another sexy broad, girlfriend of crook Lloyd Bridges, in *The Sound of Fury.*

Where did she go wrong? Soon a whole new subgenre opened itself to Adele, seducing idiots in a string of pictures: Arthur Lake (*Beware of Blondie*), Andy Devine (*Traveling Saleswoman*), Lou Costello (*Abbott and Costello Meet the Invisible Man*) and the Bowery Boys (*Blues Busters* and *Blonde Dynamite*). It was getting harder and harder for a gal to make a dishonest buck.

A slight change came with Warner Bros.' *Sugarfoot* (1951), taking over from the originally scheduled Patricia Neal. She was again a dance hall gal (dubbed on the peculiar "Oh, He Looked Like He Might Buy Wine"), but with a difference. This time she was a respectable girl who just happens to be singing in a dive called The Diana. Showing flashes throughout of being a perfect candidate for anger-management classes, she blows her top during her first meeting with new-to-town Randolph Scott. He apologizes to the demure-looking Adele for staring because "you're not what I picture gambling hall girls to look like. It ... it surprises me." Speaking for all wronged women in her line of work, she snaps, with a rising furor that startles the nervous Scott, "It *surprises* you? It surprises you that I'm a human being? You're the same as all the rest of them. Do you think I have no life or existence outside The Diana?" You go, girl.

Huntz Hall in *Blues Busters* (Monogram, 1950) is just one of a string of idiots that Adele seduced in films. What could handsome Craig Stevens (right) be thinking?

It was a good, juicy role, with the twist of not having Adele act the standard floozy; she alternated between shyness to anger to bawdiness to intense love for Scott. It was perhaps her best role in a major movie.

Did it help secure better parts? Nope. Her uncredited part as a gambling lady named Cameo McQueen, in MGM's *Show Boat* (1951) gave the impression of being cut to ribbons during the editing process. She was just barely in the picture.

She and Glenn Langan were finally wed on October 6, 1951 in New York, where he was rehearsing George S. Kaufman's new play *Fancy Meeting You Again*. A year earlier Adele had told columnist Darr Smith that "I don't want to become cynical about it through being married and divorced five times. When I was 16 I had an ideal about marriage, and what I had at 16 I'm going to keep until the right guy comes along." Apparently that was a sound outlook; they would stay together until Langan's death 40 years later. Their son Tracy was born in 1953.

After the happy occasion of her marriage, it's a shame she became involved with *Aaron Slick from Punkin Crick* (1952), singer Dinah Shore's notorious flop. Dinah and Alan Young are neighboring farmers who sing about chores, Saturday nights in town and why Young can't muster up the nerve to romance her without the aid of alcohol. Adele is an actress who's on the lam with Robert Merrill for selling phony land lots. Hiding out in Punkin Crick, they try to swindle Dinah out of her farm. Along the way Adele is chased by a bull, becoming irritable, brittle and not too fond of farm life. Probably how audiences felt back in 1952 watching this turkey.

She appeared briefly in *Somebody Loves Me* (1952), making a strong impression with her nasty segment. She was dubbed by Barbara Ames on two songs: "Honey, Oh, My Honey" and "Toddling the Todalo." No one had to dub her bitchy attitude. It was pure, unadulterated Jergens.

A break following the birth of her son, she claimed, changed her outlook. "Sexy clothes and dialog were firmly associated with me in film," Adele told Howard McClay in 1953, "and nobody would listen when I protested that marriage and motherhood had made 'an honest woman' of me. All anybody could remember was that I had a come-hither look and burned the candle at both ends and in the middle, in my screen roles. I don't think any self-respecting young mother would feel right in spending eight hours a day on movie sets displaying her baser instincts, so I turned down several parts like that.

"But eventually it became apparent that I'd have to readjust myself to that kind of portrayal if I wanted to work again, and I do like to work, so I talked myself into trying one of those parts.

"Fortunately, my first comeback part was in a television play with Paul Muni called "The People vs. Johnson" [on *Ford Theatre*]. I told myself that at least I'd be doing a tarnished type for only half an hour, and not for an hour-and-a-half, as I'd have to in a motion picture.

"After that job was finished I began to feel like my old self once more. I practiced putting a gleam in my eye and letting my hips sway when I walked around in front of my mirror, and that old feeling came back."

It's doubtful Adele felt she was losing her touch in the bad girl roles she was playing, although saying so made good copy. It was a nice try, an obvious attempt at getting better roles. She couldn't very well turn her back on such roles now—not after years of doing them so well. It was impossible at this late stage. There would be no great dramatic roles or sophisticated comedies in her movie future. Just B movies.

And television. Jergens wasn't given a substantial amount of work in the medium, but her regular appearances on Mike Stokey's *Pantomime Quiz*, starting in 1949, showed off the engaging sense of humor that motion pictures kept under wraps. Adele became a regular from 1950 to 1952. Her involvement with the show would earn her a star on the Hollywood Walk of Fame.

But, yes, on film, the old feeling was back, and was showed to full effect in *Overland Pacific* (1954), which, although minor, proved how good an actress she could be, if given half the chance. She again works in a saloon, the Silver Dollar this time, owned by the unsavory William Bishop. The brunette Adele, a tart with a heart of gold, pines for ex-lover Bishop, but he's engaged to sweet Peggie Castle. "Why don't you forget the little princess," Adele tries to convince him, "and come back to the common herd?" He doesn't. She later attempts to turn him in for a series of murders, because she loves him. He kills her instead. She gave a deep emotional edge to her role, which lacked none of the toughness she was now known for.

The Big Chase (1954), a lively crime yarn from Lippert, co-starred her again with her husband. Even though she had the female lead, Adele was lamentably domesticated as the loving housewife of patrolman Langan. While her husband goes on "the big chase" (footage from the previous year's 3-D short *Bandit Island*), Adele is stuck in a hospital suffering from pregnancy complications. Her part was not worthwhile in regard to time or substance. She and Langan would co-star only once more on screen, in the trivial western *Outlaw Treasure* (1955), produced by American Releasing Corporation (soon to be AIP). The couple also attempted two short-lived radio programs, *Stand By for Crime* (Syndicated, 1953) and *Those Young Bryans* (NBC, 1956), but it was too late for shows like this on radio.

In general, her roles were diminishing in screen time. Her slight part in *Fireman, Save My Child* (1954) didn't even warrant a character name. Hanging around *The Miami Story* (1954), she acted sexy, but did little else. She was Charles Boyer's rarely seen secretary-mistress in *The Cobweb* (1955), and showed up in a flash as a saloon keeper in *Strange Lady in Town* (1955), starring Greer Garson. Her two-minute bit allowed her to snarl, after Cameron Mitchell shoots a man in her saloon, "All right boys, take this monkey in the back." Not Shakespeare, but handled like a real pro.

She second-fiddled in *The Lonesome Trail* (1955) as the drunken floozy Earle Lyon plays around with. When he shows too much interest in leading lady Margia Dean, Adele gets riled and a slap-fest ensues between the two women as bartender Wayne Morris and various bar patrons look on in amusement. It was a small part, but not without its fun.

Her film stock went up considerably when Alex Gordon, producing for AIP, gave her roles in three now-classic exploitation features that were popular at the box office. All three contained prime, definitive Jergens performances.

In *Day the World Ended* (1956) she is one of seven survivors of a nuclear blast who come together under one roof. Adele plays an ex-stripper fatally in love with the rotten Mike Connors, who was "spawned in bilge water," according to her. When he takes more than a passing fancy in innocent Lori Nelson, good dame Adele helps the kid out, but pays for it with a ride down a cliff to her death courtesy of the not-very-amused Connors. Her best scene is the one where, drunk on moonshine, she relives her past glories in burlesque, only to break down sobbing at the end of her seductive dance.

"Funny how scum like us thinks alike ... well, I'm having some guns shipped in just in case ..." With these potent words, uttered while cooped up in her jail cell, tough dame Jergens makes it entirely believable that those guns are as good as delivered. In fact, every move Adele makes in *Girls in Prison* (1956) is plausible, or as cell-mate Helen Gilbert warns newcomer Joyce Taylor: "Don't fight her. She's cruel and vulgar, but she *is* important. She can get you anything you want from the outside." After their initial tiff, shrewd Adele plays up to Taylor, knowing Joyce is hiding a stash of stolen loot on the outside.

It's hard not to enjoy the rough-and-tumble charm of *Girls in Prison*, with its cat fights in the mud, love-starved lesbians, kooky stoolies and, especially, veteran actress Jane Darwell, as the prison matron, yelling, "It's a gang-up!!" For Jergens fans, there is the customary dominant attitude, but, as an added attraction, she also hot-wires a truck and goes out in style by shootin' it out with Lance Fuller for the dough.

She played a nothing role in *Fighting Trouble* (1956), which interrupted the flow of her AIP successes. It was a painful Bowery Boys entry, *sans* Leo Gorcey, and any kind of humor.

Adele bounced back in style, as well as displaying a little more compassion, in *Runaway Daughters* (1956), as a dance hostess who advises three teenage girls to take the right path. One girl in particular, Gloria Castillo, sister of Adele's boyfriend Lance Fuller, is the most troubled of the trio ("Maybe I've never grown up. Maybe I'm a psycho!"), and she and Adele have an instant aversion to each other. "What formula did your mother feed you on?" asks Adele. "Vinegar ... and what else?" When Fuller calls Jergens "the best little coffee-maker in California," Castillo snaps back, "Where did she learn how—state prison?" All this back and forth trashing prompts Adele to marvel, "Nice kid. I better search her for poison darts."

With angst-ridden girls brawling and smoking, burdened with unwed pregnancies and suicidal tendencies, not to mention neglectful parents, *Runaway Daughters*, tame by today's standards, is a classic of its kind. Campy, to be sure ("You can tell the principal that he can't expel me—because I *quit!*"), but diverting fun, with Jergens leaving her film work behind in a snappy, fun and, even, maternal way.

In 1956 Adele suddenly up and quit. Either she had lost interest, particularly with a child to raise, or she was receiving pressure at home from her husband. Or possibly, nearly 40, she realized her chances were getting slimmer in the glamour girl department. She still was attractive, but it was better to get out when the getting was good without ending up as an aging gun moll.

Langan continued to work off-and-on in film (his most famous: the title role in *The Amazing Colossal Man*), but stopped completely after 1971's *The Andromeda Strain*. He tried real estate for awhile, but eventually, according to David Ragan in *Who's Who in Hollywood*, "became a prosperous sales manager for the National Utility Service of San Francisco, handling all the Western states and Hawaii."

Not much was heard from Adele through the years. She turned up in late 1976 to announce, "Now that I've spent so many years in retirement, I have the urge to get back into the acting profession and have been concentrating on the TV/commercial field." Unfortunately, nothing really came through.

Their retirement years were disrupted in the early '90s when Langan succumbed to cancer on January 19, 1991, at the age of 73. Their son Tracy followed in 2001, victim of a brain tumor. Adele was especially hit hard by this last tragedy. She became a recluse and her health deteriorated. Developing a severe cold, it quickly slipped into pneumonia. Jergens passed away on November 22, 2002, four days away from her eighty-fifth birthday.

The London Times remembered her as a "sultry B-movie actress who specialized in bad-girl roles during a brief but busy career," while *The Washington Post* labeled her "a leading pinup model during World War II."

Gorgeous but deadly, the screen career of Adele Jergens might have been, to some, minor—even trivial. She was hardly an important star, but she was vividly and divinely one of the best of the floozies and bad girls who graced the silver screen.

She was pure dynamite. And possibly no one knew that better than Randolph

Scott in *Sugarfoot*, who sees his soft-spoken leading lady turn into a wildcat when his life is threatened by town baddies: "If you were taken away from me, I'll see to it that *someone* dies." Then, noticing his shock, she sneers, "Do you think I'm some tame, pampered girl from Alabama? I can hate as well as a man and I would hate more dangerously than a man."

Leaving Adele to her deadly thoughts, a dazed, but clearly loved Scott turns toward the camera, shaking his head and breathing an impressed sigh of relief. As if to say: "That's a lot of woman."

1943: Hello, Frisco, Hello (TCF), The Gang's All Here (TCF), Sweet Rosie O'Grady (TCF). **1944**: Pin-Up Girl (TCF), Jane Eyre (TCF), Together Again (Columbia), Black Arrow (Columbia serial). **1945**: Dancing in Manhattan (Columbia), Tonight and Every Night (Columbia), A Thousand and One Nights (Columbia). **1946**: She Wouldn't Say Yes (Columbia). **1947**: Down to Earth (Columbia), Blondie's Anniversary (Columbia), When a Girl's Beautiful (Columbia), I Love Trouble (Columbia), The Corpse Came C.O.D. (Columbia). **1948**: The Fuller Brush Man (Columbia), The Dark Past (Columbia), Ladies of the Chorus (Columbia), Prince of Thieves (Columbia). **1949**: Law of the Barbary Coast (Columbia), Make Believe Ballroom (Columbia), The Woman from Tangier (Columbia), The Crime Doctor's Diary (Columbia), The Mutineers (Columbia), The Treasure of Monte Cristo (Lippert), Slightly French (Columbia). **1950**: Edge of Doom (RKO/Goldwyn), Armored Car Robbery (RKO), Beware of Blondie (Columbia), Everybody's Dancin' (Lippert), Blonde Dynamite (Monogram), Blues Busters (Monogram), Side Street (MGM), Radar Secret Service (Lippert), The Sound of Fury (UA), Traveling Saleswoman (Columbia). **1951**: Sugarfoot (WB), Abbott and Costello Meet the Invisible Man (Universal), Show Boat (MGM). **1952**: Aaron Slick from Punkin Crick (Paramount), Somebody Loves Me (Paramount). **1954**: Overland Pacific (UA), Fireman, Save My Child (Universal), The Miami Story (Columbia), The Big Chase (Lippert). **1955**: The Cobweb (MGM), Strange Lady in Town (WB), The Lonesome Trail (Lippert), Outlaw Treasure (ARC). **1956**: Day the World Ended (AIP), Fighting Trouble (AA), Girls in Prison (AIP), Runaway Daughters (AIP).

Ida Lupino: Triumph of the Will

by LAURA WAGNER

Under contract to Warner Bros. (1940–47) at the same time Bette Davis was reigning Queen of the Lot, Ida Lupino showed she was no mere underling. Ida, pegging herself "a poor man's Bette Davis," was much better than that. She was a powerful actress of substance. She also, unlike the much-touted Davis, became a first-class director, writer and producer (through her own company Filmakers), in a time when that was never done. Dorothy Arzner was the only recognized female director of any importance in talkies, and a woman Lupino greatly admired. But Ida went a step further with her non-acting work, choosing cutting-edge, before-their-time material. Lupino did it all.

Her family lived and breathed show business, going back to the Victorian era; most of the family was involved with the British stage. Ida's cousin Lupino Lane was an acrobatic comic on stage and film, as well as a director. Her father, Stanley Lupino, was highly revered in revues and film for his comedic skill. It's ironic that Ida was rarely given the opportunity to show her funny side in movies.

Ida Lupino was born on February 4, 1918, in London (a sister, Rita, followed in 1921). Her maternal grandfather George O'Shea, likewise a once-popular comedian, was especially important to young Ida, teaching her to sing, draw, compose and generally develop her artistry. When she was quite young, she wrote the play *Mademoiselle*, as a school production; in typical Lupino style, she also starred. Her father, sensing his legacy passed on by Ida's obvious prodigy, began to coach her extensively. "I never had a childhood," she once noted, but that was because strong-willed Ida's purpose was always to be an actress.

Ida made her film debut as a crowd extra in *The Love Race* (1931) starring Stanley Lupino and directed by Lupino Lane. This bit bolstered her desire to become an actress, and she convinced her parents to allow her to enroll in the prestigious Royal Academy of Dramatic Arts in 1932. During her two terms, she performed in many plays, including *Julius Caesar, Pygmalion* and *The Last of Mrs. Cheyney.*

Her official film debut, *Her First Affaire* (1932) was a fluke. Director Allan Dwan said that her mother Connie had tested for the part, but it was 14-year-old Ida who perked his interest. She won the part of a young girl smitten with a married novelist. Film offers poured in.

She had a quick succession of movie roles in 1933 (including *Money for Speed* and *Ghost Camera*), and Paramount Pictures in America was advised of her potential. They were eager to obtain her services for the title role in their upcoming *Alice in Wonderland* (1933).

Alice in Wonderland. It even sounded absurd to Ida: "You can't play naive if you're not." She was the right age (15), but hardly the innocent dreamer. Regardless, she accepted the studio's invitation to come to Hollywood, mainly due to her father's counsel, which she valued. She sailed to America with her mother to play or not play little Alice.

Ida's screen test revealed what she knew all along—she was too mature. Paramount, however, was at a loss. What to do with Lupino?

The answer was simple: put her under contract (at $600 a week), promise her "great things," then slowly waste away her talent. It's disheartening today to watch these '30s Paramounts—among them, *Search for Beauty*, *Anything Goes*, *Yours for the Asking* and others of their ilk—and realize that no one had a handle on Lupino, no one knew what she was capable of, and surely no one seemed to care. Her blonde, over-glamourized look helped not a bit. As a result, she was thrown away on trivial, cookie-cutter female leads any ingenue could have handled. Around this time, dissatisfied, she

Portrait of Ida Lupino, 1940.

bitterly remarked, "If I don't get a part I can get my teeth into, I'm going back home."

Ida defiantly refused a bit in *Cleopatra* (1934) and was suspended, then turned around and surprised Paramount by accepting a small but rich part in *Peter Ibbetson* (1935). She was loaned-out to UA, RKO and Columbia in roles mirroring her Paramount output. *Variety* saw the problem when they reviewed *Smart Girl*: "In addition to being a personable girl, Miss Lupino does an elegant job of trouping; far ahead of the material offered." *Artists and Models*, with Jack Benny, her last Paramount release, was a pleasant musical comedy, but unsuited to the misplaced Lupino.

The only memorable

event from this period was rediscovering actor Louis Hayward; they had met briefly years before in England and took, as Ida recalls, an "instant dislike" to each other. Now in late 1936, they had met again and "fell madly in love." Ida and Hayward, a fine, thoughtful actor, "were a fine match," said author William Donati, "both were sensitive, emotional, and inclined to melodrama." They wed on November 17, 1938, in Los Angeles.

Meanwhile, Ida, who once stated, "I cannot tolerate fools, won't have anything to do with them," decided Paramount was the fool—and she wanted out. They never reckoned that the sweet, demure actress they initially fancied an ideal Alice in Wonderland would rebel. Ida had her own mind, always would have, and she was disgusted with playing what she thought was "pretty-pretty on the screen." Simply, she was using up precious time and energy on mere ingenue roles. Paramount released the lioness from her cage.

Her first freelance, *Fight for Your Lady* (1937) depressed her; it was the same routine nonsense. She decided it was time to take stock of herself. Her career was going nowhere fast.

It took 16 months, in which time she composed (her concert piece "Aladdin's Lamp" was performed by the L.A. Philharmonic in 1937; she would continue to write music through the years), did a little radio and, as mentioned earlier, got married. Ida, once tagged "The English Jean Harlow," let her hair grow out from blonde to its natural brown and grew in those awful pencil-thin eyebrows; she became herself. She was more determined than ever to show her acting skill in productions worthy of her.

After her self-imposed hiatus, Ida inked a two-picture deal with Columbia in 1939, and was promptly cast in *The Lone Wolf Spy Hunt* and *The Lady and the Mob*. These were hardly the prestigious products she had hoped for.

Her resolution was rewarded when she learned that Paramount was producing *The Light That Failed* (1939) starring Ronald Colman, adapted from Rudyard Kipling's 1891 novel about a famous commercial artist obsessed with finishing an artistic masterpiece before he loses his sight. Ida ached for the flashy part of the cockney wench who becomes the painter's unruly subject.

Director William Wellman was taken aback when "that crazy little English girl ... tore into my office unannounced and demanded that I watch her play Bessie Broke in the big scene from *The Light That Failed*. I did, right in my office, and I played Colman, and .... she was marvelous."

It was the breakthrough she had waited for. Meeting the challenges of the role, Ida was unrestrained, vindictive, flirtatiously grotesque and simply spellbinding. Most impressive is the scene where Colman, desperate for time to complete her portrait, tries to attain the right emotion from her, the kind that bespeaks sorrow, a "sorrow so *deep*, it's—it's laughter!" Colman tears into her, commanding her to "*Laugh, Bessie, laugh!*" Ida breaks down into an hysterical heap, a display Wellman later said "affected" him. Lupino was the talk of the town with this down-and-dirty display of virtuosity; was this really the same actress, they asked, who only a few years earlier sat blandly by as Bing Crosby crooned to her? "Ida Lupino's Bessie is another of the surprises we get when a little ingenue suddenly bursts forth as a great actress," announced *The New York Times*.

An overwhelmed Mark Hellinger, an associate producer over at Warner Bros.,

Lupino, murderously in love with George Raft, meets her competition, Ann Sheridan (left), in *They Drive By Night* **(WB, 1940). Ida's intense performance earned her a Warner Bros. contract.**

had seen *The Light That Failed.* He deemed her perfect for Alan Hale's faithless wife in Raoul Walsh's *They Drive By Night* (1940).

The film was culled from two sources, A. I. Bezzerides' novel *The Long Haul* and *Bordertown* (WB, 1935). Ida, seven years wed to boisterous trucking business owner Alan Hale, covets wildcat trucker George Raft. "I wonder what I see in you anyway," Ida purrs after he rebuffs her kiss. "You're crude, you're uneducated, you never had a pair of pants with a crease in them. And, yet, I couldn't never say no to you."

Her unrequited passion leads to Hale's "accidental" demise in their garage from carbon monoxide. With him out of the way, *surely* Raft will succumb. Ida has a marvelous closeup registering thoughts about committing the murder, by leaving her drunken husband in the running car; with nary a word, we know exactly what's going on in her mind .... and it ain't pretty.

Lupino's performance after Hale's death is a *tour de force.* Now haunted by the garage doors, Ida's mounting paranoia is a wonder to behold. She is constantly on edge, desperately trying to keep Raft within her radius ... but then she sees Raft kissing Ann Sheridan. Uh-oh. Lupino's foggy, dazed look is terrific, as she realizes it was all for nothing. When Raft reveals he'll be marrying Sheridan, Ida cracks, letting down her guard: "She hasn't the right to ya. You're *mine* and I'm hanging on to ya. I committed *murder* to get you. Understand? *Murder!*"

Ida implicates him. Nothing can top Ida's brief scene at Raft's trial; it's still a classic piece of acting. Entering the courtroom nervous, twitchy, haggard, delusional and catatonic, she ignores the lawyer's questions on the stand while she numbly rambles on about the night she killed Hale. She ends it by repeating, with rising furor, "The doors made me do it," until, laughing and thoroughly insane, she is carried out repeating those words.

She gave a strong and, in the final moments, explosive performance, one overshadowing everything in the picture. With *They Drive By Night*, stated *The World Telegram*, "she becomes one of the screen's foremost dramatic actresses."

It naturally earned her a Warner Bros. contract—how could it not? The studio, however, was in for a surprise: Ida was smart. She was burned by Paramount, and that was not going to happen again. Instead of a standard seven-year contract, Ida played it safe her first time at bat: one year, freelance rights, $2,000 a week for two pictures. She had made only one picture for Warners but was pulling down more money per week than many other contractees.

Whatever problems she and the studio would have, Lupino's intensity was completely appropriate to Warners and they gave her a range of characters few but Bette Davis received. She immediately became second in line to the throne. "They would start at the top of the list," Alexis Smith told Lennard DeCarl, "first Davis, then Lupino, then Sheridan. If they didn't want it, I got it. I got the dreck." Her ultimate problem at Warners was the competition. The studio was known for its great collection of strong women, all of whom vied for the plum parts. Of course, Davis wasn't worried, but Lupino nipped at her heels all through her stay at the studio.

With her hysteria firmly in people's minds because of her last two films, her next was a sudden turn of the dial, but no less riveting. She played opposite Humphrey Bogart's "Mad Dog" Roy Earle in the classic *High Sierra* (1941).

Raoul Walsh directed this adaptation of W.R. Burnett's novel, of old-timer Earle, just out of an eight-year stretch in the pen, attempting one last hold-up. Everyone was intent on creating a different kind of gangster movie, not just a shoot-'em-up, but one that had, said co-writer John Huston in a memo to Hal Wallis, "the strange sense of inevitability that comes with our deeper understanding of [Burnett's] characters and the forces that motivate them."

Bogie is attracted to Joan Leslie, wholesome, innocent and clubfooted to boot. He pays for her operation, then wants to marry her, but she's just an illusion, a part of the changing world around him where he doesn't fit. His friend Henry Hull tells him, "What you need is a fast-steppin' young filly you can keep up with." That would be lonely, clinging Lupino, a former dime-a-dance girl, whom Arthur Kennedy and Alan Curtis, two of Bogart's hot-headed young accomplices, fight over.

Ida gave her role a desperate gentle quality, her quiet tenderness reinforced with an inner reserve, that runs opposite to what she's supposed to be. Leslie, Bogart believes, is sweet, untouched, naive and, the word he throws in poor Ida's experienced face, "decent." Yet it is Ida who, in the end, "sticks," who really shows she loves Bogart, not oh-so-pure Leslie, who becomes engaged to an older divorced man—turning disdainful, after all Bogart's done for the sap.

Despite censorship problems regarding the sympathetic nature of Bogart's criminal, the picture was a big success.

"Her intelligent and forthright playing gives complete conviction to the role," remarked one critic about Lupino in the brutal *The Sea Wolf* (1941). This was the most famous of (at least) ten filmed retellings of Jack London's story. Edward G. Robinson's Wolf Larsen, ruthless captain of the *Ghost*, makes Captains Bligh, Hook and Queeg all look like kindergarteners. Throughout the sea voyage, he matches wits and brawn with, respectively, writer Alexander Knox and fugitive John Garfield, while beating and belittling his crew with cruel delight.

The few quieter moments below deck of the "hell ship" are supplied by Ida, also an escaped convict, and her instant soul mate Garfield. The two actors got along beautifully off-camera as well. "He was wonderful and I loved him. He and I were like brother and sister," she said in 1983. Their scenes have a luminous intensity, a strong contrast to the atmospheric savagery dished out by Robinson. "If you live, I live," she whispers to Garfield. "If you die, I die. That's the way it is with me... We crowded all our lives together in one day."

Lupino was happy about replacing Barbara Stanwyck, who declined the part, in *Out of the Fog* (1941), but she let it be known that she preferred John Garfield to the already-cast Humphrey Bogart. It sparked rumors that the two didn't get along on the *High Sierra* set. A memo to Jack Warner, from producer Henry Blanke, supports this: "Casting Garfield for the part of 'Goff' would, as you know, relieve us of the problem of convincing Lupino to play with Bogart." Years later, Ida denied hard feelings for Bogie, that her main concern was working with Garfield again.

And again it was a good fit, if on a different level. *Out of the Fog*, based on Irwin Shaw's play *The Gentle People,* first produced by the Group Theater in 1939, was one of Warners' most downbeat, moody pictures of the period.

Garfield, he of no redeeming values, and Lupino, she of the discontented spirit and desire to break out of her bleak, boring life, smolder the screen. She's unmindful of his protection racket which targets her own father; all she knows is that sexy Garfield is hotter than her bland boyfriend, Eddie Albert—a given, dontcha think? "[W]hen he talks I feel like I'm burning," she tells her startled father, adding, "I get hot and cold all over, and I feel like yelling. Nothing that ever happened to me before made me feel like this." Lupino's acting hits all the right notes. It's doubtful anyone could have matched her beauty, sensitivity and understatement.

"There is only one performance I ever gave I'm proud of: Ellen in *Ladies in Retirement* [1941]," Ida said later about this loan-out to Columbia. From Flora Robson, who played the role on Broadway, to Lupino, then only in her early twenties, was certainly a stretch. Required to play older than herself—Robson's original 60 was changed here to 45—Ida was masterfully ominous as a housekeeper protecting her insane sisters from an asylum by committing murder. "[The role] frightened me to death," she added, "because many studio bigwigs thought I was too young for the part." But Ida is magnificent, registering cold-blooded determination with compassion for her sisters.

Although her contract was redrafted at Warners ($3,000, loan privileges), Ida was unhappy. Hal Wallis claimed Ida rejected the role of the unbalanced Cassie in *Kings Row* (1942) because of *Ladies in Retirement*. When she was free, and again approached for the role, Wallis said "she told me that was afraid of the part. She had played several madwomen in a row and wanted a change of pace." Memos show the real reason: She thought the part "small and secondary," and "she didn't want second-billing to [Ann] Sheridan," though the two were good friends. Nor did she appreciate the proposed assignments *Captains of the Clouds* and *Juke Girl*. She found these movies "beneath her as an artist," firmly declining them. It ignited a battle between her and the studio that almost drove her to seek contract termination.

Peace emerged briefly when she was allowed to appear in *Forever and a Day* (1943), an all-star tribute to England's wartime spirit. Two years in the making, it eventually helped many British charities. The project was dear to her since her father still resided in England.

But at Warners she was on suspension, a common recreation for the studio's many rebels.

Ida finally made amends with Warners, agreeing to *The Hard Way* (1942), a story about a driven woman who pushes, without conscience, the life and career of her younger sister (Joan Leslie). It was a great part for Lupino and her ferocity was well-matched by the direction of Vincent Sherman. Problems were a-brewin', however.

After accepting and loving the script, Ida decided it was a mess. She was in constant friction with Sherman, screaming at him: "This picture is going to stink, and I'm going to stink in it!" Despite the antagonism between star and director, Sherman was in awe of Ida's proficiency, and certain of her excellence in the part. "She was a wonderful girl," he told Thomas McNulty in 1999, "although we got into an argument when we first started working on *The Hard Way* because she thought I was making her character too hard... She was very hard-driving in the picture, and I thought she gave a marvelous performance."

To appease Ida, Sherman altered a later scene, one showing a softer side to her coldbloodedness. Nevertheless, she was against the role.

Her mood wasn't helped when she was hospitalized with exhaustion; even on the set, various illnesses plagued her. Warners threatened to replace her with Ann Sheridan because of all the delays. Her mental state was further seriously impaired, mid-production, when her father passed away on June 10, 1942. "She was so devoted to her father and shattered by his death," related her friend Geraldine Fitzgerald. She returned to *The Hard Way* a week later emotionally drained, mad at her part, and still suffering.

Ida needn't have worried. She would win the New York Film Critics Award for her fine performance. Oddly, no Oscar nomination would be forthcoming. Nor would it ever. The Academy never saw fit to even nominate Ida in all her years as an actress, director, producer and writer. Surely the greatest piece of injustice in the Academy's history.

A bit of a letdown, she went over to Fox for the dreary *Life Begins at 8:30* (1942).

Back at Warners, however, there were more problems, alleviated somewhat by a great part in a mediocre movie.

Filmed from late 1942 to February 1943, *Devotion* would linger in the Warner vaults until 1946, mostly due to co-star Olivia de Havilland's legal problems with the studio. The movie told the overlong story of the Brontë sisters, writers Emily (Ida) and Charlotte (Olivia).

Director Curtis Bernhardt captured a mystical aura surrounding the moors— "This is *my* world," confides Lupino—that evokes the classic *Wuthering Heights*. Ida is the most serious-minded of the sisters, with deeper feelings than the frivolous de Havilland. The picture makes a point of contrasting them: Olivia, headstrong, ambitious, flighty; Ida, introverted, romantic, moody. "Love is not the tormented thing you are making it in your book," Olivia tells her, clearly not understanding. Both love the same man, Paul Henreid, yet he prefers Olivia.

"Lupino was good as Emily, the most talented of the sisters," Bernhardt said in 1977. "She was quite fun to work with. She had a fine sense of humor. She always called me 'Ducky.' Lupino was, in any case, more accessible artistically than de Havilland during the making of the film."

During a break in filming, she and Olivia participated in the all-star *Thank Your Lucky Stars* (1943). In sharp contradiction to their heavy-emoting as the Brontës, the pair joined George Tobias in the jitterbug number "The Dreamer," wildly dressed, over-singing and overacting to the hilt.

Better suited was *In Our Time* (1944), again directed by Vincent Sherman, with Ida playing an English girl who marries Polish aristocrat Paul Henreid in war-threatened Warsaw in 1939. A bit talky, it was nonetheless a literate, inspiring movie with substance. "As long as a nation preserves its honor," avows Henreid, "it will always survive." The director wasn't so pleased. "Although it had a number of good scenes at the beginning and received a few favorable reviews," remarked Sherman in his autobiography, "it was not clearly focused, nor was it an ideal subject for film: from midway to the end, it was a series of arguments about the economics and political setup in Poland and was of little interest to American audiences.

"Whatever pleasure I had from the picture," continued Sherman, "was derived from working with the actors. Ida was no longer the hard-driving, ruthless character of *The Hard Way* but a warm, shy, romantic, enchanting young idealist. The range of her talent was immense."

For her next, Ida again did a complete switching of gears.

Pillow to Post (1945) was her first and last comedy at Warners, about a woman who becomes her father's traveling saleslady. "I phoned Ida Lupino, told her the story, and suggested she might enjoy doing it," Vincent Sherman recalled. "She, too, was ready for a change. She read it and liked it... I had never done a farce comedy before, nor had Ida, but I was confident we could do it. I had seen her antics when she was in a playful mood ..."

Playful is a good word for *Pillow to Post*, and Ida proves here why comedy ran in her family—she's very funny, verbally and physically (trying to sleep on two chairs, jitterbugging). The wacky topical movie was a hit. Sherman later recalled Ida telling him that she got more fan mail from *Post* than any other film. With its success, you'd think Warners would allow Ida to let her hair down more often. Socially, Ida was known for her absurd humor, but Warners failed to exploit it. "She could do comedy very well," said Sherman. "She could do anything ... She was all-around a great talent."

At home, it was rough. She and Hayward, just honorably discharged from the Marines, were divorced on May 11, 1945. Ida still loved Louis, but the war had changed him; he suffered from depression and exhaustion, and was restless from his war experiences. It took some time for Lupino to recoup from the shock of losing her husband.

Pillow to Post (WB, 1945), with William Prince, was one of Lupino's most popular movies and her only comedy showcase.

When she finally did get back to work, it was in a movie that remains a special favorite with her fans: *The Man I Love* (1947), quintessential Lupino. It was first envisioned as the life of tragic torch singer Helen Morgan (to star Ann Sheridan), but with time it was decided to go in another direction, calling for Catherine Turney to adapt Maritta Wolff's novel *Night Shift*. Ida plays Petey Brown, a nightclub singer involved with club owner Robert Alda and tormented piano player Bruce Bennett. While the action slips and slides on occasional high-quality soap, Ida's emotionally fragile yet strong performance ("I'll land on my feet—I always do") was one of her most telling, and a big hit for Warners. Her songs, "The Man I Love" and "Why Was I Born?," were beautifully dubbed by Peg LaCentra, with Ida lip-synching with tremendous feeling.

Escape Me Never (1947) was next released, after sitting almost two years on the shelf. The flimsy plot had struggling composer Errol Flynn torn between waif Lupino and Eleanor Parker, fiancée of his brother (Gig Young). Author Doug McClelland later reported: "Ida Lupino is the cynosure, and she runs an unusually demanding gamut: from food-thief in schoolgirl drag to cafe entertainer, jilted lover to bereaved mother. That she is both convincing and appealing is a testament to the considerable ability she possessed and which Warners, glutted by Hollywood's most formidable stable of female stars, never adequately exploited."

Ida called Errol Flynn "The Baron," while he called her "Little Scout." They were the best of friends, but *Escape Me Never* (WB, 1947) was their only film together.

Although the film bombed, it gave Lupino the chance to work with her good friend Errol Flynn. He called her "Little Scout" and she named him "The Baron"; it was a friendship that endured until Flynn's death in 1959. She would remain loyal to his memory, especially in later years when he was accused of being a Nazi sympathizer.

The studio was pressuring her to sign again, but now they wanted it their way: an exclusive seven-year contract. Ida, restless by nature, and canny enough to see what that kind of imprisonment could do to her career, refused. You were meant to toe the line at Warners, but Ida wasn't playing that game.

Deep Valley (1947) was a worthy farewell. It gave Ida the unusual role of a shy, nervous, speech-impaired farm girl whose life slowly opens up after she meets escaped convict Dane Clark. It was a sensitive, beautifully crafted performance which Ida pulled off without seeping into mawkishness. Her playing seemed so simplistic, but that was the beauty of it. Ida was able to add subtle layers of deep emotion to her part, making it utterly believable. It was one of her best for the studio.

Previously Ida had been voice-doubled when her characters were required to sing on camera. For the slightly tawdry *Road House* (1948), her first freelance job, she was, after some vocal lessons, permitted to sing for herself—a brave choice for all concerned. Her songs, "The Right Kind," "One For My Baby" and "Again," were all sung in a croaking whisper. But it works. "She does more without a voice than anybody I ever heard," marvels a stunned Celeste Holm in the movie. Or as the director Jean Negulesco commented, "No-voice Lupino sang them and placed them first on the hit parade."

Ida was born for these kind of dishy roles: a sultry nightclub singer who's been around long enough to know the score, certainly no pushover when it comes to men. Her portrayal, remarked *The New York Times*, was "expertly brittle and passionate," not to mention *tough*. When Cornel Wilde tries to rough her up, Ida is more amused than abused: "Silly boy," she sasses, as she slaps him. Of course, Wilde falls hard for her, but the troubled Richard Widmark has other ideas.

She was a sought-after catch off-screen too. Among her many dates, Lupino met the man who would soon become her second husband, ex-story editor and aspiring producer Collier (Collie) Young. The two were wed on August 5, 1948. A few months later she moved over to Columbia (where Young worked as Harry Cohn's executive assistant) to appear in the unremarkable *Lust for Gold* (1949).

By this time Ida and Young were seriously contemplating producing for themselves. Ida was always driven to be creative, not only acting but the whole shebang. She wanted to be in control of her own work. Ida had read a story that interested her: *Not Wanted* (1949). Funding was hard to obtain. Columbia was not interested, and Young, in a huff, resigned. Instead, he and Ida joined Anson Bond to produce their groundbreaking film.

Ida collaborated on the screenplay with Paul Jarrico, co-produced and chose the actors. She wanted unknowns for the realistic story of an unwed pregnancy, and ended up with two young hopefuls, Keefe Brasselle and Sally Forrest.

Sally told Jerry De Bono: "I don't know if this was just publicity, but the press reported that anywhere from 200 to 300 actresses had read for the part before it was my turn. That afternoon, [my agent] Milo [Frank] drove me to the Youngs' house on Mulholland Drive, and I read from the script of *Not Wanted* for Ida and her husband in their living room. When I finished, Ida said, 'You're the one we've been looking for. You've got the part.' Well, you can imagine how I felt."

Milo Frank, who later became Forrest's husband, added, "I think she reminded Ida of Ida." Many feel that Sally bore more than a passing resemblance to Ida. It was as if Ida found a younger version of herself to act in her movies. "I can't overemphasize Ida's importance to my career," Sally continued. "She was an exuberant, brilliant, creative woman. She could do everything!" Frank seconded his wife, stating that Lupino was "the consummate actress, artist, and a terrific person."

Ida's directing career began on *Not Wanted*, *sans* credit. Elmer Clifton suffered a heart attack right before filming, forcing Ida to step in. Out of respect to old pro Clifton, who remained on the set, Ida kept his name on the picture.

Shot in eight days on a budget of $153,000, *Not Wanted*'s success led her and her husband to form their own company, Filmakers, a daring move for a Hollywood actress in 1949; she would be the first actress to produce, direct and write her own product. Filmakers' partner, writer Malvin Wald, explained to *The New York Herald Tribune:* "We are trying to make pictures of a sociological nature to appeal to older people who usually stay away from theaters. We are out to tackle serious themes and problem dramas. We don't plan to make any melodramas, musicals or westerns."

Their first release was to be *Never Fear*. It was another risky subject, that of a dancer afflicted with polio. The theme was an obstacle; they couldn't find a distributor or the financial backing necessary to proceed. The couple put all their money into the project, but it wasn't enough.

Ida, to help Filmakers' money matters, appeared in *Woman in Hiding* (1949), as a newlywed whose husband tries to kill her. It was a melodramatic trifle, but significant in that it introduced Ida to Howard Duff, an actor best known for playing Sam Spade on radio.

Never Fear (1949) finally went before the cameras, with Lupino earning her first screen credit as director. It again featured (real-life dancer) Forrest, Brasselle, and another newcomer, Hugh O'Brian. The production, which took all of 15 days to shoot, was beset with financial problems. Young wasn't able to come through with investors; her agent Charles K. Feldman loaned them $65,000, which Ida herself had to pay off. Blame was placed solely on Young's poor business sense.

Even worse was the deal Young struck with Howard Hughes at RKO to back and distribute three of their future movies, a deal which cost Filmakers half their profits. By this time, the marriage was in trouble, not helped by Ida's growing relationship with Duff. Filmakers, albeit ground breaking and artistically rewarding, caused the rift. Meanwhile, *Never Fear*, released by Eagle-Lion, bombed.

Ida began to concentrate more on directing, less on acting. She unfolded her sudden plans to Hedda Hopper in 1949: "I've never really liked acting. It's a tortuous profession, and it plays havoc with your private life. It's about time the screen got rid of the old faces, including mine. I intended to give up acting altogether eventually." She next directed two well-received gems: *Outrage* (1950), starring Mala Powers as a rape victim, and *Hard, Fast and Beautiful* (1951), featuring Claire Trevor's bravura turn as the controlling mother of tennis player Sally Forrest. Trevor called Lupino a "very warm, very sensitive, very intelligent lady." For fun, Ida did a fleeting cameo.

Cinematographer Archie Stout, who worked with Lupino at Filmakers, told *Colliers* in 1951 that "Ida has more knowledge of camera angles and lenses than any director I've ever worked with, with the exception of Victor Fleming." The respect Lupino generated as a director continues today, sometimes overshadowing her equally fine acting. In a magazine piece in 1995, acclaimed director Martin Scorsese wrote: "She was a true pioneer. The six films she directed between 1949 and 1953 are remarkable chamber pieces that deal with challenging subjects in a clear, almost documentary fashion, and are a singular achievement in American cinema … What is at stake in Lupino's films is the psyche of the victim. They addressed the wounded soul and traced the slow, painful process of women trying to wrestle with despair and reclaim their lives. Her work is resilient, with a remarkable empathy for the fragile and the heartbroken."

Needing money, Ida accepted RKO's *On Dangerous Ground* (1951). Under Nicholas Ray's stylish direction, it combined urban and rural surroundings to show detective Robert Ryan's changing moral blindness. Used to dealing with crooks, tramps and other undesirables, Ryan's jaded demeanor shatters when he meets the blind Lupino.

Having worked well with pal John Garfield in the past, Ida, whose Filmakers was producing *Beware, My Lovely* (1952), sought him for the role of the handyman-cum-psycho. But Hollywood's blacklist had not only affected his career, but also his health; before he could be cast, 39-year-old Garfield was dead of a heart attack. Robert Ryan, who had the right dazed, angry quality, was cast opposite Lupino again, she as a widow who hires the unstable man to work around her house.

It was a nerve-wracking cat-and-mouse chase with both stars, playing victims of a different sort, excellent. Also noteworthy was Barbara Whiting, playing Lupino's bitchy niece who sets off Ryan. "I was thrilled to be in that picture with Miss Lupino," Barbara says today. "That was a pleasure to work with two good people, especially Ida. She was a wonderful actress, and I'd always admired her very much. I was in awe of her, and so I did whatever she said!"

Off-screen, things were complicated when Ida became pregnant with Duff's child. She obtained a divorce from Collier Young on October 20, 1951, in Nevada. The next day she and Duff married; daughter Bridget was born about six months later. Lupino would remain friendly with her ex largely because of Filmakers; Young and actress Joan Fontaine, whom he would wed the following year, even served as Bridget's godparents.

She directed Filmakers' atypical *The Hitch-Hiker* (1953), a highly acclaimed, starkly original *film noir* that has attained cult status. Based on a then-recent murder spree, it was a harrowing, realistic movie that drew raves for Lupino's skillful

On Dangerous Ground (RKO, 1951), a tense film noir directed by Nicholas Ray, starred Ida as a blind woman who falls for violent, jaded city detective Robert Ryan.

handling of the action. Ida's dynamic sense of pace is explosive, as two men unwittingly pickup a killer. "People shouldn't be alone when they see it," Lupino told *American Film* in 1981. "It scares me even today." She often cited it as her favorite directorial effort.

The Bigamist (1953) was a breakaway from RKO, with Filmakers footing the bills. It was not a sensationalized rendering of a potentially sordid subject, but a very human story of a man (Edmond O'Brien) tangled between two women, Lupino and Joan Fontaine. It was the first time she directed herself. "I'm not mad about combining the two," Lupino told Patrick McGilligan in 1974. "It takes me morning, noon, and night to pull through just as a director, then to get in front of a camera and not be able to watch myself ... When I was acting, I still had to say, 'Cut, print, cut, print.' I think I needed a separate director."

The movie is also unusual due to the possibly sticky personal situation, considering the title—the working triangle of Lupino, Fontaine and Young. "Ida and I are old friends," commented Fontaine, defusing the issue. "I knew her before Collier did ... I'm his third wife and Ida is his second. In fact, when I go to New York I always visit the first Mrs. Collier Young. We're all good friends."

Her concentration on directing shoved her acting to the sidelines. The roles she was accepting were, it was suggested, dictated by her desire to see Duff cast also: *Jennifer* (1953), *Private Hell 36* (1954), *Women's Prison* (1955) and *While the City Sleeps* (1956), all this amid problems in their marriage. If Ida was trying to make Duff a star by insisting on his casting, it didn't work. She didn't dare direct any of these. Duff, possessor of a strong ego, would have resented it, and she knew it. Ida was especially good in *While the City Sleeps*. Her flip, flirtatious delivery and glamourous appearance lightened the mood of this tense psycho-on-the-loose thriller. Robert Aldrich's *The Big Knife* (1955), was arguably Lupino's best movie of the '50s, an adaptation of Clifford Odets' 1949 play. Her last for a while, *Strange Intruder* (1956) was interesting, slightly paralleling *Beware, My Lovely*. Filmakers went out of business after *Private Hell 36*.

Confessing to being "snobbish toward TV at first," Ida warmed up fast, spending the greater part of her ensuing years in the medium, as a director and actress. She became known as a fast, efficient, fun director, with a large body of work as proof of her capability. "Television—there's nothing rougher, nothing rougher," Ida marveled. It was so demanding of her time that she wouldn't direct again for the big screen until 1966's *The Trouble with Angels*. *Deadhead Miles* (1972), reuniting her with George Raft, marked her return to big-studio acting.

Some of the hundreds of episodic TV shows Lupino directed: *The Donna Reed Show, Have Gun Will Travel, The Untouchables, Thriller, The Fugitive, The Twilight Zone* (the classic "The Masks"), *Alfred Hitchcock Presents, The Big Valley, Gilligan's Island* and *Gunsmoke*. Lupino acted on *Four Star Playhouse, Bonanza, Burke's Law, Batman* (opposite Duff), and *Columbo*.

Doug Benton, story editor and associate producer for *Thriller*, was especially impressed by Lupino. He raved to Tom Weaver in 1996: "I'm amused by all these so-called feminine 'pioneer' directors who toot their own horns today. They couldn't carry her script case. We used to call her 'The Great Orsini' sometimes [*laughs*]— she was the package Welles. She could act, she could direct, she could write, she could *drink* [*laughs*]—she was something! She was so *serious* about it, she really was. When she acted, she was serious, when she was producing, she was serious, and when she was directing, she was *most* serious, because that's what she enjoyed more than anything else.

"I remember one time," Benton continues, "she wanted to stay on the lot overnight so she could get up early and walk the sets in the morning. Well, she did, she got up at four o'clock in the morning, went over to the stage and conned some guard into opening it up. She was climbing around on the sets and she fell down and severely sprained her ankle. And when they came to open the stage an hour and a half later, they found her down at the bottom of this thing that she had climbed up on. They took her over to the little infirmary, put her in a splint and she came *back* and *directed* that day! At that time I thought, 'I don't know anybody else who would do this.'"

Again Ida thought of Duff: She took on the added burden of a regular TV series when Collier Young, acting as executive producer, proposed the idea. *Mr. Adams and Eve* premiered on January 4, 1957, and was not only a hit with audiences, but it proved Ida a delightful comedic actress, something not seen since *Pillow to Post*; she would be Emmy-nominated. It went off the air in September of 1958 due to insider squabbles having nothing to do with the Duffs.

The marriage, long a battle of wills, came to an end in 1972. Their relationship was marked by many verbal and physical altercations, fueled by alcohol on both sides. Ida's friends were puzzled by her devotion to Duff, who seemed to dominate the relationship. The two Ida Lupinos were very different. Before and behind the camera she was in control, outspoken. At home she deferred to him until she couldn't take it any more. But she loved him enough to turn down directing jobs in Yugoslavia, Greece and England to stay close to home, and she told *Modern Screen* just before their separation: "I said to myself, 'No, Ida, you have to make up your mind. Are you going to be a wife who stays with her husband, or are you going to blow the whole marriage by spending six or seven months away from home?' So I said, 'No, sorry, I can't do it.' Some husbands follow their wives, but Howard would never do that; he is not that kind of man." It was Duff who left her for a younger woman. They would be separated for many years until Ida finally granted him a divorce in 1984.

Once very busy as a director, Ida found that screeching to a halt in the late '60s. She turned back to acting, mostly in TV movies (*Backtrack*, "gloriously camping it up as a Mexican widow," approved *Variety*) and series (*Medical Center, Barnaby Jones, Police Woman*). On the big screen she sensitively played rodeo champ Steve McQueen's mother in *Junior Bonner* (1972). Ida imbued her scenes with estranged husband Robert Preston with a restrained honesty and understanding; she conveyed so much with just her eyes—the regret, bitterness, and love she can't help feeling. It was a marvelous performance, showing that those years of directing hadn't dulled her acting senses. Other movies like *Food of the Gods* (1976), in a role requiring her to be scarfed down by a giant rat, and *My Boys Are Good Boys* (made in 1972, released in 1978) didn't show her off nearly as well.

Ida's final years were plagued by poor health, eccentricity, alcohol and an estrangement from her daughter. She faced the cameras for the last time in 1977 on an episode of *Charlie's Angels*. Ida transcended the material, as usual, but she was having trouble memorizing her lines.

She became a recluse, leading a generally quiet life away from the glare of the spotlight. She had only a few trusted friends, particularly Mala Powers, who came over to chat; Ida was still known for her wild sense of humor as she spun tales from her Hollywood heyday. Vincent Sherman, who directed her in three of her best at Warner Bros., recalled, "She asked to see me a few weeks before she passed away. I went up to see her, and we had a wonderful time. I gave her a lot of laughs, and her conservator called me later and said, 'Vincent, I just want you to know Ida said it was the best afternoon she'd had in a long time.' I was imitating how she used to come in sometimes so nervous and say 'W-wha-what are we going to do today?' And I'd say, 'Take it easy, take it easy.' But she was wonderful to work for. Very talented."

Her health started to decline by 1988, worsened by the passing of Howard Duff in 1990; many feel he was the love of her life, despite her comments to the contrary. In June of 1995 Ida was diagnosed with colon cancer, and had also suffered a stroke. She passed away two months later on August 3, at the age of 77. The press lauded Lupino for her skill as an actress and a pioneering auteur.

Honors came late. The American Museum of the Moving Image paid tribute to her November 2–24, 1996, and 2002 saw the UCLA Film and Television Archive celebrating "the strong-willed acting and directing" of Lupino with a three-week, 13-film festival of her work. It was long overdue, but well worth it to see Lupino finally gain an important place in cinema history. "She was electric," Sally Forrest told *The Los Angeles Times*. "She never had the popularity she should have had. She was a fine actress. She was beautiful. She had a fabulous figure and was a great director. Maybe she was too strong for those days."

Or maybe too independent. Ida was a woman in charge when that was unheard of. She was ahead of her time, the only female in her heyday to have complete control. What she lacked in popularity or awards, she earned back with respect and hard work from the people who worked with her.

Ida Lupino: fierce, loyal, determined, versatile, introspective. She triumphed over adversity *and* Bette Davis at Warner Bros., reinventing herself as a strong, intelligent creative force. "I like the strong characters," she told Patrick McGilligan. "I don't mean women who have masculine qualities about them, but something that has some intestinal fortitude, some guts to it. Just a straight role drives me up the wall. Playing a nice woman who just sits there, that's my greatest limitation."

Actress: 1931: The Love Race. **1932:** Her First Affaire (Sterling Film Co). **1933:** Money for Speed (Hall Mark Films/UA), High Finance (First National-British), The Ghost Camera (Twickenham Films), I Lived with You (Gaumont-British), Prince of Arcadia (Gaumont-British). **1934:** Search for Beauty (Paramount), Come On Marines! (Paramount), Ready for Love (Paramount). **1935:** Paris in Spring (Paramount), Smart Girl (Paramount), Peter Ibbetson (Paramount), La Fiesta de Santa Barbara (MGM short). **1936:** Anything Goes (Paramount), One Rainy Afternoon (UA), Yours for the Asking (Paramount), The Gay Desperado (UA). **1937:** Sea Devils (RKO), Let's Get Married (Columbia), Artists and Models (Paramount), Fight for Your Lady (RKO). **1939:** The Lone Wolf Spy Hunt (Columbia), The Lady and the Mob (Columbia), The Adventures of Sherlock Holmes (TCF), The Light that Failed (Paramount). **1940:** They Drive By Night (WB). **1941:** High Sierra (WB), The Sea

Wolf (WB), Out of the Fog (WB), Ladies in Retirement (Columbia). **1942**: Moontide (TCF), The Hard Way (WB), Life Begins at 8:30 (TCF). **1943**: Forever and a Day (RKO), Thank Your Lucky Stars (WB). **1944**: Hollywood Canteen (WB), In Our Time (WB). **1945**: Pillow to Post (WB). **1946**: Devotion (WB), The Man I Love (WB). **1947**: Escape Me Never (WB), Deep Valley (WB). **1948**: Road House (TCF). **1949**: Lust for Gold (Columbia), Woman in Hiding (Universal). **1951**: Hard, Fast and Beautiful (RKO/Filmakers), On Dangerous Ground (RKO). **1952**: Beware, My Lovely (RKO/Filmakers). **1953**: Jennifer (AA), The Bigamist (Filmakers). **1954**: Private Hell 36 (Filmakers). **1955**: Women's Prison (Columbia), The Big Knife (UA). **1956**: While the City Sleeps (RKO), Strange Intruder (AA). **1969**: Backtrack (MCA-TV/Universal). **1972**: Deadhead Miles (Paramount), Women in Chains (Paramount TV/ABC), Junior Bonner (Cinerama), The Strangers in 7A (Carliner/CBS-TV). **1973**: Female Artillery (Universal TV/ABC), I Love a Mystery (NBC-TV), The Letters (ABC-TV). **1975**: The Devil's Rain (Bryanston). **1976**: Food of the Gods (AIP). **1978**: My Boys Are Good Boys (Lone Star). **Director: 1949**: Not Wanted (Film Classics, uncredited), Never Fear (Eagle-Lion/Filmakers). **1950**: Outrage (RKO/Filmakers). **1951**: Hard, Fast and Beautiful (RKO/Filmakers). **1953**: The Hitch-Hiker (RKO/Filmakers), The Bigamist (Filmakers). **1966**: The Trouble With Angels (Columbia). **Co-Screenwriter: 1949**: Not Wanted (Film Classics), Never Fear (Eagle-Lion/Filmakers). **1950**: Outrage (RKO/Filmakers). **1953**: The Hitch-Hiker (RKO/Filmakers). **1954**: Private Hell 36 (Filmakers).

Marilyn Maxwell:
The Other Marilyn

by LAURA WAGNER

The two Hollywood Marilyns were a lot alike. Both blondes were used and abused by men, both were never taken seriously as actresses and both lives were cut tragically short—Monroe at 36, Maxwell at 49.

For all their similarities, however, gulfs set them apart. Maxwell was breezier, more unaffected and likable. She was tougher than Monroe, never seeming as emotionally fragile despite her hard life. Yet, Monroe was a *star* and has become an icon.

Maxwell never fell neatly into the "dumb blonde" image. She gave more the impression of being a cool, sometimes calculating beauty. She could sing, dance and move easily within comedy and drama, a voluptuous blonde with—is this possible?—a down-to-earth personality.

Marilyn was like that other Marilyn in that her private life garnered publicity, but didn't really help her career. Her ex-agent George Ward confirms this, claiming she "picked the wrong men, always. She brought on her own problems." Frequent co-star Bob Hope was one of those "wrong men"; he took a strong interest in her personally and professionally, but instead of helping her build a solid list of credits, he took up her time with camp shows, TV, radio and routine film roles. So close were they, she became known on the Paramount lot as "Mrs. Bob Hope." The association might have cost her a career, although certainly MGM was also at fault, mishandling Marilyn at a crucial period in her professional life.

Her stage struck mother, readying her newborn daughter's entrance into show business, bestowed upon her a marquee-worthy name: Marvel Marilyn Maxwell, born August 3, 1922, in Clarinda, Iowa. She was the second child (brother Lelland preceded her) of Hal, an insurance agent, and Anne Maxwell, piano accompanist for dancer Ruth St. Denis. Marilyn would remark that her mother "tried to fulfill her ambitions through me," while author Sally Presley, who went to Central High in Fort Wayne, Indiana, with Marilyn, noticed "she had a very pushy mother, one of those stage mothers like you read about."

The family (minus father; the Maxwells were divorced when she was just a baby) traveled a great deal with St. Denis' act. Marvel's upbringing consisted of dancing lessons and vocal studies. Her first public performance was at age three doing a butterfly dance at the Brandeis Theater in Omaha, Nebraska. Her singing was later developed with a local band made up of classmates. Instead of a normal, healthy, stable childhood, Marvel was usually found performing at local Elks and Kiwanis Clubs, and traveling with her mother.

By the age of 15, Marvel was settled in Fort Wayne, attending regular school and singing at a radio station her brother managed. Amos Ostot, small-time regional bandleader, heard Marvel on the air and promptly hired her to sing with his band for $35 a week, prompting Marvel to quit school before her junior year. It wasn't long before actor Charles "Buddy" Rogers, who fronted his own dance band, stole her away from Ostot, and a year-long Midwestern tour followed.

Some report that, after the tour with Rogers, Marvel spent some time with the Bob

Portrait of Marilyn Maxwell, 1944.

Crosby band before returning home. She got a job singing in an Indianapolis nightclub. She was again "discovered."

Marvel joined Ted Weems' band around 1939. Her stint with the band gained her regular exposure on tour and radio's *To Beat the Band*. She would record only one song with the band, the novelty "Monstro the Whale," with Red Foley sharing the vocal.

It was Weems who persuaded her to try for a Hollywood career. Marilyn later told *Motion Picture* that Weems "suggested that I go to the Pasadena Community Playhouse, and he'd finance me and pay my salary for a full year. It would be an investment for him. Then, when I was signed by a studio—as he was so sure I would be—I could pay it all back."

During her tenure at the Playhouse, Marvel kept herself busy on radio's *Best of the Week, Look Who's Here* and *The Camel Caravan Show*, as well as singing in Soundies. A Paramount test in early 1942 failed and she left the Pasadena Playhouse discouraged after six months to go on a camp show tour. But as she was entertaining the troops, MGM was entertaining hopes of signing her after viewing her failed test.

When she returned home, a surprised Maxwell found a contract from the biggest studio in Hollywood awaiting her. They also went to work fixing her teeth, eliminating Marvel from her professional name (ironically the name her mother thought would make her a star), put her on a diet and dyed her hair red, then a more becoming blonde—in short, giving her the glamour treatment.

MGM started her off in numerous bit parts, where she usually stood out (she was 5'6"). Marilyn's first featured role came in *Salute to the Marines* (1943), but it wasn't until *Dr. Gillespie's Criminal Case* (1943), playing doctor Van Johnson's flirtatiously bold love interest, that she gave audiences cause to take notice.

Criminal Case was the first of her three appearances in the popular series. Van is Dr. Randall "Red" Adams, assistant to Dr. Gillespie (Lionel Barrymore), chased by the amorous Maxwell. The movie establishes Van as a minor wolf, offering to give nurse Donna Reed a "complete examination," which she (wisely) rebuffs. Marilyn, on the other hand, is very much the aggressor, to Van's delight and fright. "Are you available?" she asks the smitten, but cautious, Johnson. He is eager at first, but her provocative remarks leave him flustered. After she puts on "lipstick that doesn't come off," Van is totally hooked, but still reluctant, fearing marriage in his future.

Van and Marilyn made an attractive couple, but although they would team in four MGM films, the studio didn't promote them—they weren't the same dewy-eyed, lush romantics the popular duo of Van and June Allyson were. Marilyn obviously had been around.

Swing Fever (1943) billed her as "Introducing Marilyn Maxwell." It was a nice showcase, but hardly the kind of movie in which a young actress wants to be introduced, especially at MGM when your romantic leading man isn't Gable, Taylor, Lawford or even James Craig, but the homely bandleader Kay Kyser. The film did give her a chance to sing, and her infectious vocalizing is well served on "One Girl and Two Boys," "Mississippi Dream Boat," "I Planted a Rose" and "I Never Knew."

Next up: *Three Men in White* (1944), again in the Gillespie series with Johnson. The relationship between the reluctant doctor and the all-too-willing socialite was advanced, just barely. "How do I know whether or not I want to get married?" whines the tormented Van. "Come around tonight and I'll *show* you," Marilyn quickly coos back, leaving Van, as usual, speechless. Gun-shy, Van refuses to kiss her for fear he'll "hear the birdies sing" and wake up married. The aggressive Marilyn is asked to behave, but without blinking, quips, "Not if I can help it."

Three Men in White concentrates on newcomer Ava Gardner (soon to be a Maxwell nemesis) and her invalid mother, but it's Marilyn who steals the show with her racy dialogue: "It doesn't wrinkle easily," she tells a panicking Van of her new dress, prompting him to run away. Even with the repetition of Marilyn pursuing and peppering Van with innuendo ("I need a doctor and *you're* the doctor"), her delivery, not really what she said, was too playful not to be totally fun; it helped a series that was so deadly serious, what with melodramatic illnesses and personal problems. Marilyn Maxwell and her "one-track mind" brightened the Gillespie films.

Abbott and Costello were not at their best in *Lost in a Harem* (1944), but for a few inspired moments. The boys, a couple of prop men in a traveling show featuring singing thrush Hazel Moon (Marilyn), get stranded in the desert. They become hypnotized pawns of evil Sultan Douglass Dumbrille, but are recruited by Prince John Conte to restore order in his kingdom. The Sultan soon falls for Marilyn, wanting her to become wife #38, but her heart belongs to the young, very attractive prince. When one of his many wives bitterly consoles the Sultan that "Blondes are fickle," Dumbrille deadpans: "Blondes are *scarce!*"

The only song she would sing in *Lost in a Harem*, "What Does It Take to Get You?," contained the prophetic line: "I can even get as far as second base with Frank Sinatra too." Marilyn would later start a famously serious romance with Sinatra.

Marilyn may have been connected with Sinatra and several other actors around Hollywood, but darkly attractive co-star John Conte won her heart off-screen. Conte, sometime actor, announcer, singer and later owner of a TV station, became engaged to Marilyn. "I was on Bing

Marilyn met first husband John Conte (right) while working on Abbott and Costello's *Lost in a Harem* (MGM, 1944). They were married from 1944 to 1946. Bandleader Jimmy Dorsey is at the left.

Crosby's *Kraft Music Hall* at the time," singer Lina Romay remembers. "She was in Los Angeles with us, and he was in New York [via hookup]. They became engaged on the radio." Lina adds wryly, "It was interesting, I'll tell you." Conte and Marilyn were wed shortly after *Lost in a Harem* wrapped in 1944. They divorced in 1946.

After her divorce, handsome heartthrobs Peter Lawford, Turhan Bey, Tony Martin and Michael North soon beat a path to the lucky girl's door, and it was around this time that Sinatra reentered her life. Insiders claim the relationship was so hot and heavy he contemplated divorcing wife Nancy for her, and that it took a gang of advisers to talk him out of it. They appeared on radio together and were discreetly photographed in the fan magazines as "just friends," but everyone knew better. Frank's buddy Nick Sevano would later recall, "She was gorgeous—simply gorgeous, and nice too. She spent hours showing me around Hollywood when I first came out because she knew that I had once been associated with Frank, and they were crazy about each other."

An incident, later reenacted for 1992's *Sinatra: The Mini-Series* (MM was played by Carol Barbee), ended the affair for good. Nancy had accidentally discovered a diamond bracelet she thought Frank meant to surprise her with. When Marilyn unwisely came to the couple's New Year's Eve party, she was seen by an incensed Nancy wearing said bracelet, and thrown out. Needless to say, after a huge argument, Sinatra cooled off seeing Marilyn.

The end of the story on her and Sinatra didn't come until 1952. At the time, Frank was married to Ava Gardner, a relationship his advisers couldn't control. Ava saw old flame Maxwell in the nightclub audience one night where Frank was performing, convincing herself he was flirting and singing to Marilyn from the stage. When the tempestuous couple got home, it became a major issue in another fight; later in her autobiography, Ava admitted to overreacting to the innocent episode.

Back at MGM, they didn't seem to need her; Lana Turner got priority on all the top roles Marilyn could have handled, and, in the musical area, well, MGM's warehouse was bursting with talent. She was assigned two production numbers in the all-star *Ziegfeld Follies* (1946), made mostly in 1944; she recorded "Glorifying the American Girl" with Lucille Ball and Lucille Bremer and "A Trip to Hollywood" with Ball and Jimmy Durante. Neither were filmed.

Instead Marilyn became a regular (February to July 1944) with Bing Crosby on *The Kraft Music Hall*, excellent exposure for a young singer. She was also doing her bit for the war effort by way of the USO. She devoted much of her time entertaining the troops, traveling extensively.

She had been featured on-screen for two years and 1945 saw Marilyn place just ninth on the Quigley "Stars of Tomorrow" poll. This delayed "recognition" (ninth is, well, ninth) did nothing to change her status at MGM—she made only one 1945 appearance, her last Gillespie, the delightful *Between Two Women*, with Gloria DeHaven as the second gal of the title. When Van becomes interested in nightclub singer DeHaven, who's coping with psychosomatic starvation, Marilyn becomes jealous. "I admit that girl isn't exactly repulsive, but anything she's good at I can do better, quicker and cheaper!" Whoa, girl.

Van's still, inexplicably, afraid to kiss her, but it finally happens when Marilyn buys $100,000 worth of war bonds for the "privilege." Presumably headed for the altar, the doctor is signed, sealed and delivered to the very patient (and very understanding) Marilyn Maxwell at the end of her third hospital drama.

A nice opportunity arose, or so she thought, in late '45 when she was tapped to play the globe-trotting female reporter in *Nellie Bly*, a play headed for Broadway. The cast was strong, featuring the popular team (*Of Thee I Sing*) of William Gaxton and Victor Moore, with music by Johnny Burke and James Van Heusen, and co-produced by Eddie Cantor. Sensing failure, MGM pulled Marilyn out of the show when it landed in Philadelphia, after only two months on the road. They were right. When the show reached New York on January 21, 1946, with Joy Hodges spelling, it tanked, receiving scathing reviews. It lasted only 16 performances.

She would finish up her MGM contract in 1946. George Kelly's popular play *The Show-Off* was filmed at least three times previously, this fourth version a tailor-made vehicle for Red Skelton. Red is a braggart, Marilyn his wife who adores him, despite his shortcomings. The pair dueted on Cole Porter's "I've Got You Under My Skin," the film's one highlight.

Marilyn, seen here with Van Johnson and Gloria DeHaven in *Between Two Women* (MGM, 1945), had her best comedy moments through her three appearances in MGM's "Dr. Gillespie" series.

What might have helped secure future, important roles at MGM was her small but overwhelming part as Belle in *Summer Holiday*. Made in the summer of '46, it was considered a hard sell, sitting on the studio's shelf until 1948, by which time, Marilyn was gone. It was a musical adaptation of Eugene O'Neill's *Ah, Wilderness*, set at the turn of the century, centering on the Miller family, headed by father Walter Huston, and including newly graduated son Mickey Rooney. He's in love with neighbor Gloria DeHaven, but when she is forbidden to see him, he travels to the seedy part of town and meets up with Maxwell.

As Belle, sixth-billed Marilyn has just 13 minutes (eight days to shoot) to make an impact, and her "pictorial and sensuous" (*The New York Times*) performance demands attention. It was her best acting opportunity in her four years at MGM, and her first "bad girl." "That was my real introduction to acting," she would say later. "For although I'd been in pictures before I played the role of Belle, I certainly hadn't been an actress. I'd been Marilyn Maxwell, going through some necessary motions for the camera and luckily getting by."

Assisting her was director Rouben Mamoulian's use of color to suggest Rooney's attitude. Mamoulian's approach to this striking sequence is described by author

Hugh Fordin in his volume about the Freed Unit at MGM, *The World of Entertainment*: "Eager to face life in the raw, the adolescent boy visits a bar and finds himself mesmerized by a pretty, vulgar barmaid, who plies him with liquor to loosen his inhibitions. Mamoulian wanted to show visually the transformation from a cheap hussy into a beautiful dream girl as seen through the boy's eyes."

Costume designer Walter Plunkett continued: "At the start Marilyn was in a pale, washed-out pink dress that blended with the indoor complexion of the customers. As Mickey drank more, her dress changed into a stronger shade of pink, better made and more stylish. As he continued drinking and the bar became hazy with smoke she kept changing ever so subtly until she was in a bright red dress, looking absolutely radiant."

Mamoulian, of course, faced problems with this unconventional, unheard of treatment. Producer Arthur Freed told him: "This is over the audiences' head—a bar is a bar and a girl is a girl."

Many consider *Summer Holiday* to be Marilyn's shining moment at MGM. She was right to be proud of her tough-talking, edgy Belle.

When the film was finally released in 1948, it became a rare flop for producer Arthur Freed; this despite a fine score by Harry Warren and Ralph Blane. Editing was a big culprit, with many choice musical numbers cut, diluting character development. The lone survivor of the cuts was Marilyn, with a stunning 13-minute sequence. The critics took notice. MGM didn't.

Her final film under contract was a minor yet attractive part in *High Barbaree* (1947), as Van Johnson's wealthy, glamourous girlfriend, thrown over for the virtuous charms of June Allyson. She was no match for the teary-eyed juggernaut Allyson, more of a fan favorite than Maxwell, so Marilyn's cool, slinky presence was lost in this mystical tale.

Then, according to the actress, sounding optimistic for the sake of her fans: "With the studio cutting down its planned schedule ... it didn't seem as though there was anything for me; so I went to Mr. Mayer and asked him to release me from my contract. The whole thing was very friendly, and the studio finally agreed to let me go."

This carefully worded statement sounds too studio-oriented to be completely true; more likely they just canned her or she had to pay her way out of her dead-end contract.

Before she left the studio for good to freelance, Marilyn was approached by director Mervyn LeRoy. Marilyn explained in a 1947 fan club journal: "He wanted to do a very dramatic test and said that producers wouldn't take me seriously in a dramatic role as long as I was a blonde. So, I went to makeup, and they fitted me with a wig, one that Lana Turner had worn in a picture. It must be a good luck wig because the test, taken from several scenes in the movie *Golden Boy* ... turned out even better than I hoped."

RKO saw the test, and the newly darktressed Maxwell, deciding she was just right for *Race Street* (1948) opposite George Raft. It was a comedown, for sure, from MGM, but the film afforded her a meaty part, the sort of dramatic role MGM never gave her. She's the duplicitous, quick-thinking girlfriend of Raft, playing him for a sucker all the way. "No, he's not stubborn," she says acidly at one point, "he's just a chump." Marilyn's a liar, a cheat, but oh-so-good at twisting Raft into believing she's a good girl.

Free from studio ties, Marilyn had been doing radio and nightclubs, also appearing with Jack Benny and his troupe at the London Palladium in 1948. Jack's daughter Joan, then only a teenager, gave a good glimpse at the real Marilyn in her *Sunday Nights at Seven*: "The engagement at Palladium was a great success and sold out every performance ... Marilyn Maxwell sang and did a skit with my father as the 'sexy dumb blonde,' similar to the role Marilyn Monroe later played once on his TV show. She had made her reputation as one of Bob Hope's 'girls,' visiting our troops during the war. Max never made it big, but her name was well-known, she had a nice singing voice and a fair amount of talent. She was soft-spoken and had a sweet quality about her, yet was a great character with a wildly funny sense of humor. Sexy and glamorous—yes, very—but hardly dumb. I liked her because she was one of the few of the many people who came in and out of my life who paid attention to me, gave me credit for brains, and treated me as an equal. We became good friends during that trip and she would often come to my room to chat ... I enjoyed knowing Max for that short time. She was a neat lady."

In addition to being the only real classic in her career, *Champion* (1949) contains Marilyn's finest acting. At the time, critical focus centered on the breakout performances of Kirk Douglas and Ruth Roman, as boxer Douglas' wife. So, again, Marilyn's excellent work was for naught, although clearly she makes quite an impact when viewing the movie today.

Star Douglas really came into his own as an actor with this small independent movie, playing his first anti-hero, boxer Midge Kelly, whose rise to the top is achieved through the destruction of those closest to him. Marilyn plays Grace Diamond, an expensive name for an expensive dame, with a self-possessed but sexy air, as she wraps the naive pug around her finger. She thrives on money, particularly if a macho boxer is attached to the bankroll. Looking cool in furs and seductive with a cigarette holder, Marilyn gets her point across after slapping Douglas: "I'm expensive, awful expensive. I didn't want you to think you could buy me cheap." Who's Kirk to argue? The assured beauty gets the boxer so mixed up, his manager (Paul Stewart) cracks, "He got himself a new manager—a blonde." (Judging from their steamy scenes in *Champion*, it's no surprise Marilyn and Kirk had an affair off-camera.)

When Kirk becomes full of himself, their relationship, which she had dictated up to this point, sours; Kirk finds himself another blonde (Lola Albright). Marilyn's confidence turns to hopelessness as she tries fiercely to hold Douglas' attention. Her best scenes follow as he throws her over. At first she insists "you're not going to shake me," threatening to expose his true nature. Catching her fingers in his arm, Kirk tells the wincing Marilyn, very quietly: "No, you're not going to do that. You're going to be a very good girl. Because if you're not, I'll put you in the hospital for a long time." Marilyn's desperation and resentment toward Douglas make these scenes the best acting of her career.

Director Mark Robson's gritty, unrelenting realism helped make *Champion* the sleeper of the year. It did wonders for Douglas' career and it should have done the same for Maxwell's. Sadly, her downfall started after her impressive work in this picture.

Key to the City (1950) led her back to MGM, but her old studio put her in support to Clark Gable and Loretta Young. It was a small part that Marilyn gamely tackled, that of Sheila, an "Atom Dancer"—MGM's variation on a bubble dancer, only more explosive—to whom Gable is briefly attracted. Lending her bubbly presence to the proceedings, Marilyn steals her scenes, especially with one suggestive dance.

Marilyn wed again on New Year's Day, 1950 to Anders (Andy) MacIntyre, owner of the Encore Room, but the couple was doomed from the start. Dancer Dan Dailey was best man at their wedding, but many in Hollywood claimed that wasn't a good sign: Marilyn, alleges agent Al Melnick, "had a crush on Dailey." She would later appear with Dailey on the *Shower of Stars* TV adaptation of the play *Burlesque* (co-starring Joan Blondell and Jack Oakie). She told reporters at the time that Mac-Intyre drank, some hinted he was abusive, but when the couple finally parted in 1951, privately the finger was pointed in the direction of, not Dailey, but comedian Bob Hope.

In June of 1950 Marilyn joined Hope to entertain in Korea, becoming the first woman to perform for the troops over there. Even though the two had known each other during the '40s, many believe the relationship started on this tour. Hope was quoted in the early '50s as to the kind of women who interested him: "I guess my top favorites are the fun girls, the ones who love to clown—among them, Dorothy Lamour, Marilyn Maxwell, Lucille Ball, Jane Russell. I like the ones who quip back." Of the actresses named, only Marilyn had a personal relationship with the comedian, which was opined by many who knew Hope to be very serious.

The gritty, realistic classic *Champion* (UA, 1949), starring Kirk Douglas, contained some of the best acting of Maxwell's career.

In addition to the Korean tour, Max found herself co-starring with Hope in their first movie together, *The Lemon Drop Kid* (1951), directed by

Sidney Lanfield; the Damon Runyon story was filmed previously in 1934 with Lee Tracy. She played Brainey Baxter, girlfriend of obnoxious racetrack tout Hope.

It was a nice, strictly supporting gig for Marilyn. She gets two songs to sing, one a duet introducing the now-classic Christmas song "Silver Bells" with Hope, a nice moment as the two stroll down Broadway. The number was added after Hope saw a rough cut of the film and wasn't happy with certain scenes and the overall pacing. Frank Tashlin did the rewrites and directed the few inserted scenes.

Hope and Maxwell were inseparable and, of course, there was talk. The rumors prompted Louella Parsons to speak out: "In an exclusive interview with Dolores Hope, I have learned that there's absolutely no truth to the current rumors that Bob Hope and his leading lady, Marilyn Maxwell, are serious about each other just because they have been seen together so much. 'Our marriage is stronger than ever,' Mrs. Hope assured me."

According to Hope's unauthorized biographer Arthur Marx, the devoutly Catholic Dolores privately pleaded with her husband to stop seeing Marilyn. In an interview with Maxwell's personal secretary Jean Greenberg, Marx asked her about the relationship, which Hope was flaunting during personal publicity trips to Ireland and England. "I will tell you this much," Greenberg replied, "Bob asked Marilyn to marry him when they were in Ireland together. But she turned him down because she knew Dolores would never give him a divorce..."

She tried to see others. Allegedly Hope caught her in a compromising position with, of all people, Jimmy Durante. If that incident made Hope laugh (wouldn't you?), another did not. One night Hope phoned Marilyn at her apartment seeking a date when a man answered. Hope demanded to know what this particular man, a popular singer, was doing there. Bob was

Known on the Paramount lot as "Mrs. Bob Hope," Marilyn had a serious affair with Hope during the early '50s. *The Lemon Drop Kid* (Paramount, 1951) was their first of three movies together.

informed that Marilyn was "upstairs getting ready for our date." When Hope shouted at him to "Stay away from my woman!," the handsome crooner told him, "Go flip yourself, we're going out!"

Alas, working extensively with Hope did little for Marilyn's screen career or reputation. She managed to appear in the low-budget Western *New Mexico* (1951) with Lew Ayres, but it was a dull venture. MM plays "Cherry, a well-known entertainer [*pause*] in the theater," who shows up in the middle of an Indian-cavalry war. The only bright spot was Marilyn singing and dancing—in the dark, mind you, as they await the Indians to attack them on a mountain—the song "Soldier, Soldier, Won't You Marry Me Now." The Indians are considerate enough to delay their attack until after the song.

It wasn't until 1953 that she finally appeared in another film, but again it was with Hope at Paramount. *Off Limits* was a mild comedy of a fight manager (Hope) in the Army training a boxer (Mickey Rooney). Marilyn plays Rooney's aunt (creative casting), owner of "The Pink Owl" bar who disapproves of boxing and Hope. She does get to sing the catchy "I Learned All About Love," and reprises it later as a duet with Bob, who does a nice tap dance on top of the piano—until he falls off.

One of her better roles came in Universal's *East of Sumatra* (1953), co-starring virile Jeff Chandler. "I came for tin, not trouble," Jeff growls to Anthony Quinn, blue-turbaned king of an uncharted island laden with unmined tin worth millions. Marilyn is engaged to Jeff's boss John Sutton. Between hairdo changes, she sashays around in improbably glamourous gowns, driving both men crazy. Marilyn's romantic scenes with Chandler (whom she was seeing off-screen) were impressively intense, but undermined the believability of his attraction to native girl Suzan Ball. Max gave the proceedings a fun, light touch.

Her work at Universal introduced her to an actor who would play a key role in her life, becoming her best friend: Rock Hudson, then just a budding contract player, whom she nicknamed "Big Sam." At this point in his career, the homosexual Hudson had to stay in the closet, so the fan magazines viewed the friendship, especially later in the 1960s, as "a love affair." Some feel that the relationship *was* sexual. "Marilyn Maxwell made the statement that even though she couldn't get Rock to marry her," actress Lori Nelson claimed, "she still wanted his child. I do recall that she really wanted to have his child," but Nelson concedes, "I was young and naive then."

Nelson wasn't the only one who was confused about their closeness. Marilyn married for the third and last time on November 21, 1954. The groom was producer-screenwriter Jerry Davis, who at first didn't know what to make of Rock's presence. He stated that Rock was "omnipresent during his marriage" to Marilyn, and that he would return home to find "this handsome six-foot-whatever man who was absolutely in tune with my wife. I felt a little like Woody Allen—'Hi, honey, I'm home.' She would get quite defensive. 'Are you paranoid? Do you actually think this man has any interest in me?'" Finally, Davis concluded that it was just "a remarkable friendship," which indeed it was. The Davis-Maxwell marriage, though producing a son (Matthew Paul, born 1956), was not a remarkable one, ending in divorce in 1960.

According to *Rock Hudson: His Story* (written with Sara Davidson, in the third person), their relationship only became sexual *after* her divorce from Davis. "I know for a fact they were having an affair," Jean Greenberg told Davidson. "Marilyn confided everything in me, and she talked about it in detail. She was in love with him. She said he always told her he loved her but he wasn't *in* love with her." But they did contemplate getting married and having a child, just as Lori Nelson remembers, but Rock told Max that she had to cope with his male lovers. She thought seriously about it, then declined, and they continued as friends. "People who saw them together said they laughed and played 'like little kids,'" wrote Davidson. "Rock had an aversion to Jell-O, and Marilyn would chase him through the house with a bowl of green Jell-O. She'd get him on the floor and tickle him, and they'd wrestle like bear cubs, laughing until tears were streaming down their cheeks."

Max had little to do in *New York Confidential* (1955). In another brief role, a favor to friend Lucille Ball, she showed up unbilled in *Forever, Darling* (1956). She performed a scene from a fictional movie *Shadows of Africa*, doing some fun overacting with James Mason. Lucy then imagines herself on-screen, dressing and vamping it up as Maxwell. It was the film's most inspired bit.

The Jerry Lewis dud *Rock-a-Bye Baby* (1958) gave her a bigger role. Movie star Marilyn, newly-widowed mother of triplets, goes on location in Egypt, foolishly trusting her children with schnook Lewis. Max is given one glorious moment, her production number "The White Virgin of the Nile," a campy bit of nonsense featuring her in a spectacular sequined Cleopatra costume. It was a breath of fresh air in a musical as moldy as Lewis' vocal chords. *The New York World-Telegram and Sun* praised Marilyn's performance as being "full of sly mirth as she takes charge of idiotic doings," while noting that she "is an old and expert hand at rowdy comedy."

She kept herself busy on TV, nightclubs and a Vegas act. She also recorded, but not for major labels. In 1953 she was heard on Forecast with "Plaid and Calico" and "Why Should I Flirt With the Blues?" Another recording during this period was her contribution of a song ("Zip") to Tops Records' *Pal Joey* studio recording. Martha Tilton, who also sang on the LP, remembered Marilyn vividly as "a funny gal. She had a wonderful sense of humor, and was extremely nice," adding with a chuckle, "She told me she was going to write her autobiography and call it *101 Night Stands*. Isn't that something? She was so fun to be around!" For Design, Marilyn shared an album with Roberta Sherwood in 1962.

Marilyn signed on for a TV series in 1961, *Bus Stop*, a project bearing scant likeness to William Inge's play or the Marilyn Monroe film of 1956. The action centered on the Sherwood Diner owned by Marilyn's character. There were high expectations for the show, but it was not to be. "It was a great experience working every week and improving my craft," she explained, "but after 13 weeks I had to withdraw. It turned out I was doing little more than direct people to the washroom and serve them coffee. In 13 weeks I had only three rousing good episodes! But it was just as well. The show went off the air."

More TV spots continued into the 1960s on game shows, where she was especially welcome because of her quick wit. She also worked on popular series like *Gunsmoke, 77 Sunset Strip, Wagon Train* and *Burke's Law*. On a telethon hosted by singer Jack Smith, viewers were treated to Marilyn's off-the-cuff, straightforward personality. Jack recalls today: "Marilyn was working the phones, and I went back to talk with her on camera. We were talking away, and she says to me, 'Are you having fun?'

And I said, of course, I was. I always enjoy doing telethons. She said, 'No, you were looking down my dress!' I said, 'I wasn't! … I would never think of…!' Marilyn looked at me, very seriously, with a twinkle in her eye, and said, 'Well, you *should!*' Isn't that wonderful? That's the way she was. A great sense of humor. Very nice girl."

Finally, a film role presented itself when Bob Hope cast her in *Critic's Choice* (1963)—probably not a wise choice. Hope is a Walter Kerr-ish Broadway critic who's been, as one character puts it, "closing shows single-handedly." When his wife (Lucille Ball) writes a play, he is expected to curb his acid pen. Marilyn plays Hope's ex-wife, an actress and past victim of his bad reviews: "The truth is, Ivy London's clothes give a better performance than she did." Our blonde tornado rustles up trouble in the Hope-Ball marriage: "I miss you too," Hope tells her wearily. "On my masochistic days." Marilyn breezes in and out of the narrative; she sparkles, she shines, she gets Hope drunk, and steals this not-worth-stealing movie.

In addition to TV and her scattered screen roles, she played in stock (*Can-Can, Bells Are Ringing*). In the late '60s she even headlined a Queens, New York, burlesque show where she stripped. About this strange career choice, she simply told the press, "The point of it all was that it was satirical and funny, and I got a good response from the audience." What she failed to mention was that probably, with a child to support, she needed the money.

Her best performance in a long time came in *Stage to Thunder Rock* (1964). She's an ex-prostitute who returns home to her family, finding nothing but disillusionment. She has endured life's hard knocks, urging her sister not to make the same mistakes. It was a rich, rewarding role in a movie that did nothing to jump-start her lagging film career.

Arizona Bushwhackers (1968) gave Marilyn a fun role as a saloon girl who "knows where all the bodies are buried," as confidant to her boss, bad guy Scott Brady. Howard Keel shows up in town to become sheriff, amid spy activities, and becomes immediately attracted to the sassy, smart siren.

She worked steadily into the early '70s, especially on TV: *The Debbie Reynolds Show, O'Hara, U.S. Treasury,* and *Men at Law.* Her last role was *Wild Women* (1970), a telefilm about five female convicts. *The Hollywood Reporter* singled out Marilyn's role, that of a "blowsy, overweight, brassy ex-madam," as "stealing the show," adding, "Miss Maxwell, in particular, has probably been dying to play a part like this for years, and she makes every minute count."

Wild Women co-star Marie Windsor replaced Marilyn in *Support Your Local Gunfighter* (1971), possibly due to illness. Marie later said, "She had been on the picture about a week, and they had shot a couple of her scenes, but apparently, she wasn't able to be feisty or bawdy enough, especially with Joan Blondell." In a 1999 interview with writer Jim Meyer, Windsor raved, "She was real, full of fun, really a regular gal … absolutely no phoniness!" She and Windsor were great friends going back to their MGM days.

Despite losing *Gunfighter,* things were looking up for Max. She was preparing another nightclub act in Chicago and two projects were being offered her: the movie *Mama's Boy* and a recurring role on the soap opera *Return to Peyton Place.*

Then, on March 20, 1972, the startling news came out over the UPI wire: "Marilyn Maxwell, who starred in numerous song-and-dance movies in the 1940s and later on television comedy shows, died today at her home at the age of 49. Miss Maxwell, who had been under treatment for high blood pressure and a pulmonary ailment, was found in the bathroom by her son, Matthew, 15 years old, when he returned home from school in the afternoon, the police said."

Hollywood was stunned. Her funeral, arranged by friend Rock Hudson, was held at the Beverly Hills Community Presbyterian Church and was packed with her show business friends. Bob Hope, fighting back tears, delivered her eulogy: "If all her friends were here today we'd have to use the Colosseum. Marilyn had an inner warmth and love for people ... and the thousands of servicemen she entertained over the years felt this. Who would have thought that this little girl from Clarinda, Iowa, would do this much and go as far as she did?

"Who knows why some of us are called earlier than others? Maybe God needed a lovely gal to sing and cheer Him up, and so He called her ... I must say it was a great job of casting."

Bob Hope's heartfelt words were shared by all who knew and worked with Marilyn. "I'd like my career to be like Ginger Rogers'," she told Louella Parsons in 1946. "Straight dramatic roles alternating with musical-comedy ones. I'm willing to work very hard to attain that." Maybe it didn't work out just that way, maybe she was never a big star, but she became well-liked with both fans and Hollywood professionals. *The Hollywood Reporter* said at her passing: "A fitting epitaph for Marilyn Maxwell: She was humble when her career was riding high, never beefed when things got rocky, and if she had an enemy in this world, she never mentioned it."

As Marvel Maxwell: 1942: This Is No Laughing Matter (Soundie), Tea on the Terrace (Soundie), Dreamsville, Ohio (Soundie), Goodbye, Mama (I'm Off to Yokohama) (Soundie), Havin' a Time in Havana (Soundie). As Marilyn Maxwell: 1943: Stand By for Action (MGM), Best Foot Forward (MGM), Pilot #5 (MGM), DuBarry Was a Lady (MGM), Presenting Lily Mars (MGM), Salute to the Marines (MGM), Thousands Cheer (MGM), Dr. Gillespie's Criminal Case (MGM), Swing Fever (MGM). 1944: Three Men in White (MGM), Lost in a Harem (MGM). 1945: Between Two Women (MGM). 1946: The Show-Off (MGM). 1947: High Barbaree (MGM). 1948: Summer Holiday (MGM), Race Street (RKO). 1949: Champion (UA). 1950: Meet the Winners (Columbia short), Key to the City (MGM), Outside the Wall (Universal), Hollywood Goes to Bat (short). 1951: The Lemon Drop Kid (Paramount), New Mexico (UA). 1953: Off Limits (Paramount), Paris Model (Columbia), East of Sumatra (Universal). 1955: New York Confidential (WB). 1956: Forever, Darling (MGM). 1958: Rock-a-Bye Baby (Paramount). 1963: Critic's Choice (WB). 1964: The Lively Set (Universal), Stage to Thunder Rock (Paramount). 1968: Arizona Bushwhackers (Paramount). 1969: From Nashville with Music (Bradford). 1970: The Phynx (WB), Wild Women (ABC-TV).

Mercedes McCambridge: Inner Fire

by RAY HAGEN

In her first movie, *All the King's Men,* Mercedes McCambridge got slapped in the kisser and won an Academy Award. That slap may have been the reason. Men had slapped women around in movies for generations and the ladies react in standard movie fashion; they gasp in wide-eyed shock, they whimper, they burst into tears, they fall down, they get lovely weepy close ups. Not this time. When John Ireland hauled off and slugged Mercedes, she cried *"Oww!"* She always believed that "Oww!" won her the Oscar. Maybe so, but whenever she's on screen, just try looking elsewhere.

I first encountered Mercedes McCambridge as a star-struck teenage fan in 1951, again in 1963 as an interviewer for *Films in Review* magazine, and finally in 1983 while she was starring in *Agnes of God* at Washington DC's Kennedy Center. (All her quotes here, unless otherwise specified, are from my taped conversations with her.) At first I was unsettled by her refusal to behave like a movie star granting an audience. Instead I'd be whisked along on a roller coaster ride of unexpected warmth, scalding intensity and ice-cool drollery as she assumed, on my callow part, an equal interest in and knowledge of life beyond movies. I kept up as best I could, mesmerized by every twist of that electric voice I'd grown up listening to on the radio.

That low, vibrant, one-in-a-billion voice, always her most distinctive asset, was central to her career from the very beginning. It was during the now-fabled "golden age of radio" that her unique name and voice first became familiar to audiences on hundreds of radio dramas and soap operas for over a dozen years. But it was that 1949 movie, *All the King's Men,* that firmly established her as a "name" player, if not a top-line superstar. She was a most attractive, slim-figured woman who bore little resemblance to the brittle, bitter, granite-featured neurotics she usually played on film, and she became one of the few character players capable of achieving a multi-media star image throughout her career.

Carlotta Mercedes Agnes McCambridge (she took Agnes as her Confirmation name) was born on a farm near Joliet, Illinois, on St. Patrick Day, March 17, 1918. Her parents, Marie and John Patrick McCambridge, were mid–Illinois farm people, as were their people before them dating back over a hundred years. Her father's ancestry was Irish and her mother's Spanish. ("God, what a Medea she could have played," Mercedes later wrote.) She had two younger brothers. One was injured in a plane during World War II, the younger became a marriage counselor in Los Angeles.

134

Mercedes emerged from childhood during the Depression. "We never were wealthy people," she said. "There were times when we were very poor, like any farmer who went through the 1930s. Franklin Delano Roosevelt is the reason my mother and father didn't go broke and the reason probably that my brothers and I were able to be brought up fairly comfortably. Not always comfortably, there were some bad times when we had to take in roomers, things like that, but that's all right, who's knocking it?"

It was Cardinal Mundelein, of the archdiocese of Chicago, who gave her destiny its major turn. He attended a performance of *The Taming of the Shrew* by the St. Thomas Apostle High School in Joliet and noticed 16-year-old Mercedes in a small part. He had her brought to him after the performance and inquired about her plans. Mercedes recalled, "I was

Portrait of Mercedes McCambridge, 1955.

frightened at meeting him, and he asked me what I was going to do for college. I told him I likely wouldn't go because there wasn't any money, and I fully expected to go to work. He asked me if I would enter the scholarship contest at his school, Mundelein College. I did, and I won it, and I got through college for the magnificent sum of $30 for four years." She won by reciting Joyce Kilmer's *Blue Valentine*, a four-and-a-half-minute semi-religious poem she'd learned in her speech class.

The head of the drama department at Mundelein was Sister Mary Leola, and she became Mercedes' inspiration, as well as her teacher. "She invented me," said Mercedes. "She is everything I know about my work. A brilliant actress, a wonderful director, a hard task-master and disciplinarian with a wildly inventive mind and a dedication to the theater. A great lady."

At Mundelein, a girls' college, Mercedes often played men's parts, since they were traditionally done by the girls with the heavier voices, "and I guess mine was the heaviest, always has been. I loved playing Petrucio in *Taming of the Shrew* because he was so flamboyant and wild. I had a mustache and everything." She also played Viola in *Twelfth Night* and belonged to Sister Mary Leola's Speaking Choir. "That was Sister's innovation at school. Eight 'darker' voices, as she called them, and eight 'lighter' voices, and I was the soloist in the choir. We would read poetry in concert. A vice-president from NBC, Sid Strotz, had to come and see us because one of the girls was a relative of his or something. He was very impressed and the next day he asked us down to NBC. We went in, none of us ever having been in a radio studio, and Sister rolled up her full outer sleeves and conducted us as a conductor would an orchestra. A half hour later the choir, en masse, had signed a one-year contract with the NBC Chicago Symphony Hour, and I had a five-year contract as an NBC actress. It happened that quickly.

"I was a sophomore, 17½, and I really didn't take it very seriously. I didn't know that I should be at their disposal. I'd go off for weekends, and then NBC would call and wonder where I was. But they weren't paying me unless I worked so I didn't see why I had to tell them where I was every minute. I did many, many programs while I was in school. We lived on the far South Side of Chicago, and I would go to Mundelein and have two classes, then go to NBC, go back for more classes, and then go home. I traveled 144 miles a day by train and bus. All the train men got to know me and respect my need to study and they'd often ask somebody not to sit in the seat next to me so I'd have room for my notebooks.

"That was necessary because I had to maintain a B-plus average. I had to take a double major for the scholarship, English and Drama, but if the marks went down the scholarship would have been lost. And while I was making money at NBC and was in no dire need of it, as I had been for the first year, still I felt that if I was given the scholarship in the first place, I ought to maintain it. And I did, but I was in an awful shape when I graduated, dreadfully tired. The doctor told me to go away for a while 'cause I needed a rest, so I went down to the travel bureau and asked the lady where I could go for $1,100 and she said Guatemala, which meant little or nothing to me.

18-year-old NBC radio actress Mercedes McCambridge, 1936.

She said I could go for three weeks and have a wonderful time, so I gave her the $1,100 and I went to Guatemala. And it was glorious, I'm so glad that I did it."

She graduated on June 7, 1937, with a Bachelor of Arts and the drama school's honor award, the Golden Rose. For the next few years she was a steadily working radio actress in Chicago, then the production center for radio's daytime soap operas. She was a regular on such NBC soaps as *Betty and Bob, The Guiding Light, Midstream* and *This Is Judy Jones.* At night she was heard on countless NBC dramas.

She met and quickly married writer William Fifield, then a CBS announcer: "Bill and I were married in 1940. We only knew each other for three weeks. I think it was a reaching out to anything that looked like permanence. I guess he believed that anyone with 16 years of a convent education should be pretty permanent, and I thought any son of a minister must surely be permanent and steadfast."

The Fifields moved to California where she continued her radio career. Their son, John Lawrence Fifield, was born there on Christmas Day, 1941.

Soon after, she received some strong advice from John Barrymore, who thought she might become a great stage actress: "We worked together on *The Rudy Vallee Sealtest Hour.* Poor John. I was there the night they carried him out, and two days later he was dead. But he kept telling me, 'This is ridiculous, why are you here, why aren't you in New York?' So I told him, 'Well, it's necessary for me to make a life for my child, and what would I do in New York?' And of course it was necessary for him to make a life for what was left of John Barrymore. We were both doing *The Rudy Vallee Sealtest Hour* to eat."

Mercedes made it to New York with her son John in June '42 to do *Abie's Irish Rose* on radio. Throughout the 1940s she was probably radio's most steadily employed actress. She had regular roles in such staple soaps as *Big Sister, This Is Nora Drake, Stella Dallas, The Second Mrs. Burton* and *Helen Trent* and appeared regularly in virtually all of radio's dramatic series (*I Love a Mystery, Grand Central Station, Inner Sanctum, Suspense, Murder at Midnight, Everything for the Boys, Gangbusters, Bulldog Drummond, Cavalcade of America,* etc.). She frequently played multiple roles—sisters, triplets, even whole families (both genders). Writer Arch Oboler used her many times on his classic CBS series *Lights Out,* saying, "She has an inner fire of a sort I've seen in only two other actresses, Nazimova and Elisabeth Bergner."

Orson Welles, on whose radio programs she frequently appeared, called her "the greatest living radio actress." "That's pretty funny, isn't it?", she later said. "What would a dead radio actress be? But I worked with Orson a long time. Orson's daughter Beatrice is my god child, and I'm very grateful to Mr. Welles."

She always recalled her years on radio with great affection: "I had such freedom. They'd let me do just about anything I wanted."

In 1944, John Huston arranged a screen test for her at MGM. She laughed as she recalled, "He thought I could play Jo in *Little Women,* but they said that I had 'flaring nostrils,' like a wild beast, I guess. They didn't like my nostrils so they made some for me. They poured things on my face and left me in total oblivion for 15 or 20 ghastly minutes, and then took it off and extracted from it some wax flaps which they attached to the extremity of my nose. I looked more like Bob Hope. Anyhow, they didn't like what they saw. Nor did I." (Five years later, MGM made *Little Women* with June Allyson as Jo.)

Nor were her stage attempts successful. Her first Broadway job was in 1945 as Sister Margaret in *The Hasty Heart*, but "nine days into rehearsal the director, Bretaigne Windust, fired me because he said I was pregnant with warmth, and until I gave birth to that quality I was as ugly to watch on stage as a woman large with child. Unquote. I never got to know Windy well enough to ask him what he meant. But I can remember walking down 44th Street after he'd fired me. It was raining, and New York seemed pretty cruel then. Later I was with one of my fancy writer friends, Sidney Sheldon, who took me to the Stork Club to forget the sorrow of *Hasty Heart* and this nice, portly gentleman across the way sent over a note saying he was Marc Connolly and could I come to the Ambassador Hotel the next day and read for him for *Hope for the Best*. I got the part. I was ecstatic. I replaced Dina Merrill. Dina had begun in it and they didn't like her, so she got what I got in *The Hasty Heart*, and I thought how ironic it was that out of somebody else's misfortune I now had the part. I went on in that lovely, euphoric way until New Year's Eve in Washington DC when we opened. The notices in Washington were the finest notices I've ever received. The next day, New Year's Day, there was a phone call. I expected it

might be the president at least, after such a glorious opening—and they gave me my notice. I was through at the end of the week because they didn't feel I was strong enough to come into New York, not having a name, and they got Jane Wyatt to replace me. So I got to be about the most replaced person going there for a while."

She did make it to Broadway, but there were more disappointments. Elliott Nugent's *A Place of Our Own* opened April 2, 1945, and closed five days later. (Robert Garland in his *New York Journal-American* review said: "There's a likely looking newcomer called Mercedes McCambridge, who reached the Royale by way of amateur theatricals and radio." Rowland Field, *Newark Evening*

John Ireland and Mercedes in *All the King's Men* (Columbia, 1949).

News: "Mercedes McCambridge, who has been curiously in-and-out of several plays before they reached Broadway this season, is finally on hand in person to show herself to be a particularly winning young actress.") *Twilight Bar* opened in Baltimore March 12, 1946 and closed in Philadelphia on March 23. A month later Sam and Bella Spewack's *Woman Bites Dog* managed to last four days. (George Freedley, *New York Morning Telegraph*: "Mercedes McCambridge has authority and humor, rather in the Shirley Booth line, as a reporter." Lewis Nichols, *New York Times*: "Mercedes McCambridge, attractive and from radio, is half the love interest; Kirk Douglas supplies the rest.") Mercedes later recalled Douglas borrowing her eyelash curler.

She and William Fifield divorced in 1946: "When war was declared he was a conscientious objector. He went away, came back some two or three years later and we were not the same people at all. It was tragic."

Mercedes continued in radio between stage flops. It paid the bills, but in 1947 she decided she didn't like what was going on around her: "Analyst couches, nose-bob jobs and Dexamyl tablets—I thought there must be more than that." So she sold her phonograph and fur coat, packed all of two suitcases and took off with her pre-school son John on a year-and-a-half adventure, first to St. Croix, Guadeloupe and Martinique, then to London and on to Dublin, Paris, Genoa and Portofino. She wrote an account of this journey, and its liberating effect on them both, in a book titled *The Two of Us,* published in London in 1960.

On her return she went back to radio. Especially notable was a superb CBS series, *Studio One* (1947-48), which featured Mercedes so often it might as well have been titled *The Mercedes McCambridge Show.* She co-starred with important theater and film names in adaptations of well-known classics and original plays. The series was directed and hosted by Fletcher Markle.

She did another play on Broadway, *The Young and Fair,* with Julie Harris and Rita Gam. It opened November 22, 1948, but she left it a few weeks later to begin work on her first film, Robert Rossen's *All the King's Men.*

Rossen and Max Arnow had held open auditions in New York for the role of political hatchet-woman Sadie Burke and Mercedes attended the call with her long time friend, actress Elspeth Eric. She was aghast at the way the hopeful candidates were quickly herded in and out of Rossen's office like so much cattle, and by the time it was her turn Mercedes was in a raging fury: "I read them the riot act about how they were in the slave business, not the theater, and if they wanted beautiful faces they should have stayed out in California, but they shouldn't come here and destroy actors' egos." Rossen was shocked, and as an enraged Mercedes was halfway out the door he gave her the part then and there. She'd unintentionally given him exactly the Sadie Burke he wanted.

The movie of Robert Penn Warren's Pulitzer Prize–winning novel told of the rise and fall of Willie Stark (Broderick Crawford), a ruthless politician patterned after Huey Long. The movie was a great hit, and Mercedes' intense portrayal of Stark's embittered hench woman (think Mary Matalin on crack) won critical raves and the Academy Award as 1949's Best Supporting Actress. Her acceptance speech, delivered with excited enthusiasm, has been widely quoted: "I'd like to say to every waiting actor, *hang on.* Look what can happen!" Crawford was named Best Actor and *All the King's Men* won Best Picture. She also won two Golden Globe Awards

Mercedes and Dean Jagger holding their 1949 Oscars, with presenters Ray Milland and Claire Trevor (May 23, 1950).

(Best Supporting Actress and Best Newcomer) and the *Look* and Associated Press Awards. Mercedes McCambridge's career was forever transformed.

A few weeks before she got her Oscar, on February 19, 1950, she married Fletcher Markle, with whom she had worked so often in radio.

Columbia, although impressed by her performance in *All the King's Men*, felt she was too specialized and did not offer her a contract, but she obtained three film roles in rapid succession, all released in 1951. But *Lightning Strikes Twice* for Warners, *The Scarf* for United Artists and *Inside Straight* for MGM were all strictly programmers.

"Ruth Roman Is All Woman In 'Lightning Strikes Twice!'", screamed the ads, which featured some of Roman's sexiest studio glamour portraits. It was Mercedes' lot to be vengeful and jealous in mannish shirts and dungarees as she terrorized the top-billed star, and it seemed that she had already become typed as a bitter shrew (and named accordingly—"Sadie Burke" in *All the King's Men*, and in this, "Liza McStringer"). But the critic for the *N.Y. Herald-Tribune* saw beyond all that. "Outstanding among the principals is Mercedes McCambridge," he wrote. "In her unrequited love she is an extremely feminine artist, whose portrayal rises in intensity to a believable denouement."

Mercedes sang professionally for the first time in *The Scarf,* a mood-piece in which she starred (for once) as a seen-it-all hash-house waitress who sang for her supper. The producers had intended to get a singer to dub her song, "Summer Rains," but Mercedes wasn't having any: "I said, 'Why? She's not supposed to be a great singer, if she were she wouldn't be working in a place like this. Let me try it.' I think that should be done more often."

In July of 1951 she made her one and only record, a single for Decca, singing "While You Danced, Danced, Danced" with Gordon Jenkins' orchestra. Jenkins, a good friend, asked her to do it as a favor and they talked of doing some more records, but nothing came of it.

She returned to radio, now as the star, playing a lawyer on the NBC series *Defense Attorney* (1951-52), and as a spinster schoolmarm in *Family Skeleton* on CBS (1953-54): "I did radio then because I couldn't do anything else. I was pregnant both times, both sons, but both didn't make it." Her friend Marlene Dietrich was to be the godmother of the first boy. The diagnosis for these stillborn births was placenta previa.

She resumed moviemaking in 1954, delivering a stunning performance as Joan Crawford's jealous, vengeful, half-insane enemy in *Johnny Guitar,* a pseudo-psychological Republic Western that has since become a full-blown camp classic. The rivalry was not all in front of the camera, and newspapers of the day gleefully reported

John Ireland and Mercedes in *The Scarf* (UA, 1951).

on the feud for weeks. Crawford had wanted Claire Trevor for the part and agreed to the younger Mercedes only reluctantly:

"She didn't want me in the beginning. But then it was all right until a scene which was shot outside in Arizona, and I had about four pages of dialogue, a monologue. And because of my background, I knew it. We shot it in one take and the crew applauded and Joan was in her trailer not more than about 50 feet away, and that's what started it. Wow. Now, it sounds as though I'd done something great. I hadn't, any girl in my speech class in college would have been able to do the same thing. Jayne Mansfield could have done it if she'd studied. It was just the fact that I got through it and the guys knew they'd get home early that night, that was all. But it made Joan mad. And she *was* the star of the picture. I guess if I were Joan Crawford I'd be mad if some Mamie Glutz horned in on the star territory that way. I'd have probably done the same thing. But when she was on the Academy Awards show a few years later she looked so great, I really thought she was marvelous, so I sent her a wire and said, 'You stole the evening, you were just wonderful.' So then she wrote me a nice letter, and now these two childish women have reverted to some kind of normalcy."

But Crawford apparently nursed her grudge. In her sugar-coated 1964 autobiography *A Portrait of Joan* (written "with" Jane Kesner Ardmore), she wouldn't even name her *Johnny Guitar* co-star, referring to her only as "an actress who hadn't worked in ten years, an excellent actress but a rabble-rouser." It was this anonymous actress, claimed Joan, who caused all the trouble.

Sterling Hayden, Crawford's leading man, called the star's treatment of Mercedes "shameful."

Mercedes, in her own 1981 autobiography, took off her gloves: "Poor old rotten-egg Joan. I kept my mouth shut about her for nearly a quarter of a century, but she was a mean, tipsy, powerful, rotten-egg lady. I'm still not going to tell what she did to me. Other people have written some of it, but they don't know it all, and they never will because I am a very nice person and I don't like to talk about the dead even if they were rotten eggs."

In 1956 the "actress who hadn't worked in ten years" received her second Academy Award nomination for her brief but riveting performance as Luz Benedict in *Giant,* directed by George Stevens from Edna Ferber's sprawling novel. She told Michael Buckley in *Theatre Week* in 1991, "People say, 'You were so mean in *Giant,*' but I *wasn't.* My father had left me the ranch. I send my brother, Rock Hudson, off to Virginia to buy a horse and he comes back with Elizabeth Taylor. What the heck is that? There goes my ranch!"

She admitted, "I would've liked to have won the Oscar for *Giant.*" (Dorothy Malone won for her absurdly overblown Jessica Rabbit turn in *Written on the Wind.*) But she got another treasured prize, her *Giant* script autographed by an admiring Edna Ferber in praise of Mercedes' skill in bringing Luz so effectively to life.

Mercedes had made her TV debut as a regular cast member on NBC's *One Man's Family* as far back as 1949. She'd continued to appear frequently on TV dramas and talk shows, but didn't sign on for another series until *Wire Service* in 1956, a series about newspaper life in which she alternated every third episode with George Brent and Dane Clark. It lasted 39 episodes and was cancelled after only one season.

In the misbegotten *A Farewell to Arms* the following year, Mercedes did a bit as a stern head nurse. Critics enjoyed Elaine Stritch and Mercedes in their nice-nurse/nasty-nurse pairing but savaged the movie. An ignominious failure, it was a sad end to producer David O. Selznick's career.

A happier experience was Orson Welles' now-classic *Touch of Evil* ('58) in which she did an uncredited cameo as a vicious leather-jacketed Mexican junkie. This was a favor to an old friend: "I did it for Orson. I was swimming one morning. They called me in the house and said that Orson was on the phone and I knew he was shooting out at Universal with Janet Leigh and so I wondered why he would he calling me in the middle of the morning. He said, 'Could you be out here at 1:30 and do you have a black leather jacket?' and I said, 'No, but I think my son has one.' So I put on some black slacks, a black sweater and John's black leather jacket, went out, shot the scene, and was back home again by 5:00 that afternoon. But it was for Orson. I'd do anything for Orson, and I think I *could* do anything for Orson. I could probably walk on water if Orson would say so."

In 1959 she was Elizabeth Taylor's mother in *Suddenly, Last Summer*—an erratic and peculiarly mannered performance—and the following year was a raw-boned pioneer woman who strikes it rich in the lethargic remake of *Cimarron*.

Angel Baby (1961) was one of her favorites. It's an uneven film, but not easily forgotten. Nor is Mercedes' performance as the sexually frustrated older wife of a young faith-healing evangelist (George Hamilton). "*Angel Baby* suffered by being released soon after *Elmer Gantry*," said Mercedes. "If *Angel Baby* had had a tenth of the money that was spent advertising *Elmer Gantry* it would have been recognized for what it is, a much better picture. I told Burt Lancaster that. Poor little *Angel Baby* got pushed around because the wonderfully trusting producers mortgaged everything but their wives and children to make it and had nothing left. It's an honest and true picture, but because there was no money for promotion nobody will ever know about it."

Mercedes and Fletcher Markle had divorced in August 1961, and early in '63 the fates almost vanquished her. Her son John, then 21, was savagely beaten by four muggers and taken to Santa Monica Hospital with a basal skull fracture. He managed to pull through, but no sooner was he out of danger than Mercedes broke a foot and then two fingers while rehearsing for a West Coast stage production of *The Little Foxes*. The very evening she broke her fingers, John was in an auto accident and his skull was fractured again. This time bone actually pierced his brain and Mercedes was told the surgeons were certain the second fracture would be fatal. She left the hospital in a state of shock and expecting John to die.

"The medical authorities say it was emotional bankruptcy, that I wrote a check and there were no more emotional funds. The two accidents of my son, breaking my foot rehearsing *The Little Foxes* and then breaking two fingers while I was still in the cast with the foot, they all happened within an eight-week period. The night before my birthday they released me from the hospital for shock, and my son was still there. I don't remember going home from the hospital. I functioned, I did all the things people do. I drove a car, don't remember doing it, wrote checks, dealt with insurance people, don't remember any of that, and I was very neat and tidy about it. I dressed in my nicest robe, put out all of the vital papers on the table and took every pill in my apartment. Luckily there weren't that many, but there were enough so that I had no pulse or blood pressure, and I was dying. Now nobody loves life any better than I do, but I wanted, I guess, to be—out—go away, I don't want any more now, enough! If I'd had a chance to recover from one of the crises before the next one came, that would have been different, but it was like a snowball, it got bigger and bigger, and it knocked me down. I let go of God's hand, I was swamped."

Not only did Mercedes survive but John did too. He had a series of serious operations and resumed his studies at UCLA, working for an MA in international trade and planning to study law.

That August, Mercedes returned to the New York stage after an absence of 15 years. She replaced Shelley Winters as Jack Warden's co-star in an off–Broadway production of Lewis John Carlino's *Cages*, which consisted of two one-act, two-character plays. In one she was a discontented career woman, in the other a prostitute. Like *Angel Baby* it was a low-paying project in which she believed. "My complete association with *Cages* has been less than three weeks," she said during the run, "and only six of those days were spent in rehearsal. To get ready in six days is pretty phenomenal. The only way I can understand it is that God must be a member of Equity."

In January '63 Mercedes took over from Uta Hagen the role of Martha in the Broadway production of Edward Albee's *Who's Afraid of Virginia Woolf*, and continued in it until it closed. Said Norman Nadel in his *New York World-Telegram & Sun* review: "Miss McCambridge brings to her role a good range of emotional response, plus a deadly effective way of holding herself in check for a few seconds before triggering her anger. It's like the good backswing of a golf club." "Anybody would drop dead to play a part like that," she told Nora Ephron in a *New York Post* interview. "I can't wait to get to the theater. Think of being paid to vent spleen and venom, all your pent-up monstrosities, every night. People pay thousands of dollars to psychoanalysts to let go that way."

If radio had been Mercedes' first love, the stage was a very close second. "Every time I get a chance I run to do anything I can in the theater, wherever it is," she said. Over the years she starred all over the country in productions of *Agnes of God, Macbeth, The Little Foxes, 'night, Mother, The Child Buyer, Medea, The Time of the Cuckoo, The Show-Off, The Miracle Worker, Candida, The Glass Menagerie, The Subject Was Roses, The Madwoman of Challiot, The Price, Black Eyed Susan* and more. Back on Broadway, Mercedes got a Tony nomination for the short-lived *Love-Suicide at Schofield Barracks* in '72 and starred in *Lost in Yonkers* in 1992.

During her marriage to Fletcher Markle they had been social drinkers living the Good Life, as was everyone around them, until Mercedes' addiction to drinking turned to full-tilt alcoholism. After a long, horrifying battle, and with the help of Alcoholics Anonymous, she was finally able to reach the stage of recovery. Then, in the summer of 1969, Iowa Senator Harold E. Hughes called Mercedes to ask a favor. He knew of her battle with alcoholism and was himself an openly recovered alcoholic. He asked if she would come to Washington and testify before the Senate Subcommittee on Alcoholism and Narcotics. He wanted a familiar face to bring attention to the need for altering a criminal code that stigmatized alcoholics but did nothing to help them. Her testimony was passionate, honest and articulate. She was certain that going public cost her much work in films, but nonetheless continued to speak

at AA meetings, on TV, and in any public or private forum that could help other
alcoholics in their recovery.

The movies Mercedes made since then were mostly of the low-budget and even
exploitation variety, done mostly to subsidize her preferred stage activities. There
was one exception, and it was a lulu.

She dubbed Linda Blair as the voice of Satan in William Friedkin's mega-
smash *The Exorcist* (1973), but it was a bumpy ride. She relished the opportunity to
use her wealth of radio experience and she called it the hardest job she ever had.
She reproduced not only the Devil's obscenity-laden dialogue but all the keening
wails, screams, growls, wheezes—every sound of agony and evil that emanated from
Linda Blair's demon-possessed body. This was done in total secret, and she was
promised, and shown, the on-screen credit card that would be used: "AND MERCEDES
MCCAMBRIDGE as THE DEMON." But when she went to the first preview, and the
final credits rolled, her name was conspicuously missing. The jeweler's credit was
there, and the furrier's, but no mention of Mercedes' contribution to the film or to
Blair's performance. Most likely this was to bolster Blair's shot at an Oscar. Mercedes' fury with Friedkin knew no bounds. She would not be silenced, and in a no-
holds-barred interview with Charles Higham in *The New York Times* (January 27,
1974) she blew the lid off. Now that the secret was out, the producers had no choice
but to add a credit to the final prints. Not quite the same as she was promised, but
now "AND MERCEDES MCCAMBRIDGE" appears at the end of the cast list. As a result,
her contribution to *The Exorcist* is now more widely known than it would have been
had they played fair in the first place. This irony amused and satisfied her.

Mercedes signed on as Artist-in-Residence at numerous universities, and a
half-dozen colleges awarded her honorary degrees. Stage and film actress Helen
Hedman was an undergraduate at Washington DC's Catholic University during
1972–73 when Mercedes taught Master Classes at their Speech and Drama Department. "The first time I met her," Helen recalls, "she looked at me, introduced herself, put out her hand and gave me an *incredibly* firm handshake. I'll never forget
that handshake, holy mackerel. And that look in her eye! She came in *close*, and it
wasn't just 'nice to meet you, blah blah blah,' it really *was* nice to meet me, she really
made me believe that. She was riveting, you couldn't turn away once she had you.
At first I was a little afraid of her, she was the most vivid person I'd ever met. It was
like she saw right through you, but not in a bad way. She wanted to engage you in
something she knew about that we didn't know about. For undergraduate theater
students, here was someone who really knew what it took, who'd had such a *life*. No
bones about how tough it was, no bones about how rewarding it was, and how much
work it was going to be. She was an in-your-face teacher, so focused on each one of
us. She came into one of my oral interp classes and brought in some old radio scripts.
Everybody had to get up and do it. She'd help us find a character's voice, commu-
nicate everything with just the voice and totally commit to it. And she taught classes
in film technique. We'd do scenes from plays and she'd teach us how to speak lines
to someone off-camera. She was *right* beside the camera, holding your gaze, and it
was like you were being hypnotized. You were in her beams, she was *on* you. She
was intimidating only because she was so direct, so right-from-the-heart. She also
did three or four lectures, all with cryptic titles. She did one called *If Not Now,*

When? I didn't know it at the time, but it's a phrase from Rabbi Hillel. Wouldn't you know she'd know the teachings of Rabbi Hillel? It was about seizing the opportunities placed before you. We thought it was going to be like 'Here's some clues to show business I'm gonna pass on to you,' but it wasn't about becoming an actor, it was about how to be a *person.* We were dumbfounded. The students loved her. She was hard on us, even relentless, but not so much as to beat us down, like some teachers who totally break students. It was totally positive reinforcement. She really had that fire and communicated that to everyone. For me as an undergrad, to see that, and to *want* that, was the greatest thing I got from her. It was great to have her there, we were so excited to have the voice of Satan at Catholic U."

Between 1974 and '78, Mercedes was heard on over two dozen hour-long episodes of *CBS Mystery Theater,* an attempt to recreate the fun and excitement of radio drama's heyday. She was happily reunited with many of her former cohorts, radio veterans thrilled at the chance to do it all again. Radio legend Himan Brown was producer-director. The series won a 1975 Peabody Award, but it didn't revive the public's interest in what was by then a dead-in-the-water art form.

Mercedes was always an outspoken "Irish farmer Democrat" and never cared who knew it. She had no patience with those who think performers should keep their politics to themselves, believing anyone in *any* profession *should* proclaim their political views if they felt like it. "I thought that's what America was all about," she said. "Perhaps I've been misinformed."

Her autobiography, *The Quality of Mercy,* was published in 1981. It's safe to say that in the annals of celebrity autobiographies there's been nothing quite like it. No mere list of show biz triumphs, it was a stream-of-consciousness rocket ride in no particular sequence, mixing rage, tenderness, torment and exultation. Startled reviewers raved. Christopher Schmering in *The Washington Post* called it "page for page, the most unusual and ambitious celebrity memoir in years...a weird kind of triumph...inspired nuttiness and bag-lady wisdom." "It has a convulsive mixture of exhilaration and dread that has no match in American show business literature," said David Thomson in *American Film.*

On November 16, 1987, her 45-year-old son John shot and killed his wife Christine, their 13-year-old daughter Amy and their nine-year-old daughter Suzanne. He wrote a two-line note saying he was responsible for the slayings, called his lawyer, aimed two guns to his head and killed himself. Three weeks later William Fifield, John's father, died of a heart attack brought on by grief and stress.

Since then Mercedes did occasional voiceovers and narrations (one for a Dr. Seuss book) but made few public appearances. She died in La Jolla, California, on March 2, 2004, two weeks short of her eighty-sixth birthday. But she could be justly proud of her legacy of a passionate dedication to her chosen profession and a unique body of work.

When I asked Mercedes if she had some overall approach to crafting a performance, she replied: "Walter Huston told me that acting is looking and listening, that's all it is. You cannot then make a false move, gesture, reading or interpretation. If you look and if you listen, you must then give a natural reaction. But, like every other truism, it's simple and therefore most difficult to learn. I surely haven't mastered it because it means so much more than it says. It embodies concentration, trust, alertness, energy, freshness, dedication, a complete lack of inhibition, honesty—it says everything. Look and listen. I think acting is a lot simpler than most people make it out to be."

1949: All the King's Men (Columbia). 1951: The Scarf (UA), Inside Straight (MGM), Lightning Strikes Twice (WB). 1954: Johnny Guitar (Republic). 1956: Giant (WB). 1957: A Farewell to Arms (TCF). 1958: Touch of Evil (Universal). 1959: Suddenly Last Summer (Columbia). 1960: Cimarron (MGM). 1961: Angel Baby (AA). 1965: Run Home Slow (Emerson). 1968: The Counterfeit Killer AKA Crack Shot (Universal), Deadly Sanctuary AKA Justine (Italian). 1969: 99 Women AKA Island of Despair, Isle of Lost Women (Commonwealth). 1972: The Other Side of the Wind (unreleased), Like a Crow on a June Bug AKA The Young Prey, Sixteen (Futurama), Killer by Night AKA The City by Night (CBS-TV), Two for the Money (ABC-TV). 1973: The Exorcist (WB) *voice only*, The Girls of Huntington House (ABC-TV), The President's Plane Is Missing (ABC-TV). 1975: Who Is the Black Dahlia? (NBC-TV). 1977: Thieves (Paramount). 1979: The Concorde: Airport '79 (Universal), The Sacketts (NBC-TV). 1983: Echoes (Continental).

Jane Russell: Body and Soul

by RAY HAGEN

"My favorite thing to do was sing, I enjoyed it more than anything else," Jane Russell told me in 1999, when we began a lengthy series of conversations about her life and career. Singing isn't what most people remember about Jane Russell.

In speaking with many of her old friends and musical colleagues, my own impression of Jane was confirmed. I'd detected a remarkably centered attitude about her sometimes rocky life and times, a bawdy and self-deprecating humor, and barely a trace of ego.

Jane became world-famous overnight in her first movie, a stardom based solely on her buxom figure and stunning appearance. It all could have died right there had she not worked hard to earn her stripes, becoming in the process an immensely likable screen presence and a fine singer with a breezy gift for comedy. Her large family and spiritual upbringing kept her level-headed and grounded, allowing her to weather her storms with wry amusement and without going "movie star nuts" when the going got rough.

Jane was not the first actress in her family. Her mother, Geraldine Jacobi, was taken on as an extra by George Arliss when his *Disraeli* played Boston and he subsequently hired her to tour in *Daddy Long Legs*. One of their stops was the Army camp in which First Lt. Roy Russell was stationed. They had first met in high school but hadn't seen each other in six years. Russell proposed, and three days later, on March 22, 1918, they were married in Kalamazoo, Michigan. She was 27.

After their firstborn, a son, died at 15 months old, Geraldine decided to return to the stage. But she again became pregnant and returned to her parents' home in Grand Forks, North Dakota. The Jacobis had a summer cottage in Bemidji, Minnesota, and it was there on June 21, 1921, that Jane Russell was born.

For years every bio of Jane has erroneously stated that her real name is Ernestine Jane Geraldine Russell. Nuh-uh. Jane explains, "Geraldine was my mother and Ernestine was her sister, my aunt. My name was just Jane Russell. I was never called Ernestine, never was supposed to be."

After some failed business ventures, Mr. Russell was hired as an office manager in the Los Angeles office of the Andrew Jergens Co. They bought a home in Burbank, and had four more children—Tommy (1924), Kenny ('25), Jamie ('27) and Wally ('29). The family moved to Van Nuys in 1932. Jane grew up as a skinny, gangly, bossy tomboy. She also learned to play piano and, with her brothers, formed a family band.

"I always loved music and we all took music lessons of one kind or another," says Jane. Jazz music was her passion and her idols included Ella Fitzgerald, Anita O'Day, Count Basie, Duke Ellington and Benny Goodman.

Jane played the lead in Van Nuys High's production of *Shirt Sleeves*, sang in the glee club, and got to know her soon-to-be husband. "Robert Waterfield was a year older but was two years ahead of me in school," she recalls. "The first time I sang solo in public was with the high school band, it was "Deep Purple." I was a senior and he was out of school, but he'd heard I was gonna do it so he came and stood in the back of the auditorium. I guess he was impressed. *I* was impressed, I'd never sung in public before." They soon began dating.

"Jane and I met in eighth grade," says her schoolmate and lifelong friend Jack Singlaub. "We were in the same class. Her

Portrait of Jane Russell, 1950.

high school boyfriend, Bob Waterfield, was one semester ahead of us. We also took a wonderful drama class at Van Nuys High. We'd all been struggling from the impact of the Depression and we didn't have a great deal, but being in extended families made us really tight and cooperative. Jane had four brothers and was a big tomboy. She'd always be involved in athletics with the guys, touch football, whatever. Jane's mother was a very practical person, and at one point our Bible teacher. Jane had a good religious background, and that was a great help."

Jane's first ambition was to be a dress designer, but her father's death in 1937, following a gallstone operation, forced her to take a $10-a-week job as a chiropodist's receptionist. She was soon able to supplement her salary by modeling dresses, coats and hats for photographer Tom Kelley (who later won fame for his calendar shots of Marilyn Monroe). Kelley taught her the basics of poise and presence for the camera and, upon seeing the photos, Jane saw to her surprise that she was no longer a lanky tomboy.

"It was a long time before Jane realized she was a girl," says Jack Singlaub.

One day in 1940 she stopped at Max Reinhardt's Theatrical Workshop to see a friend and decided to enroll. After one term there she shifted to Mme. Maria Ouspenskaya's school for six months.

Tom Kelley arranged for her to take some screen tests. "Kelley sent me to do a test at Fox," says Jane. "They told him I was un-photogenic. Then I went to Paramount and they said I was too tall. Maybe for Alan Ladd."

But her modeling paid off. Agent Levis Green saw and swiped one of Kelley's photos of Jane and took it to a few film studios and eventually to Howard Hughes, who was searching for an unknown team to star in his new Billy the Kid western, *The Outlaw*. Hughes was then a famous aviator who had dabbled in making independent movies since the late 1920s and had made Jean Harlow a star in his 1930 smash *Hell's Angels*. The multi-millionaire bachelor was also well known for romancing the most desirable actresses in Hollywood, and had now decided to create a new Harlow. He liked Jane's photo and had her tested with Jack Buetel in the haystack fight scene. Almost 200 girls and boys were tested before Hughes announced that his two new stars were Jack Buetel and Jane Russell. She received a seven-year contract and a starting salary of $50 a week.

The Outlaw began shooting on location in Moencopi (near Yuma) Arizona in 1941 under the direction of Howard Hawks, but Hughes' micromanaging of the production drove the veteran director crazy and he walked off the picture, leaving the inexperienced Hughes to direct. Hughes "didn't know how to tell you what it was he wanted," Jane said in 2000 on the TCM documentary, *Howard Hughes: His Women and His Movies*. "It was nothing to have 50 takes of any simple little scene. We took nine months to make that picture and it should have been made in about eight weeks."

Hughes had hired publicist Russell Birdwell to give Jane Russell "the build-up." For two years Jane spent every weekday from nine to five posing for publicity stills, usually with the camera aimed down her blouse. Her picture appeared on almost every magazine cover short of *Popular Mechanics*. Said Jane: "When I was on location for the picture, they started giving me the buildup. I christened boats, I judged baby contests, I reclined in haystacks, I sprawled on beaches, always in a low-cut blouse. They sold me like a can of tomatoes. There were at least 15 photographers out there. They'd say, 'Come on, Janie, bend over and pick up those two pails,' and they're aiming down to my navel. A few days before Hawks left, one of the photographers had gotten loaded and he and the unit director wanted me to jump up and down on a bed in a nightgown. I knew something was wrong so I went to Hawks and I was crying, and he said, 'Listen, you're a big girl now and you are responsible for yourself. If you don't like something, you say *no*, loud and clear.' From then on, if I didn't like what they were doing I'd just say 'No.'"

A photo session was booked with legendary Hollywood glamour photographer George Hurrell, who had a few bales of hay delivered to his studio for the occasion. Hurrell found Jane to be a friendly young girl with an experienced model's ease before the camera. He had her lolling in the hay wearing a short skirt and a tight, scoop-necked blouse and it's impossible to count how many stills were made that day. She lay back, leaned forward, turned this way and that, chewed on apples and hay stalks, sneered sullenly (even smiled once or twice) and brandished pistols, exuding attitude to burn. "Hurrell wasn't trying to get just filth," says Jane, "he was trying for something that fit the picture. He was a very nice guy." Those stills have become among the most iconic images in film history and are being reproduced to this day.

Obsessed with how Jane's chest photographed, Hughes designed a special brassiere for her to wear that wouldn't show any seams under her jersey blouse. He had inadvertently invented the first seamless bra but Jane tried it on once, found it extremely uncomfortable ("It was a contraption!"), ditched it, put some Kleenex over her own bra to mask the seams and never told Hughes.

The Hays office disapproved of Jane's cleavage, in the ads as well as in the film. Most of the promos used the Hurrell haystack photos, or cartoonish exaggerations of them. Beside her glowering countenance blazed the words "Mean, Moody and Magnificent." As Jane now explains it, "That glowering expression on my face? I'm thinking, 'What a bore!'"

One scene from the film showed Jane leaning over Billy's bed, accidentally revealing way more cleavage than had yet been seen in an American movie. Cinematographer Gregg Toland reshot the scene, but Hughes insisted that the first take be used. That scene was one of the major reasons for the Johnston Office's objections to the film. Hughes refused to make any of the 108 cuts demanded and fought all attempts to censor *The Outlaw*, realizing full well the value of publicity. As late as 1949, when the film finally had a nationwide release, Baltimore Judge E. Paul Mason commented: "Miss Russell's breasts hung like a thunderstorm over a summer landscape."

It was only when Jane returned to L.A. that she became aware of what had been going on. "That's when I saw what the photographers had been doing out on location," she says. "Here were all these magazines with all this crap in them, and I just wanted to puke. I was upset, my mother was upset, my aunt was upset. She even went to see Howard Hughes about it."

Jane had suddenly, overnight, become an internationally known movie star, a punchline for countless jokes and one of World War II's most popular pin-ups, without ever having been seen in a movie.

She continued dating Bob Waterfield on and off, and in 1942 found herself pregnant. Waterfield assumed he was the father but Jane wasn't so sure. This was highly scandalous in 1942, and Jane opted to have an illegal "back alley abortion." It was a hellish experience, and left her unable to bear children. Waterfield stuck by her, but they again separated and began dating others. Jane had a rather serious affair with actor John Payne, but she and Waterfield soon reconciled.

The Outlaw opened in San Francisco in February 1943, playing for only eight weeks. Despite poor reviews, it coined a mint. Hughes had made some minor concessions and managed to get the all-important Seal of Approval from the Johnston Office. He had Jane doing personal appearances at the theatre between showings to beef up the box office. "We did nine shows a day and I was playing straight for a comedian," she explains. "All the posters were up and the Catholic Church was saying that if you go to see that picture, you're out of the church. I didn't like what was going on, I hated the posters, I hated the whole thing. I said, 'I'm not going to do this any more,' and I left and went home." When Jane bolted, Hughes yanked the film with no public explanation.

Jane and Waterfield promptly eloped to Las Vegas and were married on April 24, 1943. Waterfield was then star quarterback for the UCLA football team (and for some years thereafter the Cleveland and L.A. Rams) and was an even bigger star in his field than Jane was in hers. When he was inducted into the Army, Jane followed him to Fort Benning at Columbus, Georgia. Hughes made her sign an agreement that she wouldn't work for any other studio or follow her husband if he were sent overseas and put her on suspension (she had been raised to $75 a week). In Columbus, she worked in a beauty parlor and for the local war bond drive under her married name.

"When she did that one movie, it changed everything," says Jack Singlaub. "I was in a parachute regiment at Fort Benning when Bob was in the infantry school, and I asked her if she'd like to come out and visit our regiment. She did, and that was a major public relations effort for us. Getting pictures with Jane Russell was a really big deal. I was just in the background and it was amusing seeing these senior officers stumbling over themselves being nice to Jane."

When Waterfield was given a medical discharge in 1945, they returned to California. Jane told Hughes she was ready to return to work and he loaned her to producer Hunt Stromberg for *Young Widow,* a routine sudser about a mopey war widow in which Jane mostly wore tailored suits. Her performance was reasonably pleasant but despite reams of here-she-is-at-last publicity, the film tanked.

Young Widow (1946) started with William Dieterle directing but he was soon replaced by Andre de Toth (who was himself replaced by Edwin L. Marin). While at work on the film, a chance meeting with de Toth's young secretary, Portia Nelson, turned Jane's career (as well as Nelson's) in an entirely different direction. "During breaks I'd go into one of the music studios to doodle around on the piano," says Jane. "One day Portia heard me and asked me if I knew a certain song. I didn't, so she sat down and played it, and I said, 'You can play anything in any key, I oughta slap you into next week!' That's how we found out about each other's singing. I told her she should never work as a secretary again as long as she lived."

The Outlaw was given a limited release in a few cities in 1946. The ads still emphasized what Jane had become famous for but had a new line of copy, "How'd You Like to Tussle with Russell?" Also quoted was Judge Twain Michelsen's remark to the San Francisco jury which acquitted the film of the charge of indecency: "We have seen Jane Russell. She is an attractive specimen of American womanhood. God made her what she is. Life is sordid and obscene to those who find it so." Which sounds like something Russell Birdwell might have written.

Jane went to New York to do some in-person appearances with *The Outlaw,* and Portia Nelson came along with her. "I took her to the Blue Angel," says Jane, "and I told the owner, Herbert Jacoby, 'You've gotta hear this girl sing,' Of course she ended up not only singing there, but she broke all records."

Portia Nelson was thus launched on a lifelong career as a highly respected cabaret and recording artist. "Jane's the best friend I ever had," she told me shortly before her death in 1999. "I don't know what I would have done without her."

During the Chicago run of *The Outlaw* at the Oriental Theatre, Jane was playing straight woman to comedian Jimmy Connally, singing a few bars here and there as he clowned around on the piano. Jane was anxious to do some real singing but Howard Hughes was extremely doubtful that his star could cut it until Portia Nelson convinced him that Jane was indeed a very good singer, and that he had no business letting her be made a fool of by a silly comic. Says Jane, "Hughes was so nervous

Bob Hope and Jane in *The Paleface* (Paramount, 1948).

and scared about it. But the theater manager asked me if I knew some more songs. I said, 'Sure, I know a lot of them,' and he said, 'Well, pick three, because that's what you're going to do. Jimmy's on the train, on his way back to L.A.' So I started singing. Portia, who was responsible for all this, ran from the wings into the bathroom and threw up afterward because she was so nervous. I wasn't a bit nervous. I just figured, well, if I make a mistake I'll just start over."

It came as a surprise to many when, in 1947, glamazon Jane Russell began appearing weekly as a singer on bandleader Kay Kyser's popular radio show for about three months. Who knew? Kyser also used her as a vocalist on a couple of his Columbia singles, which led them to offer her a solo album, released as *Let's Put Out the Lights*. Jane wanted to sing jazz but for these recordings she instead sang in a soft, romantic, occasionally bouncy pop style "because that's what the company wanted."

Still under personal contract with Howard Hughes, Jane got lucky when Paramount asked for her to co-star with Bob Hope in *The Paleface* (1948), which became Hope's biggest hit outside of the *Road* pictures. Unlike many of his leading ladies, Jane's character, Calamity Jane, actually drove the film's plot, with Hope serving as *her* foil. Her strong presence and deadpan comic delivery surprised the public and ideally suited Hope's style. They got on well together, not only in the film but subsequently in many stage and TV appearances. *The Paleface* gave some much-needed legitimacy to Jane's film career, as she freely acknowledges to this day. Hope told a critical friend who dismissed Jane as a mere sexpot: "Don't let her fool you. Tangle with her and she'll shingle your attic."

One of the reasons Jane had such a wonderful time making *The Paleface* was because it was the first movie she'd made that had just one director from beginning to end. Making movies, she discovered, could actually be fun. "I felt like I'd died and gone to Heaven."

Also in 1948, Hughes loaned her out to producer Howard Welsch for *Montana Belle*, a routine Republic Western. Jane starred as an improbable Belle Starr, who robbed banks and ran a saloon. "It was a dreadful picture," says Jane. "I said to the director, Allan Dwan, 'What does she do in this saloon, does she sing?,' and he sez, 'Well, can you sing? Good, sing a song.' So I said, 'Well, I happen to know a song that would be very good for this and I know the gal who wrote it.' So I dragged Portia Nelson in and had her sing him the song." Thus Belle Starr became a saloon singer, performing "The Man in the Moon" and Nelson's "The Gilded Lily." The latter was a bright number sung very well by Jane, but without the help of a choreographer she looked fairly awkward performing it. She gave her friend's song an additional boost by recording it as well. Hughes bought the film from Republic and put it on the shelf for four years.

Also in 1948 (by which time Hughes had taken over the troubled RKO studio) Jane did a limp comedy, *It's Only Money*, co-starring with Frank Sinatra and Groucho Marx, both then in the midst of their lowest career slumps. Jane played the girlfriend of bumbling bank teller Sinatra. When the film was finally released three years later, Sinatra (whom Hughes disliked) found himself dropped from first to third billing—raising Jane to first—and he was otherwise ignored in the ads, which pictured Groucho ogling Jane's V-zone. Lest anyone missed the point, Hughes had changed the film's title to *Double Dynamite*. Russell and Sinatra sang a duet of "Kisses and Tears," which they later recorded for Columbia.

Early in 1949 Jane won favorable attention by singing "Buttons and Bows" at the Academy Award ceremonies. It had been sung by Hope in *The Paleface* and won the Oscar for Best Song of 1948.

She and Hope were a great success in 1950 when they played an in-person engagement at New York City's Paramount Theatre, and Jane's voice got almost as much attention as where it came from. In addition to playing the Paramount, she made a personal appearance at the Broadway theater that was showing *The Outlaw*, then in its first full-scale national release. It was revealed to be an innocuous and rather tacky little affair and received predictably scathing reviews, but, thanks to nine years of non-stop publicity, was a box office bonanza.

Hughes decided to put Jane to work as an RKO star and she filmed three black-and-white, *noir*-edged adventure yarns in a row. In each she played essentially the same role, a down-on-her-luck saloon singer who'd been around too many blocks too many times, but with a gritty knack for survival. First came *His Kind of Woman* (released in '51), a sprawling, humorous action saga in which she was teamed with RKO contract star Robert Mitchum. She was merely, as she says, "the girl in the piece," but she and Mitchum were a perfect match and their flinty banter proved that Jane could easily hold her own in strong company. Although Hughes saw to it that she was costumed in the tightest and lowest-cut outfits possible, and photographed to maximize the obvious, she never appeared for a moment to take herself or her physique at all seriously. By now, "Hughes was finally convinced I could sing and wasn't afraid of it any more," so she had two pleasant songs amid the mayhem, "You'll Know" and "Five Little Miles from San Berdoo," performed with professional ease. Mitchum's on-screen assessment of these musical interludes is a flippant, "I've heard better but you sound like you do it for a living." In 1951 she cut four sides for London Records, including her two songs from *His Kind of Woman.*

She did more of the same in two 1952 releases. *The Las Vegas Story* was a dud and Victor Mature was hardly in Mitchum's laconic league, but Jane was spotlighted nicely singing a pair of appealing Hoagy Carmichael standards, "I Get Along Without You Very Well" and a duet with Carmichael of "My Resistance Is Low."

Macao, re-teaming her with Mitchum (they became friends for life), contained enough Mitchum-Russell bickering to keep things fairly lively, but was an unhappy experience for audiences, critics and cast. Jane says that director Josef von Sternberg "came to RKO to divide and conquer. We were all like family at RKO, including the crews. He was very rude to the crew, wouldn't allow any food or drink on the set, not a Coke, not anything. He'd come to me and say something nasty about Mitch, then go to Mitch and say something about me, like 'What are we going to do about this stupid girl?' Finally he was thrown off the picture. Nick Ray was a good buddy of ours, so he and Mitch re-wrote it and Nick directed it. Mitch was a wonderful writer. He and Nick wrote the best parts of that movie. Anything that sounds at all natural is what they wrote."

Again Jane was given two songs, a bright original number, "You Kill Me," and the classic "One for My Baby." For the latter, Hughes had her tightly encased in a highly publicized 26-pound mesh gown which seemed to be sprayed on. Hughes' obsessive preoccupation with Jane's anatomy, especially her breasts, was the subject of countless memos, and the results all but obliterated any chances Jane might have had to be seen as anything other than a sullen sexpot. Yet she had by now become quite popular, and reporters couldn't write enough about her.

In the midst of this turgid trio, Hughes finally released *Double Dynamite* and *Montana Belle.* They came and went without a blink.

On June 21, 1951, the Waterfields adopted the first of their three children, a newly born girl they named Tracy. Later that year, Jane and her mother went to England where Jane was presented to the Royal Family. She was at that time looking to adopt an older brother for her new daughter and went to orphanages in five different countries, seeing countless war orphans who would never be adopted. Mrs. Michael Kavanaugh, wife of a struggling carpenter foreman and the mother of three children, offered her one-month-old son Tommy to Jane to bring to the U.S. so he could "get a good home and a fine education." The British Child Adoption Act forbade the adoption of a British subject by foreigners who are not blood relations, but Jane was allowed to bring the boy home as a visitor and the Kavanaughs were not penalized by the British Courts. The U.S. courts later allowed the Waterfields to adopt Tommy legally. Newspapers here and abroad gave the story relentless coverage.

It was this experience which taught Jane about all the obstacles and red tape hindering adoptions worldwide and led to her founding the Women's Adoption

International Fund (WAIF) to legally allow American couples to adopt foreign orphans, since a sufficient number of American children were not available here for adoption. Later merged with International Social Service, WAIF eventually provided homes for over 51,000 orphans from all parts of the world, and it became what she's always considered her life's work. In a 1985 interview for *Lifestyles of the Rich and Famous* she said, "I think if I hadn't done *The Outlaw* and those kind of pictures, and had that kind of image, I wouldn't have been nearly as successful with WAIF. People would come out of sheer curiosity, then hear the story of WAIF and most of them would get hooked." She tirelessly used her celebrity to raise funds for and lobby Congress on adoption rights for the next 40 years before formally retiring from WAIF. "I really didn't do it all by myself," she said. "Somebody had to start it but we had marvelous volunteers that helped put it together while I went knocking on doors."

Bob Hope once again came to Jane's professional rescue. Paramount borrowed her for a sequel to *The Paleface, Son of Paleface* (1952), which proved to be almost as popular as the original. Jane was "The Torch," once more a bandit queen by day and a saloon singer by night, but this time with an actual choreographer, Josephine Earl, to help out. Her big saloon number, "Wing Ding," presented her in striped tights, mesh hose, opera-length gloves and a big picture hat and she socked the number over with assurance and humor, looking nothing less than spectacular. "Buttons and Bows," sung solo by Hope in *Paleface*, was amusingly reprised here as a trio (Hope, Jane and Roy Rogers), and she had a comic duet with Hope of "Am I in Love?" Again, a happy experience all around and a good career boost after her string of RKO melodramas. Hope and Jane cut duets of "Wing Ding" and "Am I in Love?" as a Capitol single.

That year she also did an unbilled cameo in the latest of the Hope-Crosby-Lamour *Road* series, *Road to Bali*, popping up in a fantasy sequence at the end. Just as Lamour rejects Hope and chooses to go off with Crosby, Jane magically appears from out of nowhere in her "Wing Ding" showgirl getup, to Hope's delight. But Jane takes Crosby's other arm and he walks off with both babes.

In vivid contrast to her entire 1940s output (three movies in nine years), between 1950 and 1952 Jane was seen in seven films. And the best was right around the bend.

In 1951, Twentieth Century-Fox bought the film rights to Anita Loos' 1925 novel *Gentlemen Prefer Blondes*, which had become a hit Broadway musical in 1949. Fox head Darryl F. Zanuck intended it as a vehicle for their '40s box office queen Betty Grable, but by 1952 Grable was on her way down and there was a new blonde on the lot, one Marilyn Monroe, who was definitely headed upward. Zanuck decided to cast her as Lorelei. Howard Hawks, set to direct, saw this as a way to finally work with Jane. Zanuck had scant faith in Monroe's musical abilities and wanted some insurance, so he approved Hawks' suggestion to borrow Jane from Howard Hughes for $200,000. She would play Dorothy Shaw, Lorelei's best friend. Dorothy had been a fairly minor character up to now, so her role was considerably beefed up and Hughes specified that Jane would have first billing.

Jane, for her part, was overjoyed that she'd finally get to work with Hawks. He'd walked off *The Outlaw* 11 years earlier before ever getting the chance to direct her, but he'd liked her from the start. Says Jane, "Before he got on his plane and left, he said to Jack Buetel and me, 'Now, don't worry, kids, we'll work together one day.'"

The press eagerly anticipated on-set fireworks between the Blowtorch Blonde and the Haystack Brunette, but they got on famously. Marilyn was then dating Joe DiMaggio and, since Jane was married to a football superstar, Marilyn wanted all kinds of advice from her on what life with a sports hero would be like.

Hawks decided to update the story to the present and went all out to make it the gaudiest and glitziest glamathon possible. Released in '53, it was a whopping success and Jane, in the traditionally thankless role of "best friend," all but walked off with it. Russell and Monroe were a dream team, both on- and off-camera, and even critics who thought the

Jane sings "Ain't There Anyone Here for Love?" to preoccupied gymnasts in *Gentlemen Prefer Blondes* (Fox, 1953).

play had been unnecessarily vulgarized poured raves on the dazzling duo. Hawks later said that whenever the script hit a dry spot, he'd just film another long tracking shot of the two girls walking.

It was while filming *Gentlemen Prefer Blondes* that Jane first worked with two men who would have a pivotal influence on her future work: the legendary Broadway dancer-choreographer Jack Cole and musical arranger Hal Schaefer.

The dance numbers were directed entirely by Cole. "*Gentlemen Prefer Blondes* was mainly fun because of Howard Hawks and Jack Cole," says Jane. "I dearly loved Jack, he was just a doll to work with. He beat his dancers, but with Marilyn and me he had the patience of Job, because he knew that neither of us were dancers. He was so patient it was not to be believed."

"I first met Jane on *Gentlemen Prefer Blondes*," says Hal Schaefer. "I'd been at Fox for about 12 years and was assigned to that movie. I didn't get screen credit, but those were all my arrangements. Jane loved good pop and jazz music and we had very similar tastes, so we got to be friends. She wanted to be a better singer, so I started coaching her. Before that I'd been working with singers like Peggy Lee and Billy Eckstine. I'd always thought of Jane as a movie star glamour girl, I didn't know about her singing, but in *Gentlemen* she showed a lot of talent, especially with that take-off on Marilyn. She surprised and impressed me and we've been friends ever since."

Jane duetted with Monroe on "Two Little Girls from Little Rock" and "When Love Goes Wrong," soloed on "Bye Bye Baby," did a wicked send-up of Marilyn's "Diamonds Are a Girl's Best Friend," and pulled out all the stops with her big number, "Ain't There Anyone Here for Love?" This was set in a ship's gym with a full chorus of actual Olympic athletes who paid way more attention to their muscles than to the Junoesque brunette trying vainly to catch their attention. The number ends with one of the divers causing Jane to take a header into the ship's pool. This was an accident and the correct ending was later filmed, but the mistake worked so well they used that take for the final cut.

Jane and Marilyn were accorded the honor of putting their hand and footprints in cement at the forecourt of Grauman's Chinese Theatre on June 26, 1953. The ceremony was lavishly photographed for the newsreels and showed the co-stars looking gleeful and gorgeous in their light summer dresses. Marilyn told Jane she thought their most famous features should be immortalized, rather than their hands and feet, by Jane leaning over into the cement and Marilyn sitting in it.

"Lookin' for Trouble," and finding it, in *The French Line* (RKO, 1953).

But, as always, one step forward, two steps back. When she returned to RKO, Howard Hughes decided to cash in on Jane's great success in *Blondes* by giving her her very own shipboard musical. *The French Line* turned out to be a dreary potpourri of necklines and nonsense shot in 3-D, and as usual Hughes missed no chance to put the focus right back on Jane's chest at every opportunity. The script even had her best pal (played by Broadway veteran Mary McCarty) address her as "Chesty." Jane played a Texas millionairess who feared that every man she met would only be interested in her money. Yeah, right.

Her mediocre songs included "Any Gal from

Texas," a duet with McCarty, "What Is This That I Feel?," "Well I'll Be Switched" and a bawdy bump-and-grind routine, "Lookin' for Trouble."

Jane's costume for the latter was a one-piece black satin affair with three big panels cut out of the midriff with spangles added to what was left. This bizarre outfit was a compromise, Jane having refused to wear the teeny-weenie bikini first handed her. But thanks to the way the song was presented, the Motion Picture Association refused its Production Code seal to the film. Just as Jane was beginning to shake off her old *Outlaw* image, a whole new censorship brouhaha erupted.

No longer afraid to speak up, Jane herself loudly and publicly agreed that cuts should be made. "I don't object to the dance scene itself," she was quoted as saying, "but some of the camera angles are in horrible taste. I had an awful time with some of the things they wanted me to wear—hardly anything at all. I fought and beefed and argued over several scenes. I don't like the accent on sex and never have." The press ate it up.

The French Line opened late in 1953 without a seal and was promptly withdrawn. In the original version, which I saw on its opening day, the camerawork for "Lookin' for Trouble" was tightly and closely focused almost entirely on Jane's bouncing, overflowing and under-covered breasts, and in 3-D yet. A somewhat edited version played the country in 1954 and was unanimously panned. "Lookin' for Trouble" was now shown entirely in long shot, and that's the version that plays on TV today. Without the mammary distractions, it can now be seen as a silly but very well-performed number, Jane's moves and steps now those of an experienced musical professional.

The ads blatantly capitalized on all the publicity: "*That* dance you've heard so much about!" and "J.R. in 3-D ... it'll knock *both* your eyes out!"

By this time, what with the *French Line* censorship wars, magazines and newspapers were going positively bonkers over the contrast between the dazzling on-screen Censorship Queen and the off-screen Jane Russell Waterfield. No born-again Christian, her spiritual foundation had been solidly in place since childhood. Jane and her brothers had built the non-denominational Chapel in the Valley in Los Angeles for their mother, who was its pastor. She had helped found the Hollywood Christian Group. She was still married to her high school sweetheart and was the mother of two children. She had founded WAIF and was its chief mover and fund-raiser. But now that sort of public attention would soar into unprecedented overdrive.

In 1954 Jane embarked on an unexpectedly successful venture with popular singers Beryl Davis and Connie Haines, all members of the Hollywood Christian Group. That all three were at their peak of success didn't deter them from embarking upon a career-within-a-career for all three, to everyone's amazement including their own. As they recalled the saga:

BERYL: "I was a member of St. Stephen's Church in Hollywood. The church needed money for a new roof, and they turned to me. I was then married to disc jockey Peter Potter so it was easy to find friends who sang. Connie had a church background and Jane had a very religious background and I knew she liked to sing. When I sang on *Your Hit Parade* with Andy Russell, I knew his wife, Della, and she sang a little, so she came along."

JANE: "At the charity benefit I said, 'Well, Connie, you're gonna sing, but what are we gonna do?' and when she said we could just greet the audience, I said, 'Well, that's ridiculous, why don't we just sing?' So Connie and I taught Beryl and Della 'Do Lord' and the four of us harmonized."

BERYL: "We went down to the basement below the stage and we learned 'Do Lord' in like three minutes. We went upstairs and closed the show with that. Well, it was a *smash*, all four of us on stage, you know, very glamourous group."

CONNIE: "I'd invited the A & R man from Coral Records to the church benefit and he was in the audience. He was so excited."

BERYL: "He came backstage and said, 'That was great, would you like to record that?' We said, 'Okay, if we can find the time.' We all had our own thing going and were terribly busy. So we picked out a few tunes, went in and recorded 'Do Lord.'"

JANE: "When Beryl's husband put the record on *Peter Potter's Platter Parade*, to decide if the song was a hit or a miss, Dinah Washington said, 'That is the most sacrilegious thing I ever heard,' but Ernie Kovacs said, 'That's terrific, that's definitely a hit.' Those were the two extremes we got."

BERYL: "So of course following that they said that now we've got to record some more. In the meantime, Della ran into some personal problems and asked us if we could find someone else. Rhonda Fleming loved to sing and wanted people to know she *could* sing, so our second recording session was with Rhonda. All the publicity about *The French Line* started at about that time and Jane was being severely criticized so the timing couldn't have been better, or worse, depending on your point of view. The publicity was fabulous [*laughs*]—I mean it was wacko. The censor wouldn't give it a clearance, and here we were singing spirituals and *this woman* is doing this movie that's being censored! The dichotomy attracted all the newspaper people and all the TV shows wanted us. Then Rhonda had to leave and we went to Capitol and did another album as a trio. We were doing four-part harmony and now we had to switch to three-part. Connie stuck to the melody but Jane and I had to learn all new parts."

JANE: "We played Vegas and started touring all around the country. We had our piano man and a drummer, sometimes a bass man, so there'd be the six of us, and we just had a ball."

CONNIE: "People didn't know Jane could sing, she was 'just a movie star.' Jane and Beryl had natural ears for harmony but I'm strictly a lead singer. We all sang together 'til, would you believe, 1984. We gave 15 percent to WAIF and gave to our individual churches too. We were godmothers to each other's kids. In all those years we never had a major disagreement. We all still talk frequently, we're like sisters."

BERYL: "We kept together through husbands, divorces and babies. I listen every once in awhile to those records and they sound wonderful, really good. I can hardly believe that we got so organized to sing harmony parts. I'd do it again in a minute."

After "Do Lord" became a million-seller, the quartet made three more singles for Coral, billing themselves as The Four Girls. All eight sides were then released as an LP album titled *Make a Joyful Noise* (four songs with Della Russell, four with Fleming). In addition, Jane recorded three more double-sided Coral pop singles on her own. After re-forming as a trio, they signed with Capitol Records to do an album called *Jane, Connie and Beryl: The Magic of Believing* (1957). By then they had added many popular songs to their repertoire as well as some self-deprecating special material spoofing their public images.

In the midst of all this, Jane somehow continued making movies. *Underwater!* was released in 1955 and had Jane swimming toward the audience from all directions in a red bathing suit. Its Florida premiere was actually held underwater as a publicity stunt. Jane, in swimsuit, aqua lung and flippers, watched it unreel with some of the hardier critics way down below. "I've had to do everything else," she remarked at the time, "I might as well do this." But for all the hoopla, the film itself was merely a standard sea adventure in which Jane had considerable trouble sustaining a Spanish accent.

This was her last film for RKO, Howard Hughes having sold the studio after completing *Underwater!* Her contract with him would soon expire, but he proposed a new and extraordinary contract that, despite the advice of others not to re-sign with him, Jane found pretty hard to resist. It would cover six films to be made on loanout over a five-year span and giving Jane director approval, plus leaving her free to do anything else she wanted. It was a million-dollar contract with the payments to be spread out over 20 years at $1,000 a week. It provided Jane a degree of long-term financial security undreamed of when Hughes was paying her 50 bucks a week.

Meanwhile, an accident of timing cost her the chance to play singer Ruth Etting in *Love Me or Leave Me* (1955). As Jane explains, "MGM had offered me *Love Me or Leave Me*, but *I'll Cry Tomorrow* [Lillian Roth's biography] was being filmed at the same time so I couldn't do them both and I'd heard that Lillian Roth wanted me to play her. MGM wanted me to play Ruth Etting but I said I'd rather do the Roth thing. I guess nobody thought I could play such a wildly dramatic part, so they finally gave it to Susan Hayward. By that time they'd cast Doris Day in the other one, so that's the way it went." She regrets that she never got to work at MGM and would have loved playing opposite James Cagney in the Etting movie.

Instead, she was next seen as Jeff Chandler's troubled wife in *Foxfire* (1955), a middling B-level Universal drama in which she suffered mightily under a new and unbecoming short hairdo.

The Waterfields had formed their own production company, Russ-Field Productions, with Jane as chief asset and Bob Waterfield as executive producer. Their first production, which turned out to be a less-than-auspicious beginning, was *Gentlemen Marry Brunettes* (1955). Jane and Jeanne Crain starred as a pair of dizzy singing sisters in Paris. They sang a slew of hideously over-arranged standards (Anita Ellis dubbed Crain's voice) and the production numbers were garishly ugly. "Everything about that picture was overdone," says Jane, "or underdone, whatever. They were just doing it off the cuff, the whole thing, day by day. I knew there wasn't enough star power to make it go but there wasn't anything I could do about it. We had a good time 'cause we spent six months in Europe with Jack Cole, but we didn't make any money."

Upon returning to the States, she had the good fortune to be teamed opposite

Clark Gable in Fox's *The Tall Men*, her final 1955 release. It was a good, big, rowdy Western in which she amusingly drawled a folksy number called "I Want a Tall Man" at four different points during the story, each version with lyrics wryly mirroring the progress of her scrappy relationship with Gable. (In one of those sequences she was shown bathing outdoors in an old tub, but only from the shoulders up and without a hint of cleavage. No other studio exploited her figure in the crude manner that Hughes had always done.) She was convincingly strong, independent and outdoorsy in *The Tall Men*, and when at one point her hoyden character was forced to don a fancy red gown she actually seemed realistically uncomfortable and gawky in it. She loved working for director Raoul Walsh ("I adored Raoul, I called him my father and always phoned him on Father's Day"), and also got on happily with Gable. Their on-screen rapport was easy and credible, despite his being 20 years her senior. The film was a success and critics paid Jane favorable notice.

Film historian James Robert Parish, in his *The RKO Gals*, commented on the difference between her work at RKO and at other studios: "It was not simply a case of Jane seeming to be better than she really was because of slick technical production values and a more high-powered cast. She actually rose to the occasion in Grade-A surroundings. Her frequently vulgar screen image (more due to Hughes's structuring of her screen presentation than to Jane's own personality) lost much of its hard-boiled crude overtones when in classier company, and she was transfigured frequently into a more brittle character exhibiting confidence, ease and experience."

In 1956 the Waterfields adopted their third child, a nine-month-old boy. He was named Robert John, at least on the birth certificate. Since Bob Waterfield had been tagged "Buck" by his teammates, their new son was called Buck from the beginning.

Hot Blood (1956) cast Jane and Cornel Wilde as

Chicken dinner with Clark Gable in *The Tall Men* **(Fox, 1955).**

Hollywood's idea of a fiery gypsy couple. There wasn't much to it but Jane did have one excellent song, "I Could Learn to Love You." Jane sang the verse live, *a cappella*, during the filming, with her prerecorded vocal of the song proper, which she does *not* lip-synch, played over the soundtrack as the stars continue miming the action of the scene. The only song in the film, it was an interesting way to move the story along and was by far the classiest sequence in an otherwise pedestrian movie. Jane's brothers were played by her real-life brothers, Jamie and Wally. (Jamie had previously done a non-speaking bit in *Gentlemen Prefer Blondes*.)

She next played the title role in *The Revolt of Mamie Stover* (1956), again being directed by Raoul Walsh. Jane, in a red wig, played a prostitute who was kicked out of the U.S. and made a fortune as a wartime whore in Hawaii. But the movie was so watered down as to seem utterly inexplicable. Mamie's whorehouse was now a dance hall headed by a blonde-wigged Agnes Moorehead, who admonished her girls that they were to provide only dancing to the avid servicemen, nothing more. Why then was the "house" an illegal military scandal and Mamie so looked down upon by "decent" people? Censorship was still strongly in force in 1956, Howard Hughes notwithstanding. Jane's leading man was Richard Egan, who had also co-starred with her in *Underwater!* As with Hope, Mitchum, Walsh and Gable, Egan became a lifelong buddy.

Jane performed a silly song for her customers, "Keep Your Eyes on the Hands," which she recorded for Capitol. On the B-side she sang "If You Wanna See Mamie Tonight" (sung under the main titles of the film, but not by Jane).

The Fuzzy Pink Nightgown (1957) was a drab and unsuccessful comedy about a kidnapped movie actress, and Jane's first black-and-white movie in five years. Director Norman Taurog saw it as a Technicolor comedy while Jane envisioned a more suspenseful black-and-white drama. "It was just as much my fault as the director's," Jane now admits. "It would have been much better if either one of us had been the boss." A resounding critical and box office failure, it was Russ-Field's final production.

A much happier experience was singing with Bobby Troup's quartet in 1958. Troup was doing a series of programs on jazz music for the Armed Forces Radio Service (AFRS) and, knowing of Jane's interest in jazz, he invited her to sing on the show every day for a week. Without any film mogul or record company to dictate terms, she was free to sing whatever she wanted the way she wanted, and acetate recordings of the series reveal perhaps the most relaxed and assured singing she had yet done. "I loved doing those things with Bobby," she says.

Also in '58 she recorded an album of 12 songs for MGM Records titled *Jane Russell*. She now had the clout to sing in the heavily jazz-inflected, harder-edged style she'd always preferred, and comparing this LP to her Columbia album from 11 years before, it's hard to believe they were done by the same singer.

Throughout the '50s Jane had guested on the TV shows of Bob Hope, Ed Sullivan, Perry Como, Jack Paar, Dinah Shore, Steve Allen, Dick Cavett, David Frost et al., either by herself or with Connie Haines and Beryl Davis. She made a pilot film for a proposed TV series, *McCreedy's Woman* (1958), but though the pilot was aired the series wasn't picked up.

Soured on producing, free of RKO and not liking the B-grade roles she was now being offered, Jane took the opportunity to play club and theater engagements here and abroad. She alternated between doing trio gigs with Connie and Beryl and putting together an act of her own with two other old and dear friends.

"Jack Cole created an act for Jane and I became her musical director," says Hal Schaefer. "I wrote the arrangements and orchestrations, coached her, played piano and led the orchestra. We toured Italy, Spain, South America and Mexico. This was around the late '50s-early '60s. You cannot imagine how popular she was. Jane has wonderful rhythm and timing, swing was very natural with her. And a *very* good ear. Play something for her once and she's just about got it. When she sang with a big band behind her, she just *blew*. The public would never have thought how good she was. She had chops. She's the absolute best I've ever met. She's a very determined lady for good causes, like when she started WAIF, that's what I most appreciate about her. She's one of the most positive people I've ever had the pleasure of working with and being friends with."

And she hit the boards. She starred in *Janus* in 1959 on tour in New England, and over the years has starred in plays and musicals all over the country, including *Skylark* ('61), *Bells Are Ringing* ('62), *Catch Me If You Can* ('62, '70 and '74), *Pal Joey* ('65), *Here Today* ('68), *High Button Shoes* ('70) and *Mame* ('73).

There were even a few more movies. As a favor to producer Aaron Rosenberg she did a cameo as herself in *Fate Is the Hunter* (1964), singing "No Love, No Nothin'" to the soldiers in a WWII flashback sequence. She was a good friend of Rosenberg's wife, who had worked with Jane on WAIF. It was the last time she sang on screen.

In 1966 she was seen in two minor A.C. Lyles Paramount Westerns, *Johnny Reno* and *Waco*, about which the less said the better.

That year she also did a picture called *The Honorable Frauds*, directed by Jerry Shaw. It was a caper movie about a group of relatives trying to cash in on an inheritance. Jake LaMotta's people produced it in an effort to launch an acting career for him, and he co-starred with Jane. It was never released. "I'm glad it never came out," says Jane. "It was a flop."

She did a Tom Laughlin biker flick, *Born Losers* (1967), playing the sort of role Shelley Winters was then doing—the blowsy, overweight, hysterical mother of a teenage girl who'd been raped. This was the sort of glamour-free character role that Jane wanted to do more of, but it didn't lead to anything.

In 1967 Jane and Bob Waterfield were divorced after 25 years. There had been many separations, infidelities and too much drinking. "It was a pretty good marriage for 23 years," Jane told Larry King in 1985. "Then everything just changed and I couldn't cope. We were both drinking a lot and that certainly didn't help. Football players drink and most actors drink after the day is over. It's not a matter of drinking all day long, we never did that, but it got worse and the last year was just impossible. After several humiliations, I realized that I could not drink any more, it was affecting me differently than it ever had before. I got to where if I had a few drinks I didn't remember things. I don't know whether your chemistry changes or you get old or what it is. I prayed about it, and just stopped."

She married actor Roger Barrett on August 25, 1968. They'd met in Chicago earlier that year while appearing together on stage in *Here Today*. The marriage seemed to be going well when, on the morning of November 18, less than three months after their wedding, he had a heart attack and died right in front of her. He was 47. Jane was thrown into a massive depression and started drinking again.

Darker Than Amber (1970) was her last movie. She had hoped for a nice character role, but most of it was cut, leaving her with just a few seconds of screen time, calling out to Rod Taylor as their boats passed each other. A sad end to what was, for Jane, a rather frustrating film career.

There was a mere handful of films she was proud of (*Gentlemen Prefer Blondes*, the *Paleface* films, *The Tall Men*) although she always enjoyed the camaraderie on the sets and liked most of the folks she worked with. She had a mentor, but Howard Hughes had neither the imagination or the story sense to guide her career in a classier direction. While she was always loyal and grateful to Hughes and liked him personally (but never in any way romantically), she has to admit that his tunnel vision of her as a buxom sexpot limited her chances to develop as an actress. He'd made her wealthy and famous, but for reasons with which she was never comfortable.

In 1971, while starring in *Catch Me If You Can* at New Jersey's Meadowbrook Theatre, Jane went with her manager Kevin Pines to see *Company* on Broadway. She loved the play and adored Elaine Stritch as the acerbic Joanne who stopped every show with "The Ladies Who Lunch." When she went backstage to congratulate Stritch and the company, the stage manager informed Jane that Hal Prince was interested in having her take over the role of Joanne when Stritch left to appear in the London production. Prince got the idea while watching Jane on *The Dick Cavett Show* and had been trying to find her. She aced the audition and agreed to do it. But her depression over Roger Barrett's death was still hammering her, and knowing that she'd have only three-and-a-half weeks of rehearsal, along with the difficulties of learning Stephen Sondheim's complex score, threw her into such a panic she wound up in a hospital. But she pulled it all together, learned it, opened and played it for six months. The New York critics raved about Jane's Broadway debut.

But Sondheim threw her a curve. "I wanted to kill him," she says. "He came up to me on opening night and suggested that I sing everything on the beat, not like Elaine did it. And I thought, 'You dumb shit, why didn't you come to me three or four weeks ago and tell me how you'd like me to sing, not on opening night just before the performance?' I didn't pay any attention to him, who could at that point, you're a nervous wreck! So I did just what I'd been rehearsing."

Nerves and curves notwithstanding, *Company* was among Jane's most rewarding professional experiences.

Also in 1971, Jane began what turned out to be a pleasant and profitable association with Playtex, doing a long series of bra commercials "for us full-figured gals." To an entire younger generation, she is today remembered chiefly for those commercials. After 15 years, by which time models were allowed to be shown on TV actually wearing the bras (rather than only showing them on mannequins), she drew the line and quit.

On January 31, 1974, Jane married 49-year-old real estate developer and former Air Force bomber pilot John Calvin Peoples. It was the third marriage for each. Peoples already had a 24-year old son, John, Jr. (called Dude), and two stepdaughters. All quickly became a part of Jane's own family. Shortly after their marriage,

John had accompanied Jane while she toured in *Catch Me If You Can* for five months, and when it was over he told her that if she didn't want to work any more, she'd never have to. That sounded great to Jane and she happily took him up on it.

One evening in 1978, she slipped off the wagon and had a few drinks, waking up pretty shaky the next morning. Nonetheless she got in her car to drive to the store but had a nasty collision. Although no one was hurt, Jane was arrested. She immediately envisioned the headlines: Jane Russell Busted in Her Cups. She'd already been pulled over on a DUI two years before, and the judge took that into account and gave her four days in the slammer. To her mortification, this did indeed hit the papers.

For about ten years Jane did occasional TV interviews but no performing until she was asked to appear in a couple of episodes of NBC's contemporary Western series *The Yellow Rose* (1984). She liked the script and her role as Sam Elliott's mother, having long admired Elliott's work.

Jane had spent a few years on and off writing her memoirs and, in 1985, *Jane Russell: My Path and My Detours* was published. It was a warts-and-all account of her life, detailing every dizzying height and fall from grace with straight-on candor.

Her mother died during her book tour. For Jane, this was a grievous loss. Back in 1960, Geraldine Jacobi Russell had her own book published, *Oh, Lord, What Next?* It was a deeply religious but often funny memoir of her own eventful life and her large family, one of whom happened to be a controversial and glamourous movie star.

In 1998 Jane's marriage to John Peoples was in its twenty-fourth year when, as he was helping his son construct an add-on garage to their home, he suddenly collapsed and died of a heart attack right in front of her (just as her second husband had 30 years earlier). Jane's high school friend Jack Singlaub had remained in touch with her over the years and had become close to John Peoples as well. "It's really been a shock to lose John," he told me in 1999, "because he was such an important part of Jane's daily activities. He was looking after her, taking care of all her managing activities. I don't know if she'll ever get back to normal."

"Jane, John, my wife Brenda and myself were supposed to go on a cruise together," says Hal Schaefer. "Jane and I were going to lecture and then I'd play a few things for Jane to sing. John had set this up. He and I had many conversations about it and were looking forward to it but John died a week before the cruise. Jane and I are in constant touch. She's very strong and deeply spiritual and she'll just go straight ahead until she joins the movie stars in the sky. I admire her greatly."

Jane didn't want to continue living in that house and was making plans to sell it when, in March 2000, her beloved stepson Dude (John Peoples, Jr.) also suddenly died of a heart attack, at age 50. "It was ghastly," says Jane. "I got drunk, stayed that way and ended up in the hospital. All my family came and stood around my bed and said that I was to go into rehab for a month. I spent 30 days in rehab, came home, and have been okay since then." During that month, her son Buck and his wife Etta moved all Jane's things into her new home in Santa Maria, California. Buck is now his mother's business manager.

By 2003, she'd started singing again. "I recently decided we should have something fun to do here in Santa Maria," she says. "Something for people over 39. There was a restaurant nearby where we started singing '40s songs with a good piano man, he's the only one who gets paid. It's like a piano bar, people just get up and sing. Most of the people in the audience are older folks who know all the '40s songs, and they grin from ear to ear."

Apart from occasionally appearing on TV talk shows, often with Larry King, and as an interviewee on various movie-themed documentaries, Jane now has no special desire to resume performing because "I'm too lazy. I'll do interviews, that's fine, as long as I don't have to learn lines. That didn't bother me while I was doing it, but 'use it or lose it' and I haven't been using it so I've lost it."

Mother of three children, grandmother of 15 and great-grandmother of ten, she keeps close to her extended family and lives in happily lazy semi-retirement. She's recently been diagnosed with macular degeneration and is part of a research program to help find a cure.

As Jane concisely puts it, "I've had an interesting life."

1943: The Outlaw (RKO). **1946:** Young Widow (UA). **1948:** The Paleface (Paramount). **1951:** His Kind of Woman (RKO), Double Dynamite (RKO). **1952:** Macao (RKO), The Las Vegas Story (RKO), Son of Paleface (Paramount), Road to Bali (Paramount), Montana Belle (Republic/RKO). **1953:** Gentlemen Prefer Blondes (TCF), The French Line (RKO). **1955:** Underwater! (RKO), Foxfire (Universal), The Tall Men (TCF), Gentlemen Marry Brunettes (UA), Hot Blood (Columbia). **1956:** The Revolt of Mamie Stover (TCF). **1957:** The Fuzzy Pink Nightgown (UA). **1964:** Fate Is the Hunter (TCF). **1966:** Johnny Reno (Paramount), Waco (Paramount), The Honorable Frauds AKA Cauliflower Cupids (unreleased). **1967:** Born Losers (AIP). **1970:** Darker Than Amber (National General).

Ann Sheridan: Oomph Without Ego

by RAY HAGEN

Few big stars were as genuinely *likable* as Ann Sheridan. It took her six years to work her way up from bit player to full-fledged star, and that was mostly the result of a silly publicity gimmick. Her studio, Warner Bros., packaged her as a sharp-tongued, smoldering siren, but she (and we) knew better. Under all the upsweeps, shoulder pads and bubbleheaded scripts they threw at her, she developed into a versatile and honest actress with brains, style and wit to burn. Her speaking voice was a uniquely resonant semi-baritone, she had the greatest laugh in pictures, had comedy timing as effective in a hash-house as in a drawing room, and she could even sing.

Clara Lou Sheridan was born on February 21, 1915, in Denton, Texas. Her mother was Lula Stewart Warren and her father was George W. Sheridan, a garage mechanic who was a direct descendant of Civil War Gen. Phil Sheridan. Their first child, Rufus, died at 18 months, followed by five healthy kids—Ida Mae ("Kitty"), Mable, George, Pauline and, finally, Clara Lou. She spent her childhood in tomboy style, riding horses and playing tackle football. "If she punched you," recalled a Denton neighbor, "she'd break your damn arm." She attended Robert E. Lee grade school, Denton Junior High and North Texas State Teachers College. (Her father died in 1938, her mother in 1946.)

While at college in 1932, her sister Kitty entered Clara Lou's photo in Paramount Pictures' "Search for Beauty" contest. She was one of 30 finalists sent to Hollywood from all over the U.S., and one of the six who were given Paramount stock contracts. (For the record, the others were Julian Madison, Colin Tapley, Gwenllian Gill, Alfred Delcambre and Eldred Tidbury, household names all.) Her first film was a ten-second bit in *Search for Beauty* (1933), and she remained a Paramount stock player until 1935. Now re-named Ann Sheridan, she signed with Warner Bros. the following year and slowly inched her way to stardom, due in part to a publicity stunt Warners contrived to have her named America's "Oomph Girl." She left Warners in '48 and made her last film in 1957.

By 1965, Ann was living in my home town, New York City, where she'd moved in 1958. She appeared sporadically on TV but kept a rather low public profile. When I got the chance to interview her for *Screen Facts* magazine I immediately began to panic—what if that sharp, funny "good Joe" that had so besotted me was just an illusion? What if she was bored to tears with talking about her movie days? What if I didn't like her? What if *she* didn't like *me?* I girded myself for disillusionment, showed up at Sardi's East at the appointed time, and she was already there—*omigawd, it's Ann Sheridan, be still my heart.* She seemed perfectly nice, even friendly, and sized me up at once. After the second or third time I addressed her as "Miss Sheridan" she slowly smiled, leveled that riveting no-nonsense gaze on me and said, "Look, please, call me Annie, because I'm much to old to call you Mr. Hagen." From that moment on, it was a day at the beach.

For the first five or so minutes she was totally fascinated by the miniature Uher reel-to-reel tape recorder I'd brought along and she couldn't stop asking questions about this newfangled modern miracle. She kept a wary eye on it, too. At one point, while talking about Olivia de Havilland, she said, "I'm sorry, I like her sister [Joan Fontaine], but Olivia was just—is that thing still on?" "Uh, yes." "Turn it off." Some stories were clearly *not* for publication.

The following transcript is edited from six-plus hours of taped interviews and phone calls between July and September of 1965.

Portrait of Ann Sheridan, 1948.

AS: I hope you'll ask me questions, so I'll know what I'm talking about.

RH: *I certainly will!*

AS: Good. I'll answer what I can. You'll be bored to death, so quit any time.

How are you on the early Paramount titles?

I'm fairly good, but I worked in so many it would be impossible to remember all of them. I worked extra in quite a few, and I did doubling—you know, hands and feet kind of doubling. They'd take me on Stage 5 and showed my hands holding a letter and it was supposed to be the star's. But I worked extra in so many things, I can see a lot of those scenes in my mind, but I couldn't tell you the names of the pictures to save my neck. Of course there was no billing. I was a stock girl all the time I was at Paramount, almost two years. At one time I had to put on a big scene to try and get my option taken up. I was going to be dropped and I heard about it.

The drama coach, Nina Mouise, didn't think I was serious enough about my career. She advised me to go back to Texas and forget the whole thing, and of course that was just the wrong thing to say. If she'd told me to try harder I might have gone back, but the minute she said go back, that gave me the incentive to prove to her that I was serious about my career. But not as serious as *she* was. You weren't supposed to laugh or have any fun, you see. Take everything *veddy* dramatically. She was the coach on the lot who had us in stock, doing plays like *The Milky Way* and *Pursuit of Happiness.* We'd do them one or two nights and the front office was called in and different executives would come by and see us. Of course, most of us were pretty horrible, because we'd had no training whatsoever. Some of the kids who did have training, who worked and starred in pictures on the lot, came and did the plays with us. So that gave us some experience.

Was this the first inkling of dramatic ambition you had?

Well, no, not really, because I'd been in dramatic classes in college and I was intrigued by it. I was going to major in art, but I didn't like trying to paint leaves and things like that and I didn't particularly like the teacher. So I decided to switch my major to dramatics because I thought it would be far more interesting. I sang with the college band and always had some idea of ending up in a chorus line on the New York stage. Never thought of pictures at all, that was too far-out. But dramatics intrigued me and I loved the teacher, Myrtle Hardy.

When Paramount held the Search for Beauty contest, was it your sister, Kitty, who sent your bathing suit picture in to The Dallas News?

That's right, they were representing the competition for that district.

You were 17, in the autumn of 1932, and you didn't know anything about it?

No, she told me later.

And John Rosenfield, the editor of the paper, asked you to come down to the office for the finals, and on to Hollywood. It sounds mythical.

It was mythical to me, I almost fainted. In those days they held all sorts of beauty contests, just for publicity purposes. And they're dreadful. They're horrible on kids, because they break so many hearts. I think every kid who wins a beauty contest thinks, "Well, now I've got a chance." Well, it may be a vague chance, but that's when your hardest work begins. And you have to live up to the producers' ideas about how you should look or photograph, and, mind you, it takes years to develop a face on the screen. I was very young and pudgy fat with kinky hair and a space between my teeth—oh God. Well, a lot of producers won't take that chance. They want someone who's been tested, who's had experience. Mind you, the New York stage means a great deal, even today. Or summer stock, anything like that. At that time, the beauty contests had the biggest publicity value. They showed a gal in a bathing suit and that meant a picture in the paper and the name of a film they were producing or releasing. They used the gimmick for so many years and got away with it. They don't do it any more.

This was during Paramount's dark days when they were going through a reorganization period, wasn't it?

Yes, I'm afraid so. And of course it was the middle of the Depression. I was very lucky to be making 50 bucks a week. I didn't know it at the time. I came fresh out of college and never worked before in my life. So it was a whole new world to me. And I was fortunate to get it, believe me.

When you first won it, was it a six-month-option contract?

Yes, and I think that on a seven-year contract like that, the six-month options would go on for about two years and then go to a yearly option, maybe with a $25 raise. Or maybe the $25 raise comes after the first year and then on the next six-month option you get another one. Maybe it goes a little higher. I know they'd start some stock people up to $150 a week at that time.

What was the difference in how they decided the rates?

Well, how long the people had been there, or how they had gotten in.

Paramount starlet Clara Lou Sheridan, 1934: "Mind you, it takes years to develop a face on the screen."

Maybe they had done bit parts in other pictures or had come from another studio that had dropped them, so because they had experience they could demand a higher salary.

When and why the change from Clara Lou to Ann?

After Paramount had taken up my second option, we were doing a play in stock called *The Milky Way,* and I was playing the part of Ann. They called me into the front office and told me that Clara Lou Sheridan was too long for the marquee. It thrilled me to death, I could just see lights all over the place. Scared me to death, too, because I don't even think I'd had a picture in the paper outside of the one with the 30 other contest winners. So they asked me to choose another name. I chose Lou at first, and they said no, that wouldn't do, it sounds too much like a boy's name. So l went back to the kids at rehearsal and somebody said, "Well, you're playing the part of Ann in *The Milky Way,* why not Ann?" So I went back to the front office and it became Ann Sheridan.

You were there for two years. If your attitude was that cavalier, running around and laughing, having fun, why were you held that long?

I think it was because I got a small part in a picture called *Behold My Wife*. Sylvia Sidney was the star, Gene Raymond was the male lead. Mitchell Leisen, the director, was a very good friend of mine, and he went to the front office and got this part for me. I think it was two scenes, but one scene was very, very dramatic. She commits suicide. He fought to get the bit for me and then took it up and showed it to the front office. And that was after I had wept my way through a scene in the front office with one of the executives, saying, "But I do take my career seriously. Certainly I love to laugh, but when I laugh in a dramatic class or something it doesn't mean I'm not taking it seriously." But I think that bit, and Mitch taking it up for me, helped me stay that long. Committing suicide was the great thing, you know, to have in a picture. It's something that draws your eye to the girl.

Then Car 99, *your first lead, was filmed after that?*

Oh God, I'd forgotten that, really I had. Yes, that was after that. It certainly wasn't an A picture, though. Fred MacMurray was in it. And then there was a Western with Randy Scott...

You mean Rocky Mountain Mystery?

Yes! I remember that. Mr. Scott cast an eye on me. He was fond of me and of course ended up by kissing the horse, but at least it was the lead. I ran around in a pair of riding britches and a pair of boots and they'd say, "Which way'd they go?" and I'd say, "That way." Or screaming at the heavy. Nothing to do, no acting, it was just playing a lead, that's all.

And then your one-line bit in The Crusades.

Oh "The cross, the cross, let me kiss the cross." With a Texas accent.

And a great weepy close-up.

Oh, tears streaming, my wig slipping—I always wanted to look like Dietrich, she was so glamorous, and I thought, "Oh, how wonderful to wear a black wig." Well, I didn't know they took 'em out of stock and they slam 'em on your head and it doesn't fit and the hair lace comes loose and they come up and glue it on just before the take and it falls off again—I was so horrible-looking! Really, it was awful, I didn't look at all glamourous.

So Paramount didn't take up your option?

No, they had no use for me. They dropped me right after I returned from doing a Western called *Red Blood of Courage*. It's the only loan-out I did while I was at Paramount. We did it at Talisman Studios. Then I did one picture at Universal. Originally it was called *Off Side*. I played a very wealthy Communist in it. I can't remember what it was released under...

Fighting Youth?

Fighting Youth, that's right. Charlie Farrell was in it.

And then Warners. Was there a fairly long period between Paramount and Warners?

Oh yes there was! An extremely long and drought-ridden period, I would say. Let's see, just after I finished that Talisman thing I was let go, and that was the beginning of 1935. Then I was very free until the agent got this *Off Side-Fighting Youth* thing for me. I think I made $125 a week on it, I'm not sure. Something like that. Amazing for me. From 50? That's all right.

What were you making when you left Paramount?

Seventy-five or a hundred dollars. I can't remember. But it was such a shock after I'd done that great thing, *Red Blood of Courage*, I thought I'd be there 'til *today*. But I'm sure they dropped me merely because the option did call for another 25 or 50 buck raise and they had other people at $50 they could use for the same things, so why bother with me? Anyway, I was on *Fighting Youth* for three weeks at $125 a week. And from early in 1935 until August of 1936 I had to live off that $375. My agent at that time, Bill Miklejohn, said they'd get me extra jobs, but somebody else told me, "Don't ever start as an extra. It's all right in stock if the studios put you in it, but don't ever start that when you're not under contract, because you'll remain an extra." So I wouldn't take extra jobs. And I dropped that agent and went with another one, Dick Pollimer. Somebody who was with him said, "Why don't you take Ann Sheridan? She looks promising." He had Tom Brown, Anita Louise, I think Ida Lupino, a list of young people, and he was nice enough to take me on. And through Max Arnow, the casting director at Warner Bros., he got me a test. Pollimer walked in and said. "Look, here are the pictures, this is the girl, and I think she may be right for this part," and Max Arnow said, "All right, we'll test her." And if you'll tell me the name of the first picture I did at Warners....

The first Warner release I have listed is Sing Me a Love Song.

Sing Me a Love Song, that would be it.

What was the screen test you had to make for them?

It was a scene from *Sing Me a Love Song*. Ray Enright directed it.

Playing the character you wound up playing in the film?

Yup. It was a bit part, the other girl. They started it off as *Always Leave Them Laughing* and then they got scared of that title, as who wouldn't, and changed it. They always passed titles around. *Always Leave Them Laughing* might have been on half a dozen pictures out there. You make it as one thing and the powers-that-be change it and you don't know what you've made, unless you go back and look, which you seldom have time to do.

Do you know what it was about your test that impressed Warners and made them decide to sign you?

I have no idea. I just did the test and on the strength of that I got the part in the picture, and Mr. Pollimer told me that Max Arnow was thinking about trying to get me a contract. Which he did, at $75 a week, here we go again. But this one ran into 12 years, so I guess I can't beef about that.

There was an incredible seesaw of billing at Warners. There was Black Legion *with Bog-art—you were the sweet young thing who warns the hero against evildoers, right?*

Oh, yes. Always. "Oh, that man is evil, they went that way." This is what I always played. Just reactions.

And The Great O'Malley...

That was just a schoolteacher who said, "He's an evil man, they went that way." These were just feminine leads and I was stuck into them. I mean *She Loved a Fireman*—God, wouldn't you know I'd do that. I did almost every B picture that was made on the Warner lot. For instance, the Mignon Eberhart series. I did those for Brynie Foy. I did *The Patient in Room 18, The Mystery of Hunting's End*—it was filmed under that title but it might have been released as *Mystery House*. I'm not sure.

You had a song in San Quentin.

That's right, "How Could You?" It was the first time I sang in a picture.

Did you ever study singing?

Well, no. I went to quite a few voice coaches, but that was through the studio. Nobody can teach me to sing, I haven't got that kind of a voice. It's kind of an odd voice.

I really like your singing.

Do you? Well, you're very nice. It's just somebody teaching you how to sell a song, it's really not singing. As far as vocalizing, to loosen up the voice, that's one thing, but to make me a singer would be absolutely impossible. I haven't got the range or anything else, and I know it. But I went to many voice coaches.

How about San Quentin? *You had third billing.*

Well, it was all right. A nightclub singer with a heart of gold who was stuck on Pat O'Brien. He'd sent my brother to prison and I finally realized that he was right and my brother was wrong, and instead of saying, "They went that-a-way," I changed direction and said "They went *that*-a-way."

During '38 there was a fantastic amount of films. Just stock stuff?

Only stock stuff. Maybe a line here and there, like in *The Glass Key* back at Paramount. I did a scene as a nurse to George Raft, giving him some medicine or putting a patch on him in a hospital with a couple of lines like, "Lie still, I don't want to hurt you." Brilliant scene.

You did a couple of films with Dick Powell back then.

Yes, there was.. .uh...

Naughty But Nice...

Oh, you dirty man. *Naughty but Nice.* You know, it's funny, the other night I was humming a number from that picture. Gale Page, my favorite Cherokee girl friend, was in it too. She finally just quit. Five kids.

Was your loanout for Letter of Introduction *on the request of Universal, or did Warners farm you out?*

It was on request, an interview with John Stahl, God love him. I went over all dressed up fit to kill. Warners had fitted me out with a wardrobe, they gave me the fox furs and the hat and all that stuff and sent me over to Mr. Stahl. I actually had five scenes in that picture. Not very big scenes, either. I played the bitch, Adolphe Menjou's girlfriend, the secret affair he was hiding from Andrea Leeds. The broad he was supporting. Me, I mean, not her.

Oh, nobody ever treated Andrea Leeds that way in her movies.

No, she was a sweet and darling girl. A very, very nice girl, too.

Did that picture have anything to do with Warners changing their opinion of you after you came back?

It did later, because I think John Stahl was responsible for getting me the part in *Angels With Dirty Faces*, which was the first A picture I'd been in there. All those others were Warner B's.

Was it after you did Angels *that you did those incredible George Hurrell photographs, which I still love?*

Oh, well, bless you, I love 'em too, He was the greatest. He and Scotty Welbourne and—oh, there were wonderful photographers at Warner Bros. Any time you weren't working in a picture, you were posing for stills. They kept you busy.

Was that a deliberate attempt at doing something different, or was it just a sitting that happened to turn out that way?

I would say that everything Hurrell did he tried to do differently. There was a lot of competition around there. Oh, once in a while you'd just get cheesecake—I mean, how much can you do? You go to the beach and stand in the wind and hold up a towel and it blows in the breeze, and so what. But I think in a portrait sitting, most of them tried to be very different. I know they worked awfully hard. I think possibly Hurrell was the best one. I think he was more sophisticated.

Did that series of glamour photos influence Warners in any way to start the Oomph thing?

Well, they might have, yes. The outfit I wore in the pictures for the Oomph Girl contest that somebody dreamed up,...

Bob Taplinger?

That's right. It had a roll-back collar and long sleeves. It was a crepe negligee, covered all the way up. Nothing on underneath, of course. On a leopard skin. And I wouldn't be at all surprised if these pictures didn't give someone the idea. Don't forget, they'd read it in Winchell's column a while before, except he spelled it u-m-p-h. He said Ann Sheridan in—something or other, I can't even remember the name of the picture—has plenty of *umph*. All they did was steal it and spell it differently.

So Taplinger arranged the dinner at the Los Angeles Town House?

That's right.

How were the 13 men who were supposedly the judges of this contest prevailed upon to get into this, to lend their names to the stunt?

I really don't know, I guess the publicity department just called them and said, "You're one of the men named on the list and we want you to participate," and they turned up at the dinner.

Can you recall who the 13 men were ?

Well, I can't remember all of them. Let's see, Orry-Kelly was there. I remember Earl Carroll and I remember Dudley Field Malone because he made some sort of crack in his cups and Rudy Vallee was going to punch him in the nose. Buz Berkeley, George Hurrell—I can't remember that evening too well, it was one of those nerve-wracking things and I actually can't remember very much of it. But anyway, it was purely a publicity stunt to get their name, Warner Pictures, and my name into the papers.

Had they decided by then, after Angels with Dirty Faces, *that it was possible to be doing more with you, or was it simply another publicity stunt?*

Simply another publicity stunt. Nothing special. My Lord, they took the back of Hedy Lamarr's head and the backs of whoever else's heads they entered in the contest, the 12 pictures of the other actresses they supposedly sent to these guys to find out who was the most glamourous. Of course it was all a set-up to pick me. They could never have had a good picture of Hedy Lamarr and said I was more glamourous than she was. The next day Jack Kelly, one of the publicists, told me that somebody had walked up to Jack Warner at lunch and showed him this shot in the paper and the publicity on it, and Warner looked at it and said, "Aw, she'll be dead in six months," and threw the paper back at him. Well, it snowballed on them, they just didn't know where to go. There was nothing but publicity, publicity, publicity.

And you've had it for the rest of your life.

Well, most of it. I think I've more or less lived it down by now. I'm old enough, I should have. But that ran away from them. The guy who got out the most publicity on a person at a certain lot was the one most looked up to, and I think this was just a silly name that caught on. Even Harvard got into it, naming me the actress least likely to succeed. More publicity.

Did you really say, or was it a press agent's invention, that "Oomph is the sound a fat man makes when he bends over to tie his shoelace in a telephone booth?"

I did not say it. It was a press agent's invention, but I adopted it wholeheartedly. Interviews were made up for me like mad by publicity people. Most of those things you read are not true, they weren't said by the people at all. Especially in those days.

It was after the Oomph thing that you did Dodge City *and* They Made Me a Criminal?

Yes, it was after that, after the Oomph campaign. I came to New York to play the Strand Theatre after opening in Washington. I played five weeks on personal appearance tours, doing a medley of old songs and publicizing some picture. And when I went back I started working on the other things like *Dodge City*. But that was a bit part too.

A bit, but you were now being prominently featured in the ads.

Yes, and don't forget billing. And *Dodge City* was the first color picture I had made, so that was important. Almost made me blind, that incredible color lighting.

You weren't in very much of They Made Me a Criminal *either, but you were given billing over Gloria Dickson, the real female lead, because of all the publicity.*

I just had, I think, one scene with Garfield. Busby Berkeley, who I loved, directed it. I once did a musical test for *Desert Song* that Buz directed, with John Boles. Anyway, John Garfield was a dear man. He was like the little guy who brought the apple for the teacher, and here I was, this hussy with the fuzzy hair and the décolletage dress. I was supposed to kiss John, but Buz said, "Hold it until I say cut, just keep kissing him." Well of course he wouldn't say it, and I had John around the neck and on the floor—he was absolutely red.

Garfield didn't come on like the hip young rebel he seemed on the screen?

Oh no, not at all. I didn't think so, anyway.

It was in 1940 that you really started working a lot in sizable roles.

Yes, I worked constantly. Everybody did. It was from one picture right into another. I read so many scripts, everybody on the Warner lot did, I don't think anybody can remember the names of them. But the parts were getting better, and more publicity. Paul Muni found me in the commissary one day screaming about this dreadful Oomph Girl thing, and he said, "Don't be silly. Be smart, use it. Use it to get parts." And I did. I think that's the one purpose it served, because the publicity itself was ghastly. If it hadn't given me a foot in the door, I probably would have never gotten the good parts. But everybody was saying, "Well all right, let's try." Including me. "Try me in an A picture, try me in good parts." And fortunately, with good directors, it started working better for me.

Did you have to battle for the good parts, or did they come easily?

Oh no. Battle, battle, battle.

Every picture a new battle ?

Almost, yes.

At this point, didn't Warners pay Louis Bromfield $50,000 for It All Came True *as a vehicle for you? Your first vehicle as such?*

Yes. I did that after I came back from that New York personal appearance tour. I'm quite sure that I was chosen because Mark Hellinger, the producer, wanted me in the picture, and because Bette Davis didn't want it.

I didn't know she was even up for it.

I don't know that she was either, but Bette got access every time, to everything on the lot. And there were quite a few others around as competition. I remember making a test for the picture, but I don't remember battling for it. Hellinger, who carried a lot of weight, saw the test and said, "I want her." But it was after that— I'm trying to straighten this out. My first suspension at Warners was some time after this. It was an eight-month suspension. Actually it was three months lay-off and five months suspension, but it came to eight months with no salary. The fight started as a salary raise, and then it got into the thing of getting the part of Randy Monaghan in *Kings Row*. Finally, all the fighting and clawing and scratching and screeching was settled. I didn't get the salary I asked for, naturally, but I did get a raise and I got retroactive pay. And I got the part in *Kings Row*. But before they'd let me do that, I had to do *Navy Blues*. Always worked out the same for me—one good one, two bad ones.

Next came Torrid Zone. *So many people I know are absolutely mad about* Torrid Zone.

I liked *Torrid Zone*, I enjoyed doing it. A good part and another song, "Mi Caballero." I'd worked in several with O'Brien before we did *Torrid Zone*, Cagney too. I assume Mr. Cagney had a great deal to do with choosing his leading lady.

Had you always gotten on well with Cagney and O'Brien?

Oh, yes! They raised me. I was a brat running around who they could pick on. I was certainly fond of them and they seemed pretty fond of me. All the people on the lot were pretty wonderful, we all got along. Then I did more B's like *Honeymoon for Three,* and *City for Conquest,* which I loved.

That was a good part for you. It gave you a lot of opportunities.

It was a very good part, and of course it was Cagney again. He sold like wildfire. To be in a picture with him was just the greatest.

And you got some excellent notices for your performance.

Yes, nice reviews for that.

And Navy Blues, *which was to get* Kings Row. *Wasn't Humphrey Bogart instrumental in your doing Kings Row?*

He was. He was the one who told me about Warners having bought the story. He said they bought it for Bette Davis, Jimmy Cagney and Pat O'Brien, and he said, "I think you ought to have it, I think you'd be wonderful as Randy Monaghan. Read it, fight for it, do anything you can." That's when I got the book. I loved Bogart, but he was a monster. After he touted me for *Kings Row,* and it worked out so well, he came down to the set of something I was doing and said, "Annie, the front office has bought the greatest story under the sun, and you've got to do it." And I'll hold the tag line for you 'til the end, because he told me the name of it, and I said, "Oh Bogie, God love you for *Kings Row,* that was the greatest part I ever had, thank you for touting me on it and tipping me off on this one, I'll get in touch with them right away." Well, this monster went to Ida Lupino and pulled the same thing, and a couple of other actresses on the lot, and if I hadn't had to go right into a scene, I would have been on the telephone too. I understand that the front office, I think it was Steve Trilling at the time, was deluged with actresses wanting to get a copy of this script. I said to the fashion editor of Warners in my dressing room, "Oh, God love that Bogie, he's just tipped me off on another thing to do," and I told her the title and I saw a strange look come over her face. She said, "Oh, well, yeah, that's wonderful," and let it go. Mark Hellinger came in a few minutes later, and when I told him he asked me what it was, and I said, *"The Story of Fanny Hill."* Well, Mark got hysterical with laughter and said, "Don't you know who Fanny Hill was?" And I said no, and I didn't. Lupino didn't know either, she's one of the ones they told me called the front office. I can imagine Trilling, shocked, horrified, groping—"We don't have such a script!" And all of us stupid dames not knowing. But Hellinger was rolling on the floor, telling me she was the greatest known madam in England. I'd heard of Lee Francis and Polly Adler, but I'd never heard of Fanny Hill in my life. Those are the kind of gags Bogart pulled on everybody. We all had laughs about it, and afterwards of course I threatened to kill him.

Naturally. You were very unlikely casting for the part of Randy at that time, what with the publicity and all. Did you have to test for it?

No, after those first tests I did, the only tests I made were wardrobe tests. Somebody decided that I was going to get a part, and the producer didn't demand that you do a test for it. Except for *The Man Who Came to Dinner.* I didn't want to do that.

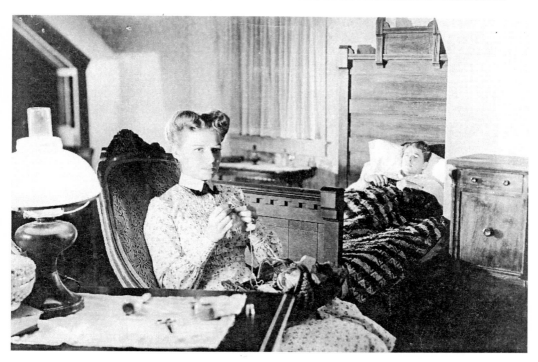

"I'd work one day on *Kings Row* and the next day on *The Man Who Came to Dinner*." Above with Ronald Reagan; below with Bette Davis, Monty Woolley (both Warner Bros., 1942).

Why not?

Because I was doing Randy. Two pictures at once.

They were both at the same time?

Yes. And my only love was Randy Monaghan. I didn't care about playing Lorraine Sheldon. I used to work, say, one day on *Kings Row* and the next day on *Man Who Came to Dinner,* or one morning I'd work as Lorraine Sheldon and that afternoon I was Randy Monaghan.

That's a treacherous switch of character.

Well, it was horrible. And more than that, the makeup, hairdo, everything. But Mr. Wallis decided he wanted me after I made the test for *Man Who Came to Dinner.*

Was it true that there were some altercations with Bette Davis during that?

Very, very little. She wasn't happy about a lot of things, there's no doubt about that.

She had a very straight part.

That's right. And I think she was conditioned at the time to remain angry at Miriam Hopkins and think that anybody on the set was going to fight with her. I wouldn't fight with her at all. I agreed with her, with everything she said. Then she got very nice and today we're very friendly. She was just—temperamental? Who isn't temperamental? I'm as temperamental as all get-out if I feel I have to be. Maybe she had a headache, maybe she didn't feel well. Maybe she wasn't satisfied with her part or her clothes or the way the director was doing a scene. Many things can enter into it.

It was common to write back in those days that every up-and-coming young actress said she wanted only to be half the actress that Bette Davis was. Was it true in your case?

Oh, certainly. All of us had the greatest admiration for her. She was the queen. One of my greatest, greatest favorites. They always tried to start a feud between Bette and me, the Warner publicity boys. You never know who plants it.

How about others on the Warner lot you especially liked?

Oh, dear. Well, of course most of them were men, I have to say that. But of the women—well, Ida Lupino is a dear, close friend. I adore her. And she's a damn fine actress, too.

Yes, she certainly is. It's a shame she was in Bette Davis' shadow for so long.

Yes, if Davis had not been on the lot, or if Ida had been on another lot and they'd had those scripts, I think a lot of those wonderful parts would have gone to Ida. I've known her since Paramount. In *Search for Beauty,* she played the lead.

Also in Come On, Marines.

Oh, no, another one I'd forgotten! Oh, you're bringing back horrible memories. Actually, though, Paramount was sheer fun, It was hard work, but this was the glitter, the glamour, stars in your eyes. I didn't care if I worked all night and started on another picture the next day. I was dead tired, but there was always the energy. But when you get parts that required a little concentration, learning dialogue at night and all that, you can't do it. You can't work all night and start another picture the next day and be too happy about it, especially if you don't care for the part, and you're supposed to carry something. At Paramount I never had to carry anything. At Warners I did, even Mignon Eberhart. I was up there and I was the one they were going to blame. Not the producer, not the director. This one. I started learning, in other words. Responsibility.

Others on the Warner lot, of the ladies, Barbara Stanwyck?

Never worked with her. She worked on the Warner lot and I knew her because she worked with my ex-husband, George Brent [in *The Gay Sisters*]. On one set we had rigged up a whole thing for Brent. They had a wedding scene, and I left the picture I was on and put on her wedding gown. George and I had just been married, two or three months. And when "Here Comes the Bride" was played, I walked down the aisle and stood beside him. You know what? I could have killed him. He didn't even break up. He out-deadpanned every one of us. I finally said, "You're supposed to laugh," and he grinned! But Stanwyck is so tiny and I'm so broad-shouldered, her wedding dress stayed open all the way down my back. She was such a tiny thing.

How long did the marriage to Brent last?

Nine months. I got the divorce exactly a year to the day, January 5, 1943.

While we're on the subject, I don't have the date for the marriage to Eddie Norris.

July 1936. It was two years, 18 days, 3 hours and 30 seconds later that we separated, that's as close as I can come. It was about two and a half years all told.

Now, Kings Row. I guess everybody thinks it's the best thing you ever did.

Well, I think so.

It was a beautiful performance. It could have been done so badly, just sweet and mawkish, or just plain hard. But it was marvelous.

Well, I thank you, I loved it. I worked so hard, I worshipped the part. [Director] Sam Wood was absolutely wonderful. And for the first time in any picture we rehearsed three weeks before one single shot was made. The sets were up and we knew where we were going, what was going to happen. Bill Menzies, the technical director, laid out every shot. The dialogue in Sam's script, and in Bill's too, was on one page, and facing it, on the back of the preceding page, were color sketches of what they were going to do. James Wong Howe followed that, and of course there's no finer photographer in the world. Every line, everything was known by that director and those people before we moved into the set.

All the work paid off, and it showed.

It really paid off. And I think Casey Robinson did a magnificent job on the script. It was a picture I could find no fault with, except that I had to do the others to get it. I loved it.

That was an astounding set of ads they used, with you in a strapless gown and those blurbs about finding love on the wrong side of the tracks.

Wasn't that something? Wouldn't you just know they'd do that? And I was told later that the New York critics gave it bad reviews because they thought it was Communistic, the poor winning over the rich! But some of them saw it later and said,

"My God, we didn't realize..." At the time everyone said it needed a comic touch. And don't forget, Warners had just done *Mission to Moscow*, and things were very touchy. If you didn't like bread and butter, it was a Commie thing.

I've read quite often that Warners had originally planned to cast you and Ronald Reagan in Casablanca *as a follow-up to* Kings Row.

No, they did not. If *Casablanca* had been announced or planned for me, I would have known about it.

This is all news to you?

All news to me. Everybody talks as though they'd been sitting at Jack Warner's side all that time. This is silly, I never heard of *Casablanca* being bought for me. Everything on the lot was bought for Bette Davis, it comes down to that. She had first choice. I spent so many years at Warners reading about them saying I was announced for things they had no intention of ever putting me in. It's just more publicity. And if it happened to be something I really wanted, I never got it.

Why in the world, after the tremendous reaction you got from Kings Row, *did they put you in* Juke Girl?

Remember I said two bad ones for every good one? You're supposed to carry it. I was under contract, it was either do it or take a suspension. I'd just come off an eight-month suspension. And I wasn't paid twice for doing *Kings Row* and *The Man Who Came to Dinner*, I was paid once. You'd have to be paid for both now, but then, no.

Wings for the Eagle *was not an awfully important film either.*

Oh that was dreadful. That was the beginning of the Dennis Morgan-Jack Carson-Jane Wyman-Alexis Smith tie-up. We became the Warner Brothers stock company of all time. We also went out to Lockheed and did speeches trying to get the people to buy War Bonds. I think it was the first film about war that was done on the Warner lot during the War.

After which you finally got another good one, George Washington Slept Here, *which was fun.*

Oh, that was fun. And of course Jack Benny and Bill Keighley—well, Bill directed *Torrid Zone*, and these are just two great people to work with. It wasn't too great a part, the only thing I did was kind of whine my way through, but it was with a wonderful comic and I had fun working with him. If the script's bad I can put up with that, I won't like it and I may beef, but I've got to have fun working with the people on the set. I don't like dissension at all. I could fight with the front office, but I never wanted to do that either. I didn't beef about *George Washington* because it was Jack Benny. I certainly beefed about *Juke Girl*. There were many things that I fought not to do. And there were many times, too, that I went on suspension and then came back and did the picture to get a salary raise.

I've heard quite often that you, Lauren Bacall and Ida Lupino were the suspension queens of Warner Bros.

Well, Lauren swears that she was on suspension more than anybody else. And I finally gave her that. More often, but I was on the longest time. The first suspension was eight months, the last one 18 months. These are the pictures I did, but you should have seen the scripts I turned down!

Remember any of the names?

Not all of them, certainly. There were several. One was *Hollywood Canteen*. They wanted me to play the lead and I refused it.

The Joan Leslie role?

You know, I'd forgotten that Joan Leslie played it. Yes, the young girl who gives the GI the come-on. The movie star he falls in love with, and she lets him think she might really love him and marry him when he comes back. And I said, "This is ridiculous! What a horrible thing to do to a GI. You're going to get every guy in the Army all upset, thinking he can marry a movie queen. He doesn't even know what he's getting into." Honey, you should have seen that script. I'm sorry, I like the man who did it, Delmer Daves, but this was dreadful! I refused to do it and took another suspension. I didn't know about this, but they had even sent my stand-in out to my place and made street shots of her walking around my property to start the picture. They would not believe that I wouldn't do it. They'd say, "It's your patriotic duty!" Well, that had nothing to do with patriotism.

Do you remember any other films you had refused to make?

Well, I turned down *Mildred Pierce*, I turned down *Caged*.

Didn't like the scripts?

Nope. But something I wanted to do very badly was *Saratoga Trunk*. Bergman did it, and she was right for it. I had made a test in a blonde wig, though, and I had a French teacher working with me all the time on the set of *Juke Girl*, trying to teach me a French accent. Can you imagine a French accent with my Texas accent? It was the most horrible-sounding thing. I didn't see the test, but I saw stills of myself in the blonde wig, and I cannot wear blonde hair, my face just sort of goes to mush. My features are too big to be a blonde.

Now we come to Edge of Darkness, *which I thought was another fine performance.*

Thank you. I enjoyed the picture very much. It was timely and I think it made a lot of money. And the people in it were just wonderful.

Walter Huston, Ruth Gordon—a brilliant cast.

Yes, and Judith Anderson. How can you ask for any better?

Did you enjoy working with Flynn?

Oh, that was a wonderful time. He was going through the Peggy Satterlee rape trial. He used to go to court in the morning and come back and report to us on the set what had happened. [Director] Lewis Milestone and all of us used to just gather around and start gurgling from the toes up at the reports of Old Dad Flynn. It was absolutely fascinating, the things this idiot child accused him of. I think what hurt him most was when she said he raped her with his boots on. This would be very indelicate and ungentlemanly for Old Dad, and he said, "My God, next she'll accuse me of wearing my top hat." No, Flynn was always strictly fun. Never any trouble. I adored him. I never had trouble with any leading men. Really, I always got along well with everybody. You see, all of us were covered. If I was in a scene with Flynn, and it was his scene, I knew that the scene was going to be played mostly on Flynn. I could only play my part to the best of my ability. I knew that I would be protected because I was also a studio property. If the scene was mine and they wanted it to go to me, they would cut to me. I had nothing to do with the cutting, or any of that. I've known other people to go in and beef at the cuttings of pictures, but I never did.

How about Thank Your Lucky Stars?

I did that under duress, because I wanted to go to Mexico and get my divorce from Brent. They didn't know I wanted one. I went immediately from *Edge of Darkness* into *Thank Your Lucky Stars* because, again, Mark Hellinger asked me to do it. So I said, "All right, can you shoot it fast? I'm doing it under protest. I don't think this is going to be a hit, with all the different stars in it, but if you want me in it, fine." I adored him. And I think we shot my number ["Love Isn't Born"] in three days. I was champing at the bit because I had reservations to take off for Mexico, and of course they were standing with another script for me to do. That never stopped, that submission of scripts. I just thought of another one. I did *The Dough-girls* for Mark because they were going to suspend me again, but I hated it. I was in New York at the time it was chosen for me, or I was chosen for it, whichever you want to call it. I went to see the play and notified the studio that there wasn't one single part that I could play with any honesty, and that I didn't think it was a good play. I figured that unless you could use the dirt of the play, which they certainly couldn't do on the screen with the Johnston Office, that it would lose all its color. Which it did. But, oh, there was a big knock-down, drag-out fight over that, threatening me with suspension. If it hadn't been for Mark, I wouldn't have taken it.

You did it just because you wanted to work with him again?

Warners knew I loved Mark, and he knew it. He wasn't trying to use me, though, he was trying to help me. They cancelled a *Bing Crosby Show* on me at the last minute, which was very dirty playing. I drove down to the radio station, but they wouldn't take me. Warner had already called and cancelled it. And he'd already given his word three weeks before. But Mark finally talked me into it. I'd get adamant, saying, "I won't be pushed around, this is dreadful!" and he'd say, "Now come on, Annie. This is assigned to me, I've got to do it. You'd be doing me a great favor." And there was another thing. I said, "All right, I'll do *Doughgirls* if after I finish it Mr. Warner will release me to do a USO tour." I had been waiting nine months to do one, I'd even taken booster shots. But every time I'd finish a picture, and Mr. Warner had given his permission for a USO tour, up would come another picture—"Well, just do this one, then you can go." So I got the promise from Mr. Warner that after *Doughgirls* I would be allowed to make my USO tour. And I was. They came to me with another script, and I said, "Uh-uh, sorry. Remember?" *Doughgirls* was finished just before I went overseas in June '44. It was released just before I got home. I remember somebody sent me the reviews on it. I came home that September and had already gotten the reviews in China. Oh, they were horrors!

Hadn't you done a tour through Wyoming, Kansas and Missouri?

Oh, Fort Riley and all that. That was just after I'd married Brent. We were on our honeymoon, in Palm Springs, dahling. I think we'd been married all of two weeks. And I got a call from my agent saying, "Mr. Warner says you have to go on a USO camp tour, it's your patriotic duty!"

They were very big on that.

Oh, they sure were. But not too big, he threatened to suspend me because I was on the CBI, the China-Burma-India tour, four months and didn't get back on time. So the agent said, "Go right ahead, suspend her." Of course he didn't. But he'd kept trying to get wires and letters through to me, but everything was censored. And I'd be in one spot when he wrote me and I got the letter three weeks later somewhere else. He kept writing, "When are you coming home?" That started as soon as I got there. But we didn't know where we were going until we were out over the Atlantic Ocean and opened our orders. We were delayed a month by some idiot special service man in Casablanca who sent us on the wrong route. We were a month late getting into Kharachi, India, and all hell broke loose. But it wasn't our fault, we had nothing to do with it. So I was a month late getting back.

You didn't mind so much as he did?

No, I didn't mind so much. I was worn out, it had been rough and I'd gone from 128 pounds down to 112, living on K-Rations, or food I was completely unaccustomed to. And the heat, travelling constantly, and sleeping in bucket seats and on the floors of planes until we couldn't sleep in a bed.

Who were the others on the junket with you?

Ben Blue, and Jackie Miles was the emcee. And there was Mary Landa, who had danced for a long time at Warners, and accordionist Ruth Dennis. We had a tough time, but we had fun, too.

What was your act?

I did a couple of songs and played straight girl in one of Ben Blue's crazy acts. The GIs absolutely adored him. And Jackie Miles has such a wealth of material. As long as they wanted it, these guys stayed on. And Mary had a tremendous amount of dancing to do. She could do almost anything, and in a few places, when the platforms on the trucks were smooth enough, she even did some tap dancing. And Ruth did a lot of accordion playing. But the weather—never cool. And sand in your teeth, sand in your eyes. The Azores was the same thing. Casablanca was a little more comfortable, and it was intriguing, French Morocco. We met all the prostitutes, and I was asked to have a drink with one of the madams, but the MPs wouldn't let us. Bob Hope told me before we left not to let the officers occupy all of our time, that the GIs were the ones we were going to entertain. You can't imagine the arguments we got into with officers, some of them with a little too much under the belt. One of them in India threatened to court-martial two MPs that were sent for us unless they brought us back. This is incredible to me, that people can do this. All those dull, stupid pink teas with the officers' wives—the minute they demanded that we go, we wouldn't. We all stuck together on that. We went to entertain the GIs.

But it must have been great, in retrospect, to have gone.

I wouldn't have missed it for anything in the world, believe me. I remember getting back to New York at eight o'clock in the morning. The first thing I wanted was milk, which we hadn't had, of course. I bought two pints of milk and an ice cream cone. I was starving to death for milk. We had boiled milk in one place. I can't bear boiled milk. And also, we had ice cream full of bugs. Night bugs that flew, little gnats. You know, I got so I didn't mind? It was ice cream. Didn't taste like ice cream, but it was cold. They froze it by sticking it into a well. Not really frozen, just crispy enough to stand up for two minutes. But I remember coming in, getting the ice cream and the milk, and going to the apartment of a friend who let me stay there. I went in, said hello to the maid and went to bed. And I could not sleep. So I took a sheet, a pillow and a lightweight blanket, got on the floor and I slept for 18 hours. Just dead. I didn't move, nobody bothered me. It was absolutely wonderful. Everyone was worn out. Jackie Miles, Ben Blue—just shadows.

Was it when you returned that you started on Shine on Harvest Moon?

No, I came back and I was signed to do *The Animal Kingdom*. We worked for five weeks on it. Then Mr. Warner found out that Barney Glazer, the producer, hadn't had it okayed by the Johnston Office. So they closed the picture because it had no Seal and couldn't be released. Irving Rapper was the first director on it. So there was a whole rewrite done. Dane Clark, who played a completely different character than had ever been in the original, was written out. They closed it and I came to New York, stayed six weeks, went back, did *Shine On Harvest Moon*, then finished this with the rewrite. They put Peter Godfrey on as the new director. It was released as *One More Tomorrow*, with Dennis Morgan, Jack Carson, Jane Wyman, Alexis Smith—the company. You can tell the difference in the scenes between the things Rapper had done and what Godfrey did. It was one of the most horrible things I'd ever seen! They bought Mr. Glazer's contract, paid him $150,000 and sent him, so they told the papers, for a rest in South America. We did *Harvest Moon* after the first five weeks on this.

Harvest Moon *was supposedly Nora Bayes' biography, but they weren't all that factual.*

Oh, they couldn't be. She had five husbands, dear, and they couldn't possibly show that. The Johnston Code said it was making fun of marriage if you even show a guy drinking too much champagne at a wedding. But I've never really seen a script for an original picture musical that had a really good story. Incidentally, I remember a very funny incident on that picture. Milo Anderson, who designed the costumes for it, was called down by LeRoy Prinz, the dance director, to see this dance thing he had done for Irene Manning, with all the fans and the hats and everything they could put on her, and 19 muscle guys lifting her and tossing her about. So Milo came in and LeRoy said, "I want you to take a look at this," and they did the number and LeRoy said, "What do you think of that? What do you think she needs?" And Milo said, "Piano wire!"

Did you especially enjoy singing in pictures, or was it just part of the job?

Part of the job. It's a different thing if I love the song, but you really get so tired, it's so much hard work unless you have a God-given voice. But when you have to work at it—oh, brother. There was a stand-by singer for me in all the pictures. All the studios did that, in case you couldn't do the song. But I did them. But it wasn't that you just stood up and did a tremendous number, like anybody with a voice. There were all those guys who cut the little pieces together. Dave Forrest saying, "Well, you did that phrase pretty well, let's go back over and add this one to it." It takes a tremendous amount of time, and it's excruciating. All of them were just a lot of hard work.

[Note: Ann never saw Shine on Harvest Moon *and was unaware that the studio decided to have Lynn Martin re-record the songs and dubbed her vocals over Ann's. Except for one brief trio number in* Naughty But Nice, *it was the only time Ann was ever dubbed.]*

I remember the advertisements for Harvest Moon, *"It's Sheridandy."*

It was pretty horrible, I just loathed those pictures. I wanted good parts and it just didn't happen.

In 1946, you were seen in only one film, One More Tomorrow, *and it would seem that at this point they would be utilizing you more.*

Suspension, dear. Over stories. Knock-down, drag-out. I went on suspension for 18 months after *One More Tomorrow* was finished. That's when the strike began for better scripts, a pay raise and a picture deal. My option was coming up, which put me in a good position.

When the strike was finally settled, what was the deal?

I had a six-picture deal, over a period of three years. Two pictures a year, paying so much for each one, with script approval.

So the first one was Nora Prentiss, *followed by* The Unfaithful *and* Silver River. *What prompted you to accept these?*

Vince Sherman, a wonderful guy and a good director, came up with the first two stories. They were the best available. And I enjoyed doing them, I liked the stories. Now, *Silver River* was not a good picture. I understand that Mr. Warner was amazed that I accepted it. I accepted it because Errol Flynn was a big box office name and women didn't get to do Westerns very often and I thought it might be a good combination, and I thought that it might turn into a good picture. Unfortunately, it didn't. They tried to get me to do another picture after *Silver River*, but I refused, and since I was on a picture deal, they couldn't suspend me. So I went out to RKO and did *Good Sam* instead. They didn't want to loan me out, but they finally did. I did *Good Sam* in '48 and then I sat for quite some time because they didn't have another story. They tried to get me to do *Serenade*, the thing that Mario Lanza did. They wanted me to play the Mexican girl. And that wasn't the only time that this came up. It had been going on for quite some time, this *Serenade* bit, and I'd keep turning it down. Can't you just see me playing the Mexican girl?

You'd get a chance to put on your Crusades *black wig again.*

Oh, that—my *Crusades* black wig! And what was that delightful thing—oh, *Treasure of the Sierra Madre*. I had a good black wig in that. I played a hooker.

You did?

I walked down the street in a big fat disguise to see if Bogart would recognize me. There's a shot where he comes out of a bar—I guess he had the toothpick, he always did, and the hat turned up—and he passes me and then turns and looks back. And you see a girl twitching down the street in a black satin dress. That's me. A bit. John Huston and I whipped that one up. Now, where were we?

You had just finished the last of your things for Warners and you went to do Good Sam *for Leo McCarey. Were you satisfied with it?*

No, I really wasn't, but I don't think that was necessarily Leo's fault. I think a lot of it might have been casting. Gary and I did not have the spark we should have had together. It was a huge, elongated picture and I worked for 11 weeks on it. It was a delight to work with Leo and Gary, I'd known them both a long time. Cutting may have had something to do with it because they stuck really to the family things. There was a lot of comedy, but so much was cut out. And then I sat for a long time because Warners didn't have anything for me. By this time, 20th had contacted me about *I Was a Male War Bride*. Well, I would have taken anything of Howard Hawks', and with Cary Grant in it, sight unseen. I read the script, which was the longest thing I'd ever read in my life, and when Howard called me back to see if I'd read it he told me to tear out the first 85 pages because they weren't going to use them. That was written off the cuff, mostly by Mr. Grant. Anyhow, my option would have been up on January 8, 1949, so I had six months to go, approximately, and I didn't want to sign with them again because I was not getting good properties. I only did three pictures. That's when I bought my way out of Warner Bros.

Do you remember the figure?
Thirty-five thousand dollars. They wanted 50, we compromised at 35.

How had been your relations with Jack Warner during all your years there?
Socially, excellent. Professionally—if I was on suspension, I wasn't to be spoken to, either inside or outside the studio.

The word went out?
Of course. All the whispering campaigns about—oh, back to my first suspension. They'd give it to all the columnists, she should be spanked, she's being a naughty girl, and after all the studio's done for her. They never take the other side into consideration. But of course these columnists had to get their information from the studios, so they're going to stay on the studio's side. I just don't think people can get to Jack in the office, he has too many people surrounding him. And of course he hates agents. I can't blame him, though, they're in there to get anything they can.

Did you deal with him personally or always through agents?
Through agents, always. Sure, that's what they're for.

No dramatic scenes, slamming into the office and throwing fits?
No, not I. I wouldn't dream of doing that. I think that's rude. He has his side to fight for and I have mine. You know, I could slam my way into his office and be kicked out, too, and that's pretty silly. But I adore Jack socially. He's a lot of fun.

Warners never really utilized you as an actress after Kings Row.
They always thought of me as the Oomph Girl, never as an actress, I could never convince them that I could act.

I know that the Oomph Girl thing stayed in their minds. Do you think the additional onus of having been a beauty contest winner hurt even more?
It certainly did. Anybody who would look over a bio of mine, any executive or producer who didn't know me, had never worked with me or seen me work with a good director, would say, "Oh my God, not a beauty contest winner! Oh, not the Oomph Girl!" Yes, between the two I think it certainly was a hindrance to my getting good parts, or better parts.

*Do you think that if you had freelanced during the time you were under contract to Warn-
ers, you would have done better?*

I'm not at all sure of that, because unless a studio could get you under contract
they didn't want to give you those nice fat, juicy, plum parts. They wanted them to
go to their contract people. So it's six of one and half a dozen of the other.

How about the contract system, are you generally for it?

I think the contract system was an excellent idea for stock people because they
had a chance to get training with good directors, even in bit parts. They did picture
after picture after picture, and whether the training you got was good or bad, you
learned something.

*But after you had gotten a name, when they had you under contract and you were estab-
lished, and knew what you wanted to go after, do you feel that it was limiting?*

I think it was to this extent. There was a great deal of jealousy among the studios and they wouldn't freely loan out their people. After Olivia de Havilland did
Gone with the Wind, she came back to Warners and took a suspension. She refused
to do a script and the front office got furious. They said, "There will never be a
loanout for you from this lot again." Bette Davis went to England and spent all her
money trying to get her freedom from Warners, and the judge was very nasty to her,
because he thought it was a *rahtha* high price for an actress to be getting. I think
he's nuts. Bette Davis was worth more than anything she ever earned, she made millions of dollars for them. De Havilland certainly earned whatever she got. All of us
did. We were highly underpaid at the time.

*Well, with the dollars your names were bringing into the box offices in scripts that would
have done nothing with unknowns...*

That's right. They were turning them out like a factory in those days, shoving
everything down the public's throat. They'd rewrite white elephants that had been
on the shelves for years, and people would do them just to get them over with. Ruth
Chatterton, for example. Now this was before my time at Warners, but I was married to her ex-husband, George Brent, so I know. She had a contract for five scripts.
They would hold up the fifth script, the one they really wanted her to do, submit
four that she had already turned down, and she had to take the fifth one or lose her
money. It's all very cleverly done. It's like the very unfair thing of Warners not releasing me from my contract for so long. They finally charged me $35,000, and two
weeks later Jack Warner gave Barbara Stanwyck her release because they couldn't
find stories for her.

Were there any roles you wanted to do for other studios that Warners wouldn't let you do?

Many. I wanted to play Texas Guinan in the thing that Betty Hutton did at
Paramount [*Incendiary Blonde*]. Probably just as well that I didn't. Oh, there were
several others, but I can't think of the names of them. You're digging too far back.

You can't recall any of the others you especially wanted to do?

Oh, well, only Scarlett O'Hara, dear, naturally. I was interviewed by George
Cukor for it, but you know what happened to that. I must admit that he was right,
she [Vivien Leigh] was absolutely wonderful. But I can't say I wasn't envious. My
not getting that had nothing to do with Warners. And I always wanted to play the

girl in a book called *The Wall*, but I don't think it's ever been filmed. Of course I'm much too old now. Then I wasn't.

Now, about I Was a Male War Bride, *one of my favorite Sheridan pictures. You and Grant were absolutely marvelous together, and I wish you'd made many more films.*

Thank you. We tried to. We were going to make sequels. We talked to Mr. Hawks about it quite often, but there was just nothing that could come up to *Male War Bride*. I know that the man and woman who wrote it, it was about them, were thinking about making a sequel. We just never found another good comedy, that's all. It's a sin and a shame too, because I think we should have done two or three.

The wit, the style, the ease between you two was just beautiful. I've seen it often and have wondered for some time whether much of the dialogue between you and Grant wasn't ad lib?

Oh, it was. Cary did it. The scene where we're in front of my commanding officer and she said, "There's a hitch," and he said "Itch? Do you itch, Catherine?" and I said, "No, I don't itch"—this was all Cary, all ad lib. He was right, he'd say, "People don't wait for somebody else to finish a line, they talk over each other." We would sit and work for hours. We were on the picture for ten months, because of illness. I got pneumonia, and when I'd finally gotten over it and was able to work, he got hepatitis. We finished in California and some of the things that were supposed to be shot in Bremerhaven, Germany, were shot at Wilmington. And we redid

I Was a Male War Bride **with Cary Grant (Fox, 1949).**

a lot of the things that we shot in England, because we had several different cam-
eramen. It took a full ten months to do it. But anyway, remember that scene in the
haystack—"Oh, you think a French girl can kiss better than I can?" That was all
Cary.

Well, it was the two of you.

No. Howard Hawks would sit on the set and he'd say, "Well, I'm not quite
satisfied with this scene, what would you say in a situation like this?" So we'd sit
and think, and it was invariably Cary. He would tell you what to say. Howard is a
very clever man. He picks brains. And he had a very clever brain to pick with Cary
Grant, believe me. If only Cary had directed. I begged him. I said, "Please, get something and direct it before I'm too old to play comedy," and he said, "No, no dear,
too much work. Not I. I want the drawing room comedies—cigarette, anyone?" It's
a shame that those comedies like *The Awful Truth*—you know, with the hands in
the pockets, the fish-and-tails, the dignified gentlemen and all, it's a way of life
that's just gone. Look at Bill Powell and Carole Lombard in *My Man Godfrey*. I tell
you, it's one of the classic films. She was such a tremendous comedienne, and you
couldn't beat Powell. He was right up there with Grant. And of course it's in the
writing.

When you went to 20th, was it on a two-picture deal?

Yes. These were the two pictures, *Male War Bride* and *Stella*, that they turned
up. They always nab you, you see, because they said, "If you can find a script we
like, we'll do a three-picture deal." Well, I submitted scripts, and they didn't like
'em.

That has a lot of holes.

Well, you can't blame them. They have to take into consideration cost and nine
million other things that, not being an executive or especially money-minded, I
wouldn't bother with. If I were going to produce it, that's another matter. But the
studio takes care of all that, and sometimes there are things that just cost too much.

Was Stella *a script you had enthusiasm for?*

I did have enthusiasm for it, I loved it. But it was a dreadful mistake, I didn't
like what I saw. It was dreary, and it shouldn't have been. Something happened
between the conception and the release of it. Now, David Wayne and Frank Fontaine
are fine actors and I thought they were very funny. Evelyn Varden, who played my
mother, is a wonderful actress. Victor Mature was a big, husky guy that all the gals
went for, but there was something chemically wrong between us. And I believe in
those set-ups. Cagney and I had it. I suppose I had some of it with Flynn. There is
a certain animal magnetism, that's all I can call it, that works between two people.

After Stella, *there were four films for Universal. Was that a four-picture deal, or was it
a longer contract?*

That was a three-picture deal. Did I do four there?

Yes, Take Me to Town, Just Across the Street, Steel Town *and* Woman on the
Run.

No, *Woman on the Run* wasn't done at Universal. That was an independent picture, Norman Foster directed it.

They just got a Universal release for it, then?

They might have, I really don't remember. Let me see, *Just Across the Street* so far has not paid off in percentages and neither has *Take Me to Town*. *Steel Town* has paid off lately. They finally had to.

I'd heard that Ross Hunter had been interested in using you for a lot more film work, perhaps the way he's been working with Lana Turner more recently.

Oh, I'm sure he was. It's just finding the right part. Ross went in with me to Universal at the same time I signed the deal with Leonard Goldstein. Ross was put on as an associate producer. Ross was an old friend of mine, and he worked with me on these three pictures. In fact, he was the one who sent me back here to New York. He was going to do *Take Me to Town* on Broadway. It was originally titled *Vermilion O'Toole*, that was her name in the picture, which I thought was absolutely fascinating, it's the silliest name I've ever heard. And some executive in the front office said, "What the hell does *Vermilion O'Toole* mean?" Imagination? Like the back end of a handball court. Anyway, this was changed to *Take Me to Town*, the title of a song in it. Ross was struggling at the time to get the rights to this for a Broadway play, and he suggested that I come East and do summer stock to learn something about the stage, which I certainly wasn't familiar with as an actress. And I did, that was 1958.

And now we come to Appointment in Honduras.

Ooh!! I never have seen that one.

Was that done under duress?

In a way. I had sued Howard Hughes at one point, and won the suit, over *Carriage Entrance*. Ava Gardner and Robert Mitchum did it later [as *My Forbidden Past*]. Well, at one time I had a deal with Colin Banks, the author of the book, to do it, and there was a big hassle over leading man. He made the deal to do it through RKO, and Howard Hughes bought the deal. Mr. Hughes and I couldn't get together on a leading man. I had asked for Mitchum, he had wanted Mel Ferrer. He had three others in mind, I had three others. I had script and leading man approval, within reason. But the whole thing blew apart. He abrogated my contract and I sued him and won, and this was the end of it, because the lawyer advised me to always settle on the courthouse steps. So I was sent this script, *Appointment in Honduras*. Again, I thought it might be an interesting thing if well done, jungles and all that stuff—oh, well. And I was tired of fighting and thought it was just about time to call everything off and say, "Oh, to hell with it." So I consulted the lawyer and he told me to do it if I thought the script was worth it, and I said, "Oh well, maybe, I don't know." So I accepted it. Never saw it. I heard it was an absolute horror.

And then Come Next Spring, *which was really lovely. Every critic mentioned you favorably.*

Thank you. I liked that very much. Unfortunately, it was not properly handled. Steve Cochran produced it but it had nothing to do with him, it had only to do with the studio release. Now in my contract, and I'm sure in his, was a clause which said that the picture would get an A picture release. Well, that can run nine different ways. I read, before I came back to New York that season, that it was released as a second feature! It didn't matter whether his contract specified an A release, it was released in an A release picture house. Shortly after this picture, Herbert Yates, who owned Republic, finally retired.

Taking Vera Ralston *with him.*

Yes, Vera Hruba. Anyhow, it was poor Steve who finally got taken, because I had a flat fee deal.

Still, Come Next Spring *was an exceptionally well-done film.*

Yes, I think it was a sweet, charming little picture. Didn't cost much, they said it cost a million, but I doubt it. It was shot in color in Sacramento during the summer.

Was The Opposite Sex *strictly on a one-picture deal with Metro?*

Yes.

And the following year, a film that puzzles me, Woman and the Hunter.

That was done for a British company. It's a horrible thing, shot in Africa in color. A silly thing about a woman who wants to marry a guy, she's his secretary, and she kills him and then takes on his son and she takes on the white hunter. It made sense in the script, but the way they cut it it made no sense whatsoever. And not even in color which was horrible, what with the color makeup, very black and very white and all that. My nephew in Dallas told me about it in 1960. He said, "I saw your African picture on TV," and I almost fell out of the chair. I didn't even know it was over here. Then later I read that it was going to be shown. I turned it on briefly that evening and said, "No, I don't think I can bear this," and turned it off. I don't believe it's ever been released. The picture was made in 1956 in Nairobi all over Kenya. I don't think it's made a dime, and of course I haven't made a dime, because that was another percentage deal. You know, I think this was really a take-off on *The Macomber Affair,* which was a dull, talky thing. Well, we thought we had action. I did anyway. And I adored Africa, would give my neck to go back tomorrow.

And that was your last film.

That's right. And should have been!

Then two things on the stage. Kind Sir *in the summer of '58....*

Summer stock, all over. Altogether I would say 15 weeks dear, don't ask me where. That's what Ross Hunter sent me back for. Gus Schirmer directed it and we opened in East Hampton, Long Island.

What led you to decide on Kind Sir?

Well, it was written by Norman Krasna, a very fine writer. And I did want to learn something about the theater. Schirmer said, and he was right, that so many of the plays are so dated. And he felt that, with some cutting, *Kind Sir* was the most up-to-date. He sent it to me, I read it, I loved it. We didn't play it at all like Charles Boyer and Mary Martin did [on Broadway]. We didn't play it straight, it was strictly for comedy. Norman Krasna gave us permission to cut any damned thing we wanted to. I think we had a fairly good success with it.

And then Odd Man In *late in '59. That didn't get awfully good reviews.*

Odd Man In was an atrocity!

Then why did you do it?

Because I was promised there would be rewrites and that it would come in to Broadway. I should have know better than to trust producers, I should have known that it wouldn't have been rewritten, but I believe people. We opened in—let me see, where did I have my first coughing fit?—Philadelphia. Opening night. The critics said the best thing about the play was Miss Sheridan's coughing fit when she had to leave the stage. And I did, because by that time I had an infected sinus. Well, we got through the play. Usually the actors got pretty good reviews. The play, never. Did I tell you we played 69 cities in five months? I think out of the five months we had six weeks altogether where we stayed in one town. The rest were just one-night, two-night, three-night stands. The hard way to learn about the theater. And with a sinus infection. I was back down to 112 pounds again.

Have you done any stage work since then?

Nope. I won't accept a bad play, I'd rather wash dishes. I made the mistake with *Odd Man In* of accepting their word, which was strictly phony. I should have learned that in Hollywood, about believing people.

How about the announcement late in '64 about your doing a show about [scandal-ridden 1920s evangelist] Aimee Semple McPherson?

That was silly. It was jumped by my agent, who was out of his cotton-pickin' mind.

Had you never agreed to it?

I agreed to talk about it.

I've heard that it was a project that has been going on for quite some time, but that they had never been able to get a clearance from the McPherson estate.

That's quite true. David Hocker, who was my agent at the time, gave this out. It had been broached to me, and I said fine, if they would do Aimee Semple as I knew about her, if they'd tell the truth. There's a brother in California who runs the temple, and a sister back here, a Mrs. David Salter. So I agreed to meet her, I said I'd love to meet Aimee Semple's daughter, so David made the appointment. I arrived, and because I didn't have my hair done I wore a white chiffon scarf over my head. I came in and the first thing she said was, "Oh, you came dressed for the part!," with an angelic expression on her face. I said, "What?" and she said, "My mother always wore a scarf." Well, you have never heard such an interview in your life! And finally somebody sitting across the table said, "Well, you can't whitewash it." I wouldn't have said it. Well, automatically—"You don't wish to do the story of my mother!" Do you know what they were going to do? They were going to have her sing songs, with that bloody tambourine, and baptize people! All purity and light. And I said, "That's not her life!" The daughter got frightened, I'm sure. I wouldn't play it that way for anything. And then, wouldn't you know, this mad agent gives it to the newspapers without my approval. They were going to save money by having me just walk out and sing spirituals. Now I adore spirituals, I can shout to the rooftops and bawl 'em out like nothing you've ever heard in your life ... [belts out] *He's got the who-ole world in His hands...*, but you can't do a musical like that. If you want music like that, you'll need a singer. I'd adore singing them, but I'm no singer. I said, "There's got to be something more. You've got to have a book and at least some of the background. The music is incidental." They wanted to cheat.

That's a shame, it's one of the great stories to come out of the 1920s. It'll be quite a while before it becomes public domain.

Well, I'll get a face lift and play it then.

Okay, can we finish up with tidbits?

Sure.

A very grand-sounding question, your opinion of your overall position in cinema history—how does it strike you?

It doesn't strike me at all. There's no position, really. It'll be just one of those things that's written off, for heaven's sake. It won't mean anything.

How about your approach to acting? Just a natural projection of personality?

That's right. Be as honest as you can. That's the only approach I could possibly answer. Hard work and honesty. I think all actors and actresses are personalities. This even applies to character actors, even they are personalities. That's why they are used.

When you were doing the bulk of your work back at Warners, and later, didn't you see yourself as considerably more than a glamour girl?

Oh, of course I did. I had dreams.

And still?

Of course I have.

That it could have been more?

Yes, and that it will be more. I think Bette's right. When they start making pictures for mature women again—I don't give a damn how old we are.

You don't intend to just up and quit?

I don't think so. I think you should always work and always have an interest. I most assuredly do. But I won't do some things that people think I should do. I won't take one or two weeks of summer stock. That's silly, and it just costs me money. I will not work with some of the general run of summer stock people. Some of them are very honest, hard-working people whom I admire, and some are liars and thieves. It's a different matter if I find a play that someone will accept for, say, an eight- or ten-week run, and they'll agree with me upon a leading man and director. I'm sorry, I will not take their directors or their local talent. I have tried that, it's pretty gruesome.

Any preferences—comedy, drama, musical?

I love comedy, I adore it. I'd like to find a good part in a straight play, I don't care whether it's a starring role or not. But these are so out-of-date on Broadway. Of course, everybody wants a Broadway production, but they're awfully hard to come by.

Any specific properties you'd like to do?

Well, I've read a story recently called *Careful, He Might Hear You.* I'd like to play the heavy in that, but I don't know how interested the public would be in a little boy and a mean, mature woman, his aunt. It seems so hard to sell things like that, unless you do something on growing old, which I think the public likes to see, like *The Subject Was Roses* and *Never Too Late*. Either you're in that category or it's for the very young people, the teenagers. Somehow or other, they're not doing in-between kind of things.

No, not any more. Well, stars are boys and girls now, and they used to be men and women. And that was nice, and I miss it.

Well, I do too. My God, you should see and hear the struggle that everyone has just to try and find a part. There's nothing for mature women, except for Rosalind Russell. She does them all, and eventually she'll get tired or something will come up that she won't want to do.

Speaking of what they're writing now, have you any thoughts about the horror cycle that Davis, Crawford, Bankhead and the others are now doing?

Wish I could find a good one. An ex-agent, Dick Levine, said they had me up for *Hush...Hush, Sweet Charlotte* before they cast Davis and Crawford in it. I didn't know my name had been even mentioned. But I love those corny things. I'm crazy about soap operas, too, I adore them. *Edge of Night* and *Secret Storm* and all that.

I just thought of something that I dimly remember from when I was a tot. Haven't seen them since, but others around my age have remembered them, too. A series of mystery books using names of stars as part of the titles, like "Ann Sheridan and the Case of the..." what?

Ann Sheridan and the Sign of the Sphinx, I'll have you know. I've got a copy that they sent me, but I haven't had nerve enough to read it. Utterly horrible, I'm sure. I flipped through a couple of pages and couldn't bear it. But you're right, it was *Ann Sheridan and the Sign of the Sphinx*. Isn't that darling? Maybe we could make that into a soap opera.

Did they do this series with stars from all the studios, or was it just Warners?

Just Warners. They had some sort of tie-in with them, like they do for advertising bicycles and spark plugs and that sort of stuff. They got a lot of publicity from those tie-ins that they wouldn't have gotten otherwise. Also a lot of people on the lot furnished their homes that way. You know, pose with the Motorola, blouses, shorts, slacks, dresses, anything under the sun they could make a tie-in with. If we'd been in the government, we'd have been accused of taking bribes.

I remember five or six years ago tuning into a Perry Como Show, *and there you were singing "Guess Who I Saw Today." Was that the only time you sang on TV?*

No, there were other times, but that was the only time I was on Perry's show.

You've been doing a few of the panel shows lately, mostly To Tell the Truth.

Yes, I did *The Match Game* one week, and *Missing Links* once. And *The Price Is Right*. That's all the panel shows I've done. But I've been on *To Tell the Truth* quite often in the past couple of years. It's a lot of fun.

Do you usually watch your films when they're shown on TV?

No! I don't.

Oh. Okay. How about favorite actors? Not necessarily that you've worked with, just that you've admired.

Oh, Paul Scofield, and Laurence Olivier, naturally. The British actors, definitely. Most of them, the top ones like Guiness and Morley. I love them. Among the American actors, I would say people like Jimmy Cagney and Cary Grant—and this is not just personality-wise, it's because I think they're damn good actors. The parts they played they gave something to, always. But I think so many people are miscast now. I think Brando is a very fine actor, but he has been miscast in quite a few pictures.

How about actresses?

Oh, dear. A lot of them. I adore Bette Davis. I love Roz Russell because she has that vitality. She really kills herself doing all these things and it doesn't seem to bother her at all. Then I go the other way to Margaret Rutherford, and who doesn't love her? Bergman I like. I think she's been miscast many times too, but that's the fault of the story, not the actress. I think Mercedes McCambridge is a fine talent, such a good actress. Anna Magnani of course I love. I've seen some of her Italian pictures that have been very bad, but somehow or other they're able to survive the bad ones. You know what everybody says, "You're only as good as your last picture," but I don't think that's always true.

I don't think they feel that way in Europe, as they do here.

No, but in Hollywood that used to be the saying. Let's see. The kid who played *Sundays and Cybele* and *Rapture* recently, Patricia Gozzi. I think she's absolutely wonderful. And Janet Margolin, the little girl who did *David and Lisa*, is a wonderful little actress. And he's very good too, I've met him [Kier Dullea]. The inimitable Garbo. Dietrich, but the greatest.

How about directors?

Well, I'd say Norman Taurog, Sam Wood—Mitch Leisen, of course, but that's possibly because he was all for me. Oh, dear, there are so many. Hank Hathaway is a very good director. I've known him for a thousand years, from when he did [*The Lives of a*] *Bengal Lancer* at Paramount, but he doesn't like to work with women, so that lets me out. We're very good friends socially. Well, there are just some damn fine ones, like Hitchcock. If they have the right property, always that.

Well, you won't believe this, but I think we've covered everything.

Oh, you poor man. How were you able to stand it?

It's been marvelous, believe me. I've loved every minute of it.

Well, bless your heart, but I don't know how you bear it. I could never sit down and do this, even if I were capable of doing it. It would bore me to death, I don't know how you have the patience. Now some people have wonderful, exciting lives. I read the article *Screen Facts* did on Davis. To me that was very interesting, because there was so much about her in it that I didn't know. It was so full of information about her early beginnings. When I first saw her she was a *star*, and a real one too. I never realized what a tough time she'd gone through. Some people have such interesting things happen to them during the knock-down, drag-out try for a career. Others, it just seems to drag along, and mine sounds so boring. If something exciting had happened I could understand people's interest, but it was just hard work, that's all.

Epilogue

Late in 1965, a month or so after our last interview, Ann began work on *Another World*, a daily NBC-TV soap-opera, in a continuing role. She remained with the show until April 15, 1966, and returned to Hollywood to begin filming *Pistols 'n' Petticoats*, a weekly TV Western comedy series that ran during the 1966-67 season on CBS.

In June 1966 she married actor Scott McKay. They had met in 1958 when he was her leading man in the *Kind Sir* tour. In October of that year they appeared in *The Time of Your Life* at the Brussels Universal and International Exposition, after which they co-starred in the disastrous tour of *Odd Man In* from October 1959 to March, 1960. They'd been together ever since.

But also in 1966, during production of *Pistols 'n' Petticoats*, Ann was diagnosed with terminal cancer. Throughout her treatments at Cedars of Lebanon Hospital she kept the news to herself and stubbornly managed to finish the season, not wanting her colleagues to lose their jobs. When her mobility became noticeably limited, she blamed it on a fall from a horse during her honeymoon. But after returning from the Christmas break, there was no mistaking how severely ill she had become. Producer Joe Connelly later recalled, "We all knew then how very sick Ann was, but nobody let on. We had to have her doing most of the scenes sitting down although she insisted she could walk." Chairs were placed so she could lean on them when standing, and costume designer Julia Hanson would pad Ann's costumes in an attempt to disguise her alarming weight loss. In a few of the later episodes, her always distinctive speaking voice had to be dubbed. Withal, she managed to complete 25 of the 26 series episodes.

Ann died on January 21, 1967, in the San Fernando Valley home she shared with Scott McKay, exactly a month short of her fifty-second birthday. Her death was front page news in newspapers across the country. (McKay died at 71 on March 16, 1987.)

It's difficult to find anyone who worked with Ann Sheridan who had anything negative to say about her. Joseph McBride interviewed Howard Hawks for his book *Hawks on Hawks* (1982) and asked Hawks about working with Ann in *I Was a Male War Bride*. Hawks replied, "Great. She outlived some of the worst pictures you've ever known and became good. People liked her. They made her a star in spite of the bad pictures. Oh, she was quick and good and everything. And when we made *Male War Bride* she wasn't so young. She'd been through the mill by that time. But if you're going to make a good picture with Cary Grant, you'd better have somebody who's pretty damn good along with him."

Frequent co-star James Cagney remembered Ann with great affection: "The leading lady of *Angels with Dirty Faces* was that lovely, talented gal, Ann Sheridan. So much to offer—and a three-pack-a-day smoker. Years later when the lung cancer hit, she didn't have much of a chance, and what a powerful shame that was. A mighty nice gal, Annie."

Sybil Jason, who co-starred with Ann in *The Great O'Malley*, recently told Laura Wagner that Ann was "one of my very favorite people. She was probably the most fun I've had working with anyone in movies. *Everyone* loved her, from the wardrobe people on up the list. She was generous, had a great sense of humor, was quick to laugh and, as far as I could see, was warm to everyone that came within her sight. Apart from her extensive career I think that is a marvelous legacy."

Marsha Hunt appeared with Ann in *Winter Carnival*, and told Laura, "I didn't really know her but I liked what I knew. My impression was of a warm-hearted girl who had a slightly tough exterior, which was wished on her probably by the industry and the sex symbol promotion she was getting. She came through as an actress, it seems to me, more than anybody ever thought she would. She certainly took her work seriously, but with humor and a good nature."

Vincent Sherman directed her in two 1947 hits, *Nora Prentiss* and *The Unfaithful*. In his 1996 autobiography, *Studio Affairs*, he wrote of Ann: "She became one of the most skillful comediennes in Hollywood.... She knew how to toss away a line, underplay it with a wry quality, and get the full measure of the laugh therein. She could also play a dramatic role with the best of them. But because she came up from the ranks, her skill was underrated. And what a joy to work with. She was genuine, no affectations and no bullshit; she loved to laugh and have fun and could, when provoked, curse like a sailor on a stormy night. Although many men made passes at her and tried to seduce her, her bedroom eyes causing all kinds of fantasies, to me she was so honest, so lacking in feminine guile, so down to earth, that I came to think of her not as a sexy female but as a good friend or a sister. I always felt that Ann was not driven to become a big movie star. It slipped up on her and she went along with it. For a short while she enjoyed the advantages of being in the limelight: money, glory, and pleasant work. Coming from a humble background, she gained inner satisfaction from being a star, and it bolstered her modest ego, but I always felt that she would have preferred being a housewife with a loving husband and children. She was a grand girl, talented, and a joy to know and work with."

In their Ann Sheridan obituary, the *London Times* said, "Without ever achieving the mythic status of a super-star, she was always a pleasure to watch, and, as with all true stars, was never quite like anyone else."

1934: Search for Beauty (Paramount), Bolero (Paramount), Come on Marines (Paramount), Murder at the Vanities (Paramount), Kiss and Make Up (Paramount), Shoot the Works (Paramount), Notorious Sophie Lang (Paramount), Ladies Should Listen (Paramount), Wagon Wheels (Paramount), Mrs. Wiggs of the Cabbage Patch (Paramount), College Rhythm (Paramount), Limehouse Blues (Paramount). **1935:** Enter Madame (Paramount), Home on the Range (Paramount), Rumba (Paramount), Behold My Wife (Paramount), Car 99 (Paramount), Rocky Mountain Mystery (Paramount), Mississippi (Paramount), Red Blood of Courage (Ambassador), The Glass Key (Paramount), The Crusades (Paramount), Fighting Youth (Universal), Star Night at Coconut Grove (MGM short), Hollywood Extra Girl (Paramount short). **1936:** Sing Me a Love Song (WB), Black Legion (WB). **1937:** The Great O'Malley (WB), San Quentin (WB), Wine, Women and Horses (WB), The Footloose Heiress (WB). **1938:** Out Where the Stars Begin (WB-Vitaphone short), Alcatraz Island (WB), She Loved a Fireman (WB), The Patient in Room 18 (WB), Mystery House (WB), Cowboy from Brooklyn (WB), Little Miss Thoroughbred (WB), Letter of Introduction (Universal), Broadway Musketeers (WB), Angels with Dirty Faces (WB). **1939:** They Made Me a Criminal (WB), Dodge City (WB), Naughty but Nice (WB), Winter Carnival (UA), Indianapolis Speedway (WB), Angels Wash Their Faces (WB). **1940:** Castle on the Hudson (WB), It All Came True (WB), Torrid Zone (WB), They Drive by Night (WB), City for Conquest (WB). **1941:** Honeymoon for Three (WB), Navy Blues

(WB), Kings Row (WB), The Man Who Came to Dinner (WB). **1942:** Juke Girl (WB), Wings for the Eagle (WB), George Washington Slept Here (WB). **1943:** Edge of Darkness (WB), Thank Your Lucky Stars (WB), Let's Carry on (Red Cross short). **1944:** Shine on Harvest Moon (WB), The Doughgirls (WB). **1945:** Overseas Roundup (Vitaphone short). **1946:** One More Tomorrow (WB). **1947:** Nora Prentiss (WB), The Unfaithful (WB). **1948:** Silver River (WB), Good Sam (RKO), The Treasure of the Sierra Madre (WB; unbilled bit). **1949:** I Was a Male War Bride (TCF). **1950:** Stella (TCF), Woman on the Run (Universal). **1952:** Steel Town (Universal), Just Across the Street (Universal). **1953:** Take Me to Town (Universal), Appointment in Honduras (RKO). **1956:** Come Next Spring (Rep,), The Opposite Sex (MGM). **1957:** Woman and the Hunter (Gross-Krasne-Phoenix). **1967:** The Far Out West (Universal; compiled from episodes of Pistols 'n' Petticoats).

Barbara Stanwyck: The Furies

by RAY HAGEN

What did all the legendary Hollywood goddesses of the 1930s and '40s have in common? Exclusive iron-clad contracts with major studios; Garbo at MGM, Davis at Warners, Crawford at MGM and then Warners, Dietrich at Paramount, Hayworth at Columbia, Grable at Fox. That's the way it worked. Studios made fortunes by building their stars' careers, publicizing them, pampering and protecting them, actually creating them. And, not incidentally, owning them.

Barbara Stanwyck, alone among the supernovas, chose to go it alone, juggling short-term contracts with all the majors but never aligning herself exclusively with any one studio. She wanted the freedom to pick and choose her roles and control her own career. She wouldn't be forced to do whatever the studio dictated under threat of suspension. That was the downside of the studio contract system. But she missed out on the great upside as well: No one studio had a vested interest in promoting her to the skies, buying the best properties for her, giving her the great roles. Creating a legend around her. She had to do that herself.

That she was actually able to do so was testament to her steel-willed tenacity, her unwavering popularity with moviegoers through good movies and (mostly) bad, and the sheer range of her talent. And it certainly didn't hurt that the bitchiest screen virago of them all was indisputably the most beloved of stars by directors, crews and fellow actors, who dubbed her "The Queen." She never threw tantrums or demanded star treatment, was always on time and totally prepared, knowing not only her own lines but everyone else's as well, and had the lifelong work ethic (and vocabulary) of a stevedore.

In his 1959 autobiography, Cecil B. DeMille paid Stanwyck his most sincere tribute: "I am sometimes asked who is my favorite actress among those I have directed. I always dodge the question by explaining that I have to continue living in Hollywood. But if the tortures of the Inquisition were applied and an answer extracted from me, I would have to say that I have never worked with an actress who was more co-operative, less temperamental, and a better workman, to use my term of highest compliment, than Barbara Stanwyck. I have directed, and enjoyed working with, many fine actresses, some of whom are also good workmen; but when I count over those of whom my memories are unmarred by any unpleasant recollection of friction on the set or unwillingness to do whatever the role required or squalls of temperament or temper, Barbara's name is the first that comes to mind, as one on whom a director can always count to do her work with all her heart."

Screenwriter Herman Mankiewicz *(Citizen Kane)* paid her a somewhat earthier tribute: "I dream of being married to her and living in a little cottage in Beverly Hills. I'd come home from a hard day at MGM and Barbara would be there to greet me with an apple pie she had cooked herself. And wearing no panties."

Her evaluation of herself: "I'm just a tough old dame from Brooklyn."

She entered the world as Ruby Catherine Stevens on July 16, 1907, in Brooklyn, New York, the fifth child of Byron and Catherine McGee Stevens. There were three older sisters (Maude, Mabel and Mildred) and one brother, Malcom Byron, two years older than Ruby and her closest companion. They lived on Clausen Street in a drab and tough neighborhood. When Ruby was two, her mother was accidentally pushed off a moving trolley car and died two days later. Her father soon deserted his children and it was left to oldest sister Millie, a showgirl, to care for them. As she was often on the road, Ruby and brother Malcom were put in a series of foster homes, sometimes together and sometimes not. It wasn't so much a cruel childhood as simply an impersonal and loveless one.

Dancing in the streets to hurdy-gurdies, common then among tenement children, was one of her rare pleasures. Another was the movies, and her idol was serial queen Pearl White, whose elaborate stunts and physical daring thrilled her. When sister Mildred could afford to take Ruby with her on her road show tours, she would watch entranced from the wings, and learn all the dance routines. Her ambition was set.

After graduating from grammar school at age 14, she got her first job as a pattern-cutter at Condé Nast, but her lack of basic skills got her quickly fired. She then spotted an ad for chorus girls at the Strand Roof and dance director Earl Lindsay hired her at $35 a week. The new chorine learned quickly, and so impressed Lindsay that he used her in future Broadway revues. Now a

Portrait of Barbara Stanwyck, 1944.

hard-working professional, between 1922 and 1925 she danced in nightclubs and cabarets, occasionally doubling in sketches and doing the odd specialty turn. On Broadway she danced in *George White's Scandals*, *Artists and Models* (both in 1923), *Keep Kool* ('24) and *Gay Paree* ('25). She also appeared in the 1924 touring company of *Ziegfeld Follies of 1923*, doing a striptease in silhouette, back-lit behind a white screen, and tossing her discarded duds into the audience. And let it not be forgotten that she was the third light to the left in a human chandelier.

Ruby was now rooming with fellow chorines Mae Clarke and Walda Mansfield. The trio were regulars at Billy LaHiff's West 48th Street restaurant, The Tavern. LaHiff was known for letting unemployed actors dine on-the-cuff and he befriended Ruby. When he learned that actor-producer-director Willard Mack needed four chorus girls for his new play, *The Noose*, he introduced him to Ruby and Mack hired her. She got him to hire her roommates as well. She played a cabaret dancer in unrequited love with a man who had been condemned to death, and she had only a few lines. But when the play was going badly during the out-of-town tryouts, Mack made some changes. A major shift concerned a scene near the end when his society girlfriend pleaded for his body so she could have him buried in a nice cemetery. When told that he has not been hanged after all, she hysterically pleads with the governor not to tell him of her visit. Mack decided to have the scene played not by the society girlfriend but by the lovesick young dancer instead. It was a powerful scene for an inexperienced actress to carry.

Mack also renamed her, feeling that "Ruby Stevens" sounded fine for a stripper but was too common for a dramatic actress. He found an old turn-of-the-century Belasco Theatre program for *Barbara Fritchie* starring British actress Jane Stanwyck, combined them, and presented Ruby with a new name to go with her new identity.

Barbara later described her transformation: "Only through Willard Mack's kindness in coaching me, showing me all the tricks, how to sell myself by entrances and exits, did I get by. It was Willard Mack who completely disarranged my mental make-up. The process—like all processes of birth and death, I guess—was pretty damn painful. Especially for him. I got temperamental. The truth is, I was scared. I'd storm and yell that I couldn't act—couldn't, and what's more, wouldn't. I think I can honestly say that this was my first and last flare-up of temperament, because Mr. Mack—who had flattered and encouraged me—shrewdly reversed his tactics. One day, right before the entire company, he screamed back at me that I was right, I was dead right. I was a chorus girl, would always be a chorus girl, would live and die a chorus girl, so to hell with me. It worked. I yelled back that I could act, would act, was not a chorus girl—was Bernhardt, Fiske and all the Booths and Barrymores rolled into one."

The Noose opened at the Hudson Theatre on October 20, 1926. Mack's show was a hit, and so was his new dramatic discovery. Her notices were uniformly splendid, none more so than the *New York Telegram*, whose critic raved: "There is an uncommonly fine performance by Barbara Stanwyck, who not only does the Charleston steps of a dance hall girl gracefully, but knows how to act, a feature which somehow, with her comely looks, seems kind of superfluous." *Variety* noted that "Miss Stanwyck ... was last season disporting herself in a side street nightclub chorus as Ruby Stevens, but she's through chorusing forever after this bit."

It was during the show's run that she went to Cosmopolitan's New York studio to test for the leading role in a silent backstage movie, *Broadway Nights*. She lost the role to Lois Wilson, but played a smaller part as a producer's dancer-girlfriend. Filmed in New York while she was playing in *The Noose*, her movie debut (and only non-talkie) was released in May 1927. As with so many other silent films, the negative has long since crumbled to dust.

Broadway producer-director-playwright Arthur Hopkins then tested her for the leading female role in his upcoming production *Burlesque*. Impressed with her quality of "rough poignancy," he cast her opposite musical comedy actor Hal Skelly. Again she was a dancer, but this time her role was substantial and demanding. She and Skelly played a pair of vaudevillians whose career and marriage go through disappointments and turmoil, their ultimate reconciliation occurring as they perform their small-time dance act in a tank-town theater. It opened on September 1, 1927. The stars were critically lauded for their fine performances, the show was a hit and, at age 20, Barbara Stanwyck became a bona fide Broadway star.

"She and Skelly were a great team," wrote Hopkins in his autobiography, *To a Lonely Boy*, "and they made the play a great success. I had great plans for her, but the Hollywood offers kept coming. There was no competing with them." In an interview shortly before his death, he described Stanwyck as "the greatest *natural* actress of our time."

Also in the cast of *Burlesque* was Oscar Levant. During the run he introduced Barbara to his friend Frank Fay, then riding high as "Broadway's Favorite Son," as he was billed. Fay, a show biz veteran since childhood and now at the peak of his fame, had recently completed a record 12-week run at the Palace. On August 26, 1928, they were married. Their marriage, Fay's third, would, in time, become the stuff of Hollywood legend.

The movies had just learned to talk and Hollywood was raiding Broadway for actors who could walk and talk at the same time. The Fays were both offered film work and they moved to California. As Arthur Hopkins later complained, "One of the theater's great potential actresses was embalmed in celluloid."

Barbara's talkie debut, *The Locked Door* (1929), a creaky old melodrama even then, co-starred Barbara with silent veterans Rod La Rocque and Betty Bronson, both of whose performances could most charitably be called dreadful. It sank like a stone, and Barbara told the *Los Angeles Times* in 1958, "They never should have unlocked the damned thing."

Although she had no experience in film acting, her own performance was remarkably simple and honest, given the chaotic surroundings. But her next opus, *Mexicali Rose* (1929), starred Barbara as the title vixen, and she was utterly at sea. Another dud, it was the first "bad girl" role she ever played and all she knew to do was sashay about with her hands superglued to her hips, her rotating elbows endangering everything not nailed down within a three-foot radius. Her Brooklyn accent didn't help. It was a disaster all around, and what turned out to be the only really bad performance of her entire career. She later said that *Mexicali Rose* "reached what I shall always believe was an all-time low."

Fay, meanwhile, brimmed with confidence as he began what he was certain would be a standout film career. Barbara was becoming more and more depressed as one screen test after another yielded no results.

By the time she was interviewed by a young director named Frank Capra for his next movie at the minor-league Columbia studio she was ready to pack it up and go back to New York. Truculent throughout the interview, she finally said, "Oh, hell, you don't want any part of me," and stomped out. But when Frank Fay showed Capra a color test she'd made under Alexander Korda's direction, her big speech from *The Noose*, he knew she was exactly what he wanted for the role of Kay Arnold, the street-smart yet vulnerable "party girl," in *Ladies of Leisure*. "Underneath her sullen shyness," Capra later wrote, "smoldered the emotional fires of a young Duse, or a Bernhardt. Naïve, unsophisticated, caring nothing about make-up, clothes or hair-dos, this chorus girl could grab your heart and tear it to pieces ... She just turned it on—and everything else on the stage stopped."

Ladies of Leisure was a great hit, a major step up for Columbia, and it made an instant star of Barbara Stanwyck. Critics raved about this lovely young actress, effusively praising the naturalness and honesty of her acting, her unique voice and her strong presence. *Photoplay* rhapsodized about "the astonishing performance of a little tap-dancing beauty who has in her the spirit of a great artist ... Go and be amazed by this Barbara girl." "Is this just a flash in the pan," asked another fan magazine, "or the beginning of a major career?"

She signed non-exclusive contracts with both Columbia and Warners and was immediately put to work in one starring vehicle after another, a pace that wouldn't slow down for the next quarter century.

Meanwhile, Frank Fay's career turned to ashes as his movies flopped and his performances bombed. Barbara's sudden ascension to stardom and his profound public fall from grace were much noted, Fay becoming unemployable and hitting the bottle as Barbara became the star (and breadwinner) of the family. It was the Fay-Stanwyck marriage that inspired the soon-to-be

With Ralph Graves in *Ladies of Leisure* **(Columbia, 1930).**

Hollywood classic *A Star Is Born*. The writers had to step very carefully to avoid being sued and many alterations were made but, at its basic core, *A Star Is Born* is very much the story of Frank Fay and Barbara Stanwyck.

Throughout the 1930s she worked like a mule, grinding out over 30 movies at all the major studios. A few were worthy of her, most were run-of-the-mill programmers and too many were out-and-out stinkers, but they had one thing in common: All were "Barbara Stanwyck movies." Along with Crawford, Hepburn, Davis, Dietrich and Garbo, it was her name that sold them and her fans that supported them. But she differed from all those ladies in some key respects. She lacked their exaggerated facial features and vocal mannerisms (mimics and drag queens never did camped-up Stanwyck impressions), cared not a whit about elaborate lighting, hairdos or wardrobe and never considered herself glamourous or even beautiful. She simply loved acting, took her profession seriously and wanted to work. All stardom meant to Barbara was that it allowed her to continue doing so.

Critics repeatedly called Stanwyck's performances "natural," "honest," "sincere." These adjectives showed up in countless reviews, and while they were meant as high praise they bespoke a drabness that came to characterize both Barbara and her vehicles, fairly or not. But a few films from this decade stood out.

She'd become Capra's favorite actress and he directed her in three more Columbia dramas. *The Miracle Woman* (1931) was an initially daring but failed attempt at telling the story of a fraudulent preacher, based on the notorious Aimee Semple McPherson. Barbara delivered a strong performance but the cop-out script sank it. *Forbidden* ('32) was nothing more than mawkish soap opera worthy of neither of them. *The Bitter Tea of General Yen* ('32) was a truly strange tale with Barbara as the captive and lover of a Chinese warlord, but casting Swedish Nils Asther as General Yen was pure racial cowardice. None approached *Ladies of Leisure* in quality or box office success.

At Warners, a studio more in synch with her slangy energy, she did a trio of films with William "Wild Bill" Wellman, who saw Barbara's strengths in a less romantic light than did Capra. After directing her as a gritty, two-fisted *Night Nurse* (1931), he cast her as the heroine of Edna Ferber's *So Big* ('32), a farm saga in which she ages 20 years with grace, skill and a minimum of old-age makeup. Her performance was widely admired but the film's scant 80-minute running time severely undercut its potential. They then collaborated on *The Purchase Price* ('32), an absurd tale that took her from hardened nightclub chanteuse (singing on-screen for the first time) to plucky, loyal, weather-worn farm wife. Early in that script she delivered a short speech that must have had an eerie resonance for her: "I've been up and down Broadway since I was 15 years old. I'm fed up with hoofing in shows. I'm sick of nightclubs, hustlers, bootleggers, chiselers and smart guys. I've heard all the questions and know all the answers. And I've kept myself *fairly* respectable through it all. The whole atmosphere of this street gives me a high-powered headache."

She always considered Wellman, Capra and Billy Wilder her favorite directors.

Also at Warners, she did three zippy pre–Code programmers that solidified her image as a sexually liberated, been-through-the-mill tough dame, equally handy with a withering wisecrack, a solid right hook or, if needed, a pistol. In *Illicit* (1931) she defiantly preferred "living in sin" to the joys of wedded bliss. *Ladies They Talk About* ('33) had her slugging fellow high-heeled inmates in a prison replete with beauticians and designer uniforms. *Baby Face* ('33) became notorious for its depiction of a totally amoral slut who escaped the coal town where her father doubled as her pimp, moving to the big city where, the ads bragged, "she climbed the ladder of success, wrong by wrong." This one, along with the advent of Mae West, was the last straw for bluenoses, and henceforth the stringent Production Code saw to it that all traces of honest sexuality would be absent from films until the 1960s. *Baby Face* and *Ladies They Talk About*, while hardly masterpieces of cinema art, are still great fun to watch and she never dogs it for a second.

In 1932 she was seen for the only time on film with Frank Fay in an all-star short spoof, *The Stolen Jools*. That year she and Fay adopted a boy, Dion (later called Tony), in the hope of strengthening their marriage.

The following year she returned to Broadway with Fay in *Tattle Tales*, financing it with her movie earnings in a doomed attempt to bolster his sagging career and ego. It opened at the Broadhurst Theatre on June 1, 1933, and limped on for 28 performances. Fay appeared in witless comedy sketches and Barbara did scenes from *Ladies of Leisure* and *The Miracle Woman*. It was her final stage appearance.

She returned to Hollywood and continued grinding out programmers, now mostly substandard sob-fests. A welcome respite was *Annie Oakley* (1935), her first Western. Her feisty energy and humor made for a welcome relief after so many weepies, and it was a much-needed hit.

In late 1935 she divorced Frank Fay, by now alcoholic and physically abusive. After winning a long and bitter custody battle, Barbara sent their son off to a series of boarding and military schools, eventually cutting herself off from seeing or even discussing him for the rest of their lives. Not her proudest achievement.

The following year was quite notable for her. She signed with Darryl Zanuck to do two Fox films with varying results. *A Message to Garcia* had her ludicrously miscast as a Brooklyn-accented Cuban senorita, but *Banjo on My Knee* was a popular riverboat comedy-drama with music that had Barbara singing with Tony Martin and hoofing with Buddy Ebsen. Martin praised Barbara in his 1976 joint autobiography (with wife Cyd Charisse), *The Two of Us*. It was his first dramatic role and he hadn't a clue how to get through a particularly difficult scene with her. As he wrote: "'It's a tough scene,' Barbara said. 'I'll tell you what let's do. I'll meet you here at eight o'clock in the morning and I'll help you.' So that's what we did. We met at eight, before anybody else was there, and she showed me how to do the scene. I'll never forget her kindness to me. Everybody liked her. She had the vocabulary of a Marine sergeant and I guess that's what made the crew putty in her hands. She catered to them. And, in return, they couldn't do enough for her." Ebsen later happily recalled that "She gave me my first screen kiss. When she finished I couldn't remember my next line."

The Bride Walks Out (1936) was her first all-out comedy, albeit a weak one, but *His Brother's Wife* ('36) had a major effect on her life. It was her first film at MGM and she was co-starred with America's new pretty-boy sensation, Robert Taylor. The picture was ridiculous but the stars had fallen in love, becoming one of the film world's glamour couples. She was four years older, not a great beauty, was from a tough, hardscrabble New York background and had been a highly regarded star actress for six years. He grew up in Nebraska, was new to big-city life in Hollywood and his beauty was such that he could have his pick of anyone he wanted. Why, everyone wondered, choose Barbara Stanwyck? His oft-quoted, classic reply: "Barbara is not the sort of woman I'd have met in Nebraska."

They again co-starred in *This Is My Affair* (1937), a period piece, by which time their romance was widely known. The ads, not to mention the title itself, didn't fail to capitalize on their relationship. They made a dazzling couple and audiences thronged to see the real-life lovers. Barbara, as a café singer, positively glowed, singing five numbers amid the melodramatic goings-on.

That same year she worked with the Abbey Players in a badly botched version of Sean O'Casey's *The Plough and the Stars* under John Ford's direction, but it was her next film that gave Barbara's career its biggest boost to date.

When Samuel Goldwyn decided to film Olive Higgins Prouty's *Stella Dallas*, it was already a dated, shameless tear-jerker of self-sacrificing mother love, but Barbara wanted the role and fought for it. Goldwyn considered her too young and inexperienced with children, but she won him over by swallowing her pride and making a test. He caved. Her portrayal of the loud and vulgar Stella who nonetheless would (and did) make any sacrifice for her beloved daughter was a personal triumph. The film worked despite its outrageous bathos because Goldwyn, Stanwyck and director King Vidor so believed in and committed themselves to the story that critics and audiences were bulldozed into acceptance. Molly Haskell, in her 1973 overview of women in film *From Reverence to Rape*, called Barbara's portrait of Stella "at once the most excruciating and exhilarating performance on film."

She copped the first of her four Oscar nominations and was profoundly disappointed at losing (to Luise Rainer in *The Good Earth*). As she later said, "I poured my blood into that one."

Her 1938 vehicles were fairly minor, though one—*The Mad Miss Manton*, a so-so screwball comedy—teamed her for the first time with Henry Fonda.

She was one of the many actresses briefly considered for *Gone with the Wind*—hard to imagine Scarlett O'Hara with a Brooklyn accent—but she wasn't a serious contender. Instead, 1939 found her in Cecil B. DeMille's *Union Pacific*, a rambunctious railroad saga co-starring Joel McCrea and Robert Preston. The focus was on the men and the trains, but Barbara was a lively and playful Irish lass who held her own through all the battles.

DeMille found her a dream to work with and, although *Union Pacific* was their only film together, he used her often on his *Lux Radio Theatre*, by far radio's most popular and prestigious dramatic series. Barbara recreated many of her film roles, eventually appearing in 17 shows between 1936 and 1954. She also starred in roles made famous by other actresses, including *Wuthering Heights, Morning Glory, Smilin' Through, Penny Serenade, These Three* and *Dark Victory*. The latter was aired in 1938 before the film was made and Barbara wanted it to be a test run for a movie version. Losing the part to Bette Davis was a crushing disappointment.

Her final 1939 film was Clifford Odets' *Golden Boy*. It had been a high-profile hit on Broadway and the movie version was severely marred by a sappy happy ending that was widely criticized, but Barbara was well received for her unflinching portrait of a hard-edged "dame from Newark" who falls for the young hero. The boy, an extremely demanding role, was played by a very nervous newcomer, William Holden. It didn't start out too well. When she got word that he was going to be fired, she threatened to walk off the picture if they did any such thing, and spent every available moment coaching and working with him so he could deliver the performance she knew he was capable of. With her help, *Golden Boy* made William Holden a star, and every year for the rest of his life he sent her flowers on the anniversary of the film's starting date.

(Many years later, when Holden and Stanwyck were introduced together as presenters at the 1978 Academy Awards, he unexpectedly ditched their prepared script, saying instead: "Before Barbara and I present this next award, I'd like to say something. Thirty-nine years ago this month we were working in a film together called *Golden Boy*, and it wasn't going well because I was going to be replaced. But due to this lovely human being and her interest and understanding and her professional integrity and her encouragement and, above all, her generosity, I'm here tonight." Surprised and overcome, her eyes filled with tears as she embraced him.)

In the midst of shooting *Golden Boy*, on May 14, 1939, she and Robert Taylor were quietly married. They became Hollywood's brightest star couple for the next dozen years.

The '40s brought a new Stanwyck to the public with her first 1940 release, *Remember the Night* (an utterly meaningless title). The short, flattened, marcelled hairdos of the '30s, never very flattering to Barbara, gave way to more softly waved, longer styles and gave her a far more attractive appearance. *Remember the Night*, beautifully written by Preston Sturges and directed by Mitchell Leisen, presented a softer, lovelier Barbara than moviegoers were used to seeing. She was a shoplifter who was reformed by assistant D.A. Fred MacMurray and the mix of toughness, tenderness and gentle comedy made for a delightful movie. MacMurray and Stanwyck were a dynamic team, and Leisen called Barbara "a woman of unlimited ability and, with Carole Lombard, the easiest woman I ever worked with."

Radio had become one of Barbara's favorite performing venues and remained so until its demise in the mid–'50s. She did all the movie adaptation series *(Lux, Screen Director's Playhouse, Screen Guild Theatre)* as well as a wide variety of dramatic and comedy shows. In 1940 she made the first of a half-dozen guest appearances on *The Jack Benny Program*. The Bennys and the Taylors were close friends and Barbara delighted in sending up her own movie star image on the Benny shows, frequently lampooning her own movies.

In 1941 she was co-starred with Gary Cooper for the first time and was happily reunited with Frank Capra in his overwrought and overweight *Meet John Doe*, a condescending tribute to "the common man" by filmmakers who were now out-of-touch millionaires. It was a big hit nonetheless, but it was her other major '41 release, *The Lady Eve*, that shot Barbara into a new realm of stardom. A brilliant and now-classic comedy, it was a joyous reunion with Preston Sturges and a fortuitous re-teaming with Henry Fonda. Critics went into astonished tailspins praising the textbook comic performances of Stanwyck and Fonda.

One other reason for Barbara's huge success in *The Lady Eve* was Edith Head's trend-setting and figure-flattering wardrobe, the most glamorous she'd ever had.

Previously, Barbara's indifference to clothes had been legendary, allowing costumers to outfit her however they wanted, feeling that was their department, standing for fittings patiently but passively with her back to the mirror. But now, after a dozen years in movies, Stanwyck suddenly became one of the sexiest babes and savviest clotheshorses in the business. She and Edith Head became friends for life and Barbara took her along on almost every movie she subsequently made.

Her third movie that year was *You Belong to Me*, another comedy with Fonda, not bad but not a patch on *The Lady Eve*. "Stanwyck can act the hell out of any part," Fonda later said, "and she can turn a chore into a challenge. She's fun, and I'm glad I had a chance to make three movies with her. *The Lady Eve* was the best. She's a delicious woman." (The 1978 *AFI Salute to Henry Fonda* prompted Barbara to make one of her exceedingly rare appearances, delivering a lovely Fonda tribute. When it came time for Fonda to speak, he expressed delighted surprise that Barbara had shown up, adding, "I fell in love with Barbara when we did *Lady Eve*. I'm still in love with her, and [his wife] Shirlee can live with it.")

Ball of Fire (1941) solidified her new glamour girl image, her naturally thin upper lip now enlarged and reshaped with artfully flared lipstick. (She retained this lush-lipped look for the next 15 years.) She was Sugarpuss O'Shea, a leggy, bespangled showgirl tootsie on the lam from the cops, hiding out in a houseful of stodgy professors and falling for the youngest of them (Gary Cooper). Billy Wilder and Charles Brackett wrote the delightful script, Howard Hawks directed, and Barbara's hyper-energetic performance was a critical and popular triumph, earning her another Oscar nomination.

Her two 1942 releases weren't quite as successful. *The Great Man's Lady* was meant to be the epic tale of a woman in the pioneer Old West, aging on-camera from 16 to 101 ("and looking 35 throughout," as one critic sniffed), but in black-and-white and at a mere 90 minutes, it didn't really jell. It was a great personal disappointment to Barbara. Her other '42 release, *The Gay Sisters*, was an overlong soap opera that just came and went. (No, the title didn't mean *that*, she was one of the three *Gaylord* sisters.)

She was a sassy stripper, Dixie Daisy, in Hunt Stromberg's *Lady of Burlesque* (1943), based on Gypsy Rose Lee's 1942 backstage mystery novel, *The G-String Murders*. It was a most agreeable, if not earth-shaking, comedy-mystery, briskly directed by William Wellman. Barbara dipped freely into her chorus girl past, singing "Take It off the E-String, Play It on the G-String" and dancing with the accomplished moves of a star showgirl, replete with full splits and cartwheels. Surrounded by a battalion of wisecracking floozies, Barbara seemed to be enjoying herself enormously.

After appearing opposite Charles Boyer in one third of the three-part drama *Flesh and Fantasy*, Barbara got the role of her life, the one that permanently redefined her star image. And she didn't want to do it. In a 1968 TV documentary, *Barbara Stanwyck: Portrait of a Star*, Barbara told of her initial reservations after Billy Wilder sent her the script of *Double Indemnity:* "I had played medium heavies, but not an out-and-out killer. I was a little frightened of it, and I said, 'I love the script and I love you, *but* I am a little afraid, after all these years of playing heroines, to go into an out-and-out cold-blooded killer.' And Mr. Wilder—rightly so—looked at me and said, 'Well, are you a mouse or an actress?' And I said, 'Well, I *hope* I'm an actress.' He said, 'Then do the part.' And I did and I'm very grateful to him."

Wilder assembled a perfect star trio: Barbara as the definitively amoral Phyllis Dietrichson, an icy schemer with the conscience of a cobra and a heart of pure anthracite, Fred MacMurray as the chump insurance salesman Phyllis seduces into knocking off her husband (whose first wife she had already knocked off), and Edward G. Robinson as MacMurray's suspicious boss. *Double Indemnity* (1944) is now regarded as *the* quintessential *film noir* and Barbara's chilling, uncompromising performance is the standard by which all *femmes fatale* have come to be judged.

But then there's the matter of that wig. Bar-

Lady of Burlesque (UA, 1943): "Take It Off the E-String, Play It on the G-String."

bara was saddled with one of the cheapest, least convincing blonde pageboy wigs ever slapped on an actress' head. When Paramount production head Buddy DeSylva came on the set and saw it for the first time, he said, "We hired Barbara Stanwyck and here we get George Washington." The wig was Wilder's idea, and he later ruefully admitted that it was a mistake.

Bad wig or not, *Double Indemnity* was a smash, and audiences loved seeing Barbara in that sort of role. She scored her third Oscar nomination, but *Gaslight*'s weepily sympathetic Ingrid Bergman took home the prize.

By now she was mainly hopping back and forth between Paramount and Warners and working non-stop at a height of popularity she'd never before attained. In 1944, the U.S. Treasury Department listed Barbara Stanwyck as the highest-salaried woman in America.

She had another hit in 1945, *Christmas in Connecticut*, an ingratiating comedy (released that summer, oddly), co-starring Warners' resident crooner, Dennis Morgan. A thespic lightweight compared to Barbara, they nonetheless made a charming and believable couple, thanks in no small part to her flexibility as an actress. Barbara never overwhelmed her leading men, instead adapting herself to their energy and rhythms, working *with* them, not merely *at* them. Frequently paired with lower-key leading men (Morgan, Joel McCrea, George Brent, Herbert Marshall), she never rode roughshod over them. Rather, they were often at their most effective when working with her.

Paramount's *The Strange Love of Martha Ivers* (1946) was a gleeful return to the shady world of *noir*, her Martha looking gorgeous—no wig this time—as she killed and schemed her way to her own eventual destruction. She now had no reservations about going the limit and her performance was neurotically succulent and corrupt. With her dancer's grace, economy of movement and venomous eyes, she was certainly by now the most dangerous woman in movies and the poor saps who got tangled in her web paid a fearsome price. No it isn't so pretty what a dame without pity can do. If *Double Indemnity* started that engine, *Martha Ivers* put it into overdrive.

Her next release that year couldn't have been more dissimilar. In *My Reputation* (actually filmed in '44, right after *Double Indemnity*), Barbara is a widow and mother of two sons who has to deal with a hidebound mother (the great Lucile Watson), lecherous neighbors and gossipy friends as she slowly begins a romance with a soldier (George Brent) while fighting off her own loyalty to her husband's memory. It was a mature, beautifully controlled and multi-faceted performance, never descending to the mawkish or the obvious. A big hit with audiences, it was one of Barbara's favorite roles.

In the middle of these high-grossing hits, *The Bride Wore Boots* emptied out many theaters. It was, not to put too fine a point on it, lousy, and, sadly, was to be Barbara's final comedy feature. But she made another friend-for-life in leading man Robert Cummings. "When we were waiting to go into our scenes for *The Bride Wore Boots*," said Cummings, "she'd whisper, 'Come on, Bob. You know you'd like to fuck me. Admit it. You'd like to fuck me.'"

Nineteen-forty-seven wasn't her most successful year, even with five Stanwyck films in release. *California* was a big, overstuffed Western with Barbara in the sort of lady-with-a-past role that Claire Trevor had made her own. It was, if nothing else, her first Technicolor film. *Variety Girl* was an all-star extravaganza with Barbara guesting as herself. *The Two Mrs. Carrolls* was a wasted chance to co-star with Humphrey Bogart with both stars wildly (in Bogart's case hilariously) miscast. She matched wits with Errol Flynn in another mystery drama, *Cry Wolf*, and neither won. And in *The Other Love*, Barbara was a famous concert pianist confined to a Swiss sanitarium where her doctor (David Niven) has fallen in love with her even though she's dying of—well, something or other, that thing Ali McGraw had. She don't ask, he don't tell. She escapes, running off with ne'er-do-well playboy Richard Conte and coughing a lot. The good doctor tracks her down and she dies, not in his arms but at least in his chalet. It didn't help that Barbara never looked more radiantly healthy or more serenely beautiful. Ania Dorfman dubbed Barbara's piano playing and coached her so she'd appear believable. She practiced the pieces three hours a day for a month.

Also in 1947 she and Robert Taylor visited New York. Frank Fay had just made a high-profile comeback in the new Broadway hit *Harvey* and a reporter asked if she'd planned on seeing it. "No," she replied, "I've seen all the rabbits Mr. Fay has to offer."

About this time, while still a certified superstar, Barbara's auburn hair started slowly turning gray. What did she do about it? She did what no other name actress in America dared to do—absolutely nothing. The press reported this shocking decision with continuing wonder. Her standard line when questioned about why she didn't hit the dye-pots: "Only the young dye good." She'd never lied about her age and wasn't about to start now, and beauty parlors weren't her style. "I simply couldn't face sitting there six hours every two or three weeks." She'd wear a wig if a script called for one, but otherwise her hair grew publicly grayer by the year until finally turning snow white. For the rest of her life, Stanwyck was the only star actress of her generation who wasn't a blonde, a brunette or a redhead.

By 1948 Barbara, along with every other female in America, had succumbed to the New Look, the fashion revolution that wiped out the '40s' padded shoulders, long hair and short skirts, substituting padded busts, short hair and long skirts. Her new short bob pretty much transformed her lushly glamorous appearance into a more mature, even matronly look (though she never lost her trim dancer's figure). The new Stanwyck was seen that year in *B.F.'s Daughter* as the wealthy and overly ambitious wife of a struggling economist. He was played by Van Heflin, her *Martha Ivers* co-star, and they paired beautifully. As with her last half-dozen films, it wasn't much of a standout.

A sorely needed hit came along that year with *Sorry, Wrong Number*. It had been an extremely successful half-hour radio play by Lucille Fletcher, featuring Agnes Moorehead as a bedridden invalid who, through an accident of crossed wires, overhears her own murder being plotted over the telephone. A one-woman monologue, it tracked her futile phone calls for help and her realization that it was her husband who'd arranged the murder, which does take place exactly as planned. So successful was the first broadcast that Moorehead repeated her live performance many times, but producers felt a star name was needed for the film version, and Barbara got it.

The attempts to "open up" *Sorry, Wrong Number* with other characters (including a miscast Burt Lancaster as her weak, vengeful husband) rather diluted the suspense, and a series of flashbacks-within-flashbacks further muddled matters. But Barbara pulled out all the stops as the doomed, frantic wife trapped in her bed, the telephone her only lifeline. It's those bedroom sequences, now scattered amidst the flashbacks, that were the heart of *Sorry, Wrong Number*, and for her wrenching *tour de force* she was Oscar-nominated for the fourth and final time. Jane Wyman *(Johnny Belinda)* won.

She closed out the '40s with *The Lady Gambles* as a lady addicted to, yes, gambling, and *East Side, West Side*, a glossy soap opera with Barbara as James Mason's wronged wife, who finds comfort in the arms of dependable Van Heflin.

The '50s were a difficult time for Barbara, as they were for all her contemporaries. There was an entire generation of younger stars by now and veterans from the '30s were having a hard time maintaining their film careers. And, then as now, women over 40 were not among Hollywood's top priorities. Barbara did keep working, but there would be fewer highlights.

Fox chief Darryl F. Zanuck considered Barbara as a possibility to play theatrical barracuda Margo Channing in Joseph Mankiewicz's *All About Eve,* but Claudette Colbert was finally signed (and due to a back injury was replaced, definitively, by Bette Davis). Though Stanwyck had perhaps a wider acting range than either Davis or Colbert, it's difficult to imagine her as Margo, a role calling for self-deluding *grande dame* artifice on an epic scale.

Instead, she had four films in release in 1950. *The File on Thelma Jordon* furthered her image as a preying mantis of easy conscience (one of her lines, "Maybe I am just a dame and didn't know it," became the tag-line of all the ads) but in *No Man of Her Own* she was an uncharacteristically passive victim of bizarre circumstances. *To Please a Lady* promisingly teamed her with Clark Gable, but the script was an eye-roller. *The Furies* was easily the class of the lot, a big-budget psychological Western in which she and Walter Huston (in his final role) were superb as bitterly competitive but fiercely loving father and daughter, fighting tooth and nail for each other's land and love. When he brings his intended new bride (Judith Anderson) to the ranch, Stanwyck hurls a pair of scissors at her, disfiguring her for life. *The Furies* is a wildly perverse masterwork.

In 1951 she divorced Robert Taylor. His infidelities had become common knowledge and her most passionate fidelity had long been to her profession. (In 1954 he married German-born actress Ursula Thiess and the following year she gave birth to a son, his first child. He died in 1969.) Barbara never remarried.

Clash by Night (1952) gave Barbara a chance to work with director Fritz Lang, and it was a rewarding matchup. She got to play the sort of hard-as-nails, seen-it-all woman she'd by now played so often but this time she's more weary and disillusioned than coldly vengeful, returning to the drab fishing village of her youth after messing up her chances for success in the big city. ("Home is where you come when you run out of places.") And for once she was evenly matched with not one but two powerful leading men, Paul Douglas and Robert Ryan.

Fourth-billed was starlet Marilyn Monroe, very much on the rise and *very* much in the news. The story of her nude calendar broke during *Clash by Night*'s production and the press was in a frenzy. Lang recounted his memories of this period to Peter Bogdanovich for *Fritz Lang in America*: "Barbara had a very difficult scene in a courtyard, hanging clothes from a laundry basket and speaking her lines ... and Marilyn had one or two lines in the scene which she fluffed constantly. I never heard one bad word from Barbara; she was terribly sweet to her ... Newspapermen came during lunch hours and, since Barbara was the star, everyone tried to make sure she was interviewed. But the reporters said, 'We don't wanna talk to Barbara, we wanna talk to the girl with the big tits.' Another woman would have been furious. Barbara never. She knew exactly what was going on."

Barbara's work in *Clash by Night* was outstanding, and even better was *Titanic* (1953). Much like the more recent megahit, it told of the disaster through the fictional stories of its passengers, chiefly Barbara and Clifton Webb as a mature couple, parents of two children, whose marriage had now collapsed. Both should have been Oscar-nominated for their beautifully modulated work but there was just a bit too much soap opera to *Titanic,* and too much melodrama to *Clash by Night,* to merit serious evaluations of her work. With her voice now deepened into the cello range, Barbara had by now slipped into the "dependable" category and even her finest performances were routinely being shrugged off with such comments as "fine as usual."

Titanic's release was bracketed that year by a pair of just-okay programmers— *Jeopardy,* a tight little thriller, and *All I Desire,* a period weepie. The supporting cast of the latter featured Maureen O'Sullivan, with whom star Barbara apparently had problems. O'Sullivan later said: "She was always so popular and everybody adored her, but I found her a cold person, and she was the only actress in my working experience who ever went home leaving me to do the close ups with the script girl, which I thought was most unprofessional. I was quite surprised. There, that's the only unkind thing that's *ever* been said about Barbara Stanwyck."

Of the rest of her seven 1953-54 films, the only one worth mentioning is MGM's all-star *Executive Suite* (1954), her final big-budget prestige release. Barbara happily accepted the smallish part because it was her first opportunity since *Golden Boy* to work again with William Holden.

For the next three years she lowered her price and ground out mostly bottom-of-the-bill Westerns, by now her favorite genre, delighting in doing all her own stunts. Her three "moderns" were notable for about one reason each; *These Wilder Years* (1956) finally co-starred her with James Cagney, but their characters allowed for no romantic connection; *There's Always Tomorrow* ('56) was a weepy soap that

With Clifton Webb in *Titanic* (Fox, 1953).

co-starred her with Fred MacMurray for the fourth and final time; and *Crime of Passion* ('57) was the last in her gallery of overwrought, steel-eyed *noir* killers.

Television was now where the work was. She'd made her TV debut on *The Jack Benny Show* (CBS, 1/27/52) in a live spoof of *Gaslight,* titled *Autolight.* They made delightful hash of the Bergman and Boyer roles, though Barbara actually seemed to be sending up her own melodramatic movie image rather than spoofing Bergman's performance.

Late in '56 she began appearing as guest star on episodes of drama and comedy series (*Ford Theatre, Goodyear Theatre, The Real McCoys, The Untouchables, The Joey Bishop Show, The Dick Powell Theatre*) and dived full-tilt into her beloved western genre, appearing on *Rawhide,* four *Wagon Train*s and four *Zane Grey Theatre*s.

She was frequently offered her own series but never the kind she really wanted, a Western that celebrated the strong women of the Old West. The network suits wouldn't go for it, so she eventually agreed to host and star in an anthology series, much like the successful *Loretta Young Show. The Barbara Stanwyck Theatre* debuted on NBC September 19, 1960, with Stanwyck starring in 32 of the 36 half-hour shows. She did mostly dramas and a few comedies, as well as sneaking in some Westerns. The opening and closing spots for each episode had her immobile, posed like a fashion model, and she was damned uncomfortable doing them. By the time she won an Emmy as Best Actress in a Series (May 17, 1961), the show had already been cancelled after only one season.

Her hair was now completely white, and she looked sensational.

Barbara was quite honest about why she was appearing on television instead of on the big screen, telling interviewer Eli Weinstein: "It isn't that I don't want to work [in movies]. The trouble is nobody asks me. Some actors and actresses in my position say they can't find the right roles, but I can't fool myself so easily ... I don't let it get me down, I couldn't retire to a life of leisure, that would drive me mad ... Acting is the only thing I'm good for. I've never been much for hobbies. I get a kick out of some stars who are afraid of growing old. How silly, everybody has to grow old ... Life is a pretty difficult thing to get through. But I'm not an unhappy person. Maybe everything hasn't worked out exactly the way I hoped it would, but I've had more than my share of good times. I'm very contented now. I have my health and all the money I need, and this comfortable house. True, I live here alone."

As she continued to guest-star on TV she made her first movie in five years, *Walk on the Wild Side* (1962), a quirkily campy but unsuccessful melodrama in which Barbara played the vicious lesbian madam of a New Orleans brothel who had the hots for her favorite hooker (Capucine) while saddled with a legless husband. In 1964 she did what turned out to be her last two feature films. She played Elvis Presley's flinty carnival boss in *Roustabout* and co-starred with ex-husband Robert Taylor in a lower-case thriller, *The Night Walker.* "Together Again!" gushed the ads, which meant nothing to younger audiences.

Those younger audiences would discover Barbara as if for the first time the following year when, on September 15, 1965, ABC premiered its new Western series, *The Big Valley* starring "Miss Barbara Stanwyck" as Victoria Barkley, matriarch of the Barkley clan—four robust sons (one sorta vanished after the first season) and one feisty daughter. For three hit seasons she did stunts to her heart's content—

jumping into saloon brawls, riding horses, doing horse drags, hurling furniture, fighting with fists and firearms, escaping burning buildings and ruling her roost, insisting all along that professional stunt people be hired so they could get a salary whether they did the stunts or not. She became a star all over again to an entire generation who never even knew her as a movie queen.

In 1966 she won her second Emmy, the Screen Actors Guild Award (for "Fostering the Finest Ideals of the Acting Profession") and was on every TV magazine cover. She'd become a Broadway star at 20, a movie star at 23 and now, on television at age 58, Barbara Stanwyck hit her third jackpot.

On March 15, 1967, the annual Photoplay Gold Medal Awards were presented on *The Merv Griffin Show*. Barbara was voted Most Popular Female Star for the second year in a row and Ginger Rogers was awarded for doing *Hello, Dolly* on Broadway. Early in the show Ginger accepted her award and then croaked out some of her movie songs. Then Barbara, after being presented her award, sat and chatted with Merv, who asked why she'd never done any TV talk shows before. Confessing her nervousness at coming out before a live audience without a scripted role to play, she noted that it was fine for Ginger to come out and sing songs from her old movies, but "all I can do from any movies I made is '*Kill! Kill! Kill!*'"

After *The Big Valley* went off the air, Barbara was seen occasionally on TV episodes and starred in three ABC made-for-TV movies: *The House That Wouldn't Die* (1970), *A Taste of Evil* (1971) and *The Letters* (1973).

Nineteen-seventy-three saw Barbara voted into the National Cowboy Hall of Fame, which she considered a great honor. She'd already been made an Honorary Stuntwoman and was adopted by the Blackfoot Indian tribe as Princess Many-Victories.

But now, for the first time in her adult life, she embarked on a five-year hiatus from acting. She was being sent scripts but didn't find any of them interesting or suitable, feeling that "I've had my day and you have to know when to quit." This, from a woman who'd always said "I want to go on until they have to shoot me." She did some traveling—the Red Sea, Russia, Istanbul and the Acropolis—but wasn't seen publicly until her appearance on the *AFI Salute to Henry Fonda* in 1978. Then, two years later and to everyone's surprise, she turned up in, of all things, an episode of *Charlie's Angels* titled "Toni's Boys," playing a female Charlie to a trio of boytoy Angels. She was as trim and energetic as always but it was a trivial use of her talents. She did it to quell rumors she'd heard that she was now an invalid, unable to walk or speak. "I figured that by going back to work, I would put an end to this rumor the fastest way I knew how."

The following year, after turning down the role Jane Wyman eventually played on *Falcon Crest*, she embarked on the inevitable, if overdue, awards circuit, beginning on April 13, 1981, when the Film Society of Lincoln Center staged a full-scale *Tribute to Barbara Stanwyck*. Her good friend, columnist Shirley Eder, talked her into coming to New York for the event. Escort William Holden joined Frank Capra, Anne Baxter and Joan Bennett in paying tribute to Barbara between dozens of clips from her films. Henry Fonda, Edith Head and Ronald Reagan, unable to attend, sent congratulatory telegrams. Barbara, at 73, looked impossibly beautiful and a good 20 years younger (yes, even up close). When she arrived there was an audible gasp from the audience, followed by the first of her standing ovations. She called her reception "a shock, but a beautiful shock."

Barbara was just as uncomfortable doing print interviews as appearing live on stage, and never did them unless she felt that she had to. On the eve of her Lincoln Center event she sat down with Aljean Harmetz for a profile in the *New York Sunday Times* (3/22/81). Asked about this reluctance, she said, "If I don't have a job, what am I going to give interviews about? 'And then I did—and then I did -' Who the hell cares?" She did admit to regretting that she'd never returned to the stage. "But I fell in love with film. Now I'm scared to try. Now I'm a coward. They keep asking me and I wish I had the courage, honey."

Early in 1982 she was given the Los Angeles Film Critics Career Achievement Award. *Then* came the *big* one. That was the year the Oscar folks announced that, to atone for their past sins of omission, Barbara Stanwyck would receive an honorary Lifetime Achievement Academy Award for being "an artist of impeccable grace and beauty," presented on April 29. Following a filmed montage of scenes from her movies, Barbara came onstage to a standing ovation. She thanked her many behind-the-camera co-workers, making special mention of "*my* wonderful group, the stunt men and women who taught me so well." She concluded, "A few years ago I stood on this stage with William Holden as a presenter. I loved him very much and I miss him. He always wished that I would get an Oscar. And so tonight, my Golden Boy [raising her Oscar up high, her voice shaky], you get your wish." Holden had died just five months earlier.

Finally! Honorary Oscar (April 29, 1982), with presenter John Travolta.

The very next day it was announced that she'd joined the cast of the ABC miniseries *The Thorn Birds*. Adapted from Colleen McCullough's 1977 best-selling novel covering 42 years of *angst* in the Australian outback, it was a formidable project that gave

Barbara the sort of role she'd been waiting for but feared would never come her way again.

At first the entire cast and crew were rather in awe of her, but she managed to gradually relax them. She would play Mary Carson, a wealthy and powerful matriarch of 75, desperately in love with the young Cardinal Ralph de Bricassart (Richard Chamberlain). That was, in fact, Barbara's actual age but because she didn't look it, it was suggested that some old-age makeup would be appropriate. She agreed, grudgingly. The younger company was impressed with her total knowledge of the entire ten-hour script, not just the first three hours in which she appears. When some cuts were made that she felt affected her character's development, she informed them that "you have just cut off my balls." They looked again, saw that indeed they had, and the scenes were restored.

Mary's constant sparring and bantering with Father Ralph called for a full range of charm, humor, anger, playfulness, frustration and sexual tension. When she finally confesses her love for him and he shrugs her off, saying he's merely "the goad of your old age, a reminder of what you can no longer be," she rages: "Let me tell you something, Father de Bricassart, about old age and about that God of yours. That vengeful God who ruins our bodies and leaves us with only enough wit for regret. Inside this stupid body I am still young. I still feel! I still want! I still dream! And I still love *you!* Oh God, how much!" Spent and shaken, trying to regain her composure, she goes to her bedroom door and closes it with as much shattered pride as she can muster. The next morning she's found dead in her bed.

Director Daryl Duke, in Ella Smith's superb book *Starring Miss Barbara Stanwyck,* said, "This was a very important scene for Barbara; she had put everything into it. It echoed so much her personal life and her position at the end of her career. Though she and I never said it, I could tell she knew it was a great, great moment, and that she might never find a script where she could unleash her full range of feeling again ... saying goodbye, in a way, to her life and her career—and she might never rise to that height on film again."

The first three hours aired on March 27, 1983. The critics raved about her performance, seemingly appreciating and understanding what this must have meant for her. Ninety-five million viewers made *The Thorn Birds* second only to *Roots* as the highest-rated miniseries ever.

Later that year she won a Golden Globe and her third Emmy for *The Thorn Birds.* The Emmys had some heavy competition that season, including Ann-Margret in *Who Will Love My Children?* When Barbara was presented her award, she did the standard gracious speech thanking the cast and company of *The Thorn Birds,* but then added: "I would like to pay a personal tribute to a lady who is a wonderful entertainer, and she gave us a film last year in which I think she gave one of the finest, most beautiful performances I've ever seen. Ann-Margret, you were superb!" The camera then switched to a shot of Ann-Margret in the audience, gasping in astonished delight. As she later said, "That moment I will cherish the rest of my life."

She was asked to appear on ABC's *Dynasty* as a member of the Colby family for a few episodes, and then to join Charlton Heston in a spin-off series, *Dynasty II: The Colbys.* She agreed and the new series debuted on November 20, 1985. She was Constance Colby Patterson, sister of Jason Colby (Heston) and aunt to his son Jeff (John James). Her contract specified that she'd work only two days a week and that she'd never have to do interviews.

In mid-season, on January 24, 1986, she was invited to the Golden Globes to accept their annual Cecil B. DeMille Award, then went back to work on *The Colbys*. After the first low-rated season she opted to quit, accurately complaining that she played the same scene every week, just in a different dress.

It was her final role.

The American Film Institute honored her on April 9, 1987, with *AFI's Salute to Barbara Stanwyck*, an all-star tribute to her body of work on film. She had recently thrown her back out and was hospitalized and in considerable pain, but worked out with barbells to be able to be there. A host of her co-stars and admirers lavished their praise, but Billy Wilder topped them all: "I learned many years ago never to say, 'This is the best actor or actress I've ever worked with,' because the next time you want a star, he or she is gonna say 'Wait a minute, you said Stanwyck was the greatest, now what does that make me?' Always say she's one of the *two* greatest stars you've worked with and whenever you approach a star, say, 'You were the one I meant.' Except, of course, for tonight. I hope nobody's watching me. *She was the best!*"

When, at the conclusion, Barbara approached the podium to accept her award, her response to all the evening's hosannas was "Honest to God, I can't walk on water." In thanking all those who helped her on her journey, she singled out Wilder, "who taught me to kill."

After the evening's festivities she returned to the hospital. For the next few years she was in and out of the hospital as her health continued to fail. She'd been diagnosed with emphysema in the early '70s and now developed vision problems and a chronic obstructive lung disease. Complications continued to mount until, on January 20, 1990, Barbara died of pneumonia at St. John's Hospital. She was 82.

Shortly before her death she told fashion designer Nolan Miller, "I never expected to become an invalid. I always thought I'd be trampled by a wild stallion or run down by a stagecoach."

Stanwyck was never given to public introspection, courting her fame, polishing her legend or glad-handing the press. She did her work, delivered the goods, never became a caricature of herself, and kept her private life private. She even kept her figure. She once briefly thought of writing her memoirs, then dropped the idea for good. What she was was a professional actress, and if that ate up the greater part of her passion, so be it. She made her choices and didn't complain.

Rex Reed had once asked her to analyze her stardom or some such folderol, but she didn't take the bait:

"What the hell. Whatever I had, it worked, didn't it?"

1927: Broadway Nights (First National). **1929:** The Voice of Hollywood (short), The Locked Door (UA), Mexicali Rose (Columbia). **1930:** Ladies of Leisure (Columbia). **1931:** Illicit (WB), Ten Cents a Dance (Columbia), Night Nurse (WB), The Miracle Woman (Columbia), Screen Snapshots #3 (Columbia short), Screen Snapshots #4 (Columbia short). **1932:** Forbidden (Columbia), Shopworn (Columbia), So Big (WB), The Purchase Price

(WB), The Stolen Jools (NVA short). **1933:** The Bitter Tea of General Yen (Columbia), Screen Snapshots (Columbia short), Ladies They Talk About (WB), Baby Face (WB), Ever in My Heart (WB), Hollywood On Parade #A-11 (Paramount short). **1934:** Gambling Lady (WB), A Lost Lady (WB). **1935:** The Secret Bride (WB), The Woman in Red (WB), Red Salute AKA Runaway Daughter (UA), Annie Oakley (RKO). **1936:** A Message to Garcia (TCF), The Bride Walks Out (RKO), His Brother's Wife (MGM) , Banjo on My Knee (TCF). **1937:** The Plough and the Stars (RKO), Interns Can't Take Money (Paramount), This Is My Affair (TCF), Stella Dallas (UA), Breakfast for Two (RKO). **1938:** Always Good-bye (TCF), The Mad Miss Manton (RKO). **1939:** Union Pacific (Paramount), Golden Boy (Columbia), Screen Snapshots #10: Stars on Horseback (Columbia short). **1940:** Remember the Night (Paramount). **1941:** The Lady Eve (Paramount), Meet John Doe (WB), You Belong to Me (Columbia), Ball of Fire (RKO). **1942:** The Great Man's Lady (Paramount), The Gay Sisters (WB). **1943:** Lady of Burlesque (UA), Flesh and Fantasy (Universal). **1944:** Double Indemnity (Paramount), Hollywood Canteen (WB). **1945:** Christmas in Connecticut (WB), Hollywood Victory Caravan (Paramount short). **1946:** My Reputation (WB), The Bride Wore Boots (Paramount), The Strange Love of Martha Ivers (Paramount). **1947:** California (Paramount), The Two Mrs. Carrolls (WB), Variety Girl (Paramount), The Other Love (UA), Cry Wolf (WB). **1948:** B.F.'s Daughter (MGM), Sorry, Wrong Number (Paramount). **1949:** The Lady Gambles (Universal), East Side, West Side (MGM), Eyes of Hollywood (short). **1950:** Thelma Jordon AKA The File on Thelma Jordon (Paramount), No Man of Her Own (Paramount), The Furies (Paramount), To Please a Lady (MGM). **1951:** The Man with a Cloak (MGM). **1952:** Clash by Night (RKO). **1953:** Jeopardy (MGM), Titanic (TCF), All I Desire (Universal), The Moonlighter (WB), Blowing Wild (WB). **1954:** Witness to Murder (UA), Executive Suite (MGM). **1955:** Cattle Queen of Montana (RKO), The Violent Men (Columbia), Escape to Burma (RKO). **1956:** There's Always Tomorrow (Universal), The Maverick Queen (Rep.), These Wilder Years (MGM). **1957:** Crime of Passion (UA), Trooper Hook (UA), Forty Guns (TCF). **1962:** Walk on the Wild Side (Columbia). **1964:** Roustabout (Paramount). **1965:** The Night Walker (Universal). **1970:** House That Wouldn't Die (ABC-TV). **1971:** A Taste of Evil (ABC-TV). **1973:** The Letters (ABC-TV). **1982:** The Thorn Birds (ABC-TV miniseries).

Claire Trevor: Brass with Class

by RAY HAGEN

Many actresses have clawed their way out of sordid, impoverished backgrounds to become "great ladies of the screen." Less publicized are those who have gone the opposite route, coming from a contented, comfortable and respectable lineage to make a profitable career out of portraying trollops, killers, gun molls, lushes and sundry tarnished belles. Perhaps the best example of this sort of "progress" is Claire Trevor, who by now must certainly possess permanent copyright to the role she played countless times: the hard-boiled Western saloon keeper–madam with a feather boa and a heart of gold. Although she played every conceivable sort of role, she became permanently identified as a hard case, and not without dipso-nympho tendencies. Most "tough babes" in movies came to be seen as camp figures, even jokes, but that was never the perception with Claire. Audiences and critics alike always regarded her with respect. Claire Trevor never became a joke.

But quiet respect rarely assures top stardom. Though often starred, she never became a true box office *star*. Her feelings about her career constantly veered back and forth from diffidence to despair, ambition to acceptance, envy to ennui. She utterly lacked the iron-willed determination of a Barbara Stanwyck or the temperament of a Joan Crawford. Perhaps that was a blessing. Her career saw a dazzling number of setbacks, disappointments and re-discoveries, but she continued to be active long after more illustrious contemporaries outlived their vogues.

She was born Claire Wemlinger in the Bensonhurst section of Brooklyn on March 9, 1910, the only child of Noel B. and Edith Morrison Wemlinger. (Her father was born in Paris, her mother in Belfast.) The family moved to New York City when Claire was two and there she attended George Washington High School. Mr. Wemlinger, a successful Fifth Avenue custom tailor, moved the family then to nearby Larchmont. Claire attended Mamaroneck High School, where she got her first taste of performing.

It was originally intended that upon graduation she attend Smith College but she enrolled instead at Columbia University where she studied art, but she had to quit after only six months because the Depression had cost her father his business and Claire had to help out financially.

Having appeared in plays in school, she'd become smitten with acting and entered the American Academy of Dramatic Arts, but after six months she left to try and obtain some paying jobs and launched her attack on the big-time Broadway boys. She often made the rounds with her long-time friend Martha Sleeper, who was already an experienced actress. For a while she called herself Claire Sinclair, having been impressed with a Sinclair Oil sign, changed that to Claire St. Clair, but soon dropped both in favor of Trevor. Armed with youth, beauty and a list of credits as impressive as it was phony, she managed to land her first acting job.

In the summer of 1930 she shipped off to Ann Arbor, Michigan, to make her professional debut with Robert Henderson's Repertory Players at the annual Ann Arbor Theatre Festival as a member of the Greek Chorus in *Antigone*. She also appeared in *Lady Windermere's Fan* as the girl who said only "Yes, mama," and had a larger part in *The Sea Gull*, which was completely beyond her grasp. The star of the company was veteran actress Margaret Anglin.

Portrait of Claire Trevor, 1945.

She returned to New York, did some modeling for photographers and impressed a Warner Bros. scout, who put her in a series of Vitaphone short subjects at their Flatbush studios. At that time, Warners was starting a stock company in St. Louis, intending, if the idea proved successful, to scatter similar companies around the country. It would also serve as a training school for future Warner stars. They sent Claire to St. Louis, where she played (with, among others, Lyle Talbot and Wallace Ford) in a new show each week for ten weeks. At $85 per week, it proved a grueling experience. She spent the summer of '31 as the leading ingenue with the Hampton Players, a little theater group in Southhampton, New York, for $5 a week plus room and board. While there she was spotted by producer Alexander McKaig, who offered Claire her first Broadway role, leading lady in *Whistling in the Dark* opposite Ernest Truex and Edward Arnold. It opened January 19, 1932. In his review for the *Herald-Tribune*, Percy Hammond wrote: "Claire Trevor, a shiny debutante, plays the pretty heroine casually."

The comedy was a hit. Claire stayed with the show in New York for nine months and subsequently toured with it. While the company was in Los Angeles, a number of film studio executives offered her screen tests. "Irving Thalberg had wanted me to sign at MGM," Claire later said, "But at the time I was all theater-conscious. I told him that I would wait until some studio brought me to Hollywood from a hit play and give me a starring role in a picture. I've often wondered if I was foolish not to sign with Mr. Thalberg then. My career might have been much more successful."

She went back to New York and got a part as a waitress in a Depression comedy called *The Party's Over*, which opened at the Vanderbilt Theatre on March 27, 1933. The critics were casually kind but the play was not doing very well, so when the New York office of Fox Films (renamed 20th Century-Fox in 1935) tested her and offered her a contract she readily accepted. She left the show at the end of April and arrived in Hollywood on May 7, 1933, a contract player with a major studio at $350 a week, a fortune to her.

Two days later Claire was sent out on location, a sandy waste, for her first movie, *Life in the Raw*, a run-of-the-mill Western in which she was George O'Brien's leading lady. After making a second Western with O'Brien, Fox decided to bring her indoors to play opposite Spencer Tracy in *The Mad Game*, a newspaper drama. She got excellent notices for her work as a cigarette-rolling reporter. At that point Sally Blane, who was frequently teamed with James Dunn, refused to play opposite him in *Jimmy and Sally*. Trevor got the part. After *Hold That Girl*, another fluffy item with Dunn, she was off on her treadmill. By the end of 1933 she had starred in half-a-dozen Fox quickies. Early in '34 her personal rave notices began piling up, but in minor films earning little or no attention. The pattern was set; Claire Trevor became Hollywood's (or at least Fox's) Queen of the B's.

She said in the April, 1934 *Picture Play*: 'The studios usually artificialize women. I vowed I wouldn't be beautified, but it's a routine you have to go through every morning out here.... Pictures seem to me like the stock market, a magnificent gamble. My wish is that I'll go to the top and then have sense enough to get out before I crash."

From 1933 to '37, Trevor starred in over two dozen low-budget Fox sausages, each one more trivial than the last. She played runaway heiresses, unhappy wives, showgirls, society belles, secretaries, colorful and colorless heroines and the sort of girl reporter addicted to hopping on running boards. She had to be as merry as Carole Lombard, as long-suffering as Ruth Chatterton, and dance as gracefully as Ginger Rogers. Only twice was she cast in A films, *To Mary—With Love* (1936) and *Second Honeymoon* ('37), but her billing was considerably lower and she merely had roles subservient to leading ladies Myrna Loy and Loretta Young.

It wasn't a total loss. Claire Trevor had become a known name and she was learning, absorbing, becoming thoroughly accustomed to delivering high-level performances under all but impossible conditions. As her income grew, so did her impatience for bigger and certainly better things. Later, in a 1946 *Motion Picture* interview, she said, "Producers decided I was older than I claimed to be and gave me snappy, severe business women, gal reporter types of roles. I played them all. I didn't know that to make a real career in Hollywood you have to become a 'personality.' You have to cultivate publicity departments and become known as 'The Ear' or 'The Toe.'"

Her patience and persistence finally seemed to pay off. She fought for, and

Claire (left) second fiddling to Loretta Young and Tyrone Power in *Second Honeymoon* **(Fox, 1937).**

won, the part of Francey in *Dead End,* a major production for United Artists, released in 1937. She had only one scene, as gangster Humphrey Bogart's innocent one-time girlfriend who had turned into a hardened, diseased prostitute. (Claire and Bogart became fast friends for life.) No one could understand why on earth she wanted to play such a part, until they saw the film. Her contribution lasted less than two minutes, but she made every second count. The press and public finally took notice and she was nominated for a 1937 Best Supporting Actress Academy Award. She didn't win, Alice Brady did for *In Old Chicago,* but Claire felt this was a definite step up.

Upon returning to Fox, however, she was sent right back to the B unit. She finished out her contract and left, preferring to work freelance. As she told *Modern Screen* in 1939: "You see, Mr. Zanuck never had faith in me. Why, I don't know. Perhaps he may even have been justified. The point is, however, that if he hasn't confidence in a player, said player might just as well up and leave at the outset. And that's what I did."

In 1937 she began a three-year run on the hit CBS radio series *Big Town,* co-starring Edward G. Robinson. Robinson was "crusading reporter" Steve Wilson and Claire was his "society editor and sidekick" Loreli Kilbourne. When Claire realized that Robinson was spending more air time expounding on weighty issues of the day and less time with Loreli, she decided she'd had enough. As she later said, her lines had now been whittled down to "I'll wait for you in the car, Steve" and "How'd it go, Steve?"

Free of her Fox contract in 1937, she gave an unusually candid interview in the June 1938 *Modern Screen*: "I owe pictures a lot. I've made an unbelievable amount of money in the last four years. But it's given me no artistic satisfaction to be in movies. I've done nothing I can point to with pride. At first I accepted anything I was handed. When the scripts turned out to be crummy and inconsistent I just did the best I could. I thought *Dead End* was going to mean everything—a beautiful script, good director [William Wyler], topflight cast—but I was disappointed in my performance when I saw the picture. I hadn't given what I thought I had ... I don't want to be just another leading lady. And I'm going to do something about it! For years I took B pictures without a murmur. Good training, I told my mother. Sound basis for a screen career, yes indeed. But they've kept me buzzing in the B-hive for four years and no relief in sight. So one of these days I'm going to surprise everybody and say, 'No, this part is not for me, this picture is not for me, I won't do another B!'"

"Perhaps I've been amiable too long," she said in the May, 1938 *Motion Picture*. "Perhaps it's time for me to put on the temperamental act and scream for better parts in better pictures. Next year I hope some really good roles in important productions will come my way. Naturally I would prefer to make three or four pictures a year which are important, rather than twice that number of the run-of-the-mill variety." The title of the interview said it all: *The Star Who Isn't a Star*.

She married *Big Town* producer Clark Andrews in July 1938. By then the last of her Fox follies were in release, and she was seen in two top-line Warner Bros. efforts: *The Amazing Dr. Clitterhouse*, an excellent gangster comedy with Claire playing a gang leader with silken ease, and *Valley of the Giants*, her first Technicolor picture and the first of many films to exploit her as a lady with a past in Western surroundings.

She was offered a Warners contract but, still smarting from her bondage at Fox, she refused. She told William M. Drew in his 1999 book *At the Center of the Frame*, "Warner Bros. had a promotional thing going at the time and they wanted me to be 'the Oomph Girl.' They wanted to sign me for five years but I turned them down ... That may have been foolish too, because I would have been 'the Oomph Girl' rather than Ann Sheridan and also Warners did more of the kind of thing that was suitable to me."

The following year gave her probably her most memorable film, John Ford's classic *Stagecoach*. She played Dallas, a town trollop who the "good" women forced to leave on the title vehicle. Her growing romance with the Ringo Kid (John Wayne) during the course of the stagecoach's journey was played by both Trevor and Wayne with tenderness and subtlety. It established definitively her hooker-with-a-heart-of-gold image and was, of course, an enormously successful film. Claire loved every moment on the picture, adored working with Wayne and Ford, and until the end of her life she considered it her favorite of all her films.

Her two follow-up pictures, however, were letdowns. As Claire told Jack Holland in 1948: "After I left Fox, some months later, I got a good part in *Stagecoach*.

In fact, I even got top billing, but the picture made a star of John Wayne and I didn't work for six months. Then I did another picture with John, a super-epic, one of the biggest RKO had ever made [*Allegheny Uprising*]. I thought I was on my way, but the film was a sensational flop. So afterwards I did a picture with George Raft [*I Stole a Million*], who was very hot at the time. That also was a charming failure."

From 1940 to '43 she fell into a pattern nearly as frustrating as the early years at Fox. She played leads in a few Westerns and B melodramas and supports in occasional A efforts, serving as second fiddle to the likes of Lana Turner and Hedy Lamarr.

In 1940 she was seen in only one film, *Dark Command*. Another Western, it had sheriff John Wayne vying with guerrilla chief Walter Pidgeon for Claire's aristocratic hand. *Texas* (1941) was a funny, bouncy western, this time with buddies Glenn Ford and William Holden vying for Claire's favors. In *The Adventures of Martin Eden* ('41) Claire was star Ford's colorless true love.

Honky Tonk (1941) was an MGM Clark Gable-Lana Turner vehicle typical of her luck. Trevor was featured as Gable's old flame, an easy going saloon hustler. She started out with a good, gutsy part, but, as she told writer Charles Samuels eight years later, "By that time I was playing second leads. I had great scenes in *Honky*

Clark Gable gets under Claire's chapeau in *Honky Tonk* (MGM, 1941).

Tonk. At least I thought I had them 'til I went to the press preview of the picture. My scenes had been scissored out. 'Where am I?,' I kept asking myself. 'What happened to me?' I cried all the way home and swore I'd never make another picture. There were a lot of nights when I felt like that. Other girls were flying past me becoming big stars. I was still just another actress, competent but not a top-notcher. Still, I didn't care too much."

Crossroads (1942) starred William Powell and Hedy Lamarr in an amnesia drama with Claire as a treacherous chanteuse (dubbed by Connie Russell). A string of unimportant B's followed. *Street of Chance* ('42) was another amnesia drama with Claire starting out sweet and ending up sour. She was back in saloon drag in *The Desperadoes* ('43), and in *Good Luck, Mr. Yates* she's a nice girl to whom Army reject Jess Barker has to prove himself. *The Woman of the Town* ('43) was another Western, a rather well done tale of Bat Masterson's ill-fated love for Dora Hand.

In 1942 she and Andrews were divorced. She married Navy Lt. Cylos William Dunsmoore in 1944, and the following year their son, Charles Cylos, was born.

Claire co-starred on radio in 1944 with her old Fox cohort Lloyd Nolan in *Results, Incorporated*. It was a light-hearted (and headed) mystery series on Mutual, lasting from October 7th to December 30th. She loved radio—no lines to learn, no hours wasted on wardrobe, makeup and hairdos—and appeared in dozens of dramas and variety shows.

After the birth of her son, Claire was a hyper-glam temptress with greed in her eyes and a gun in her upsweep in *Murder, My Sweet* (1945). It was a classic *film noir* mystery which did wonders for former boy crooner Dick Powell in his first hard-guy role as detective Philip Marlowe, and consequently all the attention was focused on his surprisingly gritty performance. Claire had a good bit of grit herself. "You shouldn't kiss a girl when you're wearing that gun," she tells Powell. "It leaves a bruise." Powell got the girl (Anne Shirley) and the publicity. Trevor got a bullet.

She did more of the same opposite George Raft in *Johnny Angel* ('45), but though she was Pat O'Brien's nice girlfriend in yet another amnesia plot, *Crack-Up*, ('46), the ads pictured her as a fancily gowned vixen. Her final '46 opus was *The Bachelor's Daughters*, about four salesgirls who move in with a rich old bachelor with Claire as the nastiest (until the fadeout). She shared screen time with "sisters" Ann Dvorak, Gail Russell and Jane Wyatt. Not much star power in any of them, and once again her career was in the doldrums.

In 1947 she played one of the bitchiest of her screen witches, a totally amoral schemer who teams up with killer Lawrence Tierney in *Born to Kill*. Now considered a *noir* classic, it was then passed by as just another RKO melodrama. She was the very spirit of evil as she hatched one sleazy scheme after another with not a trace of conscience while wearing some of the funniest '40s millenary ever constructed. As always, the high quality of her work was overlooked. By now this was exactly what people expected of Claire Trevor, and exactly the genre in which they expected to find her.

During all her years in Hollywood she had been longing to return to the stage. Each disenchantment seemed to strengthen that urge, and now seemed a pretty good time. In 1946 she did *Dark Victory* with Onslow Stevens at the Laguna Beach playhouse, following that with *Tonight at 8:30* opposite Joan Fontaine and Philip

Hilariously hatted but seriously scheming by phone in *Born to Kill* (RKO, 1947).

Merivale, and the leading role in Noël Coward's *Family Album* in August at the El Capitan Theatre.

She got a chance to return east in Sam and Bella Spewack's comedy *Out West It's Different*, co-starring Keenan Wynn. Something of a shambles, it opened in Princeton, New Jersey, and died before reaching New York.

But she did make it back to Broadway. On January 8, 1947, she opened at the Booth Theatre in *The Big Two*. Howard Barnes said in his *Herald-Tribune* review: "Claire Trevor and Philip Dorn play the leading roles with a good deal more vitality than they deserved. The former, as a woman correspondent who tries to find a traitorous American broadcaster behind the Iron Curtain of a Russian-occupied zone, brings a brittle skepticism to the part which is very right indeed." Elliott Nugent directed and Robert Montgomery produced. The critics were unanimously unimpressed. On January 25, after 21 performances, it folded.

Her legit longings squelched, Trevor returned to Hollywood. She hadn't made a film in 18 months and now decided to do anything and everything she could, and to do it as well as possible. Rosalind Russell offered her a supporting role in *The Velvet Touch*, the first of five films she turned out in breakneck procession. All were released within a few months of each other and suddenly Claire Trevor was the surprise re-discovery of 1948.

That year she discussed her career ambivalence: "Certainly I'd like to be a star," she told Jack Holland, "because the opportunity for a variety of roles is so very good. I didn't feel that way once. I thought only of all the worries the stars had; the lack of privacy, the grief and strain of worrying if each succeeding picture would be a failure. But when I see the excellent roles that Barbara Stanwyck, Irene Dunne, Olivia de Havilland, Joan Fontaine, Ingrid Bergman and others have had, I find myself wanting the same chance.... At the beginning I accepted every part that was handed to me. I was too meek. I never acted as though I was eating my heart out for a certain part. For example, I made a test for the mother in *The Yearling* and I was told I had made the best test. Then the picture was postponed, and I failed to keep my irons hot. When the production was announced again I was called to the studio for an interview, but I guess I seemed too indifferent, because I wasn't given another chance. The same meekness didn't help my chances when I wanted to play Sophie in *The Razor's Edge*."

But 1948 turned out to be a very good year for Claire Trevor. She had particularly good exposure as an acid-tongued, ill-fated actress in *The Velvet Touch*, was in unrequited love with a faithless gangster in *Raw Deal*, and had a rare non-neurotic role as Mrs. Ruth in the maladroit *The Babe Ruth Story* in which she got to do some light hoofing in her pre-marriage scenes.

Edward G. Robinson helps Claire win her Oscar in *Key Largo* (WB, 1948).

It was John Huston's *Key Largo* that cinched her umpteenth comeback, this time for keeps. It was a high-profile, star-filled drama (Bogart, Bacall, Robinson, Lionel Barrymore, all close friends), but Claire's performance as a gangster's broken-down floozie was so powerful she walked off not only with all the notices but an Oscar for Best Supporting Actress of 1948. She played Gaye Dawn, a former singer who was now Robinson's alcoholic mistress. In the film's best remembered sequence, Robinson forced her to sing her long-ago hit song, "Moanin' Low," before giving her the drink she'd been begging for, and then refused when she finished because "You were rotten." It was a wrenching scene and one of her most impressive screen achievements.

In 1983 she told John Gallagher for *Films in Review* how that scene came about: "First of all, I had no idea I was going to sing it myself, because I can't sing. I thought they were going to have a recording and I was going to mouth the words to the recording, and have a singer do it. I wanted the music department to rehearse me and train me in the gestures of a nightclub singer ... each day I'd say to John [Huston], 'When can I go to the music department and rehearse, when are you going to shoot the song?' 'Oh, we've got lots of time.' This went on and on and on... So we came back from lunch one day, and he said, 'I think I'll shoot this song this afternoon.' I said '*What*? Where's the recording? I haven't heard it.' He said, 'You're going to sing it.' I said, 'I can't!' .... He stood me up there with the whole cast and the whole crew looking. You think that's not embarrassing? And offstage is a piano, and they hit one note. Start. [*Laughter*] No time for anything except pure embarrassment and torture, and that's what came through. I tried to do it as well as I could. And when we'd done the long shot all the way through, I thought I was finished ... He said, 'All right, now we'll do the two-shot, and the close-up,' and the piano would go 'Bong' offstage and that was it. Each time I did a different set-up and then they had to blend them all together, you can imagine how many keys I was in."

She and Dunsmoore had divorced in 1947 and on November 14, 1948, she was married to producer Milton Bren. This one was for keeps. Bren had two teenaged sons, Peter and Donald, from a previous marriage, and Claire helped raise them along with her son Charles. "I didn't begin my life until I married Milton Bren," she said in 1999.

In an interview for the April 1949 *Motion Picture* titled "Change of Heart," Claire discussed her renewed interest in her film career with Charles Samuels: "I was indifferent, perhaps belligerent, when I first came to Hollywood. I was young, of course, and not very experienced ... Working in movies was just something I was doing to keep going until I got the right stage role, the one that would make me a great actress like Helen Hayes ... It was an overwhelming obsession with me that Broadway was worthwhile, Hollywood a bad joke. I was not even slightly envious of the girls who each year skyrocketed past me: Rita Hayworth, who played small bits in films in which I was starred; Betty Grable, who was just starting her sensational rise on the same old Fox lot. It's wonderful that I lasted in pictures at all with that start I made ... I'd only been in a couple of Broadway plays, but the stage had me bedazzled, bedizzied and bewitched... That old dream of returning to the stage and never coming back to Hollywood still haunted me, despite the occasional good roles I got... Actually I suppose [the Broadway failure] was the finest thing that could have happened to me... The Broadway mirage is gone, I think, for good."

In 1949 Claire appeared to rare comic advantage as Brian Donlevy's addled, breezy secretary in *The Lucky Stiff*, but Dorothy Lamour got top billing. The following year Claire starred with Fred MacMurray in *Borderline*, produced by husband Milton Bren and again showing her gift for comedy. It was a brisk, well-played adventure, though no world-beater. For the next three years she appeared in widely assorted roles, always to fine critical notice. The films may not have been top box - office, but her Oscar had extended her screen career and gave her professional reputation a permanent face lift. Her performances remained exceptional and her merit was fully and repeatedly acknowledged.

Speaking to Louis Reid in 1950 about her bad girl image, Claire said: "If I had my choice, I'd rather be a bad girl in a good picture than a good girl in a bad one. I don't care how I look—brazen, blowzy, brassy—if the role is of the bad 'un, it's all to the good. I've been all kinds of menaces—young, middle-aged, intermediate-aged, modern, old-fashioned—in big city underworlds and frontier towns. Sometimes I've had a heart of gold but more often my heart is only tarnished gilt. The idea is to look tough, live hard, be dangerous … I never knew any women as bad as those I've played on the screen. Never have I had the slightest acquaintance with a female dipso such as I depicted in *Key Largo.*"

Between 1951 and '53 she did a variety of starring and supporting roles in mostly programmers: standard Trevor duty in a pair of Westerns *(Best of the Bad Men* and *The Stranger Wore a Gun)*, a sour farmwife harridan *(My Man and I)*, an underworld siren patterned after celebrated mob babe Virginia Hill *(Hoodlum Empire)* and a former gun moll trying to crack society in a misfired Damon Runyon comedy *(Stop, You're Killing Me)*. Best of the lot was *Hard, Fast and Beautiful*, directed by Ida Lupino. Claire was the calculating, overly ambitious mother of tennis champ Sally Forrest, and she imbued the role with a stunning harsh reality.

On December 31, 1953, Claire made her TV debut in a filmed half-hour drama for NBC's *Ford Theatre* titled *Alias Nora Hale.* It was the beginning of a lengthy and extremely well-handled TV career, working irregularly in roles carefully selected.

In 1954 she was seen as May Holst, the overblown, warmhearted broad in *The High and the Mighty*, Warners' mega-hit with John Wayne and Robert Stack co-piloting the imperilled, star-filled plane. This was the prototype for every all-star this-plane's-going-down saga that followed. Despite Claire's role having been severely truncated, both she and Jan Sterling earned Oscar nominations (Trevor's third).

The following year she did *Lucy Gallant* (second fiddle to star Jane Wyman) and *Man Without a Star* (her final fling in a Western saloon), and in '56 she won an Emmy as Best Actress in a Single Performance for her role as Fran Dodsworth on the *NBC Producers' Showcase* production of *Dodsworth*, broadcast live on April 30. She co-starred with Fredric March and scored a tremendous personal success. (She had been nominated for a previous Emmy in 1954 for *Ladies in Retirement* on *Lux Video Theatre.*) She later called this her favorite of any performance she ever gave.

In 1956, Claire told Kevin Delany: "In television I can do what I can't do in pictures, which is to play sympathetic, normal roles. Of course, if the part has enough facets, I don't mind playing the bad girl. Bette Davis played designing woman after another for years, but they were such marvelously interesting people. I'm tapering off in pictures. I think three or four TV shows a year are enough too. As for a TV series, never. Life is too short, and frankly I'm not terribly ambitious."

She did a small part opposite Spencer Tracy in *The Mountain* (1956). It starred Tracy and Robert Wagner as *exceedingly* unlikely mountain-climbing brothers, with Tracy turning to Trevor for some brief affections. She won particularly impressive critical response for her incisive turn in *Marjorie Morningstar* (1958) as Marjorie's shrewd Jewish mother, one of her finest performances.

Jack O'Brian wrote in his March 11, 1957, TV column: "Lana Turner is beginning to look like Claire Trevor, which is our notion of growing up gracefully." Claire was indeed looking effortlessly sensational well into the next decade, while most of her contemporaries were battling the clock all too visibly.

In 1957 the Brens moved from Beverly Hills to Newport Beach, California, and Claire was by now spending more time painting than acting. Long one of the more gifted painting talents of the Hollywood set, she worked constantly at it, mainly doing portraits. "Painting," she noted, "is a lot cheaper than going to a psychiatrist."

Her next film was in 1962, the disastrous *Two Weeks in Another Town*, in which she let fly with one of the nastiest in her gallery of screen witches, once again paired with old friend Edward G. Robinson. A year later she was seen as Richard Beymer's well-meaning mother in *The Stripper*, in which she got over-the-title billing for the first time in years. It was also the first film she'd done for 20th Century-Fox since walking out on them 26 years earlier.

In 1964 she was Eddie Mayehoff's wisecracking take-charge wife in *How to Murder Your Wife*, a middling Jack Lemmon comedy, and in '67 she was in the little-seen *The Capetown Affair*, made in South Africa. This was a remake of 1953's *Pickup on South Street*, with Claire in the Thelma Ritter role as a weary, doomed bag-lady.

She wasn't seen on the big screen again for 15 years.

In 1968 Claire again took to the boards in a pair of regional tours. She starred with Rock Hudson and Leif Erickson in Charles Laughton's adaptation of *John Brown's Body* and startled everyone by playing the fierce, cigar-smoking title lesbian in *The Killing of Sister George*.

For the next ten years she devoted herself to painting, charitable causes and enjoying the good life in happy unofficial retirement. Then, in 1978, Claire's son Charles, 34, was killed in an airplane collision over San Diego, and a year later Milton Bren, her husband of 31 years, died of a brain tumor. Claire was devastated by these twin tragedies within one year. She later told the *Los Angeles Times* that Bren's death "was the biggest loss except for our son, who was killed. That was something you never get over. But losing my husband left me without anybody. I mean, I felt completely alone."

Needing to break away from Newport Beach and her memories there, she moved to a Fifth Avenue apartment in New York in 1981 and gradually entered into a busy social life. The Brens had long been active in charity work with the March of Dimes and Claire chaired the Orange County Arthritis Foundation. She'd lent her name to many charitable causes and by now had limited her public appearances to fundraising events. Now, in the eighties, she became active in furthering AIDS education well before it became widely acceptable to do so.

She returned to the screen (and to Fox) in 1982 for *Kiss Me Goodbye*, a remake of the 1978 Brazilian hit *Dona Flor and Her Two Husbands*. She played Sally Field's tart-tongued, poker-playing mother. Actually old enough to be Field's grandmother, she was still looking improbably youthful and was altogether delightful and convincing. But the picture tanked, to Claire's disappointment.

In 1984 Claire was among the actresses featured in James Watters' photo-essay book *Return Engagement*. "I'm lucky I don't have to work," she told Watters, "and while there are still a lot of things for me to do, keeping up my name is not one of them." Horst's accompanying unretouched portrait of Claire showed her looking serenely trim and beautiful at 73.

Claire's final acting role was in an ABC television movie awkwardly titled *Norman Rockwell's Breaking Home Ties*, seen on November 27, 1987, playing a lame, middle-aged spinster-schoolteacher.

By the '90s she had moved back home to Newport Beach and was keeping a low public profile. In 1999 she met the Dean of the University of California, Irvine, School of the Arts, who invited her to come by and visit their theater. Claire took an interest in the program and began doing some off-the-cuff, informal master classes for the students. She didn't care for the theater's outdated physical setup so she donated $500,000, enabling them to renovate their 30-year-old playhouse, which they renamed the Claire Trevor Bren Theatre Stage.

It was in the midst of these activities that Claire died at age 90 on April 8, 2000, in a hospital near her Newport Beach home. She'd been hospitalized for respiratory ailments.

It was then announced that she had bequeathed her entire estate to the University of California, Irvine, School of the Arts. Along with additional bequests from the Bren family, the amount totaled $10 million. In her honor it has been renamed the Claire Trevor School of the Arts.

At the formal dedication, her stepson Donald Bren said, "Claire last appeared publicly on this very stage, on a blustery day in January almost three years ago. That's when a wonderful group of students brought tears to Claire's eyes with their performance and then she came up on stage and answered their questions about her many years of acting opposite such stars as John Wayne, Humphrey Bogart, Clark Gable and Spencer Tracy. She stole the show and she stole their hearts. Then she opened her heart and gave a [$500,000] gift to the theater, and I'm thrilled to be able to help students achieve their goals." He then added, "Claire was a remarkable person in every way." Bren concluded his speech by presenting the school with Claire's Oscar and her Emmy.

Now *that's* giving back.

1931: The Imperfect Lover (WB-Vitaphone short), The Meal Ticket (WB-Vitaphone short), Angel Cake (WB-Vitaphone short). **1933:** Life in the Raw (Fox), The Last Trail (Fox), The Mad Game (Fox), Jimmy and Sally (Fox). **1934:** Hold That Girl (Fox), Wild Gold (Fox), Baby Take a Bow (Fox), Elinor Norton (Fox). **1935:** Spring Tonic (Fox), Black Sheep (Fox), Dante's Inferno (Fox), Beauty's Daughter (Fox). **1936:** Sunkist Stars at Palm Springs (MGM short), My Marriage (TCF), The Song and Dance Man (TCF), Human Cargo (TCF), To Mary—With Love (TCF), Star for a Night (TCF), 15 Maiden Lane (TCF), Career Woman (TCF). **1937:** Time Out for Romance (TCF), King of Gamblers (Paramount), One Mile from Heaven (TCF), Dead End (UA), Second Honeymoon (TCF), Big Town Girl (TCF). **1938:** Walking Down Broadway (TCF), The Amazing Dr. Clitterhouse (WB), Valley of the Giants (WB), Five of a Kind (TCF). **1939:** Stagecoach (UA), I Stole a Million (Universal), Allegheny Uprising (RKO). **1940:** Dark Command (Republic). **1941:** Texas (Columbia), Honky Tonk (MGM), The Adventures of Martin Eden (Columbia). **1942:** Crossroads (MGM), Street of Chance (Paramount). **1943:** The Desperadoes (Columbia), Good Luck, Mr. Yates (Columbia), The Woman of the Town (UA). **1945:** Murder, My Sweet

(RKO), Johnny Angel (RKO). **1946:** Crack Up (RKO), The Bachelor's Daughters (UA). **1947:** Born to Kill (RKO). **1948:** Raw Deal (Eagle Lion), Key Largo (WB), The Velvet Touch (RKO), The Babe Ruth Story (Allied Artists). **1949:** The Lucky Stiff (UA). **1950:** Borderline (Universal). **1951:** Best of the Badmen (RKO), Hard, Fast and Beautiful (RKO). **1952:** Hoodlum Empire (Republic), My Man and I (MGM), Stop, You're Killing Me (WB). **1953:** The Stranger Wore a Gun (Columbia). **1954:** The High and the Mighty (WB). **1955:** Man Without a Star (Universal), Lucy Gallant (Paramount). **1956:** The Mountain (Paramount). **1958:** Marjorie Morningstar (WB). **1962:** Two Weeks in Another Town (MGM). **1963:** The Stripper (TCF). **1965:** How to Murder Your Wife (UA). **1967:** The Capetown Affair (TCF). **1982:** Kiss Me Goodbye (TCF). **1987:** Norman Rockwell's Breaking Home Ties (ABC-TV)

Marie Windsor: Face of Evil

by LAURA WAGNER

Her face gave her away: the half-smirk, her shadowy eyes and that *look* were sure signs that she was up to no good, even if she wasn't. You somehow suspected her motives might just be tainted. Not an asset for an actress who wants to play traditionally romantic leading roles, but great viewing for her fans who *wanted* her to be bad, *wanted* her to gun down the next dope who came along. Marie Windsor was at her best when she was ruthless or just plain tough; she made her roles interesting—heck, she *looked* interesting—giving them a visceral, raw energy many of them didn't deserve. Yeah, she couldn't be trusted, what of it?

She was born Emily Marie Bertelsen on December 11, 1922 to Lane and Etta Bertelsen in Marysvale, Utah. She recalled in interviews that acting was an early passion, attending silent movies with her grandmother (Clara Bow was her favorite) and taking dancing and dramatic lessons, before reaching her teen years. By the time Marie was in junior high she was the captain of the school's basketball team "because of my height," which was 5'9".

Marie graduated high school a year early and entered Brigham Young University. She studied art and drama and participated in campus productions. After two years she, along with her family, traveled to New York, where she wanted to study acting with the famed coach Maria Ouspenskaya; she was frustrated to find that Mme. Ouspenskaya had moved to Hollywood.

Back in Marysvale for a spell, Marie was still determined, and windows of opportunities opened for her. "Marysvale somehow got me named Miss Utah," she laughed, "even though no such competition existed." What the fictitious title did was act as a stepping stone, as did being named "Miss Covered Wagon Days" and "Miss D. & R. G. Railroad." Her prize for the latter was 99 dollars in silver, which was spent on luggage for the journey west.

With renewed vigor, the family all drove to Hollywood in 1940 in search of Mme. Ouspenskaya, who, when finally found, agreed to coach the budding actress. Marie said in 1991, "She seemed to like me very much, but was always working on me to deliver more 'inner energy.' It's interesting that after I spent ten summers studying with Stella Adler, I discovered that she was also a student of Ouspenskaya's."

Settling in with her acting lessons, Marie moved to the Hollywood Studio

Club, while her parents went back to Utah. At the suggestion of "a royalty buff" at the Studio Club, she also changed her name to Windsor.

She was working at the Mocambo as a cigarette girl when she was spotted by producer Arthur Hornblow, Jr. He alerted producer LeRoy Prinz, who gave her a bit in *All-American Coed* (1941). It led to numerous bits during 1941–43. Notable during this period was the East Side Kids' *Smart Alecks*, where she gave Leo Gorcey his first screen kiss, a dubious distinction.

In addition to her brief movie roles and various modeling assignments, Marie was involved with the revue *Henry Duffy's Merry-Go-Rounders* in 1943 with Sid Marion; the 13-week show played in Detroit, Buffalo and Washington, DC. In another show, *Star Dust*, an out-of-town flop, she understudied Gloria Grahame.

Marie busied herself in New York on radio during this period, employed, she estimated, in at least 400 largely uncredited on-air assignments. Her longest-lasting gig was

Portrait of Marie Windsor, 1950.

on the soap *Our Gal Sunday* for nine months. On the show *Amanda of Honeymoon Hill*, she met bandleader Ted Steele, who would later become her first husband. (They wed in 1946, and it was annulled after eight months.) But it was another Broadway production in 1944 which proved her ticket back to Hollywood.

Follow the Girls was a smash hit musical revue (eventually running two years), set in a serviceman's canteen. It starred pre–TV Jackie Gleason and Gertrude Niesen, and was drawing crowds mainly because of its vaudeville-flavored skits. Marie was a replacement several months after the show opened in April of 1944. After she was with the show six months, Vladimir Vetlugen offered her an MGM screen test and then a short-term contract.

The contract with MGM was high-profile for the young actress, but she was basically low-profile on-screen. It was back to tiny parts, albeit in major movies; her roles as salesladies, train passengers, nightclub patrons and script girls wasted the potential Marie exuded. She seemed to indicate in these movies that there was something more waiting to be told, something smoldering just below the surface, but MGM had no idea how to bring out that quality.

It was left to the independent company Enterprise to give Marie her breakout performance, her first featured part. John Garfield, Bob Roberts and Abraham Polonsky had seen a test she had done of Jean Cocteau's one-person play *The Human Voice*, which Marie's friend Otto Preminger had directed for her. She was dropped by MGM, but cast in the now well-regarded *Force of Evil* (1948).

It was unappreciated at the time, perhaps because of its "autopsy on capitalism," as director Polonsky (who was later blacklisted) called the original source material, Ira Wolfert's novel *Tucker's People*. Garfield is a mob lawyer involved with a corrupt numbers racket. Marie plays mob boss Roy Roberts' sexy wife, trying to seduce Garfield. The unforgettable Windsor was a sharp contrast to the bland female lead, Beatrice Pearson.

Due to financial struggles imposed by the failure of their other major 1948 release *Arch of Triumph*, Enterprise was forced to seek aid from MGM. In turn MGM, who distributed the film, cut ten minutes from the final print and sent the finished product out as a second feature. Enterprise would suffer, but Marie's edgy talents had at last been on display and she was now ready for larger roles. She finally was given a role to sink her teeth into, and from then on would generally attack each part with the same ferocity. Unfortunately, since her work was mostly seen in lowercase productions, A features largely eluded her.

After Garfield and the powerful *Force of Evil*, did Marie deserve *Outpost in Morocco* (1949)? There was something a tad obscene about George Raft starring as a dashing Legionnaire, with every female, including Windsor's Princess Cara, daughter of the evil Amir, falling madly—deeply—incomprehensibly—in love with him. Marie's glacial, exotic beauty (minus accent), her regal bearing and fiery temper elevated the silly, banal story.

"Bill Elliott saw the test I'd made as well as the George Raft film," Marie recounted later, explaining how she was cast in Republic's *Hellfire* (1949), "and when he learned I was a horsewoman, he fought the studio to use me instead of one of their contract players. He later taught me how to twirl guns, and I did a lot of stunt work in this Western that normally an actress simply would not do."

Marie considered the film one of her three top favorites (alongside *The Narrow Margin* and *The Killing*). "*Hellfire* had a particularly wonderful script and a fabulous part for a woman, namely me. I got to play a woman disguised as a man in the first part of the film. Then my character turned out to be extremely feminine. On top of that, I really enjoyed a chance to use my ability as a horsewoman," an ability honed while growing up in Utah.

"Take a good look, Lou—while you've still got a look left," Marie growls to the man she's about to out-draw. This is how her character Doll Brown is introduced, and, naturally, everyone shudders at her mere name. Everyone except Bill Elliott, a gambler-turned-preacher.

While the brothers of the man she killed aim to kill her, Marie is looking for her long-lost sister and Elliott is after her $5,000 reward to build a church. Along the way, Marie pistol-whips Elliott, plays poker, knocks back two straight whiskeys, rolls her own cigarette and sings two songs ("Shoo, Fly, Don't Bother Me" and "Bringing in the Sheaves," dubbed by Virginia Rees).

Her final scene, finding faith while trying to save Forrest Tucker's life, is one

Marie is about to assist William Elliott (center) in *Hellfire* **(Republic, 1949) by gunning down Marshall Forrest Tucker. The ruthless part was one of Marie's favorites.**

of the finest she ever played. Holding the wounded Tucker's bullet-hole with a tight compress, and unarmed herself, she reads from a Bible as the two brothers come closer with guns drawn. Her arms full of lead, but still praying, the seriously wounded, barely conscious Marie is finally saved by Elliott. The intensity of this scene (played mostly in closeup) has impressed many through the years.

In a perfect world, *Hellfire* would have made Marie a major star, but this was Republic. Its lack of success with audiences never deterred Marie, who mentioned *Hellfire* in just about every interview she gave. "I dearly loved that role," she stated, with good reason.

She would later play opposite Bill Elliott again in *The Showdown* (1950). Marie is the tavern owner and cattle investor who Elliott may or may not be able to trust. Figures.

From over-the-top to second fiddle—to Vera Ralston, yet—Marie showed up next in *The Fighting Kentuckian* (1949), doing what she did best: acting the innocent but double-crossing everyone in sight. When we first see Marie she's all sweetness, strumming a guitar and singing "Let Me Down, O Hangman" (dubbed by Virginia Rees). She speaks *so* delicately, *so* demurely to star John Wayne, you know something's going to happen. The greedy, callous Windsor gets hers at the end when Grant Withers catches her picking the lock to his safe. Wayne finds her dead body lying half in the safe, her cold, dead hand open wide as gold coins spill into it.

Fox next gave her the title role in *Dakota Lil* (1950) about a Treasury agent (George Montgomery) on the trail of the Hole-in-the-Wall Gang (led by Rod Cameron). Marie is a "counterfeiter, expert forger, skilled engraver and plate printer," not to mention saloon singer (her songs "Matamoros" and the fabulous "Ecstasy" were voice-doubled by Anita Ellis); unaware that George is an agent, she helps get the goods on Cameron. Of course, there's a mutual attraction between her and the gorgeous Montgomery. "What's a smart girl like you doing in a broken-down cantina like this?" is his pickup line.

Though soft-spoken, Marie is no weepy Western maiden. Finagling with Cameron over her cut of some stolen loot she plans to put signatures on (as part of her and George's plan), he offers her a quarter of the $100,000 because "you're so beautiful." Marie, giving him a steely look, cracks, "You're so repulsive, I'll take 50."

The major studios viewed the unconventional Marie only as a B-movie babe—great in Westerns and crime melodramas, where her commanding presence gave the low-budgeter class. "Playing heavies is fun," she admitted in 1991, "and the parts usually have meatier dialogue to chew on." But, naturally, she craved diversity. Insisting that she "wanted to be Greer Garson" and "play things like Mrs. Miniver," she knew that was never a possibility, because even when she was "the good girl" there was that interesting element of defiance in her makeup. "My height has always

"What's a smart girl like you doing in a broken-down cantina like this?," sexy federal man George Montgomery asks Marie in *Dakota Lil* (TCF, 1950).

handicapped me. And my 'look' with my prominent eyes. I look more like the madam of a brothel than I do the girl next door!" she laughed. The studio system was breaking down and Windsor had no studio to prepare the proper big-budgeted vehicles for her. Instead, her stock was in inexpensive productions, some of dubious merit.

There's little to brag about during the early '50s. *Hurricane Island* (1951) at least had some camp value, with Windsor creditably and terrifically cast as a treacherous lady pirate. Marie called her supporting role of Don Taylor's bigoted sister-in-law in *Japanese War Bride* (1952) "the bitchiest dame I've ever played," which is saying plenty. Windsor had less than ten minutes in the classic *The Sniper* (1952), as the first of five victims of the disturbed, woman-hating Arthur Franz, but she's extremely effective.

Her next film, no mere triviality, contained perhaps her best performance. It would solidify Windsor's reputation with film fans.

The Narrow Margin (1952) was meant as just a little picture at RKO. Filmed in 13 days in 1950, at a budget of around $230,000, it came to the attention of Howard Hughes, who was running RKO at the time. He adored it, running it continually in his private screening room. The director, Richard Fleischer, who was nervous about the movie's downbeat ending, was sent for by Hughes personally to discuss the picture. "Hughes was so impressed with this little film that he wasn't going to bother about fiddling around with the end of it," Fleischer wrote later. "What he was contemplating doing was remaking it in its entirety—make an A film out of it, with stars. Instead of Charles Mc-Graw and Marie Windsor playing the leads, it would be Robert Mitchum and Jane Russell. [It would now] cost $1 million. Instead of being the tightly wrought gem of a *film noir* we all believed it to be, it would now become—well, something else."

Hughes eventually lost interest because, says

The classic *The Narrow Margin* (RKO, 1952) pitted Charles McGraw against a ferocious Marie Windsor.

Marie, "he was involved more deeply in other business matters and had little interest in any film." His initial enthusiasm held up its release for a good 18 months and *The Narrow Margin* was delivered to theaters without much fuss. It nonetheless became a sleeper, whose classic status is well-deserved today.

The actress thought *The Narrow Margin* "would thrust me into big stardom. But it took several years for the word-of-mouth to prove it was a great little picture." Director Fleischer later raved to Karen Burroughs Hannsberry of the "brilliance" of Marie's performance, continuing, "It was a great part for any actress to play, but it fitted Marie perfectly and she was able to give it the bite and the high-tension performance it required. I was fortunate to have such a talented actress in the picture."

Her outwardly nasty character, seemingly a gangster's widow, rocks the screen, as she goes toe-to-toe with virile detective Charles McGraw. Marie is specified as "a dish, 60-cent special. Cheap, flashy, strictly poison under the gravy." Marie is more than capable of standing up to the rugged detective. He doesn't know she's a decoy, therefore he resents her, finding her cheap and sordid—exactly the point. McGraw and Windsor, their friction touched with electricity, turned in their most exciting screen portrayals in *The Narrow Margin*.

From the riveting *The Narrow Margin*, she became one of the *Outlaw Women* (1952). Marie is the leader (Iron Mae) of a group of lethal ladies taking over a town, with the ad campaign promising: "Meet the Babes Who Put the *Bad* in the Bad Men!" Shot in New Mexico, *The Tall Texan* (1953), refers not to Marie, but to her leading man Lloyd Bridges. It had the unlikely scenario of Bridges reforming bad girl Windsor. In his dreams.

Marie landed a supporting part as John Wayne's ex-wife in *Trouble Along the Way* (1953), but this excursion to the big studios ended when she was cast right back at Republic for her next, *City That Never Sleeps* (1953). Shot in Chicago, it cast Marie as an ex-waitress married to lawyer Edward Arnold, regretting her indiscretion with shady William Talman.

She played temperamental actresses in two major screen biographies: *So This is Love* (1953), the story of songstress Grace Moore, and *The Eddie Cantor Story* (1953). These small parts served only as bookends to one of Marie's most famous movies: *Cat Women of the Moon* (1953).

Windsor called *Cat Women of the Moon* "one of the worst pictures I was ever in." She told Tom Weaver in 1996 that she knew instantly that things would not bode well for her or her fellow actors "the minute I walked on the set and saw that we were traveling to the Moon seated in desk chairs with wheels on the bottom! We were strapped into those chairs and off we went, into outer space! And I thought, 'Gee, can't they figure out that these chairs would be rolling and floating around?' It was so silly!" Marie is the navigator of a crew on a rocket landing on the Moon. Their scientific expedition is made even more troublesome by giant spiders (with visible strings) and the appearance of a race of low-rent "Cat Women."

The deadly females, who "have no use for men," have been mentally bending an unaware Windsor to their will. Their motive is to seize control of the ship and take over Earth, with Marie in tow. Marie tries to fight their strong mental control, her desire to help the women ("You are one of us") clashing with her desire for the supposedly macho Victor Jory ("You're smart, you have courage and you're *all* woman," he growls). Marie's best acting moments are the ones where she lapses between good and evil, grappling with her conflicting feelings—a classic case of an actress rising above her material. She would have made Mme. Ouspenskaya proud, even in this trash, with her "inner energy." Surely she also deserves points for making her inconceivable romantic triangle with Sonny Tufts and Jory plausible.

On a personal note, Marie met realtor Jack Hupp, son of silent screen actor Earle Rodney, in August of 1954, on a blind date arranged by actor William Bakewell. Four months later, on November 30, they were married. The union produced a son, Richard, born in 1963; Hupp had a son, Chris, from his previous marriage. They would remain happily married until Marie's death 46 years later.

Funnier than its reputation suggests, *Abbott and Costello Meet the Mummy* (1955), the team's last for Universal, contained a fabulous part for Marie. She plays it straight and wicked as Madame Rontru, oozing pure evil—every inch the Egyptian villainess. Seeking the mummy Klaris and the sacred Medallion of Ra, she isn't fazed one bit by the curse placed on it: "There is no curse that a gun or a knife can't cure." Flanked by two henchmen, she lets nothing—not even a mummy on the loose—stop her from her goal. Going *mano a mano* with the monster, Windsor first empties her gun into it and, when that fails, she beats the hell out of it with a torch and finally tosses a stick of dynamite his way. All in a day's work. "Remember," one of her followers foolishly warns her, "he's dangerous." Meaning every word, Marie snarls, "So am *I*."

Roger Corman helmed *Swamp Women* (1956), a potent piece of camp co-starring Beverly Garland and Jil Jarmyn. Together they're "The Nardo Gang," felons who break out of prison to reclaim a diamond stash hidden in the swamp marshes.

Filmed after *Swamp Women* but released before, *The Killing* (1956), based on Lionel White's novel *Clean Break*, is one of Marie's most notable movies and director Stanley Kubrick's first major work. Her part as Elisha Cook, Jr.'s, sultry, spiteful wife earned her *Look* magazine's Best Supporting Actress Award in 1956 ("my happiest moment as an actress"), an honor that should have extended to the Academy.

"That's my Sherry," Marie remembers Kubrick saying after he saw her in *The Narrow Margin*, even turning down Ida Lupino and, thankfully, Zsa Zsa Gabor to get her. And he was right. Marie is flawlessly cast as Cook's seductive, treacherous, two-timing (with Vince Edwards) spouse who impairs a $2,000,000 payroll heist arranged by Sterling Hayden and his gang. She gave a portrayal that exploded through the screen, scorching the celluloid. Hayden sizes her up, calling her a "little tramp," branding her as someone who'd "sell out your own mother for a piece of fudge."

It was a part that in lesser hands (Gabor) could have sunk into conventionality. Marie explained in 1999 her approach: "I never believed that Sherry meant to be so cruel, but she felt that life just hadn't given her a fair shake, and she was determined that it would ... so I tried to approach her from that point of view." An impressed Kubrick later tried to get her for a role in his *Lolita* (1962), shot in England; Marie was unable to obtain a work permit, losing the role.

With no promotion (due to Kubrick's dispute with UA), *The Killing* slipped into theaters, eventually developing a strong following, especially with *noir* enthusiasts. Again, Windsor had turned in a star-making performance in a film of high quality, but it changed nothing. The movies offered to her continued to be of lesser caliber, with Marie eclipsing her material. Not an easy task when your 1957 titles are *The Parson and the Outlaw*, *The Unholy Wife* and *The Girl in Black Stockings*.

Another of Marie's 1957 releases, *The Story of Mankind* bears notice, not because of its excellence, but for its reputation as one of Hollywood's most notorious all-star bombs. Screenwriter Charles Bennett, known for writing some of Hitchcock's finest, was caught up adapting Hendrik Van Loon's best-selling 1921 volume with producer-director Irwin Allen. Bennett, bristling at the memory, complained in 1993 that he "didn't realize quite how dreadful it was going to be. I didn't realize when I was starting off that it was really going to be just a collection of snippets from old pictures and things like that. It was dreadful, I hated the picture. But I'm a writer, I wrote it, I was being paid quite handsomely, so that was it."

Marie thought the movie was a good idea—at first. "But it's the kind of idea that demands top-notch quality, with better writing and production values than our film got. In some ways, it almost seemed like a glorified high school movie with a

The all-star dud *The Story of Mankind* (WB, 1957) featured Dennis Hopper and Windsor's two-minute bit as Napoleon and Josephine.

great cast." Some of the actors were able to rise above the inept dialogue and situations (Ronald Colman, Vincent Price, Hedy Lamarr), while many more did not (Peter Lorre, Virginia Mayo as a giggling Cleopatra, the Marx Brothers). Marie—nineteenth-billed above the title—belongs in the former category. Acting as Josephine to Dennis Hopper's Napoleon (don't laugh—it *works*), the two actors turned their two-and-a-half-minute spot into a powerful, restrained vignette, worthy of a better movie.

Jack Warner requested that she be tested as Vera Charles for *Auntie Mame* (1958), with Rosalind Russell; the chic part would have been ideal. Marie was disappointed when Coral Browne was cast.

Work on television kept her increasingly occupied. She had made her TV debut as far back as 1950 on *Pantomime Quiz*, and followed that with dramatic shows (*Ford Theatre, Pepsi-Cola Playhouse*), comedy (Eddie Cantor, Red Skelton) and Westerns (*Cheyenne, Maverick*, and, as Belle Starr in *Stories of the Century*). Marie's professionalism graced other shows like *Perry Mason, Lassie, Hawaiian Eye, Batman*—literally hundreds of episodic TV roles well into the 1970s, stretching to 1991 and her final TV gig, *Murder, She Wrote*.

She did a little theater work starting in 1959 with *Would-Be Gentleman* at the Ritz Theater in Los Angeles with Buddy Ebsen and Anna Lee. Another around this time was George S. Kaufman's *Fancy Meeting You Again*, in which she played four roles, at the La Jolla Playhouse with Joan Caulfield and Richard Crenna. Marie's stage roles allowed her the chance to do comedy.

However, her movie parts began to slip permanently into the supporting bracket when she returned in 1962. "I hate to admit this, 'cause it really isn't a very classy statement," she divulged later, "but I never turned a picture down unless they asked me to *strip*! So I'd take anything, unless it was too tiny. *Now* I don't care how tiny, I just would like to work."

In *Mail Order Bride* (1964), with Lois Nettleton in the title role, Marie was quite touching as a widow (and saloon keeper) who eventually finds love with Buddy Ebsen. She played the owner of "Polly's Palace Saloon" in *The Good Guys and The Bad Guys* (1969). Both were directed by Burt Kennedy, who clearly saw Marie in those surroundings. He later cast her in *Support Your Local Gunfighter* (1971) as, yes, a bawdy madam.

Marie was *another* madam in *Chamber of Horrors* (1966). It was "made from a TV pilot called *The Hook*," she revealed to Jim Meyer at the time. "It was a wonderful pilot film, but too gruesome for TV ... no one would buy it." It was released to theaters.

Windsor's motion picture parts were no longer giving her satisfaction, and her choice to be with her family and to do TV led to more rigid casting decisions and less opportunities. "I wanted to work," she explained, "and TV had faster turnaround and quicker paychecks." But that didn't save her from the screen parts she did get: she was a sharpshootin' con in *Wild Women* (1970), and ran ever more brothels in *One More Train to Rob* (1971) and *Manhunter* (1974). She was to be yet another madam in Disney's *The Apple Dumpling Gang* (1975), but reportedly Disney execs were so abashed at her *too* realistic portrayal that her scenes were completely cut. She owned a bar in *The Outfit* (1974).

Good, if still smallish, roles continued to find their way to her. She was cast opposite old friend John Wayne in *Cahill, U.S. Marshal* (1973), warmly sincere as a widow in love with Wayne. She did an amusing turn in *Hearts of the West* (1975), a nostalgic piece set in 1930s Hollywood, about B-western movie making. She was funny in *Freaky Friday* (1977), a Disney movie she wasn't cut out of. Instead of a madam, they made her a schoolteacher.

The suspenseful Stephen King vampire saga *Salem's Lot* (1979), a four-hour TV mini-series directed by Tobe Hooper, reunited Marie with *The Killing*'s Elisha Cook, Jr. She said of her one-time co-star: "Elisha was a real character. He was pleasantly off-the-wall, full of energy ... he brought me a white orchid with a sweet note about how happy he was about our reunion."

Her movie appearances started winding down. Her last was *Commando Squad* (1987), where *Variety* found her "hilarious" as the owner of a memorabilia store (a front for illegal activities).

During this slow stretch of movie making in the '80s, Marie made a triumphal return to the stage, mostly in Los Angeles. Among the plays she appeared in were *The Vinegar Tree* and *The Shadow Box*. She won the L.A. Drama Critics' Best Actress Award for *The Bar Off Melrose* (1987), in a part playwright Terry-Kingsley Smith wrote with her in mind. Marie's work in the latter drew raves, with Jack Holland of *Drama-Logue* mentioning her "amusing and sharp-edged performance": "Windsor, with her deep husky voice, tosses off the lines with acid delight. It is a potent reminder of one talent that was wasted by the studios." Her work on the stage would earn her four *Drama-Logue* Awards.

Marie got more attention during her later years. "It's mind-boggling," she mused in 1991. "For [an] actress who ... never became a genuine name-above-the-title star—there's consolation in belated recognition." She got a star on the Hollywood Walk of Fame in 1983, the Golden Boot Award (for excellence in Westerns), "The Woman of Western Fame Award" at the 1993 Sonora Film Festival and the Bronze Halo Award. The Screen Actors Guild, with which she was a board member of good standing for almost 30 years, honored her with their Ralph Morgan Award for distinguished service in 1990; she also helped establish the SAG Film Society. When she retired from the Guild, she was made Honorary Chairperson of the Film Society and awarded a SAG Lifetime Membership.

She was involved with the Thalians, a group dedicated to helping troubled children, and WAIF (Women's Adoption International Fund), while also serving on the board of the women's auxiliary of the John Tracy Clinic, dedicated to teaching hearing-impaired children to speak.

The flow of her career was seriously hampered during the '90s with numerous illnesses and physical complications: arthritis, botched eye surgery, a brain concussion, heart surgery, shoulder replacement and back surgery that left her paralyzed for a time; she was only able to walk after several operations and intense therapy. Marie's optimism never failed through it all. "I just think that every day will be better," she asserted in 1999. But even the toughest lady on film couldn't surmount all the physical problems troubling her, even though she put up a valiant fight. Marie passed away peacefully on December 10, 2000, a day shy of her seventy-eighth birthday.

Her approach to her career was very simple: "If it wasn't meant to work out— if I never got the star-making part—that's just how it goes. I'd forge on."

And forge on she did, through cat women, mummies, fast-guns and brothels. She was strong, possibly too strong for her own good, but clearly having a ball overpowering everyone in sight ("I wasn't afraid to dirty my hands with tough, unsympathetic roles"). Windsor was unconventional in looks, height and manner; she could never be classified as an ingenue. Marie was a good actress relegated either to B movies or supporting parts in major movies. Fair? Not at all. But despite this, she, through her work in *film noir*, Westerns and sci-fi, will always be remembered fondly as one of the great screen *femme fatales*.

"I like him because he's so good," Marie seductively coos in *Hellfire*, one of her favorites, "and he likes me because I'm so *bad*."

1941: All-American Co-ed (UA), Weekend for Three (RKO), Playmates (RKO), Four Jacks and a Jill (RKO). **1942**: Joan of Paris (RKO), Call Out the Marines (RKO), Smart Alecks (Monogram), Parachute Nurse (Columbia), Eyes in the Night (MGM), The Lady or the Tiger (MGM short). **1943**: Chatterbox (Republic), The Iron Major (RKO), Three Hearts for Julia (MGM), Let's Face It (Paramount). **1945**: Good, Good, Good (soundie). **1947**: The Hucksters (MGM), I Love My Wife, But! (MGM short), Romance of Rosy Ridge (MGM), Living in a Big Way (MGM), Song of the Thin Man (MGM), The Unfinished Dance (MGM). **1948**: On An Island with You (MGM), The Pirate (MGM), The Three Musketeers (MGM), The Kissing Bandit (MGM), Force of Evil (Enterprise/MGM). **1949**: Outpost in Morocco (UA), The Beautiful Blonde from Bashful Bend (TCF), The Fighting Kentuckian (Republic), Hellfire (Republic). **1950**: Dakota Lil (TCF), The Showdown (Republic), Frenchie (Universal), Double Deal (RKO). **1951**: Little Big Horn (Lippert), Hurricane Island (Columbia), Two-Dollar Bettor (Realart). **1952**: Japanese War Bride (TCF), The Sniper (Columbia), The Narrow Margin (RKO), Outlaw Women (Lippert), The Jungle (Lippert). **1953**: The Tall Texan (Lippert), Trouble Along the Way (WB), USSR Today (Artkino Pictures documentary), City That Never Sleeps (Republic), So This is Love (WB), Cat Women of the Moon (Astor), The Eddie Cantor Story (WB). **1954**: Hell's Half Acre (Republic), The Bounty Hunter (WB). **1955**: The Silver Star (Lippert), Abbott and Costello Meet the Mummy (Universal), No Man's Woman (Republic). **1956**: Two-Gun Lady (Associated Film), The Killing (UA), Swamp Women (Favorite Films). **1957**: The Parson and the Outlaw (Columbia), The Unholy Wife (Universal), The Girl in Black Stockings (UA), The Story of Mankind (WB). **1958**: Day of the Bad Man (Universal), Island Women (UA). **1961**: Paradise Alley (Sutton). **1963**: Critic's Choice (WB). **1964**: The Day Mars Invaded Earth (TCF), Bedtime Story (Universal), Mail Order Bride (MGM). **1966**: Chamber of Horrors (WB). **1969**: The Good Guys and the Bad Guys (WB–Seven Arts). **1970**: Wild Women (TVM). **1971**: Support Your Local Gunfighter (UA), One More Train to Rob (Universal). **1973**: Cahill, U.S. Marshall (WB). **1974**: Manhunter (TVM), The Outfit (MGM). **1975**: Hearts of the West (MGM). **1977**: Freaky Friday (BV). **1979**: Salem's Lot (TVM). **1980**: The Perfect Woman (Cable). **1981**: Lovely But Deadly (Juniper). **1987**: Commando Squad (Trans World). **Cut Footage: 1942**: The Big Street (RKO), George Washington Slept Here (WB). **1943**: Pilot #5 (MGM). **1975**: The Apple Dumpling Gang (BV).

Bibliography

Books

Arnaz, Desi, *A Book*. New York: Morrow, 1976

Behlmer, Rudy, ed. *Inside Warner Bros.* New York: Simon & Schuster, 1985

Blondell, Joan, *Center Door Fancy*. New York: Delacorte Press, 1972

Brady, Kathleen, *Lucille: The Life of Lucille Ball*. New York: Hyperion, 1994

Brooks, Tim and Earle Marsh, *The Complete Directory of Prime Time Network TV Shows, 1946–Present*, New York: Ballantine Books, 1981

Cagney, James, *Cagney by Cagney*. Garden City: Doubleday & Company, 1976

Capra, Frank, *The Name Above the Title*, New York: Macmillan, 1971

Cohn, Art, *The Nine Lives of Michael Todd*. New York: Random House, 1958

Crawford, Joan with Joan Kesner Ardmore, *A Portrait of Joan*. New York: Paperback Library, 1964

Curcio, Vincent, *Suicide Blonde; The Life of Gloria Grahame*. New York: William Morrow & Co., 1989

DeMille, Cecil, *The Autobiography of Cecil B. DeMille*. Englewood Cliffs NJ, Prentice-Hall, 1959

Dickens, Homer. *The Films of Barbara Stanwyck*. Seacaucus NJ: Citadel Press, 1984

Donati, William, *Ida Lupino: A Biography*. Lexington: University Press of Kentucky, 1996

Dunning, John, *On the Air: The Encyclopedia of Old-Time Radio*. New York: Oxford University Press, 1998

Fitzgerald, Michael G., and Boyd Magers, *Ladies of the Western*. Jefferson NC: McFarland, 2002

Fleischer, Richard, *Just Tell Me When to Cry: A Memoir*. New York: Carroll & Graf, 1993

Fordin, Hugh, *The World of Entertainment!* Garden City NY: Doubleday & Co., 1975

Guilaroff, Sydney, *Crowning Glory: Reflections of Hollywood's Favorite Confidant*. L.A. GPG, 1996

Hannsberry, Karen Burroughs, *Femme Noir: Bad Girls of Film*. Jefferson NC: McFarland, 1998

Haskell, Molly, *From Reverence to Rape*. New York: Holt, Rinehart and Winston, 1974

Higham, Charles, *Celebrity Circus*. New York: Delacorte Press, 1979

_____. *Lucy: The Real Life of Lucille Ball*. New York: St. Martin's, 1986

Hudson, Rock, and Sara Davidson, *Rock Hudson: His Story*. New York: William Morrow, 1986

Kiersch, Mary, *Curtis Bernhardt: A Directors Guild of America Oral History*. Metuchen NJ: Scarecrow, 1986

Kobal, John, *People Will Talk*. New York: Knopf, 1985

LaSalle, Mick, *Complicated Women: Sex and Power in Pre-Code Hollywood*. New York: St. Martin's, 2000

McBride, Joseph, *Hawks on Hawks*. Berkley, University of California Press, 1982

_____, *Frank Capra; The Catastrophe of Success*. Simon & Schuster, 1992

McCabe, John, *Cagney*. New York: Knopf, 1997

McCambridge, Mercedes, *The Quality of Mercy*. New York: Times Books, 1981

_____, *The Two of Us*. London: Peter Davies, 1960

McCarthy, Todd, *Howard Hawks: The Grey Fox of Hollywood*. New York: Grove Press, 1997

McClelland, Doug, *Eleanor Parker: Woman of a Thousand Faces*. Metuchen NJ: Scarecrow, 1989

____, *Forties Film Talk*. Jefferson NC: McFarland, 1992

McGilligan, Patrick, *Film Crazy: Interviews with Hollywood Legends*. New York: St. Martin's, 2000

McNeil, Alex, *Total Television, Third Edition*, New York: Penguin Books, 1991

Martin, Tony and Cyd Charisse, *The Two of Us*. New York: Mason/Charter, 1976

Marx, Arthur, *The Secret Life of Bob Hope*. New York: Barricade Books, 1993

Miller, Ann, and Norma Jean Browning, *Miller's High Life*. Garden City NY: Doubleday & Company, 1972

Morella, Joe, and Edward Epstein, *Lucy: The Bittersweet Life of Lucille Ball*. Secaucus: Lyle Stuart, 1986

Neal, Patricia, *As I Am*. New York: Pocket Books, 1988

O'Neil, Thomas, *The Emmys*. New York, Perigee, 1998

Oppenheimer, Jerry, and Jack Vitek, *Idol: Rock Hudson, The True Story of An American Film Hero*. New York: Villard Books, 1986

Parish, James Robert, *The RKO Gals*. New Rochelle NY: Arlington House, 1974

____, and Ronald L. Bowers, *The MGM Stock Campany*, New Rochelle NY: Arlington House, 1973

____, and William T. Leonard, *Hollywood Players: The Thirties*. New Rochelle NY: Arlington House, 1976

____, and Don Stanke, *The Leading Ladies*. New Rochelle NY: Arlington House, 1977

Rogers, Ginger, *Ginger: My Story*. New York: HarperCollins, 1991

Russell, Geraldine Jacobi, *Oh, Lord, What Next?* New York: Vantage Press, 1960

Russell, Jane, *Jane Russell; My Path and My Detours*. New York: Franklin Watts, Inc., 1985

Sherman, Vincent, *Studio Affairs: My Life as a Film Director*. Lexington KY: University Press of Kentucky, 1996

Shipman, David, *The Great Movie Stars: The Golden Years*, New York: Hill & Wang, 1970

Smith, Betty, *A Tree Grows in Brooklyn*. Philadelphia PA: The Blakiston Company, 1943

Smith, Ella, *Starring Miss Barbara Stanwyck*. New York: Crown Publishers, 1985

Thomas, Bob, *King Cohn: The Life and Times of Harry Cohn*. New York: G.P. Putnam's Sons, 1967

Thomas, Danny, with Bill Davidson, *Make Room for Danny*. New York: G.P. Putnam's Sons, 1991

Wallis, Hal, & Higham, Charles *Starmaker*. New York: MacMillan, 1980

Watters, James, *Return Engagement*. New York, Clarkson N. Potter, 1984

Weaver, Tom, *Attack of the Monster Movie Makers: Interviews with 20 Genre Giants*. Jefferson NC: McFarland, 1994

____. *Monsters, Mutants and Heavenly Creatures: Confessions of 14 Classic Sci-Fi Horrormeisters!* Baltimore MD: Midnight Marquee, 1996

____, *John Carradine: The Films*. Jefferson NC: McFarland, 1999

Wellman, William A., *A Short Time for Insanity*. New York: Hawthorn Books, 1974

Articles

Atkinson, Brooks, "Ghosts" review. *New York Times*, Feb. 17, 1948

Barnes, Howard, "A Highland Fling" review. *New York Herald-Tribune*, April 29, 1944

____, "The Big Two" review. *New York Herald-Tribune*, Jan. 9, 1947

Barthel, Joan, "Quartet of Queens." *Life*, Feb. 19, 1971

Briggs, Colin, "Exclusive Interview with Lynn Bari." *Hollywood Studio*, Dec. 1987

Buckley, Michael, "The Quality of Mercy." *TheaterWeek*, Oct. 7, 1991

De Bono, Jerry, "Sally Forrest: Stepping Out of the Chorus in a Big Way." *Films of the Golden Age*, Spring 2000

DeCarl, Lennard, "Alexis Smith." *Films in Review*, June-July 1970

Delany, Kevin, "Claire Trevor Has Sane TV Outlook." *New York World-Telegram*, June 22, 1956

Ephron, Nora, "Closeup: The Busy Actress." *New York Post*, Feb. 18, 1964

Field, Rowland, "A Place of Our Own" review. *Newark Evening News*, April 3, 1945

Freedley, George, "Woman Bites Dog" review.

New York Morning Telegraph, April 1946

Gallagher, John, "Claire Trevor: An Interview." *Films in Review*, Nov. 1983

Gardella, Kay, "Yes, Hope Still Loves Lucy." *New York Daily News*, Sept. 22, 1989

Garland, Robert, "A Place of Our Own" review. *New York Journal-American*, April 3, 1945

Golden, Eve, "Shoes With Wings On: A Conversation with Ann Miller." *Classic Images*, Jan. 1994

Haas, Dorothy, "Lynn Bari: My Five Year Plan Worked." *Hollywood*, Aug. 1942

Hagen, Ray, "A *Screen Facts* Interview with Ann Sheridan." *Screen Facts*, 1966

_____, "Claire Trevor." *Films in Review*, Nov. 1963

_____, "Gloria Grahame." *Screen Facts*, May 1964

_____, "Jane Russell." *Films in Review*, April, 1963

_____, "Jean Hagen." *Film Fan Monthly*, Dec. 1968

_____, "Mercedes McCambridge." *Films in Review*, May 1965

Hammond, Percy, "Whistling in the Dark" review. *New York Herald Tribune*, Jan. 20, 1932

Harford, Margaret "Barefoot in the Park" review. *L.A. Times*, Jan. 27, 1966

Harmetz, Aljean, "Barbara Stanwyck: I'm a Tomorrow Woman." *New York Times*, March 22, 1981

Higham, Charles, "Will the Real Devil Speak Up? Yes!" *New York Times*, Jan. 27, 1974

Holland, Jack, "Claire Trevor, Hollywood's Neglected Star." *Screen Guide*, Oct. 1948

Johnson, Marsha, "Catching Up with ... Ida Lupino." *Modern Screen*, Nov. 1972

Lee, Sonia, "Claire Trevor: The Star Who Isn't a Star." *Motion Picture*, May 1938

McClelland, Doug, "Ann Dvorak: Underground Goddess." *Film Fan Monthly*, May 1969

McNulty, Thomas, "Vincent Sherman: From the Director's Chair." *Films of the Golden Age*, Summer 1998

Maltin, Leonard, "FFM Interviews Joan Blondell." *Film Fan Monthly*, Sept. 1969.

Meyer, Jim, "Marie Windsor." *Screen Facts* #16, 1967

_____. "Marie Windsor: A Shining Light." *Classic Images*, Nov. 1999

Miller, Mark A., "Marie Windsor: This Actress Knew How to Survive ... with Style." *Filmfax*, Dec. 1991-Jan. 1992

Morehouse, Ward, "Another Part of the Forest" review. *New York Sun*, Nov. 20, 1946

Nadel, Norman, "Cast Change Gives 'Woolf' New Tone." *New York World Telegram & Sun*, Jan. 15, 1963

Nichols, Lewis, "Woman Bites Dog" review. *New York Times*, April 1946

O'Brian, Jack, TV Column. *New York Journal-American*, March 11, 1957

Oettinger, Malcom, "Claire Trevor: Kicking Over the Traces." *Modern Screen*, June 1938

Pontes, Bob, "Interview with Marie Windsor." *Classic Images*, June 1988

Reid, Louis, "Claire Trevor: A Really Good Bad Girl." *Screenland*, June 1950

Roberts, Barrie, "Lynn Bari: The Siren Call." *Classic Images*, Feb. 1997

Samoiloff, Zepha, " Claire Trevor: Nasty But Nice." *Motion Picture*, Oct. 1946

Samuels, Charles, "Claire Trevor: Change of Heart." *Motion Picture*, April 1949

Schmering, Christopher, "Mercedes McCambridge: Acting Out a Life." *Washington Post*, March 29, 1981

Scorsese, Martin, "Behind the Camera, a Feminist." *New York Times Magazine*, Dec. 31, 1995

Tell, Drummond, "Claire Trevor: Three-Alarm Blonde." *Picture Play*, April 1934

Thomson, David, "No Surrender, No Mercy." *American Film*, April 1981

Van Neste, Dan, "Glenda Farrell: Diamond in the Rough." *Classic Images*, May 1998

_____. "The Shrink Who Didn't Blink: The Story of Columbia's *Crime Doctor* Series." *Films of the Golden Age*, Fall 2002

Wagner, Laura, "Marilyn Maxwell: The Other M.M." *Classic Images*, Feb. 2000

Watts, Richard, "Ghosts" review. *New York Post*, Feb. 17, 1948

Woodward, Ian, "About Town." *Woman's Weekly*, 1979

Index

Numbers in *italics* indicate photographs.